PROBLEMS OF YOUTH

PROBLEMS OF YOUTH:

Transition to Adulthood in a Changing World

Muzafer Sherif and Carolyn W. Sherif
editors

ALDINETRANSACTION
A Division of Transaction Publishers
New Brunswick (U.S.A.) and London (U.K.)

First paperback printing 2009
Copyright © 1965 by Muzafer Sherif and Carolyn W. Sherif.

This book is printed on acid-free paper that meets the American National Standard for Permanence of Paper for Printed Library Materials.

Library of Congress Catalog Number: 2008027972
ISBN: 978-0-202-36288-5
Printed in the United States of America

Library of Congress Cataloging-in-Publication Data

Problems of youth : transition to adulthood in a changing world / [edited by] Muzafer Sherif and Carolyn W. Sherif.
    p. cm.
Originally published: Chicago : Aldine Pub. Co., [1965].
Includes bibliographical references and index.
ISBN 978-0-202-36288-5 (alk. paper)
    1. Youth. I. Sherif, Muzafer, 1905- II. Sherif, Carolyn W. III. Sherif, Muzafer, 1905- Problems of youth.

HQ796.P755 2008
305.235--dc22

2008027972

CONTRIBUTORS

All affiliations are given as of the original publication of this book.

DAVID P. AUSUBEL, Professor of Educational Psychology, Bureau of Educational Research, University of Illinois

WENDELL BELL, Professor of Sociology, Yale University

DANIEL S. CLASTER, Research Associate, Hawthorne Cedar Knolls School, Hawthorne, New York

ROGELIO DIAZ-GUERRERO, President, Centro de Investigaciones Sociales, A. C. de Monterrey and Professor, National University of Mexico, Mexico City

DAVID GOTTLIEB, Associate Professor, Department of Sociology and Anthropology and the College of Education, Michigan State University

WAYNE H. HOLTZMAN, Professor of Psychology, University of Texas and Associate Director, Hogg Foundation for Mental Health

JOHN E. HORROCKS, Professor of Psychology, Ohio State University

LEWIS W. JONES, Coordinator and Research Sociologist, Race Relations Department, Fisk University

BERNICE M. MOORE, Associate Director, Ford Foundation Grant for Consultation Services for Local Foundations, and Assistant to the Director, the Hogg Foundation for Mental Health, University of Texas

ARTHUR PEARL, Associate Director in Charge of Research Center for Youth and Community Studies, Howard University

HOWARD W. POLSKY, Assistant Professor, Columbia University School of Social Work

FRANCIS THOMAS RAFFERTY, JR., Associate Professor in Psychiatry, University of Maryland, and Director, Child Psychiatry Service, the Psychiatric Institute, University Hospital, Baltimore

CAROLYN WOOD SHERIF, Research Associate, Institute of Group Relations, University of Oklahoma

MUZAFER SHERIF, Director, Institute of Group Relations, and Research Professor of Psychology, University of Oklahoma

JAMES F. SHORT, JR., Director, Sociological Research Laboratory, Washington State University and Dean of Graduate College, Washington State University

PREFACE

The topic of this book is one of the most timely of our age. Today's youth have to achieve adulthood in a world fraught with gigantic problems of rapid social change. In the throes of their own personal transition from childhood to adulthood, youth also face a *world* in transition. The problems that this changing world presents to them include a conflict of values. They include unequal opportunities that place large segments of the new generation in underprivileged positions for educational, vocational and cultural development. They include prejudicial arrangements among human beings belonging to different ethnic, racial or national groups. Unbounded promises for the future exist side by side with discriminatory treatments and facilities that set low ceilings for achievement and future goals.

These circumstances of the changing world are the context for the behavior and misbehavior of its youth. Youth's attitudes must be viewed and evaluated against this background, whether these attitudes are socially acceptable or objectionable. For this reason, several chapters of this book concern youth in different sociocultural circumstances. The authors present their analyses and findings on adolescents living in cultures that represent different levels of technological development as well as privileged and underprivileged positions in the United States.

The particular problems of youth vary in different sociocultural settings according to the opportunities afforded, the privileged or discriminatory practices prevailing in them, their cultural values, their complexities, and the contradictions they present. However, these variations in the concrete problems of particular youth cannot be treated theoretically by improvising separate and distinct psychological "laws" or "psychodynamic principles" uniquely applicable to each setting or subculture. For example, different psychological formulations have been proposed for the formation of attitudes and goals by lower class youth and upper class youth, by youth who behave in desirable and undesirable fashions, and by youth in different cultures. These proposals usually turn out to be circular descriptions of behavior translated into elaborate terminology or, worse yet, moralistic verdicts from the viewpoint of a particular class or culture.

For this reason the book starts and closes with emphasis upon general principles common to youthful behavior and misbehavior. Whether youth behave or misbehave, set low or high goals for achievement, conform or rebel against adult values, they must ultimately be understood with reference to common psychological principles operating in different social environments. Within such a framework, the unique development of individual personalities may be explored more fruitfully and may be appreciated more fully. The chapters dealing with youth in trouble with adult agencies of society treat their problems with explicit reference to their social situations in urban slums or treatment centers.

The challenge for researchers in social psychology is the search for operational means to specify both youthful attitudes and behavior, and the salient features of the environments in which youth develop. One of the distinctive characteristics of this book is the presentation of efforts made to meet this challenge by research centers and programs studying youth and their families, youth subcultures, age-mate groups, and adolescent values and attitudes in different cultures and subcultures. Because the sociocultural context of attitude and behavior is so complex and varied, precise specification of its salient aspects is a notable achievement, as represented by the Shevky-Bell social area analysis. This book is indebted to the Thomas Y. Crowell Company for permission to summarize a previous report of the analysis. In his chapter, Dr. Bell has brought research employing social area analysis up to date, including the specific computational procedures (which are not readily available since their original publication is now out of print).

The Shevky-Bell analysis, in turn, was used to specify the sociocultural settings of adolescent members of natural groups in urban areas of low, middle and high socioeconomic rank in our own research program, first presented in our book *Reference Groups*, and brought up to date in Chapters 12 and 13 of this volume. These two chapters constitute the second published installment on research in progress since 1958. They include both experimental studies and observational data on natural groups obtained recently in a project supported by the National Science Foundation, for which support we are grateful. Because this research program endeavors to study youthful attitude and behavior within reference groups of age-mates located in different sociocultural settings, the reader will find that the generalizations derived from research in the last two chapters have much in common with the major conclusions in previous chapters.

Most of the chapters in this volume were based by the authors on papers they delivered in May, 1964, to the Fifth Social Psychology Symposium at the University of Oklahoma, organized by the Institute of group Relations. Our greatest debt and appreciation go to the contributors of chapters, both for their lively stimulation during the symposium and for their labors in preparing their original contributions to this book.

After the symposium, we requested Dr. David P. Ausubel to prepare a chapter based on his research reported in *Maori Youth* (Wellington, New Zealand: Price, Milburn, 1961). We are grateful to him for spending part of a sojourn in Italy to summarize and abstract his analysis and findings on the problems of these youth in becoming acculturated to a modern society. The striking similarities in their problems and those of certain minority youth in the United States help to broaden our perspective on youth problems.

The last two chapters were also written after the symposium, the first based chiefly on Muzafer Sherif's invited address to Division 9 of the American Psychological Association at the annual meetings in Los Angeles (September, 1964), and the second on the paper presented to the symposium by Carolyn Sherif incorporating new material still unanalyzed at that time.

The Fifth Symposium, like its predecessors, was made possible by the generous support of the administration, faculty, staff and students of the University of Oklahoma. The atmosphere encouraging such intellectual events at the University was created by its administrative officers: Dr. George L. Cross, President; Dr. Pete Kyle McCarter, Vice President; and Dr. Lloyd E. Swearingen, Vice President for Research and Development.

The bulk of the financial support that made possible the Fifth Symposium and the preparation of this volume came from the University of Oklahoma's Social Psychology Seminar Fund, derived chiefly from the royalties of the previous symposium volumes. We are grateful to the Alumni Development Fund and to R. Boyd Gunning, Director of the University of Oklahoma Foundation, and Ronald K. Green, Director of the Fund, for an additional grant. Our friend Boyd Gunning was most helpful in making the Symposium possible and effective. We are also indebted to Dr. John Griffith, Psychiatric Director of the Oklahoma Mental Health Survey, who through his office contributed travel funds for two participants.

Practical arrangements and public announcements were effectively handled by Mrs. K. C. Suggs, Mrs. Betty Frensley, and Elizabeth Stubler, who were ably and enthusiastically assisted by the following University students: Mike Lauderdale, Don Granberg, Mark McNeil, Sam Shurtleff, Kay Phifer, Joan Rollins, Harry Bird, Pat McCabe, Carol Jensen, and Merrilea Kelly.

Much of the success of the symposium was due to the lively discussions among the speakers and the participants, which are reflected in some of the final versions of chapters as revised by their authors. Nearly five hundred participants—students and faculty from the University, from neighboring institutions, from the Southwest region, and from as far away as New York—attended its various sessions, to the mutual benefit of all. Afterward, many letters came from far corners of the country requesting access to the papers, which is provided in this volume.

The proceedings were enlivened and enriched by the contributions of the chairmen and discussants of various topics. We are grateful to the following persons for fulfilling these functions: Sol Tannenbaum, University of Houston; Arthur Pearl, Howard University; George T. Hauty, Civil Aeromedical Research Institute of the Federal Aviation Agency; William Schottstaedt, University of Oklahoma School of Medicine; Jerry Miller, University of Arizona; Robert Scofield and Nicholas Pollis, Oklahoma State University; John Griffith, Oklahoma Mental Health Survey; and our colleagues from the University of Oklahoma, Henry R. Angelino, William E. Bittle, C. Stanley Clifton, Alfred Glixman, Roger E. Nebergall, and Joseph Pray.

Steering the entire proceedings was a dedicated faculty committee collaborating with the Institute of Group Relations in the many decisions and details involved in the conduct of the symposium. Readers of this book, as well as its authors and those who participated in the symposium, may properly thank the following members of the arrangements committee who gave generously of their time to make the symposium possible: Henry R. Angelino, William E. Bittle, C. Stanley Clifton, Jack E. Dodson, Alfred F. Glixman, R. Boyd Gunning, and Roger E. Nebergall.

Most of the manuscript was typed by the alert and indefatigable Betty Frensley of the Institute of Group Relations, with assistance from Mary Lou Shurtleff. In preparing the manuscript and proof, we were materially assisted by Sam Shurtleff, Don Granberg, Mike Lauderdale, Kay Phifer, and Joan Rollins, all research assistants at the Institute of Group Relations.

MUZAFER SHERIF
CAROLYN W. SHERIF

The Institute of Group Relations
The University of Oklahoma
Norman, Oklahoma

CONTENTS

ILLUSTRATIONS

PROBLEMS
OF YOUTH

INTRODUCTION

PROBLEMS OF YOUTH IN TRANSITION

Muzafer Sherif and Carolyn W. Sherif

This book is about human beings, their circumstances and their problems during a crucial period of their lives. During adolescence, a person's body changes from that of a growing child to that of an adult. Every known human society recognizes this change in physical status by according new standing to the person vis-à-vis his fellow humans. In fact, the dictionary definition of the word *adolescence* refers to the social change. Adolescence is defined as the transition period between puberty (boyhood or girlhood) and adult stages of development. In the different societies known to man, the timing of the transition varies, as does its duration and the kind of recognition accorded to the changed status of the individual. Yet everywhere, it is the youth emerging from adolescence who, ultimately, define the future of their peoples.

It is small wonder, therefore, that in generation after generation history records the concern of adults over the state of their youth. The concern is translated both into poetry glorifying youthful adventure and romance and into stock phrases like "Youth is going to the dogs." Today's adults are no exception. Problems of the adolescent years are a major source of concern to parents, educators, youth leaders and policy makers. At times, these adults forget that the problems also concern youth themselves.

Concern about youth today is, in one sense, a paradox. In the major populated areas of the world, the young people of today face a future of unprecedented opportunities for creative activity and new knowledge, if their elders can fulfill their promise of a future world by avoiding the holocaust of major national conflicts. In the modern, industrialized and more "affluent" societies, more young people have opportunities for education, for the arts, for entertainment and leisure than any other generation in history. Why, then, the outcry about youth problems?

Perhaps it is partly that each generation of adults conceives of youth problems in the context of its own image of a brighter future. This

1

is not all. Adult concern about youth today also reflects changes in our societies which have altered the transition period itself, which have exposed the myth that "affluence" eliminates problems, and which have heightened the differences in opportunity for youth according to their parents' location or station in life.

The chapters of this book were written by researchers whose life works have included active study and theorizing on youth and their problems. To introduce the book, let us first introduce the adolescent and the problems he faces, relating these to more general problems of human behavior.

THE INDIVIDUAL DURING ADOLESCENCE

Despite the misgivings of parents and many specialists, the adolescent is a human being, male or female. With due regard for variations in physiological and social conditions, it is safe to say that he has at least a decade of human life and development behind him, usually a few years more. Depending on these same conditions, he has from one to about five or six decades of life to live. Within such bold general strokes outlining past and future, the picture of adolescence varies enormously in different societies, different times, and different circumstances. Still it is a period that epitomizes the lifelong interplay between the development of a human being, with his strivings and emotions, the face-to-face social process of living with other human beings, and the surrounding sociocultural arrangements and images.

In any known human society, adolescence is the period of change from the physical and social status of "child" to that of "adult." As noted earlier, in different human cultures this transition is strikingly different, both in duration and in the manner in which it is achieved. But everywhere, the period signifies changes in the individual's position relative to others, a shift in his loyalties and responsibilities. It signifies new activities, different behavior patterns, different attitudes, even changes in the way he looks and stands and walks. None of these changes can be accomplished unless the individual redefines his relationship to his world. Otherwise, despite a manly or womanly figure and voice, he would behave as he did in childhood or respond to immediate aspects of each situation, necessarily hindering any consistency in relationships with others.

In short, the adolescent period presents the individual with the problem of reformulating his concepts of himself as being different in many significant respects from the now-familiar childhood image. This is the fundamental problem in the psychology of the adolescent, and it represents a general problem for theories of human behavior—the formation and change of the self-conception, or ego.

Whether in adolescence, childhood, or old age, the problem of self or ego involves specification of the concrete social situations which the individual encounters, as well as the more general cultural setting in which he functions. The problem may be thought of fruitfully as the process of forming (and changing) conceptions about one's self relative to the many persons, objects, groups, institutions and values that constitute one's social environment. Better still, these self-conceptions may be called *attitudes,* since they not only define denotative ties with aspects of the environment, but also imply their evaluation. By self or ego, we mean the constellation of such attitudes, which become intimately related to one another within the person and which, accordingly, define his personal experiences of psychological stability or instability, as the case may be.

THE ADOLESCENT PREDICAMENT IN MODERN SOCIETIES

In adolescence, the problem of redefining one's self relative to others is aggravated, even forced, by the bodily and biochemical changes of the period. These changes are dramatic ones. They are universal to the human species, varying only in detail. Even if others took no note, the adolescent would know from his own body that he was changing. The changes associated with sexual maturation are reflected in new psychological experiences, though these may be poorly understood. It is ironic that the Freudian movement, which liberated social science from traditional taboos in studying problems of sexual development, regarded sexual changes during adolescence as much less important for character formation than bodily sensations and adult treatment in early childhood. Perhaps this is one reason why the problems of sexual maturation in adolescent development are so neglected.

Faced with an identity shaken by profound biochemical and structural changes, what does the adolescent learn about who he is from the adults in his society? In most industrialized societies, the developing youth faces years during which he is neither child nor adult, girl nor woman, boy nor man, neither wholly dependent on adults nor wholly independent of them. He is betwixt-and-between for a prolonged period, which is becoming more and more extended as the skills needed to be an adult grow more complex and require increased training. During this period, the length of which varies markedly even within a society, he is traditionally supposed to *prepare* for adulthood. But unless the process of preparation is clear-cut, what he hears most is that he must *postpone.* He must wait.

To be betwixt-and-between is not a comfortable experience, as we know from the studies of individuals caught in conditions where they must endure uncertainty or conflict. The more the period is prolonged without establishing stable bearings, the more painful it becomes. The adolescent's changing body experiences new and more powerful urges. The longer he is betwixt-and-between, the harder it becomes to ignore these urges and his strivings for some new personal stability.

The shift from the status of childhood to adulthood implies, in varying degrees, a different relationship with adult figures who hitherto had been in charge of one's fate. In modern societies, the change has been referred to aptly as "psychological weaning" from parents. Whenever there is social change underway, the young person may find that the adult generation provides few clear-cut solutions which are acceptable to him as to how the change is to be accomplished. Inevitably, he is more impatient to prove and test himself as an adult or near-adult than adults are for him to make this "test."

Thus, there is a rift between his own conceptions about himself and those of adults. As many studies have shown, the rift between the adolescents' and the adults' conceptions of the procedures to be followed in becoming grown-up is roughly proportional to the change in conditions from the time when the adults themselves experienced the proceedings. The classic example is the immigrant parent and second-generation youth in the United States. With gaps so wide between the parent's traditional notions and the adolescents' conceptions, active conflict occurs between the generations. It is a mistake, however, to think that the conflict of generations is confined to such dramatic instances. In our own research, reported in the last chapters of this book, we found, for instance, that the majority of boys and girls in neighborhoods of low, middle and high socioeconomic rank disagreed with their parents on the time to come home on week nights and, especially, on weekends.

To the extent that the adolescent period is a prolonged period between childhood and adulthood with unclear or unsatisfactory procedures for progressing to adult status and responsibilities, it produces a dilemma for the individual. The dilemma is a personal one, colored by strong emotions and motivational urges. Such dilemmas are not entirely unique to adolescents.

What do individuals facing a motivational dilemma do? Like any human being caught in a dilemma and striving to reestablish himself with some stable ties in social life, the adolescent looks around him. What he finds will vary enormously from one social setting to another. If adult solutions are unsatisfactory and there is no possibility of going out into his environment for a solution, he will daydream, engage in fantasy life, or write a diary to give vent to "true" feelings. But, in most modern societies today, contact with age-mates is permitted and even encouraged, so that the adolescent soon finds that he is not alone in his plight—alone with a diary or his misery, as the case may be. He finds that his age-mates are in much the same boat.

Thus, the adolescent gravitates toward his age-mates—more intensely, more frequently and more significantly than in childhood. These are the people who can understand him, since they are in the same boat themselves. They become his *reference set* for sizing up his own problems, his own strivings, and his own ambitions. In this country, young people are encouraged in this process by the general accentuation of social activities in national life, by adults, by schools, and by mass communication which deliberately feeds on appeals to adolescents.

CHANGE IN PERSONAL TIES: NEW REFERENCE SETS

The actual movement toward age-mates during adolescence in modern societies is symptomatic of a general shift in psychological ties. For the time being, one's conception of himself is linked firmly with the domain of other adolescents, the ties with adults and children being proportionately less salient. Thus, adolescents are much more concerned about how they stack up with other adolescents in certain respects, than with what their families, teachers, and other adults think about these matters. Other adolescents are a major reference set even for youth who are not members of clear-cut groups or cliques.

The products of the increased intensity and frequency of interaction among adolescents—the "youth cultures," the fads, the proliferation of clubs and informal groups—are frequently viewed as phenomena distinctive to the period. Viewed in broader perspective, they are not unique phenomena at all. The tendency of human beings to gravitate toward others who seem to be facing a common dilemma or predicament is not at all specific to adolescence. It is a general tendency whenever people see a common problem which is incapable of solution by single individuals. Adults in such prosaic settings as the office, the factory, the military, and the community follow the same tendency when they can. In less usual circumstances, too, such as a disaster or a prison camp, people generally turn toward others and organize their efforts if possible. It is a way of doing something about a dilemma rather than submitting to it.

Hence, like any individuals during a period of prolonged problems for which common effort may provide comfort or solution, adolescents tend toward *group formation*. Although adolescents may live in what is called a "mass society," they do have a social life that is far more patterned than adults are willing to believe. It seems to be part of the ethic of being adult to believe that social life is expressed only in forms that adults sponsor or approve—schools, churches, clubs with officers and planned meetings. Any other social life is, from this view, casual, haphazard, unpatterned, and even frightening, especially if it manifests itself in, for instance, a case of vandalism in a quiet neighborhood. In our own research, we have found reports and have heard the earnest protests of parents, teachers, and officials that there are no relationships of any special significance among teen-agers. The protest is epitomized in the phrase: "We have no gangs here."

CHANGE IN PRIMARY GROUP TIES: ADOLESCENT REFERENCE GROUPS

The adult belief that informal social contacts among adolescents are unpatterned, that youth "gangs" are unnatural or pathological phenomena, and that only certain neighborhoods have "problems" involving "gangs" does not square with the facts. There are patterns of regular and recurrent interaction among adolescents in neighborhoods and communities of all descriptions. Nor is this general phenomenon unique to adolescents.

When individuals come together and interact with reference to a commonly experienced dilemma or problem for any period of time, the result is not merely a unique combination of individuals. As part of a general social process, to which unique individuals contribute, such regular associations become patterned. The interaction among individuals produces certain properties which are reflected in the attitude and behavior of all the individuals, but which are distinguishable from the behavior of any one of them. These "properties" are the features marking a collection of persons as a *group*, wherever they may be found and whatever their age.

The patterning among individuals that earmarks a group is a matter of degree, for it is always dependent on interaction over *time*, and on the conditions in which interaction takes place, the problems which brought individuals together, and their personal characteristics relative to one another. Among the patterns to be found is one reflecting power relations among the individuals, according to which each occupies a differentiated relative status. Even in the most casual and informal association continuing over time, say, one of adolescent girls, the individuals come to differ more or less consistently in how effective their attempts are to initiate activities and shape the trend of interaction. The differences in *effective initiative* are usually accompanied by differences in deference and prestige, so that the individuals can be ranked according to relative status. This is one essential property of any human group.

Invariably, when individuals interact with reference to a common dilemma or problem, over a period of time they will produce common ways of approaching, tackling, and dealing with problems. They develop customary procedures, private jokes, signs of dress or decoration, nicknames for individuals, ways to refer to "us" and "not us," and so on. These common products of interaction are handled in sociology and anthropology under the titles of "social norms," "cultural values," and the like. There is no theoretical reason to reserve such terms for gang codes, exotic tribal customs, or far-distant societies. Every human group has its normative regulations for the behavior of those who belong to it.

In short, associations among adolescents that continue with regularity for any length of time are patterned, in some degree, by organizational and normative properties marking this cluster of persons as a human group. Like any human group, an adolescent group does not form overnight by spontaneous generation, nor is it totally isolated from its environment. Therefore, the characteristics of adolescent groups, the specific concerns which bring members together, and even the criteria for being accepted vary in different sociocultural and socioeconomic settings.

The values cherished by adolescents, their customs and fads, cannot be divorced from the cultural and organizational context in which their groups function, including the mass media of communication. The desires and aspirations of the individual members, as well as the ramifications of their personal dilemmas, are referable to the physical and social arrangements in their ken. The kind of leadership a group requires for its activities, the definition of what constitutes the behavior of a "good" member, as well as routines and techniques for carrying out activities, are decisively affected by relationships with other groups of age-mates, with established figures in their setting, and even by the discrepancies between what they have in their setting and what they see proffered in others.

From the beginning of this chapter, with its outline of the common dilemma of adolescents in modern industrialized societies, we have found it necessary to stress the dependence of youth problems on the social arrangements, the predominant values in larger society, and the immediate circumstances of living. Within the range of variations provided by these conditions, we find that the psychological problems of adolescents, their reactions to problems, and their forms of association fall within the scope of human problems at any age, despite the unique body changes and surges of energy which make the words "adolescence" and "youthfulness" nearly synonymous in the language.

THE DIVERSE INFLUENCES ON BEHAVIOR

Our look at the adolescent has shown that youth problems are problems of human beings and the human condition during a period not only set off by society, but also marked by notable physiological changes. Adequate study of adolescent behavior must, therefore, include all sources affecting the individual—physiological functioning, psychological functioning, interpersonal relations, the formal and informal arrangements for living, the cultural values prevailing locally or permeating all localities, and the goals toward which human effort is expended.

Academic life has established special fields or disciplines to study each facet of the gamut of influences shaping behavior. Such division of labor is necessary, if only because of the limits of human effort. A bulky and substantial research literature on adolescence and adolescent behavior has accumulated in the academic disciplines of psychology, sociology, and anthropology, as well as in the applied fields of psychiatry and social work.

At times, however, theories about youth problems have been built by representatives of one discipline or specialty as though the aspects and facts known to them in their specialization were all that was necessary for full understanding. Like the child, seeing the world through the eyes of a child, we who specialize are in constant danger of seeing youth problems exclusively through the eyes of our specialty. As the world does not conform to the child's vision, so problems of youth will not conform to the narrowed viewpoint that sees all adolescent phenomena through the favored etiology in one's specialty. When the problems of youth are diagnosed through such restricted viewpoints, research into them and practical steps to send youth forth better equipped for the future are bound to be insufficient or to fail utterly.

In addition to popular theories which merely praise or denounce youth, there have been ample supplies of theories from the academic disciplines, based exclusively on narrow or one-sided views. In one, the sole focus was on motivational complexes and their resolution. In another, the social definition of the adolescent period received credit for all adolescent problems. In still another, the characteristics and values of the particular class or ethnic grouping were regarded as sufficient etiology for the diverse phenomena of youthful behavior or misbehavior.

This book was prepared with the conviction that an adequate theory of the behavior of youth, or of any other period in human life, must seek the etiology of its problems in the whole range of major influences that actually affect behavior. If this book succeeds in demonstrating the need for research and theory that accommodates this diverse etiology, it will have fulfilled its purpose; however, the various chapters offer more than such a demonstration.

PLAN OF THE BOOK

The chapters were written by scholars whose backgrounds and research activities have centered on psychological, sociological, or anthropological aspects of youth problems. They consider different aspects of these problems in both theoretical and factual detail. Yet each writer represents a growing group of workers in the social and psychological sciences who consider particular problems and the aspects most pertinent to them in relation to *other* problems and other aspects. Both in topics and in the authors' orientation, the views of youth and their problems in this book are intended to be *inter*disciplinary.

The chapters have been arranged under four general headings, though the reader will find chapters under each heading which refer to problems encountered in others. This is as it should be, for none of the topics is insulated from others in the interplay of factors shaping youthful behavior.

Part I of the book, the first block of three chapters, concerns problems traditionally and justifiably assigned importance in youth study. Chapter 1 by John E. Horrocks discusses adolescent attitudes and goals within the framework of a general orientation to adolescent behavior. In many respects, the reader will find this view of adolescent problems similar to that outlined in this introduction. Those who are acquainted with Horrocks' notable text on adolescent psychology will appreciate the broad empirical basis for his discussion.

In Chapter 2, David Gottlieb, a sociologist by training, considers the similarities and differences in the prevailing values or norms of youth in varied sociocultural and class settings. Similarities are seen in the strivings of youth, but differences in particular goals, in views of other people (especially adults), and in the probable outcomes of their strivings. Like several other authors in this book, Gottlieb is particularly concerned with the contrasts in present and future opportunities for youth in different social classes. Chapter 3 is the only chapter focused on the important problem of youth attitudes with reference to the family. From carefully controlled analysis of findings from a large-scale research project, Wayne H. Holtzman (a psychologist) and Bernice M. Moore (a sociologist) draw forth structural properties of families which are important in understanding adolescent outlooks, along with the variations attributable to class and ethnic background.

Part II concerns variations in youth problems according to the socioeconomic and cultural backgrounds of development and behavior. In Chapter 4, Lewis Wade Jones draws on his own lifetime of research and on findings by many others as the basis for an account of the "new world view of Negro youth." Scarcely a decade after the 1954 Supreme Court decision, Jones finds changes in outlook among young Negroes, reflecting the sociopolitical movements of these years even more than changes in the conditions in which these youth actually find themselves. Of diverse socioeconomic class and residence, Negro youth differ in outlook and in reaction to the adult world, itself full of divergent trends. But all of these reveal the impact of cruel discriminatory arrangements beginning, slowly, to change.

Many Negro youth are among those discussed by Arthur Pearl in Chapter 5: youth in lower class settings. But Negro or not, youth in impoverished circumstances face a past, present and future very different from those of their more fortunate counterparts. Pearl, a psychologist by training, draws on the findings and projections of economists to define both the present lot facing youth whose first misfortune was to be born in poverty, and the grim future facing them in an increasingly technological

society. His critical appraisal of social and educational schemes to prevent waste of human talent in lives of poverty is the basis for his own
action research reported in the chapter.

Youth in lower class settings and Negro youth in this country are all
members of the same larger culture, albeit with distinctive values generated through generations of living apart from the dominant stream of
life. Chapters 6 and 7 both concern adolescents with quite different
cultural backgrounds. The former is based on research conducted by
David P. Ausubel (both a medical doctor and a psychologist) among
Maori youth in New Zealand. In both urban and rural areas, Maori youth
grow up in a culture that traditionally defines adolescence quite differently from the dominant white society, despite years of contact between
Maori and *pakeha*. Despite discriminatory treatment, Maori youth are
becoming acculturated to dominant white values, but differentially so.
Ausubel's research shows us the clear interplay of culture, class, and
residence in shaping youthful patterns, an interplay sometimes obscured
in youth research in this country.

Chapter 7 traces the intellectual struggle of a Mexican scholar, who
is both a psychologist and a psychiatrist, with the problem of reconciling
cultural variations in values and traditional theories of mental health and
disturbance. Through his own research on Mexican and American youth,
Rogelio Diaz-Guerrero concludes that these traditional theories have to
be changed if they are to be equally applicable in different cultures. He
shares with the reader the problems of conceptualization and research
encountered in moving toward an approach accommodating both personal and cultural factors.

Part III, chapters 8, 9 and 10, constitutes a natural cluster concerned
with youth whom society has officially designated as "in trouble." In
Chapter 8, James F. Short, Jr. offers penetrating insight into current
sociological formulations on social class and group processes in explaining
delinquency. Through findings from a large-scale research project by
Short and his collaborators on "delinquent" gangs in Chicago, we learn
in detail why oversimplified theories and typologies of delinquent behavior are inadequate. Some theories regard delinquency as a strictly
psychopathological problem; others as a mirror image of an insulated
lower class culture; still others as a mechanically triggered reaction
against society. But Short shows that even outbursts of violence by
youthful gang members are linked to status problems within groups and
to their relations with other groups. Though cut off in many significant
respects from "middle class" life, the members of such groups appear less
ignorant of its ways than was once believed.

In Chapter 9, Howard W. Polsky and David Claster continue
Polsky's earlier studies on adolescents in a residential treatment center
for delinquent youth. In this more recent research, the focus is upon the

give-and-take between youth in residential units and the adults who supervise and otherwise are supposed to treat them. After outlining a conceptual scheme that they found useful in studying adult-youth inter-action, the authors summarize research showing the differential behaviors of adults and youth in different patterned relationships.

Frank T. Rafferty, a psychiatrist, makes a similar analysis of adult staff and youth relationships in Chapter 10. His work deals with youth in an inpatient clinic whose behavior is so severely disturbed as to earn the label "mentally ill." Rafferty's researches on severely disturbed youth led him to problems of social interaction, group formation, and social structure in institutions, problems traditionally considered sociological. But he soon found that further concepts were needed, particularly because the youngsters were so erratic and inconsistent that their interactions seldom developed toward stable or regular patterns. One of the few problems conducive to stable interaction was relationship to adult staff, and it is striking that role relationships were first observed when patients jointly defied the staff. His research gives new insight into the etiology of mis-behavior by youth who *are* able to maintain consistent relationships with their fellows. For, consistent regulation of behavior toward others is essential for membership in any group, whether or not its activities are antisocial.

The last three chapters, Part IV, represent attempts to specify, through research procedures and measurements, the major sources of the many influences affecting youthful behavior. Chapter 11, written by the sociologist, Wendell Bell, summarizes a mode of analysis developed by Shevky, Bell, and their colleagues to specify the major properties of urban social areas. Bell surveys the accumulating research that utilizes social area analysis to show how a detailed description of the ecological setting may clarify our understanding of individual behavior. Despite the known effects of the social setting on the people living in it, there was, prior to social area analysis, a lack of precise and convenient methods for specifying its major characteristics for research on behavior.

Social area analysis also permits the researcher to pinpoint what he means by "low" or "high" socioeconomic rank, and for this reason, it was used in the research program reported in Chapters 12 and 13 by Muzafer and Carolyn Sherif. Chapter 12 presents the theoretical approach and methods developed to study, in a single research design, youthful attitude and behavior as a function of sociocultural setting and age-mate reference sets. It includes several experimental studies undertaken as part of the research program to clarify relationships between individual behavior and the patterned properties of human groups.

If we are to develop a theory of adolescent behavior, along with research to assess and expand that theory, we must begin to study care-fully the interrelationships between psychological factors (background, motives and goals), the interaction patterns and norms of adolescent groups which matter to the individual, and the sociocultural setting of the person and his groups. Only in this way can we gain realistic leads for preventive and ameliorative programs to aid youth in progressing toward adulthood and prevent serious waste of human potentialities. The last chapter of the book summarizes representative findings in the research program studying groups of adolescents in low, middle and high rank neighborhoods.

If as citizens, social scientists or practitioners, we are to understand youthful behavior adequately, there must be collaboration among all disciplines and specialties. Theory must be based on factual knowledge of the many-faceted influences shaping adolescent behavior and their interplay. Undertaking the necessary tasks is a great challenge to our own potentialities, and their accomplishment is the greatest gift we can pass to the youth of future generations.

PART I

THE INDIVIDUAL ADOLESCENT, YOUTH SUBCULTURES AND FAMILY

ONE

ADOLESCENT ATTITUDES AND GOALS
John E. Horrocks

This chapter will discuss adolescent attitudes and goals and consider some of the major motivations characteristic of the adolescent period, particularly as they are displayed in a social context.

In considering the attitudes and goals of adolescence it is necessary to remember that the adolescent is first a human, and only secondarily a member of a specific category of humans. Thus, he is not unique to the extent that much of his psychology separates him from other humans. The essential bases of his motivations, the structural aspects of his personality, the mechanics of his attitude formation, the processes by which he learns do not differentiate him from other humans. Yet there are differences, so particular and so dynamic that we are justified in saying that there are behaviors and interpretations specific to adolescence, and that these must be included in the consideration of an adolescent operating either in isolation or in concert with his peers.

DEVELOPMENT OF THE SELF-CONCEPT

The adolescent is normally a highly reactive person in the process of building and consolidating his impression of the world about him. Equally, since birth he has been in process of building a concept of self— a concept still in formation during the second decade of life, although already structurally complex and beginning to exhibit aspects of its ultimate inflexibility. And here we have one of the basic problem areas of adolescence. As the adolescent confronts the world and as he gains an impression of it, he must relate it to himself, and himself to it, so that it seems, as he construes it, relatively compatible with the self-concept he has been developing since birth. Where he perceives incompatibility the adolescent has the difficult task of explaining this incompatibility to himself, as well as of coping with it in such a manner that his developing self-concept and system of values remain intact or at least self-consistent.

But all of this is not a solitary matter. The adolescent's environment contains persons as well as objects and concepts, and the impact of others (socialization) is a major force shaping the developing individual.

The end product of his personal evolution must, ideally, be a concept of self that is not static but constantly shifting and re-evaluating as it moves toward consolidation in a context in which personal needs and reality must be brought into at least a working relationship, if not into harmonious congruence. However, the adolescent is typically an idealist who seeks a harmonious congruence hardly possible of attainment. In the area of personal relations he finds a proving ground for the kind of person he conceives himself to be. This is the period when the individual child develops strong loyalties and equally strong rejections which he feels are not only just, but immutable. Actually, with the passing of years these loyalties and rejections do, of course, change or find modification, but while they last they are of tremendous significance and act as exceedingly strong motivators.

But the problem of integrating self and environment, as the adolescent must live with it, is far from simple, and there is great need for help and support. Because he is embarking on many new experiences, because he is assuming new values and new attitudes and trying to integrate these with ones previously held, because he is undergoing new and strange sensations and changes, and above all, because he is not sure how to cope with his environment, the adolescent tends to feel insecure in many areas of his daily living. As a result he looks for an anchor to help him find a measure of security and ego defense.

The most available anchor—and most tempting because of its potential for self-assertion—is the peer group. Among those of his own age the adolescent can find others in a situation and a state of mind similar to his own. In such company he can either ignore his problems or even imagine they do not exist. In the peer group, as in no other context in his environment, he can find "belonging," affiliation, and acceptance as well as status as a nondependent person that he so strongly desires. The peer group has the further advantage of offering the young person the experiences and training for which he is striving. It offers him a stage on which he can play out the role of self relatively unhampered by the inhibitions and child-adult assumptions of the adult world. For this reason it is little wonder that the peer group becomes so important to an adolescent and that exclusion from it or lack of adequate status within it often constitutes a traumatic, or at least a thwarting, experience.

SELF-ASSERTION

To this point I have contended that the prime business of growing up is the development of a self-concept and the relating of that concept to both the outer and the inner environment. I pointed out the potential problem posed to the adolescent as he attempts a harmonious relationship between the realities of his environment and his developing concept of self. In doing this I have implied the adolescent's need for self-assertion and his quest to find a place where he may assert himself as an independent individual in his own right. In my opinion the drive for self-assertion is a prime motivating force in a child's development as, indeed, it is in a different way during the years of maturity. The difference is one of control, of perspective, and, in the case of the adult, of freedom from the complication of coming to terms with a developing self. Here we have, of course, the background for the development and consolidation of many of the attitudes an individual acquires.

Perhaps at this time it would be well to pause a moment and examine the matter of self-assertion as a fundamental need. The concept is, of course, not a new one. A perennial question in psychology has to do with the impulsions to behavior. Various lists have been composed, usually with some attempt at categorization, as "innate" versus "acquired," or "learned" versus "unlearned." Commonly appearing on such lists is the "power drive," which from my position I would amend in somewhat less drastic terminology to read "need for self-assertion." Although I would not, for example, place this need for self-assertion in as central a position in a behavior system as the Adlerian concept of mastery, I would not deny its importance or its motivational role in the development of self concept. In his *Conquest of Happiness* (1930), Bertrand Russell says, "Speaking more generally, one may say that some kind of power forms the normal and legitimate aim of every person whose natural desires are not atrophied. The kind of power that a man desires depends upon his predominant passion." Russell lists among his impulsions to power, "power over actions of men," "power over their thoughts," "power over their emotions." He notes that some persons desire to "change the material environment," others desire "intellectual mastery," and so on. I would add to these the generalized desire to assert oneself over the environment by construing it in accord with the self-concept that one has built, and even by bringing the environment to serve and nourish that self-concept. The adolescent's problem is that the process is reciprocal, and the environment is even more likely to change the self-concept than the self-concept is to change the environment. The environment's change of the self-concept must, of course, be resisted, and when it occurs it must be explained and rationalized if mental health is to be retained. Naturally, for some the self-concept is powerful enough to enable the individual to effect changes in his environment. For others we find a retreat to fantasy and the construction of an artificial environment which does not test reality and does not exist except in the minds of its inventors. To some extent every adolescent lives for a time in such a self-constructed, self-defensive world. It is an individual matter as to how all-pervasive and how consistent across the modalities of behavior such a construction becomes.

In any event, men's apparent hope for mastery or power over their environment, or for self-assertion, is a common phenomenon. But it is not very helpful to let it rest at that. The prior question must be asked: "Why do they want this power?" Survival is one reason, prestige another, curiosity a third, and ego-defense a fourth. Looked at in this manner, the power drive may be conceived as a second order rather than as a truly primary impulsion. Power impulsions appear to be a result of environmental necessity and of social or personal pressures. Returning to Russell's position quoted previously, the impulsion to power can hardly be assumed to be an inevitable universal human attribute common to all cultures and all periods of history. It certainly does, however, appear valid for western culture. This is particularly true when one considers how western culture is ordered and how it grants and withholds its rewards from earliest childhood on. To say that the power drive is necessarily innate is going beyond the data. But this is not to deny either its importance or its fundamental relationship to other motivations. In a sense power is only a technique for manipulating the environment in such a manner that one may achieve the major desires that one's self-concept and one's biological necessities have promulgated. The peasant wishes, for example, to dominate nature, his fields, and his animals to the end that he may through these means achieve his wants. The adolescent wishes to operate in and be accepted by a milieu which will reinforce not only his feelings about himself and his importance as a person but which will also permit behavior that will simultaneously enable him to role-play the concept he has of himself and reassure him that his construction of the world is correct. In this sense the power or self-assertion drive is fundamental to other drives since it is the operative or implementing means to their achievement.

I have been speaking of the power drive in individual terms, but there is also the social or "effect-on-others" aspect of the power drive—an aspect that must certainly be taken into account in any consideration of the social psychology of adolescence. Russell speaks of the good and the bad aspects of the power drive and notes on the positive side that it is ". . . in part the equipment of the kind of men out of whom a good community can be made." He sees it, if not thwarted, as representing "a correlative form of effort." He warns, however, that a certain amount of selective resignation must be in the picture for those whose power drives are not attained or for whom they are unattainable. That is, good adjustment is partly composed of resignation, in the sense that one must consider reality in one's role playing. Unfortunately one hardly expects resignation, even of a constructive or of a selective nature, to come easily for the young. Resignation, or at least reasoned acceptance, is an attribute of maturity, and the adolescent must tilt at his windmills as he attempts to make sense of himself and his world.

The consequences of the frustration so often experienced by the adolescent in self-assertion and self-rationalization are important in understanding adolescent attitudes and behavior. A person frustrated in power satisfaction in one direction is likely to turn in another direction. For example, in adult life we may turn from our occupations and find our satisfactions in our hobbies. Similarly the adolescent may turn from school or from some other constructive effort to delinquency or some other less approved activity. He may turn from the adult to the peer world. Or he may have to embark upon the task of changing his whole structure of attitudes and interpretations of himself and his environment.

INFLUENCE OF THE FAMILY

Much has been said about the relationship of an adolescent with his parents and of the importance of these relationships upon the attitudes and goals he possesses. Any valid consideration of childhood or of adolescence must sooner or later deal with the problem of these relationships—usually in terms of the effect of parental activities and attitudes on a child's behavior and character formation, as well as the economic and social benefits which parents provide or fail to provide the child. During the first decade of life the home is certainly the center of the child's existence. It is the place in which he spends the vast majority of both his waking and his sleeping hours; and it is the place in which he initially learns about other people and how to cope with them as the process of socialization and of self-conceptualization begins in the days immediately following his birth.

The family transmits and interprets the culture to the child, at the same time evaluating it for him. It is here that the child forms his first sense of values, both personal and social; it is here that he encounters security and insecurity, punishments, and rewards; and it is here that he experiences acceptance or rejection. In his family he observes human contact and gains direct knowledge of the methods of control—whether democratic or autocratic or their variations—that we use on each other. When he first encounters the outside world it is from the vantage point of his family circle and in a real sense he views the outside world through his family's eyes; and if it is only with their consent, it is equally with their protection. As Bossard notes, the family is "the place from which the child goes to participate in the larger social life," and it is "the place to which he returns after his social experience." But not only is the home an experience-defining agency, it is also a status-defining agency. As a member of a family a child takes on the caste and class of his parents; their socioeconomic status defines him to others, while from the viewpoint of this status, he in turn defines them. Many of his attitudes, his interests, his values, and his activities are based upon the family socioeconomic position in the community. In effect their position becomes his position. As Hollingshead points out, there is "a functional relationship between the class position of an adolescent's family and his social behavior in the community." It is no exaggeration to say that in the first years of life there is nothing in his world that he questions less. To him the family is inevitable and he sees no alternatives.

But time passes. The first decade merges into the second, and with the advent of puberty the world has enlarged to include many other elements, many of them competing with or inconsistent with the family stand. There are new desires for independence, experiences outside the scope of the family's interest, knowledge, or approval, and a growing need for self-assertion. The developing self has become more complex, more uncertain, more insecure, and is now beginning to face head-on the realities of the non-family-dominated world. Rebel can meet rebel and compare notes, and family opinion is no longer the criterion of right and wrong. Increasingly it becomes apparent that there is a frequent lack of common ground in adolescent-parental relationships. There are many reasons for this lack, such as maturity, interests, responsibilities, role, etc., but there are some that are not so obvious yet are probably just as pertinent. Himmelweit, Halsey and Oppenheim astutely mention one. They write:

The Upward Steps of all American families, taken together, constitute the American standard of living . . . But one serious disadvantage of the Upward Step is that it means that parents and children can not live in the same world. The child starts off on a higher social and economic level than the one his parents inhabited when they were children. Consequently, parents and children do not share a common experience of childhood. To the child, his parents' childhood seems remote, unfamiliar, and rather meaningless—if indeed he can bring himself to believe that they had one at all. Nor does the gap ever close. If the child grows up into a conscientious, purposeful American who has advanced himself in life, his relationship with his parents in maturity is as necessarily superficial as it was when he was young.[1]

In short, the new generation has arrived, and the old slowly and sometimes reluctantly begins to leave the scene. It is not easy for the old generation to recognize that it is old and, in the eyes of the new, already obsolescent. Nor is it easy for the new generation to accept what they regard as outmoded behavior.

THE PEER CULTURE

Thus, the major area around which an adolescent focuses his behavior tends to become that of his interpersonal relations with his peers.

[1] Himmelweit, Halsey and Oppenheim, *British Journal of Sociology,* 1952, 3, 148-172.

The family—important as it is as a defining and limiting agency, and as much as it is the central focus of any child's existence—nevertheless cannot usually transcend, nor, indeed, in many cases even meet, the achievement of the peer group in shaping values and in providing perceived personal security as an individual.

Research has suggested that within the group situation the adolescent can feel a sense of power, belonging, and security; he can make decisions in collaboration with his peers that he would never be capable of making alone. Parents may try to restrict their children's activities in these respects, but such attempts at restriction will more often meet with failure than with success. The rewards of prestige and freedom of movement seem to be more valid if bestowed by the group and it is, perhaps, because of this that group influence can overwhelm and negate parental instructions or prohibitions.

Thus, we may see the peer world, for most adolescents, as a tremendously important source of attitudes, the inhibitor as well as the initiator of action, the arbiter of right and wrong, and the dispenser of acceptance and rejection. The adolescent argument, "I want to do such and such because all of the other kids are doing it" is the strongest and most cogent reason that any adolescent can give an adult in justification and explanation of his desires and activities.

In addition to providing emotional bulwarks for the adolescent in the form of security, prestige, and so on, the peer group has the further function of acting as a proving ground—a place to test oneself, to try things out, and to learn to cope with others. The peer group offers the adolescent an opportunity to initiate, to distill, and to refine his social movements in such a manner that later in life social adaptation and participation may be approached on an easier and surer ground. This aspect is, in effect, the offering of social learning experiences. Tryon writes of the peer group, "It is in this group by *doing* they learn about the social processes of our culture. They clarify their sex roles by acting and being responded to, they learn competition, cooperation, social skills, values and purposes by sharing the common life." Obviously, the group has its own means of insuring learning, which it may accomplish in a variety of ways. The surest method at its disposal lies in the need for group conformity with its reward of acceptance. If the adolescent refuses or is slow or obstinate in learning or abiding by the laws and mores of the group, he faces the prospect of expulsion, partial rejection, or at least of reduced status. Even in the relatively unstructured informal play or recreational group, conformity to the prevalent code of behavior is jealously guarded. Occasionally the group may withhold its acceptance of an individual if he is perceived by the group members as one who will not readily adopt the current code governing such matters as manner of speech, dress, and approval-disapproval of the significant figures and objects periodically central in the adolescent world. As one sixteen-year-old said, "Of course we all want Corvettes. That's the thing to have. I wouldn't want a compact car or a station wagon as a gift—I'd be ashamed to drive it. If you really know what you're doing you just have to have a Corvette. But not a new one—it's better to get an old one and fix it up yourself so it will run the way you want it to. There just isn't anything I wouldn't do to get a Corvette."

Of course, in many of these respects adolescent groups are not crucially different from adult ones in terms of purposes, standards, values, and rules of behavior. The difference is one of focus, of emphasis and of the presence or absence of testing behavior. For the adolescent, acceptance by the peer group and possession of the good opinion of his peers *on their terms* is what he believes to be the most important thing in the world, and he is prepared, quite beyond the readiness of most adults, to allow himself to be governed and to have parameters set to his behavior and his beliefs and values by peer opinion and group sanction. Small things are more important to the adolescent than they are to the adult. He lacks not only experience, but even the perspective to view the experience he has had.

Thus we see the peer group as security inducing. It is a prime source of experience. It is an arbiter and a dispenser of acceptance and rejection. It tells the adolescent what is done and what is not done, what is acceptable and what is not acceptable. It is the milieu which he knows best and it is the context, if he is accepted, in which he feels most comfortable. Its position is his position, its jargon his jargon. Through it he achieves status as an individual, and in it he finds support in his struggle for emancipation from adult authority and controls. It provides, perhaps to press the matter a bit far, the glasses through which an adolescent views and interprets his world. As one adolescent said, "My friends are my life." Could anyone say more?

It is fruitless to attempt any further substantiation of the importance of the peer group to the adolescent, either in terms of his perceptions of its importance, or in terms of its actual role in his psychological and social development. Instead it would appear expedient to examine the nature of the groupings so prominent in the lives of teenagers.

To this point I have spoken of "the peer group" as though there were only one kind of peer group, and in positing its importance to adolescents it may have appeared that all adolescents are striving members of a single kind of peer group. Of course, such is not the case. Not all adolescents are peer-group centered, nor do all of them find the peer group necessarily the most available or successful means of self-assertion and experience. In actuality, adolescent peer society is composed of a variety of different types of groups. Peer groupings may be categorized along a continuum of formal-informal, or of large-small, and may be described by such terms as *crowd, clique, gang,* and *spectator.* Some are adult-sponsored and some are not. Categorization may also be based upon membership, as heterosexual and unisexual. Single pairings, either heterosexual or between members of the same sex, may also be included as a part of peer society. Obviously groups may also be classified in terms of their activities or in terms of the personal attributes and need-inspired behavior of their members. In one study conducted by the author and his students each of the informal peer groups of an entire community were identified under nine more or less mutually exclusive behavioral headings defined in terms of pressures. The headings were:

1. Pattern of pressures leading to assumption of the adult role, emancipation from the home, and satisfaction of heterosexual interests.

2. Pattern of pressures assuming the form of a moral code approved by the school and upper socioeconomic home.

3. Non-emancipated, home, school, and community .centered activity pattern.

4. Pattern of activities and social values deriving from a very low socioeconomic status.

5. Pattern of pressures leading to the assumption of an upper socioeconomic, quasi-adult social role.

6. Pressures toward social conformity manifested by a concern for good appearances and rejection of noisy, "show-off" type of behavior.

7. Pattern of pressures and needs involved in playing a masculine role.

8. Pattern of pressures resulting from adult domination and lack of emancipation from the home.

9. Need for approval and status growing out of pressures applied by the middle class family.

Here we have a number of adolescent groups with relatively little overlapping membership—groups who tended to reject each other overtly, or at least to ignore each other. A member, accepted and playing a leading self-assertive role in one group, would find little acceptance in one of the other groups, and indeed would often be likely to meet with active rejection. Here we see a peer-group society composed of a variety of sub-groupings, each one operating in terms of the needs of its members. All groups did have the common element of group cohesiveness and loyalty, rejection of others, and a rigid standard of conduct which could not be deviated from. All groups were proving grounds for interpersonal relationships, and all existed in a non-adult world, even the group of the non-emancipated whose adult-relationships were more like those of the first, not the second, decade of life. From this it would appear that any consideration of adolescent peer groups must recognize within the larger peer culture a considerable amount of inter-group divergence. Adolescents tend to seek out those groups which best permit them to gain their self-assertive needs and to construct an environment most satisfactory to their concept of self and their construction of reality. Selective group seeking—and joining—is one way in which an adolescent is able to manipulate and control his environment. Parents and other adults prepared to accept the importance of the peer group are often perturbed at the particular grouping most appealing to a particular adolescent. They may feel that his particular groups are perverse, atypical, or decidedly undesirable. Any peer group may well be undesirable by some adults' criteria, but hardly perverse in his own perception and certainly, looking at the overall peer culture, not atypical in terms of what the members use them for. In general all peer groups get at the same thing—a matter having little connection with the specific activities in which they may indulge. It is a mistake to interpret the effect of a group in terms of its overt activities rather than in terms of each individual member's interpretation of those activities with reference to his own self-concept and opportunity for self-assertion and proving behavior. In view of this it is questionable to what extent an analysis of the peer groups an adolescent is most loyal to, or wants to be included in, is effective in understanding his needs structure and concepts of self and reality. The approach, rather, is to learn how he perceives the group and how he role-plays in the group's activities.

In the study of group behavior one must eventually turn to the individual. Whatever the classification of the group, membership is composed of individuals and the group is only the field in which each plays his own individual role. In actuality no group has any essentially real existence outside of the individual minds of those who compose it or who, without being themselves members, perceive an aggregation of individuals as a group. Thus, any group is only what its individual members or observers conceive it to be. And there will be as many different perceptions and conceptions of any given group as there are individuals involved. That these perceptions are often diametrically opposed is a potential source of misunderstanding and conflict. Any adolescent's perception of his group will usually differ widely from that of his parents, his teachers, and other adults. In a real sense the adult's perception of an adolescent group tends to be in operational terms—what, grossly, he observes them doing and saying. In contrast, the adolescent's view is in terms of a fellowship often romantic and idealistic in character, and his interpretation of ends and means is always based on his own developing self-concept and the various roles he is trying out, using the group as a background. It is unwise to take adolescent peer group behavior at face value—but when an attempt at control is involved it is usually a mistake for an adult to align himself against the group if he can possibly avoid doing so. Equally, it is unwise for him to attempt to intrude to too great an extent into the life of the group. Parent-child togetherness, essentially a concept promoted by women's magazines and bleeding heart writers, is well enough up to a point, and doubtless conducive to security in the child if not carried too far. But when carried to the lengths of excessive and uninvited adult intrusion into the adolescent peer world it becomes highly non-facilitative and interferes with some of the most basic functions of the peer group as the adolescent wants and needs it to be.

Adults who attempt to deal with the peer group often approach it as an entity having a separate existence apart from the individuals who compose it, and forget that while the group may have physical being as an aggregation of individuals, its physical being is a time-space phenomenon and is a single event that exists only when those individuals are gathered in one place at one time. When the members depart, the group has no existence except in their thinking, and the group has as many separate existences as it has members, meaning to each of them only what he, and he alone, perceives it to mean. It is then that the group has no existence in reality. It is a myth, a figment of several imaginations. I sometimes think that the major benefits of belonging to a group may come from an individual's thinking about it when it has physically scattered.

HABIT REPLACEMENT

As I have discussed the adolescent to this point I have endeavored to present a picture of an individual in transition—an individual who is building and trying to interpret a world and to relate it to a self that is still developing. Yet even as the adolescent builds he has to tear down or to alter. The old must constantly be replaced by the new. One of the reasons for the difficulty of being an adolescent in western culture is the problem of replacement. Certain habits were acquired in childhood and were even promoted by adults. Many of these habits represented security and approved ways of socialization. But in adolescence these childhood habits had to be replaced by ones more appropriate to older children and adults, and such replacement often happened under pressure from parents and other adults, from peer group pressure, and from the examples set by reading and other experiences.

Unfortunately for ease of transition, many of the habits that have to be replaced do not exist in isolation. Most of our habits are interrelated, and interact and influence each other both positively and negatively. One habit may lead to and facilitate the acquiring of another habit. Or it may inhibit the potential of an already existing habit by changing reward values, by causing it to operate only with difficulty (latency) or by decreasing its tendency. One habit may change or alter an existing habit. Any individual is a complex of habits, many of which have become an integral part of his self-concept. Where habits have become integrated into the self-concept, replacement can represent a very severe problem, assuming at times traumatic proportions.

Of course, the influence of habits extends even beyond the individual, as his habits and customs—or their results—influence those with whom he comes in contact, and theirs in turn influence him. The action of customs and habits is thus both an individual and a group matter.

There is an interesting parallelism between the period of habit replacement following the advent of puberty and the period when the small child is passing from the period of initial habits to the period of socialization. One difference is that the adolescent brings to the current replacement the experience of his previous transition, which may have been good or bad. An hypothesis might be that transition to adolescence is easier when the earlier transition was favorable, and difficult when the earlier transition was difficult.

EQUILIBRIUM ATTAINMENT

To end this chapter, I would like to posit another motivating force, probably even more primary than self-assertion. This is the drive to attain a state of equilibrium or homeostasis in both the psychological and organ functions. Equilibrium attainment is a vital force for any living individual, not only for adolescents, but acceptance of the equilibrium-striving hypothesis gives the observer an additional vantage point from which to view and interpret adolescent behavior and attitude formation. Equilibrium may to some extent be equated with satisfaction or even euphoria. When a need, as self-assertion, is unsatisfied—when the individual has not attained closure—there must be a continuing effort on his part to achieve equilibrium by satisfying his need. Not to do so represents an abnormal condition, and a person who deliberately (sometimes the situation is unconscious where he is concerned) refrains from seeking equilibrium is displaying maladjustive behavior that may well have serious repercussions.

There is a paradox here, however. Just as there is a straining toward equilibrium, so, once attained, there is a straining toward disequilibrium. The functioning organism avoids a static state—and so there arises the counter-need for a movement away from an attained equilibrium. This, of course, is in turn followed by the return quest for equilibrium again as the circle completes itself. Robert Frost speaks of the expansion and contraction of the biological aspects of the universe.

Another problem arises in the person who attains equilibrium and then adjusts his needs system so that this equilibrium lessens, or at least becomes something that must be renewed and added to. For example, a person may attain success, but then discount the first success and strive for further success. One would presume that some persons go through life attaining or trying to attain goals, never being satisfied with an attained goal, but always striving for an even greater one. Others no sooner reach their goals than they relinquish or modify them, and in a sense never go ahead, but always have to start over again. There are, of course, goals that are never attained. Here we have a matter of reality testing and of self-concept in the goals that are established. There are also people who deliberately avoid goal attainment—those who are, as I have previously mentioned, abnormal.

Throughout this discussion I have emphasized that the adolescent is, after all, a human and that his psychology is human psychology. But, it is equally true that he is a special class of human, and where the mature adult is concerned he is an incomplete human in process of development, striving to attain a state that is not yet within his grasp. He has problems peculiar to his existence as an adolescent; he is seeking experience and relating it to his self-concept as well as his self-concept to the experience; and together with his fellow adolescents he is trying to make sense of himself and of the universe. Under the circumstances, it is fair to say that a general psychology of adolescence may be isolated and that, since peer society is the focal point of the adolescent's life, one of the best approaches to an understanding of the adolescent period may be found in the study of his sociopsychology.

TWO

YOUTH SUBCULTURE: VARIATIONS ON A GENERAL THEME

David Gottlieb

Youth culture is a universal phenomenon. Whether a society be primitive or highly complex, it attempts to assign certain roles and behavior limits along an age and sex dimension. As a youngster moves from one stage of biological growth to another, adult expectations as to what is proper and "good" will change. What is tolerated at age five, for example, may not be considered acceptable when the same behavior is performed by a fifteen-year-old. Along similar lines, we can see how our evaluation of observed behavior is very much influenced by the sex of the actor. What we are willing to accept as normal for girls is in many instances not the same for boys.

When adult expectations are fulfilled by youth, conflict between the generations is kept at a minimum and there is little concern for the future of the society. When, however, attitudinal and value expectations of the adult governing body are not in harmony with the system of beliefs endorsed by youth there may be serious consequences for the functioning of the society. The reasons for concern should be apparent, since the most crucial task faced by any society, once it has established an efficient system of social control, is the training of the young for responsible adulthood. If the society is to survive and flourish over time, it must socialize its youth so that a continuing supply of human resources is available to meet societal goods and needs. The purpose of this chapter is to explore how youth have been classified by adults and to propose a model which might be fruitful for future studies of adolescent behavior.

This task of preparing the young for future responsibilities is neither unique to our society nor to contemporary man. Every nation, and this is no doubt most apparent in those undergoing rapid industrialization, encounters some difficulty in the training of adolescents. England has its "teddy boys," France its "blousons noirs," while in Sweden the more expressive youth are called "raffare," in Germany they are identified as the "halbstarken," and Japan has its "thunder boys." The Russians are not spared, and the "stiryagi" present numerous problems for the authorities.

28

There is additional evidence that even before industrialization, urbanization, and highly organized mass media, youth were a problem for the adult society.

Within the Old Testament, in the section titled Proverbs, the words of Solomon have a familiar ring:

> Hear my son, the instruction of thy father
> And forsake not the teaching of thy mother:
> For they shall be a chaplet of grace unto thy head,
> and chains about thy neck.
>
> My son, if youthful sinners entice thee, Consent
> thou not. If they say: 'Come with us.'
> Let us lie in wait of blood.
> Let us lurk for the innocent without cause;
> Let us swallow them up alive as the grave
> And whole, as those who go down into the pit;
> We shall find all precious substance
> We shall fill our houses with spoil;
> Cast in thy lot among us; Let us all have one purse.
> My son walk not thou in the way with them
> Estrain thy foot from their path;
> For their feet run to evil.
> And they make haste to shed blood.
>   (Proverbs 1: 8-16)

This passage reflects two themes that prevail in our own society: the first a plea for conformity to the values of one's elders, and second, recognition that age peers do have the potential of moving the child toward behavior considered inappropriate by adults.

CONFORMITY TO PEER GROUPS AND SOCIAL CLASS

How and why youth can and will come together in their own groups and operate in a manner unacceptable to adults has been discussed by many authors, both the novelist and the behavioral scientist. A central point in these writings, especially those published since the turn of the century, is the impact of industrialization as the stimulus for the breakdown of traditional mores and customs which had acted to assure a peaceful transition from youth to adulthood. The early 1900's and the years immediately after are portrayed as a period of social upheaval in America. Not only were thousands coming to this country from various sections of the world, but there was in addition an internal migration which marked the emergence of our complex urban society. The emphasis in the writings of this period, therefore, was on the special problems faced by youth who suddenly found themselves in a relatively new and frequently unstructured situation.

The literature pertaining to youth for this period of American life is indeed rich. There are not only numerous case studies but also a number of descriptive accounts of youth groups. Among the case studies are several which have become classics for students of adolescent behavior. Included are Clifford R. Shaw's *The Jack-Roller* (1929), the autobiography of a young delinquent, and *The Natural History of a Delinquent Career* (1931), a study of the effect of family life, gang association, and neighborhood conditions on the evolution of a criminal career.

A third study dealing with gangs is the monumental work undertaken by Frederic M. Thrasher which appeared in 1927. Thrasher's discussion of the origin and dynamics of the gang was based on a survey of some 1,300 Chicago youth gangs and clubs.[1]

In discussing the "roots of the gang," Thrasher stated that "the gang represents the spontaneous effort of boys to create a society for themselves where none adequate to their needs exists" (Thrasher, 1927, p. 37). Indirectly he took the position that the various agencies responsible for the socialization of the child, *i.e.*, the family, the church, and the school, have failed in fulfilling the needs of the young, hence their involvement in gang associations.

Thrasher concluded:

The gang functions with reference to these conditions in two ways: it offers a substitute for what society fails to give; and it provides a relief from suppression and distasteful behavior. It fills a gap and affords an escape. (Thrasher, 1927, p. 39)

Although Thrasher made only brief mention of a separate youth society, his work appears to anticipate contemporary adolescent research which places great emphasis on the existence of distinct adolescent subcultures.

As noted earlier, social scientists were not alone in identifying the breakdown of social institutions as the major force for moving youth into intimate peer associations. The American novelist James T. Farrell, who created the character Studs Lonigan, took a position very much like that expressed by Thrasher. In discussing his conception of Studs—an American boy of Irish-Catholic extraction—he notes the following:

The important institutions in the education of Studs Lonigan were the home and the family, the church, and the school, and the playground. These institutions broke down and did not serve their desired function. The streets became a potent factor in the boy's life. (Farrell, 1932, p. xiii)

---

[1] The definition of a gang as used by Thrasher would be questioned by some investigators currently studying delinquent gangs. Thrasher used a broad categorization which included all boys, despite variations in behavior, who interacted with peers over a period of time. The term gang, then, was applied to both acting delinquents and boys involved in some informal athletic activity.

With the gradual absorption and integration of these ethnic groups into the dominant American culture the research emphasis on youth shifted from those groups to studies dealing with the impact of social class on youth behavior.

Hollingshead, for example, in his study of *Elmtown's Youth* (1949), took the position that the high school acts as a source for furthering the gap between certain groups of youth—namely, the children of working or lower socioeconomic groups—and the society. In this case the society is viewed as endorsing a certain set of values and norms identified as middle class, and as penalizing those who are unable or unwilling to accept these norms.

Variations in social class and the end product as observed in the aspirations, values, norms and behavior of youth has been the primary research emphasis during the past three decades. For the most part the findings of these investigations are similar, tending to validate the observations of Hollingshead. Socioeconomic status is reported as accounting for much of the variation observed in adolescent behavior, with youth from the lower class falling at the bottom of most scales dealing with educational and occupational values. The explanations offered are again twofold: lower class youth are penalized by the shortcomings found in their socialization, and middle class institutions fail to fill the gap created by their social origin and background experiences.

It is interesting to note that concern with the dynamics of lower class youth behavior is not so much a reflection of theoretical interest as it is a concern with understanding and resolving deviant or non-desirable behavior. In other words, since the most distressing behavior is that of the delinquent, the drop-out, and the rebel, and since this behavior is more visible among lower income youth, the research emphasis and dialogue has been with this segment of the population. At both the local and national level we can see manifestations of this concern in programs of prevention aimed at delinquents, drop-outs and the culturally disadvantaged.

As a result of this research direction we have a variety of propositions interpreting why lower income youth who do rebel do so, but we have little knowledge as to why some other youth from similar backgrounds conform and why some from more affluent backgrounds do not.

Concentration on the deviant behavior of youth has given us a variety of insights about certain kinds of adolescents but few propositions from which to build a foundation for the general study of adolescence as a distinct age group within our society.

This restricted focus in youth research may help explain why there is a lack of consensus among behavioral scientists as to how far we are willing to go in accepting the notion of there being a distinct youth culture in our society.

ASSESSING YOUTH SUBCULTURES

In an earlier work, with my colleague Jon Reeves, an attempt was made to survey a group of social scientists in order to determine whether they accepted the proposition of an adolescent culture as well as the criteria used to establish the validity of a subculture. Each of our respondents was presented with an excerpt from James S. Coleman (1961), who certainly endorses the notion of a youth culture, and a statement from Elkin and Westley's article (1955) entitled "The Myth of Adolescent Culture." With few exceptions, most of our respondents were willing to accept the proposition that there is indeed an adolescent culture in our society. A few went on to point out that in all probability there is more than *one* youth culture and that others can be identified once we look for variations in socioeconomic, ethnic, and religious background.

Next, there was general agreement as to the operational criteria which should be used in identifying or establishing the existence of the subculture. For the most part, these investigators felt that observed differences in values or behavior between adolescents and some other age-grade group would be sufficient for the acceptance of the subculture proposition.

While these statements indicate a real agreement in view, the matter is not so simply handled. It would appear that a number of authors hold some reservations as to how far out on the limb they would be willing to go on this question of adolescent subculture and validating procedures.

In summary then, it would seem that while we are willing to accept the notion of adolescent subculture, we are not really clear as to just how and where it departs from the total or more universal culture. The difficulty, it seems, stems from the fact that many investigators allow the subcultural hypothesis to stand or fall on the degree of differences observed between adolescents and some other age-grade group. In other words, if the investigator finds deviation from some base level of norms or values, he sides with the subcultural proposition. If, on the other hand (as was the case with Elkin and Westley), he does not find such deviation he rejects the proposition. Obviously this approach leaves much to be desired since the results are virtually predictable, given the sample of youth studied and the base values or norms being investigated. As several of our respondents indicate, this technique creates a number of other methodological and analytical hazards:

First, what do we mean by differences? Second, differences in what? Third, how do we separate values or behavior which are solely the product of adolescent peer group contact from those which are learned from adults? Finally, what is accomplished if we do note areas of differences between adolescents and adults? Will this prove that the adolescent peer group influences educational aspirations more than parental influence? Will this allow us to predict in what direction an adolescent may go when faced with the pressures of his peers and the desires of his parents? On the contrary, it would seem to me that a presentation of differences will do little more than show where young people are in agreement or disagreement with their elders.

To my mind, there is yet another—and from a research and theoretical angle, a more productive—way to view and measure adolescent subcultures. The question of whether an adolescent culture or subculture does or does not exist should not depend on degrees or types of differences found between adolescents and adults. Differences may at times be sufficient but they are hardly a necessity for establishing the significance of a particular phenomenon. In the case of adolescents the question is not deviation from some established norm, but rather, first, how and why adolescents enter into certain types of peer associations; and second, how involvement in, and commitment to, the adolescent group influences the behavior and beliefs of the participant. Once we can identify why youth enter into these peer associations and how these groups influence and operate, we will be in a better position to evaluate the meaning of adolescent subcultures. This approach would get us beyond the descriptive accounts of adolescent behavior which, although highly dramatic at times, tell us little about how the adolescent perceives himself, his peers, adult referents, and the world in which he lives.

Following this thesis I have attempted in my own research to learn more about the dimensions of youth associations. More specifically, I have been concerned with the emergence of different kinds of youth social systems; how these systems operate; and the characteristics of those who enter. In reporting certain findings of these studies it will be apparent that I do not think in terms of a single youth culture. Rather, I view adolescence as one of a series of transitions which every individual in every society must undergo. How each individual will react to this period will of course be dependent on a variety of factors, both psychological and sociological. As a sociologist my concern is with how different groups of youth in different places go through the process of attaining adulthood. From the sociologist's perspective it is essential to view both the social climate or structure of the society and the characteristics unique to a specific group of youth. In other words, while the necessity of child training is incumbent on all societies, the means by which this training is accomplished vary greatly. Obviously there will be differences between youth in societies incorporating a caste system and those in a setting where upward mobility is not only encouraged but demanded. In addition, we can expect variations between youth in the same society who, because of their background experience or ascribed status, perceive their position in the society in different ways.

At the same time, it is important to recognize that even with the variations among social structures and individuals there will be certain continuities and similarities in the transition process.

COLLEGE STUDENT SUBCULTURES

The research reviewed here is based on a study of college students and student groups (Gottlieb and Hodgkins, 1963). Our primary concern was with noting the impact of the college on the behavior of students. We began with the assumptions that the student bodies at most colleges represent a heterogeneous population and that the college itself could be viewed as a distinctive sociocultural system, with a value orientation that contains a variety of goals for the student.

Given recognition of these assumptions, a study of the influence of college life upon students should be concerned with the subsequent effects of the dynamic interaction of these factors in the college milieu. Such interaction does not always result in the uniform embracing of university values, with all that this implies, but it may rather result in a subgrouping of the student body based largely on the student's response to the college environment. Such subgroups are here identified as "subcultures." Because there are no phenotypic criteria for differentiating such groups, their subtle influence is often overlooked by others.

A method of identifying these subcultures is both desirable and essential. The classification system adopted is one suggested by Clark and Trow (1962). Briefly, this posits the existence of four subcultures: the academic, the vocational, the nonconformist, and the collegiate. The choice of this particular taxonomy is predicated upon (1) the appropriateness of the terms for what are perceived to be the major goals of most college communities; and (2) the degree to which they characterize the different student types observed by the author and others. Within the scope of the preceding discussion, the specific subcultures are identified as follows:

Academic. These are the students holding a value orientation closely similar to that of most college sociocultural systems. They emphasize the "well-rounded" approach to education. Thus, while primary interest is on a broad education, vocational proficiency and social adeptness are considered desirable and are actively sought.

Vocational. These students, accepting the vocational goal with its emphasis on class attendance, study, and good grades, tend to withdraw from both intellectual pursuits and social activities offered by the institution. Being "job-oriented," the non-applied aspects of academic life will appeal little to them.

Collegiate. The students within this subculture value highly the ability to get along with and manipulate other people. Their value orientation is such that, besides enjoying social activities, they perceive of them as indispensable for their later success in life. Accordingly, the intellectual and vocational aspects of academic life tend to be minimized.

Nonconformist. The students of this subculture are in a sense unique, for, although coming closest to an intellectual value orientation traditionally associated with academic life, they reject the vocational or social phases of it, and further tend to reject the prescribed means for attaining their intellectual goal. They are intellectually curious, but non-disciplined in their approach, as far as conformity to the prescribed "balanced" approach to college is concerned.

I have noted the existence of a unique sociocultural system at institutions of higher learning. As a result of socially heterogeneous student bodies attending these institutions, with value orientations different from that of the college sociocultural system, subcultures develop within the student body that are instrumental in determining the effect college ultimately has on the student. The manner in which these subcultures develop is explained in terms of the strain for self-consistency by the individual, which is achieved largely by self-alienation from that part of the sociocultural system incongruent with his perception of self and the social system of the college.

Since the cognitive system of the individual was the key to adequate classification, an instrument was developed whereby the individual could classify himself into one of the four categories. The results presented here then are based on the subcultural choices of the respondents, 977 college students.

In summary, the findings of this research indicate that significant differences exist in the proportion of students who identify themselves as belonging to the four subcultures. As was expected, lower class students were found to the greatest extent in the vocational subculture, although a sizable percentage of them are found in the academic category. While few are found in the collegiate subculture (as expected), they constitute proportionally about as many as those coming from the middle and upper class. Middle class students, as anticipated, were found in the largest proportion in the academic subculture. Yet, as in the case of the lower class, a sizable number of them were vocational. For the upper class the predominant category was academic. The proportion of the upper class in the collegiate culture was little different from those of the middle and lower class.

Contrary to expectations, nonconformists, as have been defined here, do not come only from the large metropolitan centers, but in many cases from rural areas or small towns.

In terms of religious background, there were few differences, except that Jews are scarce in the vocational category.

Academic performance was significantly related to subculture identification. Based on a four-point grade scale, the Nonconformist had a mean average of 2.72; the Academic 2.66; the Vocational 2.49; and the Collegiate 2.32.

As for expressed attitude change from the time they entered college, it was found that nonconformists became less dependent on peers than other groups; less committed to religious beliefs; less interested in the need for a religious identification; and less respectful toward the role of school administrators. For all these dependent variables there was little variation between the other student groupings.

A major difference between the four groups was in their evaluation of the importance of certain aspects of the college community. Generally the collegiates stressed the importance of extracurricular programs and activities; the vocationals ranked courses that gave direct and practical experience related to their chosen occupation; the academics tended to rank all activities, both extracurricular and academic, as important; the nonconformists limited their choices to books and certain activities such as the lecture and concert series, foreign films, and the university theatre. In addition, the nonconformists were highest in indicating a preference for more informal contact between students and faculty.

Although this research was restricted to students at a single university, the results have some value for future efforts in the study of youth.

The proposition that background differences, goals, and perceptions will be related to how students react to a particular social milieu is certainly supported by the data. Of greater significance, however, are the implications the results hold for the formulation of theoretical propositions. We see that all our respondents, regardless of subcultural choice, are behaving in much the same fashion. The student moves into the subcultural setting which comes closest to fulfilling his own goals. Involvement in activities and commitment to certain phases of the college system are a reflection of the students' own needs and desires. This observation would suggest that youth will become involved in those activities which they perceive as being related to their own goals, and will tend to reject those in which they fail to see a connection between personal goals and the potential activity.[2]

From a more critical analysis of these data we were able to arrive at two other relationships which are seen as having certain theoretical implications for the study of youth behavior.

The first is that young people will become involved with those referents whom they perceive as having the *ability* to help them attain their goals and will tend to avoid those whom they perceive as not having this ability. Hence, in our college student research, we find differential patterns of involvement and evaluation based on the student's perception

[2] The relationship between alienation from a social system such as the school and perceived consensus between individual goals and institutional goals is described in beautiful fashion by Arthur Stinchcombe (1965).

of the degree to which the activity will aid in goal attainment. Secondly, young people will become involved with those referents whom they perceive as having the *desire* to help them attain their goals. Again borrowing from the student research, we saw many incidents of peer and faculty choice or rejection based on the respondent's belief that particular referents lacked the desire to help the student attain his goals.

Three factors then have been identified as being salient to the socialization of youth and the emergence of youth subcultures.

Briefly they are: the adolescent's perceptions as related to goal consensus between his goals and those of potential socializers; the adolescent's perceptions as to the desire and ability of the potential socializer to help him attain his goals. Carrying this orientation a step further, we are proposing that maximum involvement between an adolescent and some potential socializer will occur when the adolescent perceives *goal consensus* as well as *desire* and *ability* on the part of the referent socializer. Conversely, alienation from, and lack of involvement with, a particular referent will occur when the adolescent fails to perceive any of these three factors.

Currently we are involved in a series of research projects directed at testing the validity of these propositions. Since these studies are at various stages of completion, only some scattered findings are available at this time. Prior to this presentation, however, there are certain comments which should be made.

I am taking the position that adolescents behave much the same anywhere (that is, in any sociocultural context) in that they will become oriented to (involved with) referents whom they perceive as having the desire and ability to help them attain skills, goals, and ends, and that they will not become oriented to referents whom they perceive as having neither the desire nor the ability to help them attain these same ends. In addition, I am proposing that prior to evaluation of a potential referent the adolescent must sense some meaningful "pay off" between involvement with the referent and his own goals.

Any research or theoretical analysis necessarily begins with such predilections and orientations for stating the problem to be investigated, and for developing certain kinds of hypotheses, assumptions, and postulates (Gottlieb, Reeves and TenHouten, 1964). When this orientation reaches a certain level of specificity, it may be described as an explicational model.

Assumptions, by definition, are not directly under investigation; but an empirical study using a certain set of assumptions may possibly generate findings that would demand they be modified or discarded. The formulation here begins with the following assumptions:

1. The adolescent wishes to attain skills, goals, and ends.
2. The adolescent perceives referents in terms of a certain end.

3. The referents are perceived as having differential power means (ability) and intentions (desire) to help the adolescent attain an end.

4. Adolescent goals may vary from one society to the next and within subgroupings of any particular society.

5. Nothing is said here about the criteria used by the adolescent in the selection of goals.

6. No statement is made about the "objectivity" (validity) of the adolescent's perceptions with respect to goals or referents.

7. Perception precedes involvement: perceptions can be made without involvement, but involvement cannot occur without prior perception.

8. The adolescent is the initiator in his involvement.

An explicational model, employing Guttman's facet theory and design, has been developed (Guttman, 1959, pp. 130-132). The model is consistent with these eight assumptions; it exhausts the variables and classes of variables to be used, and provides a formal procedure for combining and interrelating variables. Of course, an explicational model is not itself a theory; it is rather the forerunner of a theory.

All propositions constructed from these variables (elements and combinations of elements) involve decisional processes on the part of the adolescent. An adolescent's perceptions, and in particular his information about certain properties of potential or actual referral categories, is an important behavioral property. It is assumed that the adolescent has knowledge about the relevant aspects of referents in his social environment with respect to his attaining goals. This knowledge may or may not be objectively valid, but it *will* be organized in a relatively well-ordered set of preferences. It is also assumed that the adolescent has evaluative (ranking) skills that will enable him to "calculate" alternative choices of referents with whom to become involved.

To the extent that the adolescent optimizes referent-choosing (on the basis of his perceptions) he is rational. It is not hypothesized that the adolescent is always rational. On the contrary, it will be hypothesized that the adolescent will be more rational under some conditions than others.

THE MODEL—TWO EMPIRICAL APPLICATIONS

COLLEGE STUDENTS

On the basis of the explicational model and the preliminary assumptions in the preceding discussion, it was possible to develop and empirically test some propositions generic to the general orientation. In this phase of the research our concern was with noting the relationship between perceptions of referents and levels of interpersonal involvement.

A written questionnaire was administered to 447 undergraduates at a state university. The respondents were asked a series of questions about their occupational goals. This was followed by questions dealing with five types of referents with whom respondents might be involved in an interactive attempt to attain their occupational goals. The referents were parents, siblings, spouse, peers, and teachers (TenHouten, 1963).

Four substantive hypotheses were developed, all of which are supported by the data.

Hypothesis I ($\bar{D}$, $\bar{A}$): If a referent is perceived as having no desire and no ability to help the student attain an occupational goal, the student will be involved with the referent at a low level.

Hypothesis II (D, A): If a referent is perceived as having both desire and ability to help the student attain an occupational goal, the student will be involved with the referent at a high level.

Hypothesis III ($\bar{D}$, A): If a referent is perceived as having ability but not desire to help the student attain an occupational goal, the student will be involved with that referent at an intermediate level.

Hypothesis IV (D, $\bar{A}$): If a referent is perceived as having desire but not ability to help the student attain an occupational goal, the student will be involved with that referent at an intermediate level.

The latter two cases need further clarification since both lead to intermediate levels of involvement. The frequency of interaction (involvement) with a referent is determined by the extent to which the respondent has a *role* with that referent. The goal of the respondent refers to a perceived future state of affairs involving *new* role relationships. New roles are attained through two broadly defined interactional processes: *intentional instruction* and *incidental learning* which operate conjointly. *Intentional instruction* refers to formal institutions of role socialization for the performance of prescribed acts. *Incidental learning* refers to processes of identification with, or emulation of, role models in the imitator's behavior field (Sarbin, 1954, p. 226).

Different goals will correspond to different socialization processes. An instrumental goal, such as an occupation, will be primarily obtained through intentional instruction. Social goals, on the other hand, are more informally learned.

Given this relationship between learning processes and kinds of goals, it seems reasonable to hypothesize that the relevance of a kind of referent will depend on the goals sought. A teacher provides intentional instruction for attaining an occupational goal; an older sibling provides a role model for learning social skills. Here, for occupational goals of college students, ability was somewhat more predictive of high involvement than desire.

HIGH SCHOOL STUDENTS

In research currently being conducted we are taking a more detailed look at the model and relationships between adolescent perceptions and certain background characteristics as well as structural factors (Gottlieb, 1964).

The data to be discussed here are based on a written questionnaire administered to the following samples of youth: (1) all students from two Negro segregated Southern high schools, one in a rural community of some 14,000 people, the other in a community of over 100,000; (2) all students from a white segregated high school from each of the two communities described above; (3) a 25 per cent random sample of Negro and white students in an interracial high school located in a fairly large, newly industrialized midwestern community; (4) a 25 per cent random sample of Negro students in an all-Negro high school in a Northern community of over one million. This type of sample allows for recontrolling race, socioeconomic status, region, and the racial composition of the total school system.

Within the theoretical framework of the model it was hypothesized that involvement between students and teachers would reach a maximum level where the student perceived goal consensus and ability as well as desire on the part of the teacher in the goal-attainment process. Conversely, minimal involvement would be found where the student did not perceive these factors.

Based on an initial (and by no means complete) analysis, we find the following: As was the case with the college student sample, there is a significant relationship between perceptions and involvement with referents. Both perceived goal consensus and perceptions of desire and ability lead to high involvement with referents.

Of perhaps greater interest are the relationships between class, race and perceptions: between Negro and white students in that, regardless of class background, Negro students see the greater discrepancy between their goals and those they believe are held by teachers. This discrepancy is expressed in part at least by the fact that Negro youth—significantly more so than white students—state that they frequently are unable to see the day-to-day value of school, in terms of their goals and expectations. Here is a situation where the student feels that while education is important to the better life there is much in the educational process which is incomprehensible.

There is little difference between racial and class groups in perceptions of the teachers' *ability* to help the student attain certain goals. Socioeconomic status as well as race causes significant differences in perceptions of the teachers' *desire* to help the student attain certain goals. Not unlike the first relationship (goal consensus), lower socioeconomic youth, especially Negro youth, are least likely to perceive the teacher as someone with a desire to facilitate goal attainment.

The preliminary analysis of the data would suggest that the perceptions of Negro youth are not unrelated to the race of the teacher. It seems quite likely that Negro students are more apt to see Negro teachers as understanding their goals and as having a desire to help them attain goals. This more favorable perception should not be too difficult to understand. Certainly there is much in the experience and observations of Negro youth to lead them to believe that many whites do not have a desire to facilitate goal attainment among Negroes.

There are, in addition, significant racial and class differences with respect to the number of potential referents who students think have both a desire and ability to help the adolescent attain his goals. White middle class youth were more likely than any other group to perceive all four potential referents (older siblings, parents, peers, and teachers) as having an ability to help them attain their goals. Negro youth at each social class level had fewer positive perceptions of referents than did their white counterparts. Perceived desire to help followed a similar pattern. In other words, given a limited number of reference group alternatives who could and would facilitate goal attainment, the world looks best to the middle class white adolescent. The fewer perceived adult referents on the part of the lower class adolescent should help explain why the peer groups of children from this class are more tightly knit than those from more affluent families (Gottlieb and Ramsey, 1964).

The findings might also provide some understanding of why alienation from the school setting is reportedly high for lower income youth. As hypothesized earlier in this paper, detachment from, or avoidance of, a particular activity will be related to perceptions of goal consensus. Since it is the lower class adolescent who is least likely to see the relationship between what goes on in school and his immediate goals, we would anticipate that he would have a higher level of alienation from the school. Finally, the data present some insight as to why lower class youth, particularly Negro youth, view the school and the society with some hostility. It is this group which perceives the greatest discrepancy between the ability and the desires of adult referents. No doubt these are the sentiments of many Negro college youth who are involved in protest movements taking place throughout the country. They see a society and its institutions which have the ability to facilitate legitimate goal attainment, but they see at the same time little evidence of a real desire.

SUMMARY AND CONCLUSIONS

In dealing with variations on the theme of youth cultures I have touched a number of bases and covered a variety of materials. Here I would like to summarize briefly my position and raise certain action program implications.

Generally, it is my position that our research emphasis on the behavior and characteristics of certain kinds of youth has prevented the development of sociological theories dealing with the general dynamics of adolescence. This restriction in research emphasis has led to an abundance of descriptive and quantitative data stressing where and how adolescents differ from their peers, but little information about the continuities and similarities between youth.

In this chapter, my aim has been the proposal of a model dealing with the decision processes of adolescents in regard to goal attainment. The position taken is that, despite certain background characteristics and influences, young people tend to behave in pretty much the same way. Variations in behavior are not so much related to the goal attainment process as to the goals themselves and the adolescent's perceptions of those who play a part in his socialization.

The theoretical system discussed here is not of course in a final stage of development nor has it been subject to any national validation. Research related to the model has consisted only of studies dealing with groups of college students and comparative studies of Negro and white adolescents in different kinds of school settings. The initial analysis of data from these studies and the application of the model to research done by others in other cultures would, I propose, indicate that the model is viable and worthy of further study and commentary.

Having covered several dimensions of adolescent cultures and the perceptions of different kinds of youth in different places, we come to the most difficult task of all—the proposing of ideas that might be employed in order to facilitate the successful integration of these youth.

Coleman (1961), in his study of adolescent behavior, proposes that there is, in fact, a distinct youth culture, a self-contained adolescent society with "only a few threads of connection with the outside adult society." While we might view the conclusions drawn by Coleman as disturbing—since he sees many American adolescents as frivolous and more likely to be concerned with personal popularity than intellectual curiosity—there is some evidence that these youth, in due time, will become part of their community and society.

There is further evidence that the great majority will finish high school and many will go on to college; they will acquire skills and abilities which will enable them to compete in our complex and highly technological occupational market. Although these youth may be growing up in an absurd manner, products of a society that makes adolescence a rapidly vanishing phase of life, the prognosis is fairly good that they will become part of the middle class culture.

There is, on the other hand, a second group of youth for whom the future is not so certain. These are the youth who have been described as "impoverished," "culturally deprived," "lower class," "working class," "socioculturally deprived," or "socially and culturally disadvantaged." Whatever name we might choose it is clear that this group is in need of specific and unique kinds of assistance. For this reason, and because these are the youths about whom I am particularly concerned, I will direct my comments at this group.

In noting that neither the disadvantaged Negro or white youth is likely to see goal consensus between what goes on in the classroom and his own ends, it is important that certain curriculum and pedagogical techniques be altered. The emphasis, it seems, should not always be on long-range or future-directed programs, but rather on showing the adolescent the more immediate benefits of the formal educational process. In part, this could be accomplished by using the classroom as a setting for discussing and possibly resolving current concerns and problems. Since the culturally alienated youngster, and especially the Negro, perceives few around him who have a desire and ability to help him attain his goals, there is a need to alter our program in the selection and training of those who will be working with these youth.

There is no reason to believe that every individual, by merely completing certain formal educational requirements, is able to work with this group of youth. On the contrary, there is every reason to believe that it takes a certain kind of person with certain kinds of abilities and feelings to do an effective job. As we are cautious in whom we allow to work with the emotionally disturbed or the physically handicapped, so must we practice discretion in whom we assign the task of socializing the impoverished. There are people who are not able to function with these children. There are adults who are not able to perceive or identify with the plight of this group. There are some people who do not have the patience or the physical stamina to work on a day-to-day basis with youngsters who live by standards and conditions quite unlike those of the middle class. It is better to recognize this factor before we allow an individual to work with these youngsters, rather than take the disappointment. It is not an admission of defeat to recognize that one would do better with a different kind of clientele. It is, in fact, an admission of one's own insights and professional status to declare that, in terms of the growth of the child and his eventual integration within the society, it is better that "I do not become a part of his world at this time."

Aside from the process of professional selection, there is a great need to alter our current practices in the preparation of professionals—be they teachers, social workers, therapists, or guidance counselors—who are to work with the culturally alienated. It is a waste of time and funds to teach all professionals as if they were all going to go out and work with the same kinds of youth. The professional who is assigned to the inner city area must have special training in the sociology and psychology of this group. He must be shown beforehand what to expect in terms of the home conditions of these children, how they perceive the world in which they live and what their world is really like. The professional who is to work with this group must be made familiar with the neighborhood and social institutions of the culturally alienated. A term of practice teaching or field work experience of several months is not sufficient for the individual to know what his professional duties will be like nor is it sufficient for him to gain insights into a world in which he has little exposure. It is essential that those who feel that they might want to work with these youth have more extensive pre-professional contact with professionals already in the area. Let us keep in mind that not all children in our society represent the middle class, and that the techniques appropriate for the middle class youngster will not always suffice in the context of the deprived.

We must, by our actions, make it clear to the child that we not only have the ability to help him attain the better life, but that we have the desire to do so. This is not a simple task, since words alone will not be enough. We must indicate by our actions that we are committed to the freedom and equality of all men, regardless of their background. We must show the child and his parents that the good life is not the exclusive right of any one class or people. We must also point out that the job cannot be done by the professional himself but must be carried out by the individual who seeks to attain a life of dignity and productivity. We must declare by our actions that we recognize the pain and deprivation that has been encountered by this group but that we also are firmly convinced that the situation is not futile and that change can be accomplished. Again, I emphasize that words alone will not alter the situation. These people have heard all the words—what is needed now is a symbolic act or deed.

Finally, there is a need for more systematic and realistic research with adolescents. This will mean a working arrangement between educators, counselors, therapists, and the behavioral scientist. The task of socializing our youth is not the problem of any one group, but rather a responsibility of each of us, no matter what our professional identity.

REFERENCES

Clark, B., and M. Trow, 1962. Determinants of college student subculture. In "The Study of College Peer Groups: Problems and prospects for research" (Mimeographed).

Coleman, J. S., 1961. *The Adolescent Society.* (New York: Free Press of Glencoe.)

Farrell, J. T., 1932. *Studs Lonigan.* (New York: Modern Library.)

Elkin, F., and W. Westley, 1955. The myth of adolescent culture. *Amer. sociol. Rev.*, 20.

Gottlieb, D., and B. Hodgkins, 1963. College student subcultures: their structure and characteristics in relation to student attitude change. *The school Rev.*, 71.

Gottlieb, D., and J. Reeves, 1963. *Adolescent Behavior in Urban Areas.* (New York: Macmillan.)

Gottlieb, D., and C. Ramsey, 1964. *The American Adolescent.* (Homewood, Ill.: Dorsey Press.)

Gottlieb, D., J. Reeves, and W. TenHouten, 1964. *The emergence of youth societies: a cross cultural approach.* (East Lansing, Mich.: International Programs, Michigan State University.)

Gottlieb, D., 1964. Goal aspirations and goal fulfillments: differences between deprived and affluent American adolescents. *Amer. J. Orthopsy.*, 34, no. 2, 214-216.

Guttman, L., 1959. Notes on terminology for facet theory. *Proceedings of the fifteenth international congress of psychology.* (Amsterdam: . North Holland Publishing Co.)

Hollingshead, A. T., 1949. *Elmtown's Youth.* (New York: Wiley.)

Sarbin, T. R., 1954. Role theory. In Gardner Lindzey (ed.), *Handbook of Social Psychology*, Vol. I, *Theory and Method.* (Reading, Mass.: Addison-Wesley.)

Shaw, C. R., 1929. *The Jack-roller.* (Chicago: University of Chicago Press.)

———, 1931. *The Natural History of a Delinquent Career.* (Chicago: University of Chicago Press.)

Stinchcombe, A., 1965. *Rebellion in a High School.* (Chicago: Quadrangle Books.)

TenHouten, W. D., 1963. Methodological innovations and models on the structure of reference group behavior. (Unpublished M. A. thesis, Michigan State University.)

Thrasher, F. M., 1927. *The Gang.* (Chicago: University of Chicago Press.)

THREE

FAMILY STRUCTURE AND YOUTH ATTITUDES

Wayne H. Holtzman and Bernice Milburn Moore

A unique opportunity arose in 1954 to study the problems, concerns and attitudes of high school youth throughout the state of Texas by means of a large-scale random sample. For some years the departments of home economics education in Texas colleges and universities and in the Texas Education Agency had hoped to undertake a thorough study of youth which would form the basis for a revision of the high school courses dealing with home and family living. At the same time, the Hogg Foundation for Mental Health at the University of Texas had reached the stage in its own development where it was ready to support major research programs dealing with youth, their families, their schools, and those aspects of their community environment that play an important role in personality development. It soon became apparent that these several goals could be achieved in one comprehensive project by combining the technical and financial resources of the Hogg Foundation with the large, well integrated network of professors and field supervisors of homemaking education who were deeply interested in learning more about youth attitudes, interests, and problems. Thus did the Texas Cooperative Youth Study come into being.

DESIGN OF THE RESEARCH

A preliminary review of existing youth inventories and attitude scales indicated that new instruments would have to be developed, involving a fresh approach to the whole problem. In addition to being fairly simple and objective, the instruments had to contain items phrased in the language of youth. They had to be focused on sensitive problem areas without being offensive or unduly negative. Parental misunderstanding or

The material presented in this chapter has been drawn largely from the more extensive publication by the same authors: *Tomorrow's Parents* (Austin: The University of Texas Press, 1965). The authors wish to thank the University of Texas Press for granting permission to reprint the graphs here. Only a few highly selected findings are reported here, chosen because of their relevance to family structure and youth attitudes and their value in illuminating the research methodology.

community resistance would be disastrous in a large-scale project where a truly representative sample of the whole state was of paramount importance. Professors of home economics participating in the project were asked to collect statements from youth themselves. Hundreds of teenagers met in small groups where they openly discussed the kinds of problems they encounter in all aspects of personal and family living. More than three thousand statements were collected in this manner, providing a basic pool for the writing of items to be included in the preliminary forms of the inventories. A small number of items was also drawn from existing inventories and attitude scales to round out the picture.

Most of the statements fell into one of two major categories. One kind could best be answered by indicating the amount of agreement or disagreement. The other kind represented problems, feelings, or ideas about which a person could respond "true" or "false" as applied to himself. Two different forms were constructed.[1] The first, called "Attitudes Toward Personal and Family Living," consisted of attitude-type items with a five-choice response continuum ranging from "Strongly Agree" through "Undecided or Uncertain" to "Strongly Disagree." The second form was called "Concerns and Problems in Personal and Family Living" and contained items with the following five choices: (1) "False, or does not apply to me in any way"; (2) "True, but of no concern to me"; (3) "True, but of little concern to me"; (4) "True, and of much concern to me"; and (5) "True, and of greatest concern to me." By combining an "importance" scale with the usual true-false dichotomy, it was believed that subtle but significant variations in response could be detected, making the problem inventory more sensitive to varying degrees of concern among youth.

Preliminary versions of the attitude and problem inventories (Forms I and II, respectively) were administered to several hundred teenagers to test the feasibility of this approach. In addition, at annual state conferences they were given to 696 home economics teachers who were asked to respond as though they were teenagers, to revise the wording, and to suggest other items. Analyses based on these preliminary data reduced the item pools still further. Refined versions of the instruments were given to 2,163 teenagers in fifteen schools across the state representing a wide variety of sociocultural settings. Data from this pilot study were employed to carry out a rigorous item analysis and empirical verification of fourteen scales that had been developed earlier. A large number of

---

[1] A third form consisted entirely of items designed to record the degree of interest of teenagers in a variety of topics and activities that often constitute the content of homemaking courses in high school. Called the "Personal Interest Checklist," this form provided information of special value for curriculum revision and need not be considered further here.

judges were asked to sort statements into meaningful clusters according to content. Item-scale correlations were computed, as well as the inter-correlations among the fourteen scales. Minor adjustments were made in the items to improve still further the internal consistency of the scales, and the final versions of the two forms were printed for use in the major phase of the research program.

TABLE 1

Descriptive Name, Number of Items, Median Item-Scale Correlation, and Sample Item for Each of the Final Fourteen Scales in the Attitude and Problem Inventories

Scale Name	Number of Items	Median Item-Scale Correlation	Sample Item
FORM I (Attitudes)			
1. Orientation to Society	8	.56	These days a person doesn't really know whom he can count on.
2. Authoritarian Discipline	9	.56	Too much affection will make a child a "softie."
3. Criticism of Education	10	.64	Most teachers are too rigid and narrow-minded.
4. Criticism of Youth	7	.47	Silliness is one of the worst faults of most teenagers.
5. Family Problems	6	.61	I can always count on my family for help when I get in trouble or have a problem.
6. Self Inadequacy	9	.54	I just never seem to get anything done.
FORM II (Problems)			
7. Family Tension	20	.67	My parents quarrel and fight much of the time.
8. Personal Adjustment	23	.54	I would like to get married as soon as possible.
9. Social Inadequacy	12	.72	I am always afraid in a crowd.
10. Resentment of Family Life Style	9	.69	My parents don't like to have me bring friends home.
11. Social Conformity	4	.70	Sometimes I tell dirty jokes when I would rather not.
12. Social Isolation	4	.77	Even when I am with people, I feel lonely most of the time.
13. Financial Troubles	4	.70	I can never save money.
14. Resentment of Dependency	6	.75	My parents treat me as if I don't know right from wrong.

Table 1 contains the descriptive names of the fourteen scales, the number of items in each scale, the median item-scale correlation as a rough index of internal consistency, and sample items to illustrate the content. In addition to the fourteen scales, there were fifty-two statements in Form I and eight in Form II that were retained as individual items of interest in their own right. A simple face sheet, the Student Information Blank, was also devised to obtain information about parents' occupation, education, family structure, family dwelling, and other background factors of importance.

Defining the sample so it would be truly representative of high school youth in grades nine through twelve throughout the state proved to be a major undertaking. It was estimated that a 5 per cent sample would yield over ten thousand cases, a sufficient number for the type of controlled analysis contemplated. The state was broken down into three major categories: (1) five geographic regions; (2) classification of the school as white or Negro; and (3) size of community—rural (population under 2,500), metropolitan (urban areas in counties having population greater than 100,000) and medium-sized cities (the remainder). Using the fifty-one population cells resulting from this procedure, a proportional stratified random sample of junior and senior high schools was compiled, together with an alternate panel of schools to be used if difficulties were encountered in seeking the cooperation of any particular school in the primary sample. The individual classroom was used as the basic sampling unit for collection of data.

The final sample of 12,892 teenagers came from 182 high schools which participated in the major data collection during the winter and spring of 1956. The extensive network of homemaking educators, the skill of the field research team, and the painstaking developmental work the year before paid off handsomely. With only minor exceptions, every school which was invited to participate did so wholeheartedly. No major biases appeared anywhere in the sample. Only a small handful of completed inventories (less than 2 per cent) had to be discarded because of failure to understand or unwillingness to comply with the instructions.

No claim is made that Texas is a microcosm of the nation, but such a claim might be substantiated. Within the state's seventeen metropolitan counties and five major regions may be found everything from desert sands to deep forests, from rich black lands to arid caliche, from industrial and business complexes to the most isolated rural areas. Urbanization has come to most of the state, with over 70 per cent of the people living in communities with more than 2,500 population. However, there remain back country and backwoods, settlements as untouched as can be found anywhere.

Texas, then, is an agglomeration of East Texas with a mixed white and Negro population, and its forests, family farms, and growing industrialization; the Gulf Coast, with intensive industrialization and extensive large-scale farming and ranching; South Texas, with valleys of commercial fruit and vegetable production, enormous ranches, and a heavy Latin-American population; Central Texas with an old-line, multi-ethnic culture and trading and business centers, rich blackland farms, and growing industrial development; and West Texas with its wide-open spaces, industrialized agriculture, ranching, and even cases of petrochemical and other manufacturing. The state offers as much variety in peoples, their settings, their economic and social situations, as can be found anywhere in the United States. Data from the Texas study, therefore, may be considered as more applicable to other areas of the country than would appear possible at first glance.

METHODS OF ANALYSIS

Two broad approaches were developed for analysis of the massive amount of data. First, a sample of one thousand cases was carefully selected from the total sample in such a manner that each of the geographic regions, community types and racial groups contributed students in exact proportion to population figures obtained from the 1950 census. Such descriptive statistics as means, standard deviations, frequency distributions, and intercorrelations were computed. A detailed analysis shed considerable light on the characteristics of Texas youth.

The second approach involved rigorously controlled analyses of variance in order to test hypotheses about the relationships between personal-background characteristics of the teenager and his attitudes and problems as measured by the fourteen scales in Forms I and II. For this type of analysis, special samples were drawn carefully from the entire pool of data in such a way that certain major variables were held constant or were systematically varied as independent variables in the design. Given nearly thirteen thousand cases from which to draw samples, a number of important variables can be controlled in a manner that is not possible when samples of even a few hundred cases are used. In this respect, the Texas Cooperative Youth Study provides a really unparalleled opportunity to disentangle personal-social factors that are usually hopelessly confounded and to test rigorously hypotheses about the effects of such background factors upon the attitudes and problems of youth.

Several dozen separate studies were designed and carried out employing analysis-of-variance methods. In each case, certain restrictions were placed on the sample to insure clear meaning in the results. In every analysis the dependent variables or scores that were used consisted of all fourteen scaled scores plus occasional selected items that had been stored on the master IBM card. Altogether, more than four hundred such complex analyses were carried out.

One of the major analyses provides an excellent example of the multivariate statistical design repeatedly employed. Many of the findings concerning family structure as related to youth problems and attitudes are based on a design involving 1,440 cases selected to control four major background variables—sex of the student, parental pattern, number of siblings in the family, and level of father's education. Parental pattern consisted of three variations of special theoretical interest: (1) students with both parents present in the home; (2) students with only the mother present because of divorce, separation, or death of the father; and (3) students with a mother and a stepfather present. The number of siblings varied systematically from none to nine in five categories. Level of father's education consisted of three categories: (1) elementary grades only; (2) at least some high school but not beyond; and (3) at least some college level of study completed by the father. Only white students were used. Age variation within school grade was controlled by eliminating students who were too young or too old within each of the four grades. No cases were used in which roomers or relatives outside the primary family were present in the home.

The use of all possible combinations of the four independent variables yielded a four-way factorial design with ninety cells. The advantages of such a design are obvious. Not only is it possible to consider each of the four main effects alone while the other three are held constant, but the interactions among the four independent variables can also be examined systematically at any level. In this particular analysis, four main effects, six first-order interactions, and five higher-order interactions can be tested for significance. When the same analysis is repeated across all fourteen scales, a total of 210 separate F ratios are computed. Some sources of variance will appear significant by chance alone because of the large number of comparisons made in such an analysis. Consequently, one has to be careful to choose rather conservative statistical cutting points for deciding that a finding is significant. In the present instance, a finding was deemed significant only if it represented a consistent trend significant beyond the .01 level.

Specific findings concerning family structure and youth attitudes serve to illustrate both methodology and results of the larger study. Potentially confounding variables have been rigorously controlled by these analysis-of-variance methods.

FAMILY STRUCTURE AND YOUTH RESPONSES

The availability of a very large sample and the use of complex factorial designs makes it possible to study a variety of family structure variables as they affect the responses of youth to the problem and attitude inventories. Family size can be varied from no siblings to nine or more brothers or sisters while at the same time parental pattern, sex of respondent, and other factors in the same design are being considered.

Some highlights of findings concerning family size are presented first, followed by several studies involving different parental patterns. The results of two studies dealing with grandparents living in the same household are summarized next. And finally, variations in sibling order, sex distribution of siblings, and type of siblings are discussed.

FAMILY SIZE

Public opinion would appear to indicate that the more brothers and sisters with whom a person was raised, the better would be his development. This idea is tied in with the belief that children learn from one another and, of course, they do. However, if the above premise ever did hold, the modern urban family tends to refute it.

Youth from the largest families, with six to nine children or more, were consistently more negativistic and less egalitarian in their attitudes. They were the most pessimistic about the world and its people. They were distrustful of relationships with others. For them, authoritarian discipline was more often accepted as the "better way." Criticism of education was more prevalent among them. In addition, these youngsters in families with six or more children resented their dependence upon the family to a greater degree than did youth from smaller families. Family tension was also recognized as high among members of such large households. They felt problems were more numerous between them, their parents, and their peers. Resentment of family life style was most pronounced as well. These findings do not mean that all large families present major difficulties for their children. Rather, they indicate that family size does create real problems for some of today's youth.

Many of the largest families in an urban and technological society are living with economic strain, if not in real poverty. The "culture of poverty" has as one of its indices the number of children in the household. In these family constellations of numerous members, the actual social-emotional distance between parents and children tends to be greater. Person-to-person contact between adults and youth is diluted in proportion to the number of others with whom it must be shared. In "teen" years, companionship and conversation with parents add stability to this highly transitional period of human development.

Moreover, in the largest families, surrogate parenthood is the rule rather than the exception. Older children are forced by circumstances to assume adult parental roles with younger children, while they may still remain emotionally immature themselves. In addition, separation from normal peer group activities would appear to be real, since these older children must assume home and parent-like obligations which cut them off from many of the usual activities of their own age group.

Figure 1 illustrates the interaction between the sex of the respondent and the number of siblings in creating family tension. Girls from large

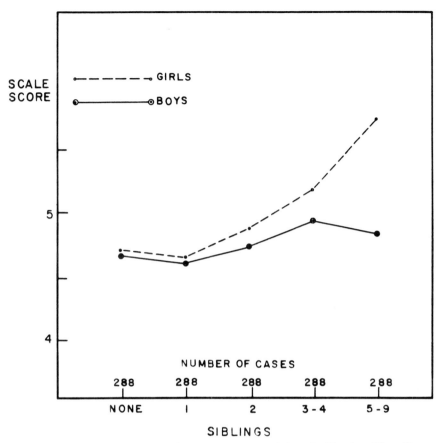

FIGURE 1. Girls in Large Families More Aware of Family Tension Than Boys

families are apparently more concerned about tension in the family than are boys who live in similarly crowded homes. High school girls find themselves in peculiar positions within larger families. They are economic and social necessities to the operation of such households. Demands upon their time for housekeeping assistance, for child care, and for other aspects of home life are especially heavy as brothers and sisters increase in numbers. When a girl's unfulfilled desire for more independence and for a personal life "like the other girls" grows in adolescence, the family relationship cannot help but become more tense. Boys from large families, on the other hand, are quite apt to enjoy more rather than less independence. They may even acquire relative economic self-sufficiency by holding a part-time job. Within the traditional large family, it is the teenage daughter, rather than the son, who tends to feel overburdened with family responsibilities.

PARENTAL PATTERNS

Systematically varying the parental pattern while holding other variables constant revealed some striking trends, including several complex interactions of special interest. Young people living with both natural parents were substantially more authoritarian in their concepts of child-raising than were youngsters living with their mothers alone or in families with stepfathers. When the natural father was replaced by a stepfather, both boys and girls rejected dictatorial management of children more strongly than ever. On the other hand, youth who were living in homes with stepfathers showed greater conflict within the family than either those with both parents or those living with only their mothers. Stepfathers are sometimes viewed as interlopers by children, who resent

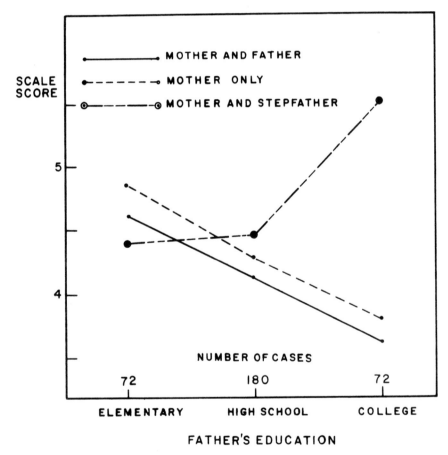

FIGURE 2. Interaction of Parental Pattern and Father's Education for Resentment of Family Life Style

the loss of the real father and the presence of another man in his place.

The nature of the differences between the three parental patterns becomes clearer when other factors are taken into account. Figure 2 shows the interaction between parental pattern and level of real father's education when considering the young person's resentment of family life style. The degree of resentment drops off markedly as the father's education increases, when both mother and father are present, or when the mother remains as the sole parent. But when the mother remarries, the trend is reversed. Replacement of the real father by a stepfather causes no problems when the original father is uneducated. But when the father is college-educated, the intrusion of a stepfather is more strongly resented, providing a source of tension within the new family.

A well-educated father who has been supplanted by a stepfather provides the teenager with a high-level standard against which to measure the intruder. Given any basis in reality for pointing with pride and longing to the real father, the youngster can find fault more easily with the stepfather and the new family pattern. When the mother fails to remarry, the real father still reigns supreme in the fantasies of the teenager, even though he may be present no longer. While this hypothesis is highly appealing in many respects and certainly fits the results obtained, it must be remembered that the hypothesis has been generated from the analysis, not proven by it. Additional studies of a different nature are necessary to get at the underlying personality dynamics responsible for general trends.

Still further insight into the meaning of parental patterns can be obtained by examining a second significant interaction as outlined in Figure 3. The number of siblings present in the family is directly related to the degree of resentment when a stepfather is present, but is unimportant for situations with either a mother alone or the mother and father together. When the respondent is an only child, the resentment of family life style is essentially the same regardless of parental pattern. The presence of one brother or sister significantly increases the level of resentment where a stepfather is concerned. The degree of resentment due to a stepfather goes still higher when there are three children instead of only two. Apparently there is a "ganging up" effect; resentment of the family life style with stepfather present grows more intense, or at least can be expressed more directly, when there are brothers or sisters with whom to share one's resentment.

Is there any evidence that the number of siblings and the level of the father's education reinforce each other in affecting the degree of resentment with a stepfather present? Apparently not. The second-order interaction consisting of parental pattern, number of siblings, and father's education was clearly insignificant in every case. Although both the number of siblings and the level of the father's education have similar effects

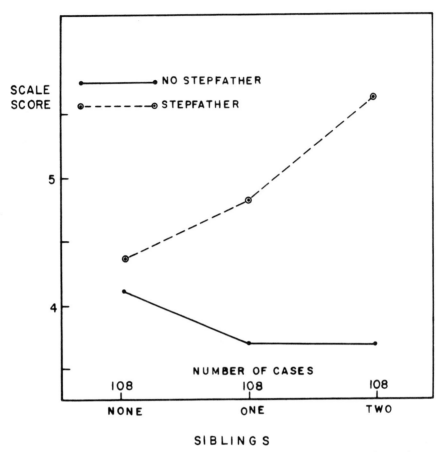

FIGURE 3. Interaction of Parental Pattern and Number of Siblings for Resentment of Family Life Style

on resentment of the stepfather, the effects are of a simple additive nature. Both variables operate independently.

In another study, parental pattern was varied in order to determine the effect of situations involving a father alone and a stepmother, the mirror-image of the previous analysis. Not only do stepfathers turn out to be emotional liabilities in some families, but so do stepmothers, though not to the same degree of severity. As in the case of mothers only, the outcome on the Family Problems scale for lone fathers did not differ from the intact family with both mother and father present. However, when a stepmother entered the picture, a sharp increase in the Family Problems score occurred.

Resentment of family life style was also highest when stepmothers were present. But unlike the previous situation, teenagers with lone fathers showed just as much resentment as when the father remarried and a stepmother was present. The absence of the real mother brings about a noticeable rise in resentment of life style in the family, regardless of whether the father tries to manage the family alone or remarries. Taken together with the earlier finding that resentment did not rise when the mother was alone, these results strongly suggest that the presence of the mother is much more important than the presence of the father in keeping the household functioning smoothly, maintaining a proper level of family "manners," and providing a family life style with which the teenager can identify proudly.

Still another variation in parental pattern was examined systematically in another study, an analysis-of-variance design involving 32 youngsters living in orphanages, 192 living with foster parents, and 528 control cases living with their own parents. Sex of the youth and educational level of the true father were matched across the three variations in parental pattern. All four of the family scales showed highly significant differences according to parental pattern. Generally speaking, the differences between the foster homes and the intact homes were minor, with only the scales for resentment of family life style and family problems showing any significant difference at all. For youngsters in orphanages, however, the rise in family problems, family tension, resentment of family life style, and resentment of dependency was marked, a not unexpected finding in view of the institutional setting characteristic of orphanages. These results confirm the widespread belief of many case workers that foster home placement is generally a better plan than placing a youngster in an orphanage.

GRANDPARENTS IN THE FAMILY

Having nearly thirteen thousand cases from which to draw select samples for special analysis is a decided advantage when dealing with relatively rare family events. Among the respondents in the Texas study were a few who had two, three, or even four grandparents living in the same house as their nuclear family. Several studies were done in which other variables were held constant or systematically varied in a standard design. The presence of one grandmother or one grandfather made no difference whatsoever when compared to intact families with no grandparents present. However, with two or more grandparents in the same household, the amount of family tension and resentment of dependency rose sharply.

In a more refined analysis, using a matched block design to control a number of background factors, the forty-six families with three or four grandparents present were compared with families having only one grandparent and families having none at all. Family tension, resentment of family life style, resentment of dependency, and the scale for personal problems(personal adjustment) increased significantly for youth living in families with three or four grandparents. No differences were noted on any scales between families with one grandparent and those with none. Only when several grandparents are living in the same home, especially when both maternal and paternal grandparents are represented, is there any cause for concern about possible adverse effects upon the problems, concerns, and attitudes of high school youth.

VARIATIONS IN SIBLING PATTERN

Much has been said and written about the personality differences and attitudes of first-born children compared with the second or third child in the family. Although the kinds of personality traits measured by the fourteen scales in the Texas study are quite limited, the large number of cases does make it possible to examine rigorously the effect of sibling order upon response, holding other factors constant by careful selection of the sample. Only intact families having three children were used in one study of 1,020 cases. The sex of the youth who was the respondent; the sex of the two siblings—both male, both female, or mixed; and the ordinal position of the respondent in relation to the age of the other two children in the family served as the primary independent variables in the design. Because of the unusual nature of this analysis and its relevance to much current speculation about the importance of sibling order, all of the higher-order interactions were tested for significance, as well as the main effects.

In spite of the large number of cases, not a single F ratio involving ordinal position proved significant. It made no difference whether a youngster was first, second, or third within the family. First-born children revealed neither more nor less family tension, resentment, personal problems, or negative attitudes than did the second or third child. The same generalization applies regardless of the sex of the respondent or the sex pattern of the siblings. Though indeed there may be some differences in personality due to ordinal position, certainly none were revealed in the present study.

A new factorial design was constructed to extend the possibilities for studying sex of the respondent and sex of patterning of the siblings. Only intact families with six children were used. Four variations of sex distribution among the siblings were employed: (1) five brothers, (2) four brothers and one sister, (3) four sisters and one brother, and (4) five sisters. A total of 130 cases was drawn for this analysis.

Only one of the four sibling patterns stood out markedly from the rest as reflected by mean scale scores—the pattern involving five sisters and no brothers. The totally feminine sibling pattern resulted in a marked rise in scores on seven of the fourteen scales—negative orientation to society, criticism of education, family problems, resentment of dependency, resentment of family life style, social isolation, and personal adjustment problems. The existence of only sisters and no brothers in a large family of six children is a relatively rare pattern which, for some reason, leads to trouble more often than the less extreme patterns or the presence of only brothers. Because of the small number of cases in this all female sibling pattern, only eight families, the results may be somewhat unstable in spite of the fact that the difference is statistically significant.

The interaction between sex of the respondent and sibling pattern proved significant for only one of the scales, financial problems. In Figure 4 it can be seen that the relationship between sex distribution of the siblings and concern for financial troubles is quite different among high school boys than it is among girls. For boys, the degree of worry over money rises sharply in a regular trend as the sibling pattern changes

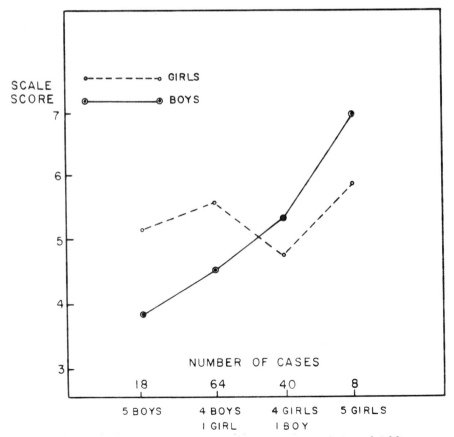

FIGURE 4. Relation of Financial Problems to Sex and Sex of Siblings

from five brothers, through a mixture, to five sisters. No such relationship is apparent for girls. With more sisters in the family, less money is probably available for boys to meet their own special needs.

A final study of sibling pattern focused upon the type of sibling rather than the sex, ordinal position, or number of siblings. A special sample was drawn, consisting only of respondents living with the real mother and a stepfather. The type of sibling was classified in three categories: (1) only true siblings present, (2) only step siblings present, and (3) only half siblings present in the family. The sex of the student and the level of the father's education constituted the second and third variables in the factorial design. A total of 242 cases was needed to fill the 18 cells of the design.

No differences whatsoever could be found among the three types of siblings. As far as the high school youth is concerned, it doesn't matter particularly whether his brothers and sisters are true siblings, step siblings, or half siblings. Much more important than the type of sibling is the parental pattern, especially the presence or absence of a stepfather, as indicated in the findings reported earlier.

SUMMARY

While Texas may serve as a prototype for the nation as a whole, given the wide range of ethnic, socioeconomic, and geographic variation in the Texas Cooperative Youth Study, no claim can be substantiated that today's families are small societies within themselves. Family structure is indeed important in shaping the attitudes of youth. Number of siblings, parental pattern, presence of grandparents, and sex distribution of siblings are all significant factors influencing the kinds of attitudes acquired by youth. Yet the family is really only one aspect of a complicated whole, a social subsystem within the life space of the growing adolescent. Peer group pressures, sociocultural variation in the environment, and ethnic, religious, and educational factors are at least as influential as the structural aspects of the family.

The present discussion has been limited to the more formal or structural aspects of the family and their influence on the problems, concerns, and attitudes of youth. Responses by nearly thirteen thousand high school youth to specially designed attitude scales and problem inventories constitute the basic data for analysis. Only a few highlights of the Texas Cooperative Youth Study are given here, the bulk of the findings having been presented elsewhere in the full report of the research. By working with very large samples randomly drawn from the total population, many variables that usually obscure the meaning of family structure have been adequately controlled or systematically varied as part of the research design. Only in this manner can one approach the precision of experimental methods where experimentation is unfeasible. While it is not possible to probe deeply into the reasons for the relationships and trends that are discovered by such an extensive design, the findings themselves are relatively unequivocal. It remains for other investigators employing quite different research methods to explain more fully why some family structure variables are important factors shaping the attitudes and personalities of youth while others are not.

PART II

ADOLESCENCE
IN DIFFERENT SOCIAL
SETTINGS

FOUR

THE NEW WORLD VIEW OF NEGRO YOUTH

Lewis W. Jones

One of the considered limitations of formal education is the transmission of knowledge and skills that are already outmoded when the youth of the society are given instruction in them. In a slowly changing society, the traditional thought forms and action patterns of the culture continue to be useful as they serve to reinforce stability. But sudden or rapidly accelerated change in a society produces disjunction between what its youth are taught and what they experience. This contradiction can assume the proportions of a psychological and a sociological cataclysm when youth answers the question, "Who am I?" with negations such as "I am not my parents' child" and "I am not my teachers' pupil." Behavior, in this circumstance, provides empirical evidence with which to elaborate Muzafer Sherif's reference group theory (1953).

As young people look about them and change the weighting of the valences attached to others who are significant to them, their world undergoes a transformation that may be in consonance with, or contradictory to, technological and institutional change in process.

The 1963 annual report of the Federal Reserve Bank of New York considers a major challenge to the nation to be the finding of "ways of dealing with the problems created by the accelerated rise in the labor force and by technological progress."

The challenge of stepping up the rate of growth of our economy appears even greater for the years ahead because of the more rapid increase that is expected in the labor force. Some glimpse of the coming surge in job applicants was already apparent in 1963, as the youths who were born in the baby boom following World War II began to reach the age at which many seek either permanent or part-time employment. Thus, the number of sixteen and seventeen-year olds in the labor force jumped by about 250,000 in 1963, in contrast to decreases in this age group in the two preceding years. By 1970, according to Labor Department projections, the prospect is that there will be nearly 20 million persons under twenty-five years of age in the labor force—an increase of 6 million persons, or 45 per cent, over the number in this age bracket in 1960; during the 1950's, the size of this age bracket grew by only 370,000 or less than 3 per cent (Federal Reserve Bank, 1963, p. 18).

In a recently published collection of essays edited by Eli Ginzberg under the title *Technology and Social Change,* there is a statement that poses a challenging hypothesis for us with its suggestion that Negroes in this expanded young population will be acutely disadvantaged. The second essay in this volume is "The Post-Industrial Society" written by Daniel Bell. He says:

> The greater emphasis placed on educational competence will mean that groups which lose out early in the educational race will be quickly excluded from society as a whole. In the next twenty or thirty years the economic situation of the Negro may become relatively worse, simply because the rate of economic change is such as to outrun the increase in educational opportunities available to him. Apart from a thin stratum who do have better educational opportunities, a large part of the Negro population, more than half, continues to live in the South, many in the agrarian sector. This agrarian population has been relatively excluded from society. In this sense coming into the industrial work force was a way for the Negro to enter modern society. The fact that a large proportion of the Negro population continues to live in this agrarian situation, many of them functionally illiterate, some of whom will emigrate to the North, means that the position of the Negroes will worsen. A disturbing indication today is the dropout rate for Negroes in schools in New York and Detroit. This rate is an indicator of the position of the Negro thirty years from now.
>
> Lastly, the growth of technical specialization creates a strain on the cultural level of society; the term is used here not in its anthropological sense but in the sense that culture is the symbolic expression of what is occurring in society. People try to symbolize their experiences in order to make them intelligible to each other. This is the way nineteenth-century culture developed, a culture that arose out of an awareness of social mobility. The novels of the time represented the way in which the awareness of the new experiences of society found symbolic expression. It will become more and more difficult to find common symbolical expressions of the forms of specialization that are now developing. As a consequence an increasing disjunction between the culture and the society may arise. This is not just a problem of the political alienation of the intelligentsia but a much more pervasive problem of the inability of the society to find cultural terms for expressing what is occurring in the realm of science and in life itself. This is not just the 'two cultures' problem presented by Snow because it is not just a matter of the education of people. It is, rather, the problem of the inability to find symbolic expressions for the kinds of experiences that take place in the work life created by the new forms of intellectual technology. (Bell, 1964)

In our discussion here, we need not accept the limitations Professor Bell sets for himself in focusing on work, technology and science. We may be extravagant in undertaking the appraisal of a population, its existential circumstances, and an array of symbols meaningful to it. Of course, nothing conclusive or even definitive can be presented, but questions will be raised and an unresearched universe will be suggested.

Several fundamental propositions require specification to preclude expression of intellectual racism.

1. There is now, and there will be an increasingly greater youth population in the United States in the age group at which transition to adulthood is anticipated according to established folk belief.

2. These youths expand the labor force of an economy that is already reducing the man-hours required to produce an increasing volume of goods.

3. Because of an obsolescent educational system, only a fraction of these youths will, in the foreseeable future, have marketable skills.

4. Perhaps no previous youth generation has been so inculcated with anticipation of opportunity and affluence as this one.

5. The disjunction between their goals and their means can be nothing less than confounding to a young population that has been encouraged to expect so much.

6. Historical circumstances make Negro youth a graphic illustration of the process by which disadvantage may be built into a society.

7. Ambivalence in many culture traits describes the raising of expectations and thwarting of their realization characteristic of the entire disadvantaged population, of which Negro youths are a disproportionate element.

The focus of attention on the Negro by social scientists may, by inference and implication, add up to intellectual racism in favor of or against the Negro. Social scientists need to consider the effects of social action which rewards the disabilities of Negro youth, but not undertake the prodigious tasks of attacking the problem of disadvantage in society.

NEGRO YOUTH AND DISADVANTAGE IN SOCIETY

The conduct of Negroes both in the South and outside since 1960 has challenged the elaborate mythology about their personal characteristics, their conception of the world and their accepted way of life in the American social matrix. Formerly, the behavior of Negroes, as they followed unplanned and apparently unconscious modes of action in their everyday living, as they obeyed a time-honored etiquette in their contacts with white people, seemed to indicate accommodation to a subordinate status. However, there were deviations, and planned and deliberate action by some Negroes. Under the aegis of the National Association for the Advancement of Colored People they went into the courts to challenge the legal status prescribed for them in local and state laws.

In the now current emphasis on direct action to remove inequities affecting the circumstances of Negroes, the importance of the preparatory redefinition of the legal status of the Negro may not be recognized for what it was. The vision of a promised land of unrestricted citizenship came into focus when the courts declared it to be Negroes' for the taking. Hesitation to undergo the hardships which occupancy of their title-hold would entail stirred a restiveness in a bold, usually young, Negro minority. Some recognized that the monolithic system of segregation, though under-girded by laws and customs and supported by a common property of attitudes and belief system, was not impregnable. Yet many feared the cost to them of an assault upon it.

What the traditional world of Negro youth has been is no mystery. As a matter of record we have its documentation in an articulated group of studies made just a generation ago, between 1935 and 1940. I refer to the studies commissioned by the American Council on Education for the American Youth Commission. Results of original field research were pub-lished in the following volumes:

Children of Bondage: The Personality Development of Negro Youth in the Urban South, by Allison Davis and John Dollard (1940).

Negro Youth at the Crossways: Their Personality Development in the Middle States, by E. Franklin Frazier (1940).

Growing Up in the Black Belt: Negro Youth in the Rural South, by Charles S. Johnson (1941).

Color and Human Nature: Negro Personality Development in a Northern City, by W. Lloyd Warner, Buford H. Junker, and Walter A. Adams (1941).

Each of these studies is based upon conditions as found in the particular area and uses methods of research especially adapted to those conditions. All, however, are pointed at the central problem: "What are the effects upon the personality development of Negro youth of their membership in a minority racial group?" The studies supplement each other in the insights which they contribute to an understanding of this problem.

Analysis and re-specification of the generalizations offered in these studies might provide a base line including hypotheses for research that could now be undertaken. Furthermore, social scientists are by no means limited to these four volumes in seeking to clarify and specify personality configurations or societal structures in the search for testable hypotheses to guide research into the present world and present self-images of Negro youth. There are Frazier's studies of the Negro family, Powdermaker's *After Freedom* (1939), John Dollard's *Caste and Class in Southern Town* (1937), Davis and Gardner's *Deep South* (1941), as well as Davis' sub-sequent research on Negro children.

Although research is in progress, some segmented and some inclusive, I still do not have empirical findings to justify the ambitious title given to this chapter. I should, in addition, call attention to research on child rearing being done in Washington, D.C. by Hylan Lewis, the most respected sociologist who happens to be Negro. Being initiated now is a study in child rearing in Nashville, Tennessee, by S. O. Roberts, a psychologist of superior competence, with whom I am collaborating on a study of *The Education and Outlook of College Students* in five Negro colleges. Certainly the work of Kenneth Clark is known to most people interested in this concern. There are, or will be, more programs of amelioration of the psychological stresses and the sociological impact of economic and social circumstance on Negro youth. There should be a paradigm for research in this area to whose subdivisions empirical findings collected might be allocated, interpreted and re-specified in an agreed-upon theoretical context.

To describe the base line of geographic distinctions in the world of Negro youth, let us take the American Youth Commission categories:

1. Rural South
2. Urban South
3. Border urban
4. Northern urban

Add to this what Hylan Lewis gave us in *Blackways of Kent* (1955), namely:

5. Southern small town

Thirty years ago, the preponderance of Negro youth was being born in the rural South. Many would not arrive at maturity there, and fewer would remain when adulthood permitted their choosing a place of residence. Still, in 1960, according to the U.S. Census, 63 per cent of Negro youth under age twenty lived in the South, with 37 per cent outside. Accepting the census limitations by the prescribed enumerative categories of Southern Negroes under age twenty, 30 per cent were "rural non-farm," 13 per cent "rural farm," and 57 per cent in Southern urban areas.

There is a mass of demographic data, important to sociologists, that would provide the skeleton of social structure: family income, ratio of persons under age twenty to persons over twenty, educational level of persons under twenty. Much could be made of this, with accompanying inferences as to comparative status, achievement performance within age-group level, and aspiration potential which would be formidable.

In terms of geography, I venture that the Southern city is *the place* where a Negro child has the best chance for socioeconomic mobility. The most insecure and, potentially, the most frustrated Negro child is the one who lives in the rural non-farm South. There he lives in economic insecurity; his education is patently substandard; his recreational provisions are crude or nonexistent; there, for him, the future is a boring,

depressing present. There, in the rural non-farm South, the Negro youth
is aware that he may not mature into a social entity he would accept.
He is painfully conscious that he has no hope of being what he would
like to be in the place to which sooner or later he must go. May I remind
you that except for *Blackways of Kent* there is, to my knowledge, no
research being conducted on these youth. Where better could a study
of frustration be conducted?

The question raised here is not solely of the Negro. It is of an
interstitial and insecure segment of the American population that is
faced with loss of its former significance. The Negro is in dire straits in
this milieu, but his situation only exaggerates the straits of all the people
of the milieu. Economic problems, political reapportionments, and out-
migration mark the decline of rural non-farm communities all over the
United States.

I have an overpowering urge, as sociologist transcends Negro, to
suggest that we reject considerations of prejudice and discrimination
against the Negro. A more fruitful research orientation is that in which
deprivation, of whatever variety, is studied as process, and the resultant
disadvantage as the social product. Diminution in social growth is a
function of the rejected "we" in accepting the norms and values of the
favored "them." On the basis of this hypothesis, we move from the
demographic to the economic tangent. At this point we suggest a
hypothesis contrary to popular pronouncements.

Negroes were aware of the change in their value as the slave system
gave way to the tenant system. Under slavery they had value and were
protected, as valuable possessions are protected. They came to interpret
the philosophy of the new class of masters, who had no investment in
them as persons:

> Kill a mule,
> Buy another—
> Kill a nigger,
> Hire another.

They felt that these new southerners were concerned only about
their labor. So long as they could work, the landlords did not care about
their well-being. There was no appeal to be made from a government of
landlords or their agents.

That they could laugh at the exploitation about which they were
helpless may be strange human behavior, but laugh they did and took
pains to put their laughter into rhyme. One of the universally quoted
jingles was:

> A 'aught's a 'aught
> And a figger's a figger.
> All for the white,
> None for the nigger.

Still, however exploited the Negroes were in the plantation system that replaced the slave system, they remained essential to agricultural production until machines were invented to do the tasks they had done. Then, by about 1940, the Negro agricultural worker became expendable.

By 1960, the Negro was relatively poorer than he had ever been before at any historical point in his presence in America. During slavery each Negro knew his worth: he had a price determined by age, weight, sex, and the intermeshing of skills—fecundity, appearance, occupation. He was a commodity, and as such, he was valued and protected. In freedom, his economic worth went through changes because his world had changed.

Despite the oratorical flourishes about the progress of the Negro, the foreboding projections of Dr. Bell are substantiated by 1960 census figures on income. In 1940, the median white family had $838 more per annum to feed, clothe, house and educate its children than the median Negro family did. In 1960, the median white family had $2,366 more per annum. True, the statistics show increases in the median income of Negro families, but reports since 1960 show this to have dropped back. Negroes have made dramatic progress, but the economic progress of the white population has been greater. Negro youth are aware of their disadvantaged economic position in a more meaningful sense than statistics convey. Until a very few years ago Negro youth prepared to enter the labor market under severe restrictions about which they saw themselves impotent. They received poor preparation which did not really matter because those with superior preparation found no demand for it in the labor market.

EDUCATIONAL DISADVANTAGE

Another changing dimension of the world of Negro youth is the institutional. The first massive assault on the old world order was directed at schools and the educational disadvantages of Negro youth.

According to its special issue on ten years of public school desegregation, *Southern School News* reported in May, 1964, that the percentage of Negroes attending schools with whites in the Southern and border region was 9.3 per cent at the end of the 1963-64 school year, and for the South alone, 1.18 per cent. In the border areas, the percentages were more impressive, ranging from 28 per cent in Oklahoma to 84 per cent in the District of Columbia; but the numbers of Negro children enrolled in schools in the border states were about one-sixth of those enrolled in Southern schools. The speed of desegregation in the public schools of the South has been more than "deliberate."

The principle underlying the educational policy governing what was offered in the Negro school has been "Education for Present Opportunity." This was interpreted as education for the community in which the

child lived. It was described as preparing for a fuller and more constructive life where you lived by being able to perform efficiently what you
might expect to do in life. This was regarded as practical education and
demonstrations of it were applauded. Spokesmen for the white community
had high praise for the Negro schools' offerings in home economics,
trades and agriculture.

Another principle that had a strange appeal for support came in the
motto, "Take what you have and make what you want." This amounted
to Negro children taking nothing and making something out of it. In
trades and home economics classes, orange crates were made into kitchen
cabinets; potato sacks were made into rugs; and animal feed sacks were
made into dresses. Used tin cans were made into drinking cups, biscuit
cutters, or metal scoops. These creations were produced in the courses
that were offered under the title, "Resource Use Education." The Negro
child came to see that the resources of the community available to him
were to be found in the refuse heap.

What the Negro child had learned when he completed high school,
or had stopped at any point below high school graduation, was certainly
not the same thing that the white child at the allegedly comparable level
had learned. The same was true of instruction at the college level in tax-
supported institutions. Examination of the catalogues of instruction
offered in the state colleges still shows immediately that there is no intent
or attempt to provide for Negroes what is provided for white young
people.

Many instances may be reported to illustrate psychological disabilities and distortions which those who have been previously excluded
show in their first experience of inclusion. The South has "sown the wind"
by broadcasting the seeds of ignorance of human relations and social
skills, and many whirlwinds of personal and social friction are the harvest
outside of the South.

The current hue and cry over the educational deprivation of lower
status youth and the "drop-out" problem point up no new problem. It is
simply an old social-psychological problem whose cumulative results
are being bewailed in a deafening crescendo. As long ago as 1947, Charles
S. Johnson wrote:

> There is a lack of any discernible relationship between the formal content
> of instruction designed to relate the youth to his ongoing past and to provide
> him with the manual and intellectual tools for dealing with his environment—
> and the traditions and status definitions of the Negro youth.

The rural youth meets school with mixed attitudes toward the value of
education. On the one hand, the school is either expected to provide a formula
for escape from a status, or it is casually accepted for its social satisfactions
without serious regard for the subject matter presented. Studies have revealed
that considerably more than half of the youth are uninterested in school; that

most of them view American and European history as remote and unrelated to their own past or future careers; that they lack the psychological set and self-confidence for using numbers; that they read poorly and without a will to translate the printed page into familiar experiences; that they lack the elements of precision and exactness in manual manipulation; and in general make little or no connection between school and everyday life. Most of the youth eventually drop out of school before reaching the 7th grade; and of those who remain, the extent of the success of the education which they receive can be measured by the expressed desire to leave the setting entirely. (Johnson, 1963, p. 44)

Martin Deutsch, discussing the urban Negro child, says:

It is highly unlikely that any one factor could account for the poor performance and deprived psychological state of the experimental group; it is more realistic to see the urban Negro child as subject to many influences which converge on him, all contributing to the effects noted. Among these influences certainly not the least is his sensing that the larger society views him as inferior and expects inferior performance from him, as evidenced by the general denial to him of realistic vertical mobility possibilities. Under these conditions, it is understandable that the Negro child—the experimental group in the present study—would tend strongly to question his own competencies, and in so questioning would be acting largely as others expect him to act. This is an example of what Merton has called the "self-fulfilling prophecy"—the very expectation itself is a cause of its fulfillment. The middle-class orientation of the school helps little in recognizing the realities of the problem, and contributes little toward the development of value systems and activities directed toward breaking this circular dynamic process. (Deutsch, 1963, p. 65)

As in no other area of institutional activity, there has been greater change in higher education. This is particularly true at the college level. Elaborate efforts are now being made to enroll Negro students in traditional white colleges in and outside the South. This beckoning to Negro college students, rather than forbidding them, is encouraging higher esteem of himself by the Negro youth.

ACCOMMODATION AND CHANGE

For nearly a century following emancipation, the Negro accommodated himself to the social restrictions which hedged him about. An intricate etiquette of race relations sustained this accommodative system. Negro children were taught by their parents that they must accept the condtion in which they found themselves and warned of the painful punishments to be meted out to them if they should not. Parents themselves punished young children for violation of the etiquette, following the logic that, in so doing, they were conditioning the child to save himself from the dire consequences that such transgressions would bring from the outside when he was older.

Negro children were actually told: "This is the white man's country, he makes the laws, he has the guns. You are helpless." Generations of youths grew to adulthood and, becoming parents themselves, gave their children the same indoctrination in subservience. How to get along, and to win such rewards as might be won were taught and demonstrated. Even when opportunity came to the individual youth, he was unbelieving and hesitant about taking it.

Negroes who have been indoctrinated with a belief in their own inadequacy and dependence, if not inferiority, present a problem of adjustment. Any white face becomes that of the persecutor. The white person disposed to be friendly may be alienated by the Negro's responses to "whiteness" developed over the childhood years. Outside the South, this resentment may take some form of aggression that was denied in the South. Outside the South, Negroes in the lower economic positions help in the preservation of the ghettos because of the deep feeling of needing to band together for protection, or simply of a desire to be removed from those they feel will use them ill. Many others remain in the ghetto because of devices on the part of whites to confine them there. To seek refuge in the ghetto is the other side of the coin of segregation outside the South.

Meanwhile, the Negro middle class increased in numbers and significance. For the Negro child new models appeared, especially in the widely publicized *first* and *only* achiever who had breached a barrier past which others could go. There came more and more individuals who expressed protest and dared action against powerful proscriptions.

There came leaders of protest and positive action that included some Negro businessmen, physicians, dentists, and college professors, who placed their loyalty to their Negro followers above any relationship with the white power structure. State and city employees, college and public school teachers, are deterred in many places in the South from taking active roles in the organizations and activities for furthering desegregation. Most presidents of local NAACP chapters, and other organizations pressing the cause of desegregation, are now drawn from those who depend for a livelihood on a Negro clientele and against whom the local whites can take fewer reprisals.

Population changes, expansion of the Negro middle class, emergence of a new leadership among Negroes, adoption of direct action once their prerogatives were legally clarified, and new policies of the federal government in the protection of civil rights—together, these have effected some improvement in Negro status in the South.

It was not until 1960 that young Negroes discovered and began to use social action measures that meant taking a strong initiative. Discarded were the acceptance of subservient rewards and the acceptable means of obtaining them. Rejected was the slow pressure against limits and boundaries. Gone was the hope to be the individual who escaped as first or only. The new tactics and strategy adopted by Negro youths themselves began the revolution to change the Negro's world.

The hopes of Negro youth today about their tomorrow are in striking contrast to the hopes their fathers held. Negroes below the age of twenty know what immediate drastic change means. These children see respected Negro adults and courageous Negro children in front-page news, in contrast to the old newspaper practice of ignoring Negroes except for criminal acts. The quickened concern of Southern legislatures over their education, heretofore neglected, has projected Negro children into a sudden prominence they had never known. They realize that the eyes of the world are on this drama as it unfolds, with Negro children playing stellar roles for the first time in their lives, supported or opposed, as the case may be, by their white contemporaries as they make their personal decisions in a new relationship. This generation of children lives in a climate of change and they will increasingly influence its course.

The greatest change since 1940 has been the redefinition of the Negro's legal status in the South through a succession of judicial decisions that progressed from removal of specific, negative legal sanctions to a positive affirmation of legal protection of common opportunity without distinction for Americans.

The second institutional area on which attention has been focused is the political. As in the case of educational inequities, there was recourse to the courts for removal of state and local legalisms that denied the vote to Negroes. When the legal questions had been answered in terms of the federal Constitution, the struggle for the vote was only begun. Negro youths took responsibility for instructing prospective voters to meet local requirements for registration, and carried on a campaign still in progress to secure registration of qualified voters. Intimidation and bald violence against would-be registrants, as well as undisguised brutality toward the youthful workers for voter registration, is one of the harshest lessons Negro youths have learned. Obstruction to use of the ballot by state and local police power, and by state officials, has made clear the need for free exercise of federal power to protect the politically deprived citizen in southern citadels of segregation.

Circumstances of cultural change over the past quarter of a century have produced new functions and new roles for both whites and Negroes, and new relationship patterns between them are emerging. The many changes that might be described are affecting the young even more than their elders. They are learning and experiencing without the need for unlearning or forgetting. Their normal expectations in many things exceed the vague fond hopes of their parents' childhoods.

During the past decade, young Negroes have learned more about schooling from outside experiences than from class instruction. As an

institution around which controversy has centered, the public school has
come up for reassessment. Negro children now know more about the
provisions and operations of public schools than most adults did ten years
ago. They have had to go through hostile crowds into classrooms where
they were unwelcome. No parent or friend, or even advocate, can do this
for them. They have done it for themselves in Clinton and Little Rock
and Charlotte. When Negro teenagers made these pioneering journeys,
with television following their progress for other Negro children everywhere to see, the Negro child got another kind of preparation for the
future. These children are aware that others may make opportunities
possible for them, but they alone can take advantage of them. They must
be prepared for this as an unpleasant experience.

The Negro child in the South today has a better understanding of
the Supreme Court, the Presidency, and the Congress than foregoing
generations had. It is, moreover, an understanding that relates these
institutions directly to *his* fortunes and welfare. Experiences of Negro
youth in this decade, and their own discussions of them, have provided
an uncommon education in the value content of American culture, including political principles and processes of the government under which we
live. Perhaps no other generation of young people has had so intensive
an indoctrination in the American value system, and certainly none has
had the inconsistencies and contradictions so clearly presented to it.
Southern children and youth have had conflicting social expectations
defined for them and negations of these expectations spelled out in detail.
No other generation of the young has been so confronted with the bright
illusions of our political institutions or has had these illusions so ruth-
lessly attacked.

I cannot say better than I said in my paper for the 1960 White
House Conference on Children and Youth what the basic changes in the
self-image of Negro youth have been:

The experiences of Negro children in the South during the past decade
might well be expected to have affected their conceptions of themselves. Their
behavior and conduct offer evidence of some attributes of their self-image.
Their self-esteem ranges from pride to bumptiousness. Ideas they hold about
their opportunities are expressed by some in striving to realize an ambition and
by others in a demand for unearned rewards. Consciousness of having powerful
and influential advocates of their greater opportunity is expressed by some
in quiet confidence, and by others in a challenging arrogance. Encouragement
to venture where their parents did not dare has affected the respect shown
for those parents and teachers who urge caution and restraint. As in all revolutionary circumstances in which a new freedom is gained, there is considerable aimless, random, irresponsible behavior on the part of those who
have no constructive goals. Uncertainty and a sense of inadequacy are revealed
in a truculence that challenges any imposed discipline.

FEATURES OF THE NEW SELF-IMAGE

The one clear feature of the new self-image of Negro youth, of whatever status, is a sense of security expressed by assuming positive and sometimes aggressive attitudes and postures. A Southern white man, who recently returned to the South after eight years in other parts of the world, said that the most startling change he noticed was that "Negroes look you straight in the eye now." The newly gained confidence that young Negroes have in themselves, and their feeling of security in expressing their aspirations, appear to be disturbing facts of contemporary Southern life that many Southern white people are loath to face.

Charles S. Johnson wrote in 1956 what would become the valedictory to his long career of studying race relations. He said:

The present-day Southern Negro does not share the belief of the Southern white that he is inferior as a human being, even though he may earn lower wages and have fewer years of schooling. . . . What is for white Southerners' most difficult to understand, in these days, is the absence of both the belief in inferiority and the simulation of this belief. The Southern Negro viewpoint is more broadly national than regional. There are very few, if any, Southern Negroes who do not want full American citizenship, even though there are undoubtedly those who, if they had it, would make no better use of it than some of their white counterparts. In philosophy the Southern Negro identification is with the nation and not with the Southern region, which is, in spirit, separatist. (Johnson, 1956)

Negro youth strive to give the impression that they do not feel inferior, even though the behavior of some is clear evidence that they are overcompensating for such feeling. Unfortunately, a type of juvenile delinquency among Negro children and youth is appearing in the South. It is expressed in challenges to the traditional authority of whiteness and to those Negro adults who occupy their positions through white authority.

Perhaps the most unfortunate aspect of the young Negro's conception of himself is that he must depend upon himself to carry his battle with the support of few, if any, white people in his local community. Those whites who are sympathetic to his cause are silent for very good reasons of their own. Those who most loudly declare their "friendship" for him are those who do so while confidently asserting they know no "good" Negro has aspirations of equality, and who denounce his heroes and threaten mayhem if he persists in pursuit of his ambitions. A state official in high office expressed this often repeated opinion: "I'm the best friend the Negro ever had, but integration will come only over my dead body." If such are the Negro's white "friends," no wonder he is convinced he has none. It is certainly unfortunate when Negro youth get the idea that they must protect themselves, or be prepared to do so, because the duly constituted authority for preserving the security of citizens in their home communities leaves them at the mercy of enemies who would do violence to them. Although their elders caution them to turn the other cheek, many come to feel that their security lies in their readiness to meet violence with violence.

Another feature of the new self-image is that young Negroes are seeing themselves as leaders rather than as being in preparation for leadership. Students who suffered indignities as the first ones to enter desegregated schools, with the responsibility for persisting in their attendance despite discouraging experiences, feel this way. Students who challenged bus segregation in Tallahassee, those who staged a boycott in Orangeburg, and those who mounted a campaign to desegregate business establishments in Oklahoma have some of the feeling. The problem growing out of such a self-conception is the danger of intemperate actions that may draw reprisals.

A third feature of the new self-image is that young Negroes do not feel themselves to be a helpless minority. Instead they consider the diehard segregationists to be the minority, whatever their positions may be in the community or however important may be the political offices they hold. And they scoff at them as ludicrous buffoons clinging desperately to a lost cause. The young Negro in the South sees himself as belonging to the majority that includes the federal government, Negroes who have advanced outside the South, and white people of powerful influence outside the South. Some of problems posed by this feature of the new self-image are the following: (1) an obstruction to an early rapprochement with young Southern whites, and (2) the disenchantment possible if their allies give them too little or too tardy support.

A fourth feature of the new self-image is the belief that they hold to the great human values uncompromisingly. This is especially true in relating their struggle to the independence struggles of Asia and Africa. A problem raised by this conception is the possibility that some may join the divisive black nationalist movements in the United States, which would be a rejection of all the arduous struggle for integration and would bring further tension and conflict.

The major question raised by the Negro youth's new self-image is what positive approaches can be taken in order that a constructive productive humanism can mature out of the current personality conflicts in a setting of social confusion.

Lester F. Carr (1964), a clinical psychologist, has undertaken a review of student social action in terms of personality and culture. I am giving excerpts of this review with his permission:

Some social scientists have pointed to cultural factors as significant determinants of involvement in social problems (Powdermaker, 1939; Davis and Dollard, 1940; Jones, 1961; Frazier, 1957). Others such as McLean (1949), Goff (1950), Grossack (1957) and Rose (1959) have looked to personality dynamics as related forces, while Moore (1925) advanced the proposition that "neuromuscular machinery" may predispose one to engage in "social action." Also, efforts to equate social action involvement with emotional maladjustment have not proved too fruitful, as for example, Murphy (1937), Nelson (1938), and Kerr (1952). In sharp contrast to this position, there are those who view social action interest as the mark of the more healthy personality: Maslow (1954) has put forth the concept of "self-actualization"; Hollander (1958) posited "idiosyncrasy credits"; and Jahoda (1959) has laid stress upon "personal involvement in an issue." Solomon and Fishman (1961) see sitting-in activities as a "passive-aggressive" act. They feel that the philosophy and practice of "non-violence" is well in line with the traditionally submissive role of the Negro in the face of social and personal abuses.

For Solomon and Fishman, protest demonstrations represent a new way for the "new" Negro to channel deep-seated feelings of hostility and hate—although, as they indicate, such aggressive strivings are to be distinguished from the acting-out of delinquents and other anti-social personalities. As these authors pointed out this is action "consciously based on moral imperatives." Still other investigators have emphasized "social situational field forces" as significant determinants of individual involvement in social issues. Such social forces range from rapid socio-political changes to social pressure, small group dynamics, and roles. In a later paper, Solomon and Fishman (1962) view the civil-rights movement, a la Erickson (1956), as serving as an external superstructure upon which some attempt at identity resolution can be based. "When this identity crisis is successfully passed through, the results should be a new self-awareness, dignity, self-esteem and goal-directed work consonant with their abilities—in short, successful identity formation and movement to new maturity."

In the fall of 1961, Roberts and Carr made a study of Negro American college students attending a Southern, predominantly Negro university and factors related to their involvement in "sit-in" demonstrations. The study sought first to determine a three-way social action classification of a small sample of students as "Active," "Students in General," and "Apathetic." The second task was to seek possible differences among these groups in terms of such variables as regional and socioeconomic background, intelligence, knowledge, adjustment and personality, and academic achievement. It was found that "Active Students" were only slightly different, if at all, from "Students in General," except for a greater amount of social aggression and a group academic record not quite as good as would be expected from their ability. It was suggested that the involvement of "Active Students" in sit-ins may be an outlet for energies not fully used in the class-room, and hence, their participation serves as a form of personal and possible social fulfillment. It was also conjectured that these students have a strong social conscience and, therefore, seek fulfillment of their ideals with little regard to personal consequences in their role as "crusaders."

Employing all freshmen and sophomores at this same university, a more comprehensive investigation was made by Carr and Roberts (1963). Utilizing social attitude, self-concept, and background variables—few differences, if any, were found between 332 Negro American students at three levels of social action participation (actively involved, moderately involved, and non-involved). In fact, examination of all 124 variables (including the 1961 study) revealed no "individual characteristic" which was significantly related to social action behavior (*i.e.*, accounted for more than 9 per cent of the variance). In addition, intensive interviews of a small number of students suggested that "social situational field forces" were also related to participation; but even here there was no variable, or combination of variables, which could account for the social action involvement of a "majority" of students. Some reasons given by students for not taking part in protest demonstrations included: (1) general apathy—"Students seem to be a living-dead almost and have a lack of interests in an awful lot of things"; (2) parental pressure—". . . parents would be faced with an embarrassing situation if the student's name would come out," "my parents have definitely advised me against involving myself"; (3) pressure from teachers and university officials to make high grades; and (4) complaints about the confusion and disorganization of civil-rights local and national groups. Some reasons given by students for participating in demonstrations included: (1) "inspired"—by an activist's talk, mass meeting, television or newspaper accounts; (2) individual persuasion—friend, roommate, date "talked me into it"; (3) value system—"It was in line with my philosophy of life"; and (4) curiosity and thrill-seeking—"exciting, breaks up the monotony of life, a lot of fun." (Carr, 1964)

ORIENTATIONS OF NEGRO YOUTH

Negro youths themselves are divided into groupings with distinctly different ideological orientations, each with its own means for attaining the common goal of unrestricted aspiration and achievement by young Negroes. These groupings may be placed on a continuum.

1. ACCOMMODATERS

Negro youth who appear to accept the improvements within the traditional Negro status, and who receive an education to return to teaching or other traditional occupations with satisfaction.

"My aims, ambitions, and goals in life are to become an educated and well-informed citizen of my community. I desire to obtain my Master's in education and do other graduate work in history and economics, or both. Marriage and a family is an idea that often concerns me. Social equality is too a concern of mine; thus, I may say that my goals include those things that will enable me to have a fairly well-rounded life, which for me includes education, religion, marriage and social activities."

2. TRANSCENDERS

Those youth who accept new opportunities open to them in education and occupations and strive to meet the qualifications required to take advantage of these new occupations. These positions carry with them status achievement that means no invidious distinctions. These are the "study-hard," self-development youth who have no time for demonstrations or other activities that would slow down their personal development.

"My ambitions are an education (college and medical school), marriage, and a better understanding of myself. I am working on these goals every day. I presently attend Fisk University (sophomore) and I plan to attend Meharry Medical College upon graduation. I have worked in hospitals and my father's office. To attain a happy marriage is a task I have undertaken—I have no immediate plans for this goal—that is, I am too young for marriage. I wish to marry upon graduation from Fisk. Achieving a better understanding of myself seems to be a goal that will take a lifetime, but it is important."

3. SOCIAL ACTIVISTS

Youthful activists committed to the Student Nonviolent Coordinating Committee point-of-view. They, in cooperation with white youths, carry on an activist campaign involving different tactics to achieve desegregation and integration. For the most part these youths accept the philosophy of Martin Luther King. However, deviationists and revisionists are conspicuous in this group.

A. Secular Integrationists. Committed to integration because it is desirable to remove restrictions that hedge them in a disadvantaged sphere of activity.

"Well, you see, I'm very confused about my role in life. I have an inferiority complex about being Negro and about being me. I have tried to gain respect by participating in the movement (civil rights, SNCC). Last year working in SNCC, putting my heart into demonstrations gave me purpose. As a result of my actions (plus others) many places were opened up to Negroes. My reaction to this has been, 'So what! So what if a few places do serve my people now; that really doesn't help the problem.' I believe the only answer to Negroes, the world's problem of exploitation is socialism. And I'm confused about my role in bringing this about. I can't stand reading because it makes my mind feel imprisoned. Yet, I feel I must in order to learn."

B. True Believers. Zealots who fit integration into a strongly felt religious or political conviction.

"I feel my aims and goals in life are my most cherishable ideals and I cannot and will not stop until I have served my purposes to humanity, mankind, God, and myself."

C. Autistic Participants. Serving themselves by finding in integrationist activity self-expression as psychological or social satisfaction.

"Some of my friends were demonstrating and I didn't go at first, but the next time they went I didn't have anything to do so I decided to go with them, especially since it looked like they were going to have trouble with them Paddy (white) boys and might need me."

4. APARTHEIDS

Nationalist youth who accept the Black Muslim ideology.

A. *The Identity Seekers* who want to segregate themselves and belong to a cult of blackness.

(Youth selling *Muhammed Speaks,* the Black Muslim Magazine) "Read it; it'll open your eyes like it did mine. Lot of things I used to do, I don't do now. You have to be clean in mind and strong in body to deal with the white devils."

B. *The Actor-Outers.* Extremists who are committed to aggression against whiteness including violence to individual white persons.

(No contact with this type as reported in news accounts from Northern cities).

5. BLACK WORLDERS

Afro-American youth who are to the right of the Black Muslims and who have a "black internationalist" view, seeing the world they want brought into being by darker peoples becoming an effective majority that will reduce the Caucasian minority to its fitting minority status. Follow an erratic course of action, holding aloof and joining in the activities of integrationist groups.

"My goal in life is to be a black woman and to become part of a revolutionary force that will change the world. To be a black woman means to be able to direct and fortify a black man in the direction of his goal. In order to achieve this I have been searching my inner self for the knowledge of what I am. Daily I look through my mental thoughts in search of my true self, not the facade the world forces me to create. To become a force of change I must know myself and my capabilities, so introspection is my method of achieving this, along with learning the inner motivated forces of other people. I observe and try to analyze why people are the way they are. When I am able to know the inner workings of people, I will be able to implement the ideas of change in them. So far my progress has been slow but certain, for now I realize what I have to do to achieve my purpose. *This is progress.*"

These divisions among Negro youth indicate that the commonly referred-to "Negro youth movement" is complicated, and not at all a single movement. However, youths in all factions move in a *now* that is vastly different from yesterday, however they may envision tomorrow.

It may be well to indicate briefly the metamorphosis of the college student movement initiated in 1960 into the youth movement of 1964. The sit-ins and attendant demonstrations in the spring of 1960 were campus-oriented and supported in the local community. The second phase was sporadic stand-ins, kneel-ins, etc. Attempts were made in each successive school year to revive the campus-oriented activities despite counteracting influences of loss of leadership by graduation, parental pressure on the students themselves and on college administrations to control student actions, and the demands for satisfactory academic performance. The third phase was the Freedom Rides, when the movement left its campus orientation. The fourth phase came when former students began operating as professional youth leaders in many types of communities in organizing and directing activities. Controversy over strategy and tactics produced schisms that made for the divisions described.

Changes in the Negro's status are functionally related to basic culture changes including technological and economic changes, changes in social structure and organization, and changes in the value system and belief pattern. Changes in the Negro's status involve changes in his conception of group and individual functions in the economy and of roles in the society. The character of "race relations" is defined by the interplay of changes in the culture as they impinge on group and individual functional and role relationships.

Understanding and appreciation of change depend on understanding and appreciation of the basic satisfactions and the rewards sought in the order of things experiencing change. The psychodynamics of culture shows that people behave the way they do because the patterns of cultural activity set up patterns of expected behavior which yield rewards to the performer. Cultural patterns are no longer practiced or else they are changed when the old practice does not yield rewards, and/or new practices yield greater rewards.

Professor MacIver (1945) has written: ". . . the thought forms, the valuational constructs . . . perpetuated among the members of a group serve as the group focus of dynamic assessment." Since we began this chapter with a description of purposive action, we should point out that in terms of MacIver's classification of these types of social phenomena as socially conditioned thought forms are related to them, we begin with his second type. Of this he says:

Our second type includes statutes, regulations, administrative policies, organized social movements, political revolutions and demonstrations, social agreements of every sort. The distinctive feature of this type is that individuals who are more or less in accord in their assessment of a situation take concerted action, either directly toward a common objective, some change in the social structure, or in the conditions to which they are subject. Here congruent individual assessments are the basis of a collective determination. A particular objective is formulated and "blue-printed." It is of the kind that admits actualization through a specific agency in fulfillment of a preconceived design (p. 123).

Essential to change is propaganda, which has been described by Talcott Parsons (1945) as essentially a technique capable of use in the service of any goal. From the point of view of the present paper, that of relevance to the state of integration of a social system, three kinds of propaganda may be differentiated according to their orientation to different goals (cf. Parsons, 1945, pp. 301-302).

1. "Revolutionary," oriented to the "conversion" of people to a pattern of values and definition of the situation which is specifically in conflict with fundamental aspects of the existing basic institutional structure and its attendant values and definitions.

2. "Disruptive," aimed not at winning people over to an alternative set of values and definitions of the situation, but at undermining their attachment to the existing institutional system as such.

3. "Reinforcement," strengthening attachment to the basic institutional patterns and cultural traditions of the society, deliberately and systematically counteracting the very important existing deviant tendencies.

So it came to pass that in pursuing certain common goals, in the common interest and for the common good, some aspects of race relations and Negro status changed. The circumstances of life changed. The "message to the people," or propaganda, changed. The institutional patterns, at some times and in some places regarded as being sacred, changed. Parsons has said for us:

> Since institutional patterns consist of norms defining what action and attitudes are legitimately expected of people, they are, in one respect, actually part of the cultural tradition. In the aspect of institutionalized patterns they have, to quote Durkheim, a "constraining" or controlling influence on action, while in the role of part of the cultural tradition, they are involved in the different standards by which its elements are evaluated and subject to selective pressures, in terms of cognitive validity, moral judgment and conformity with human interests and sentiments.

Negro youth are certainly no longer invisible, accepting their lot and condition in silent resignation. There is the ferment of change but not heartening change in either quantity or quality. In a recent discussion of school segregation in the North, Dr. Herman H. Long (1964) referred to the monolithic social structure in the South and remarked:

> Though less repressive, more permissive and nothing like as monolithic, there nevertheless was a body of Northern school segregation law which helped set the stage and create the expectations for present patterns. We must not at the same time, overlook the fact that legal and ecological influences toward racial segregation do not work independently. In the North as in the South, they were concurrent and, undoubtedly, mutually reinforcing, factors. Continuous in-migration of Negroes and the other "New Minorities" into the big cities, following existing nationality and religious enclave patterns, settled down into the institutional fissures which Northern "racial law" had helped to create.

The world of Negro youth remains for him, dishearteningly, a segregated world. This is true, North and South. Six out of every ten schools outside the South with 90 per cent or more minority group en-

rollment were located in six great cities—New York, Chicago, Philadelphia, Detroit, Cleveland, and Los Angeles. Of course, prating of
progress in school desegregation in the South places inordinate value
on token efforts. There remain for all practical intents and purposes two
separate school systems in the South.

Social scientists have expressed alarm at the results of research in
many and varied communities. Public officials find themselves in a dilemma between increasing harrassment for change and an established
structure that requires greater efforts for manipulation than they deem
feasible immediately. Meanwhile, in scattered instances where desegregation education has actually been tried, its salutary effects have been
demonstrated.

Token gains in many places affirm the conviction of youth that
desegregation can be achieved with good results for the whole community as well as for Negroes. Obstruction and resistance to change,
which at times take the form of brutal repression, convince Negro youth
that before them is a long and arduous campaign. In the South they are
losing hope that the implacable opposition will have a change of heart.
This enemy must be reduced to its hardest core and defeated. To achieve
this victory some Negro youths see the need of white allies, and all agree
on the need for great recruitment to the active forces that are pushing the
struggle. The actionist youth groups all stress recruitment, even though
they differ in whom they welcome to their ranks. All of them emphasize
the need for discipline and self-denial among the forces they marshal.

There has been shift from the belief that an educated middle class
elite might accomplish desegregation and set integration in process. All
three action groups are making their distinctive kind of appeal to the
masses of Negroes. The Black Internationalists are beginning organizational and propaganda efforts. The Black Nationalists are recruiting,
educating and disciplining. The Integrationists are educating for literacy
and training for citizenship participation, while they grope for effective
economic reforms that would improve the employment and income of
Negroes generally. Meanwhile, general recognition of the imperatives of
reform to forestall revolution is given by all who care to admit the
presence of a disadvantaged population juxtaposed to the affluent.

For all the groupings of Negro youth, there is the realization of
opportunities heretofore not present, of the massiveness of the old established social system, and of the possibility that they might be able to do
something about it. Meanwhile, their doing is challenging and exciting
with hazards and rewards, sometimes small and sometimes considerable.
The integrationist youth are conscious of groundwork laid for changing
the old order by governmental definition of new principles which are
sterile unless implemented. They are heartened by the shift of more and
more sympathizers into roles of action, while conscious of the alienations

of some former sympathizers. From all indications Martin Luther King's "summer of discontent" will be followed by winters and more summers of discontent, with youth vociferous and unrestrained in expression of their discontent.

A PLEA FOR SYSTEMATIC APPROACH

In this chapter, I have undertaken to raise questions for research suggested by both such studies as have been done, and by unstructured but perceptive observation. Reports in preparation, and rife rumors of forthcoming reports, on the activities of Negro youth since February, 1960, in the so-called "Movement" lead us to anticipate a rash of literature on the subject. If hearsay is partially accurate, a plethora of studies of Negro youth of varying age groups, in a variety of social settings, from diverse economic and social circumstances may be expected. From the political hullabaloo over poverty there will no doubt come a considerable body of writing.

If social scientists are to avoid intellectual racism or some other orientation that will distort or compound confusion, heed may be taken of Merton's (1949) emphasis on the need of an analytical paradigm in another social science area.

To introduce a basis of comparability among the welter of studies which have appeared in this field, we must adopt some scheme of analysis. The following paradigm is intended as a step in this direction. It is, undoubtedly, a partial and, it is to be hoped, a temporary classification which will soon disappear as it gives way to an improved and more exacting analytical model. But it does provide a basis for taking an inventory of extant findings in the field; for indicating contradictory, contrary and consistent results; setting forth the conceptual apparatus now in use; determining the nature of problems which have occupied workers in this field; assessing the character of the evidence which they have brought to bear upon these problems; ferreting out the characteristic lacunae and weaknesses in current types of interpretation.

The following general questions are posed to suggest a scheme for data collection and analysis that may lead to development of a useful paradigm for the study of youth and social change.

1. What measures of social change to determine direction and rate may be used? Since economic changes may be charted, how may changes in other areas of social life be described and analyzed so as to relate them to the economic? How may contradictions and ambivalence be described?

2. What disjunctions and stresses within an order—economic, political, social, etc.—and between orders may be located, and their significance measured?

3. What differential impingements are experienced by sectors of the population in what phases of change?

4. What reactions to changes may be identified and described?

5. What are the contents of cultural and subcultural beliefs, norms and expectations that influence reaction to change?

6. What are the cultural thought forms that shape the youth's dimensions of the world, his identification of himself and his role expectations?

7. What conformity and diversity is there in identifiable segments of the youth population? What communication and interaction takes place within and between identified segments?

8. How are behavior and conduct related in the action-patterns of different segments of the youth population?

9. In what way are the experiences of youth influencing personality development and role expectations?

To answer these questions in a fully developed paradigm is a large order that can be justified only in the hoped-for intra- and inter-disciplinary results. Studies of the Negro conceived and carried out specifically within such a scheme would serve as a diagnostic isotope in locating causal or contributory influences on social processes and social products.

Otherwise, much that may be written may be likened to the work of many craftsmen, each using the Negro as an indication of his own special preoccupation. In that event, the results will be like a confusion of neon signs with eye-catching declarations about the mystique of prejudice, the cult of personality, the structural design, ideological barrooms, or individual variations of myriad colorations.

REFERENCES

Bell, D., 1964. The post industrial society. In E. Ginzberg (ed.), *Technology and Social Change.* (New York: Columbia University Press.)

Carr, L. F., 1964. Social action: an existential approach. (Unpublished manuscript.)

Davis, A., and J. Dollard, 1940. *Children of Bondage.* (Washington, D.C.: American Council on Education.)

Davis, A., and J. Gardner, 1941. *Deep South.* (Chicago: University of Chicago Press.)

Deutsch, M., 1963. Minority group and class status as related to social and personality factors in scholastic achievement. In M. M. Grossack (ed.), *Mental Health and Segregation.* (New York: Springer.)

Dollard, J., 1937. *Caste and Class in Southern Town.* (New Haven: Yale University Press.)

Federal Reserve Bank of New York, 1963. *Forty-Ninth Annual Report.*

Frazier, E. F., 1940. *Negro Youth at Crossways.* (Washington, D.C.: American Council on Education.)

Johnson, C. S., 1941. *Growing Up in the Black Belt.* (Washington, D.C.: American Council on Education.)

————, 1956. "A Southern Negro's View of the South." *New York Times Magazine,* Sept. 23, 1956.

————, 1963. The guidance problems of Negro youth. In M. M. Grossack (ed.), *Mental Health and Segregation.* (New York: Springer.)

Jones, L. W., 1960. Negro youth in the south. In E. Ginzberg (ed.), *The Nation's Children.* Vol. 3, Problems and Prospects. (New York: Columbia University Press.)

Lewis, H., 1955. *Blackways of Kent.* (Chapel Hill: University of North Carolina Press.)

Long, H. H., 1964. The meaning of segregated education in the North. (Unpublished manuscript.)

MacIver, R. M., 1945. Social causation and change. In G. Gurvitch and W. B. Moore (eds.), *Twentieth Century Sociology.* (New York: Philosophical Library.)

Merton, R. K., 1949. The sociology of knowledge. In *Social Theory and Social Structure.* (Glencoe, Ill.; Free Press.)

Parsons, T., 1945. *Essays in Sociological Theory, Pure and Applied.* (Glencoe, Ill.: Free Press.)

Powdermaker, Hortense, 1939. *After Freedom.* (New York: Viking Press.)

Warner, W. L., B. H. Junker, and W. A. Adams, 1941. *Color and Human Nature.* (Washington, D.C.: American Council on Education.)

FIVE

YOUTH IN LOWER CLASS SETTINGS

Arthur Pearl

The actions, life patterns, and characteristics of the poor have intrigued social scientists for a great many years. A major avenue of interest and study has been the social groups that emerge among the lower classes. A mountain of data has been amassed on the academic performance and failure, the incidence of deviance and social pathology among poor youth, together with a spate of theory and quasi-theory to explain the statistics. Since in this chapter I intend to argue against a number of the apparent findings, a brief review of some conclusions derived from various studies of the poor is in order.

There appears to be general consensus that low-income youth, when contrasted with more affluent counterparts, are characterized by the following: a poorer self-image, a greater sense of powerlessness, a more fatalistic attitude toward life, a lack of future orientation, a greater potential for impulsive "acting out." Most studies have found low-income youth to be nonverbal, anti-intellectual, and at best primitive in conceptual ability. The young lower class person is held to have unrealistically high aspirations and at the same time more depressed expectations than his middle-class counterpart (Miller, 1958; Lewis, 1961; Cohen and Hodges, 1963; Deutsch, 1963b).

The attitudes and outlooks listed above are supposedly responsible for a complex of behaviors which further hamper the expectations of poor youth. Low-income youth tend to be more likely to leave school prematurely and to achieve little even when they persist in their schooling (New York State Division for Youth, 1963). The poor, in disproportionate numbers, are remanded to correctional and mental institutions (Hollingshead and Redlich, 1958).

Students of social problems usually assume that intrapsychic variables—attitudes, identifications, and values—are the independent variables, while the indices of social pathology are the dependent variables. They draw the conclusion that a change in the way of life of the poor would produce significant changes in behavior.

Empey and Rabow (1961), in their Provo experiment, state this quite explicitly. The goal of the Provo experiment is to convince lower class gang youth that conventional behavior has greater utility than delinquent ways. Such a goal may be possible in Utah, but it is not truly meaningful for the youth of New York, Chicago, Washington, D.C., or Los Angeles, for reasons which will be described later in this chapter.

This interpretation and suggested solution for the problems of low-income youth places the onus on the poor and calls for the non-poor to provide services to produce changes in their self-concept, aspiration, and style. There is, however, a more parsimonious explanation of the available data, which is that the aforementioned styles of life among the under-privileged are dependent variables stemming from their efforts to deal with an insoluble problem, the essence of which is forced exclusion from functioning society. It is only when this dilemma facing the poor is analyzed that it is possible to make sense of their behavior and styles. Our solutions for changing behavior must lie in opening up the *possibilities* for a different existence—possibilities which are currently nonexistent.

The poor of today are faced with a situation uniquely different from that faced by the lowest classes of previous generations. The traditional mechanisms for absorbing the unschooled and unskilled into the productive fabric of society are no longer operative. To indicate the nature of this situation, a number of economic and social factors must be identified, if only in the simplest terms.

The year 1963 was a magnificent one for the general economy. There was a healthy increase in gross national product; a new high was set for median income. But in this same year, rising unemployment widened an even greater economic gap between the poor and non-poor, the Negro and the non-Negro. Between 1957 and 1962, 500,000 fewer workers produced significantly more goods, and one million jobs were eliminated in agriculture although farm surpluses continued to accumulate (U.S. Department of Labor, 1963).

Automation must be recognized for what it is, a permanent fixture in American life which will enable private industry to produce efficiently, increase the gross national product, and—eliminate jobs. John I. Snyder, president and chairman of U.S. Industries, Inc., estimates that two million jobs are eradicated a year by automation. Most relevant to the issue of low-income youth is that the jobs that are being eliminated are those which the poor can perform; whereas, the jobs that are being created in our society are those to which the poor are denied access. The result of this is as Snyder states (1964):

We are already feeling the enormous impact of the clash of what I regard as the two surging forces of our time: the growth of automation and the eruption of the Negro's demand for equality. It seems to me there is little doubt that in eliminating the jobs of youth who have not yet even come into the labor market, the technological revolution has intensified the social revolution.

The impact of the changes wrought by programs of cybernation and automation is reflected in the coping mechanisms of low-income youth today, in the action and reaction surrounding civil rights, and in new expressions of national concern over poverty in this land of affluence.

THE NEW ELEMENT IN POVERTY

Poverty is not new—but there is something new in poverty—there is no way out. In the not-too-distant past the poor could enter functioning society by three paths. The *unskilled labor market* was open to many, since all technological change then took place at the expense of skilled labor, actually increasing the relative number of unskilled jobs. Today, however, the technological impact of automation is felt most severely by the unskilled, whose functions are fast becoming obsolete. The unskilled poor can no longer use their labor to gain entrance into productive society in significant numbers.

In the past, little capital was needed to make a start in agriculture, sales, or even small-scale manufacturing. Individual members of the lower classes could venture into *entrepreneurial enterprises* with some hope of achieving success. Technology and current business practice has erased this possibility too. Small business mortality—even for established enterprises—is extremely high in this country, and the capital and "know-how" necessary to implement even modest ventures are beyond the means of today's current poor.

Education for professional and business roles was in the past the third way for aspiring lower-class youth to improve their economic and social status. Higher education for some members of lower-class families was often made possible because other family members had attained an economic toehold through the other productive avenues described above. But today education of the extent and quality required for most rewarding occupations is systematically denied the poor.

To obtain a marketable skill, youth of today must be prepared to stay in school four or five years beyond high school. For most of the poor, this is not a possibility. Even if scholarships were provided, the indirect costs would make college prohibitive. However, most of the poor do not even have this choice. They are simply not offered a secondary education which can lead to college. They are neatly detached from the educational through train and shunted off onto tracks which lead nowhere.

One of these "educational" sidetracks is vocational training. In many cases the trades for which such training is intended are rapidly being made obsolete by automation. In other instances modern tooling, equipment, and techniques are lacking in a secondary trade school, and an already inadequate technical schooling is compounded by failure to provide even the minimum basic skills—reading and mathematics—necessary to face the current scene. Another fallacy of vocational education is its tendency to be occupation-specific. The vocational student is securely "locked" into a job for life, which means, conversely, that he is *locked out* of opportunities to gain entrance into other fields. The products of an occupation-specific vocational curriculum who lack adequate basic learning skills must become casualties when there is technological change and dislocation.

"Special ability classes," "basic tracks," or "slow learner's classes" are various names for another means of systematically denying the poor adequate access to education. These special programs rarely yield literacy and they most certainly do not prepare the student for any productive role in society. Students assigned to the "basic track" in most metropolitan schools are simply counted and kept in order; they have been relegated to the academic boneyard and eventual economic oblivion. In certain high schools over 40 per cent of the student population has been assigned to the basic track.

It is not fully appreciated that present teaching procedures are insuring and even accelerating a trend to segregation in our society. The inequities of open racial segregation in schools have been brought to public consciousness, but other kinds of segregation are creating similar inequities. Segregation by alleged ability brings with it the same lack of stimulation and dearth of association that the Supreme Court proscribed in declaring racial school segregation unconstitutional.

Nor is it generally recognized that from another viewpoint there is virtually total segregation in the school systems of this country. Nearly all persons currently teaching school are middle class by income, identification, and residence. The entire administrative and teaching staffs of schools in urban slums are alien to the population which they serve—identification and rapport between pupil and teacher is characteristically absent in this situation.

Teachers of the urban poor are discouraged by their students' lack of response to curricula which are geared to neither their interests or experience. Students are oppressed by what is for them an alien imposition—dull and uninspiring at best. City schools typically provide poor youth with little opportunity for developing status, dignity, or a sense of self. The school, in microcosm, represents the dilemma which faces the poor in society. They are not a part of it, it is simply an oppressive authority.

The school is an integral part of the insoluble problem of low-income youth. On the one hand, the school denies them education with any promise for access to success, yet they are urged and warned that they must stay on to graduation if they expect to get any job. They are lectured about democratic processes but have little or no choice in determining their own course of study. In the process they are denied dignity and often stigmatized or ostracized.

REACTIONS TO AN INSOLUBLE PROBLEM

The response of low-income youth to schools which present such bitter contradictions resembles the behavior of other organisms presented with insoluble problems. When rats are placed on a platform and subjected to electric shock whether they remain still or jump, they cease to attend the problem, engage in random behaviors, and sometimes flail out wildly, biting the cages and even the experimenter (Mowrer and Viek, 1948). Studies with human subjects who have been asked to resolve insoluble problems show that their response is variously regressive or aggressive behavior (Lewin, 1951). In both social and experimental settings, the behavior of subjects is understandable when the nature of their problem is fully appreciated. In both contexts we note that a variety of apparently irrational behavioral responses are generated from the same problem.

The problem for poor youth is not that they lack future orientation but, indeed, that they lack a future. They are made aware of this early because there is so little meaning in their present. A limited gratification exists in striving for the impossible, and as a consequence poor youth create styles, coping mechanisms, and groups in relation to the systems which they can and cannot negotiate. Group values and identifications emerge in relation to the forces opposing them. Poor youth develop a basic pessimism because they have a fair fix on reality. They rely on fate because no rational transition system is open to them. They react against schools because schools are characteristically hostile to them.

Despite the seeming hopelessness of their chances in life, poor youth do develop coping skills and strengths. It is a mistake, for instance, to characterize them as inarticulate, or non-verbal. Although their academic command of language may be lamentable, urban low-income youth possess a colorful and complex verbal style (Riessman, 1962). In the face of a forbidding system in which they seem to have no stake, they struggle to establish codes, groups, values, and goals which will provide a basis for identity, a standard for behavior, a status, a competence.

The problem facing the poor is simply that they lack the skills and education necessary to make a living in society which is becoming ever more technological and specialized. They are unable to take the hurdle into productive existences since their sole commodity, unskilled labor, is not in demand, and no amount of pluck or hope will change this. They are increasingly relegated to the sidelines as spectators of society.

A QUICK CRITICAL LOOK AT SOME PROPOSED SOLUTIONS

Proposed solutions to the problem of the poor take several forms and we shall briefly consider those with most current importance.

1. *Economic Manipulation*—One solution to poverty is the proposition that stimulation of the economy is beneficial to all classes. Economic manipulation of tax schedules and interest rates is often the method advanced, but it is safe to say that the poor are not the beneficiaries of such measures (Harrington, 1962). They have neither the income base nor the credit status to profit by them. And since inflation is a likely after-effect of tax reduction, the poor may actually be disadvantaged by having to pay more for goods with no increase in income.

2. *Educational Reform*—A more widely acknowledged approach to solving the problems of the poor is that of improving educational techniques and staff and providing compensatory education. Advocates of this solution argue that there are plenty of jobs for people with proper training but that the poor are not equipped to fill the unmet needs of the modern labor market. Therefore, by improving school facilities and training of teachers—by increasing the status of teachers to attract and hold the best qualified—the poor can be educated out of their current dilemma. Galbraith (1964) suggests that the solution to poverty rests in paying teachers a salary of $12,000 to work with the poor children of Appalachia and Harlem.

Even allowing that paying teachers more will insure the poor an improved education (which is somewhat unlikely since most able teachers prefer closer-to-home assignments in middle-class areas), there is no assurance that the poor will find a future in the economic system.

3. *Compensatory Education*—A more alluring variation on the educational theme is proposed by advocates of compensatory education. It is claimed that the poor fail to negotiate the educational system because they enter it with an acute cultural handicap. Further, if remedial education is not initiated at a very early age, the proponents of this theory state, poor children can never bridge the ever-increasing cultural and academic gap which separates them from more economically favored youth.

Martin Deutsch (1963a) has marshalled an impressive array of data to support this thesis. He demonstrates conclusively that the poor are already at a comparative disadvantage at school-entering age and that this comparative disadvantage increases as they progress through school. Deutsch suggests that poor children must be stimulated and trained starting at preschool age—prepared for reading and the development of intellectual interests—if they are to overcome the strictures which seemingly doom them to academic failure. He has devised exciting tasks for the children in his experiments and clearly substantiates that markedly improved accomplishment results from use of these techniques. The incontrovertible evidence to be drawn from Deutsch's work is that a potential for enterprise and achievement exists in the poor.

It is possible, however, to contest his conclusion that the cumulative or increasing differential in achievement is a simple progression stemming from initial lack of stimulation. The growing failure or increasing deficit exhibited as poor children grow older is not necessarily due only to accumulated environmental deficit. Their growing failure may be also in part due to a growing recognition that there is no pay-off in the system for them. Motivation is crucial in inspiring the poor child to make the necessary effort to master skills which are perhaps harder for him than for the youth with more solvent parents, who receives encouragement and rewards within the family for his success.

THEORETICAL FOUNDATION FOR COMPENSATORY EDUCATION

The underlying theoretical formulations in the compensatory education thesis deserve to be examined in some detail. The basic thesis has its foundation in experiments in sensory deprivation. Laboratory studies with primates have provided evidence that pronounced deprivation of stimulation from a very early age has devastating results (Riesen, 1947; Harlow and Harlow, 1962).

Primates kept in total darkness for their first two years may develop irreversible retinal abnormalities. Harlow, in a series of interesting and profound studies, has shown that denial of peer or maternal association from birth will produce hopelessly psychotic monkeys.

Deutsch and his co-workers see an analogy between these studies and the conditions which surround poor children. The poor child, they insist, is starved and stunted by lack of intellectual stimulation; he has parents who do not engage in complicated verbal interactions; his home contains no books; and the environmental noise level is so high that adaptation to it produces a functional hearing disorder in the child. They hold that, if not soon counteracted, the effects of such an environment are irreversible (Hunt, 1964).

While this formulation is enticing and seductive, it is based primarily on argument from analogy. Sensory deprivation means denial of stimulation, which to date has only been systematically induced experimentally by rearing or maintaining subjects in isolation. The poor are not reared in isolation; the opposite is true—poverty is characterized by overcrowding. Not only is there no evidence of lack of sensory input, it has not even been conclusively demonstrated that the poor are victimized by an analogous condition—sensory overload. All that can be stated definitely is that the poor child is stimulated *differently* than the non-poor child.

CHANGING EDUCATION TO MEET THE CHILD

The poor child learns to negotiate his world. That world stresses physical accomplishments and downgrades styles which are not functional. The differences between social strata, however, are relative, not absolute. The low-income child is not isolated from verbal exchange and cognitive excitation. He might not get as much, and what he gets may be different than the middle-class child (Riessman, 1964).

If his skills and coping abilities lead him toward physical activity rather than verbal manipulation in his adaptation to environment, then why must they be judged inferior or worthless? It is suggested that learning experiences in the early grades be amended to fit the special abilities and approaches of the poor child (Riessman, 1964). Why must the child be reshaped to negotiate even the initiation into education when the system might more easily be adapted to appreciate and build on his experience?

Schools should be prepared to meet and treat with poor children on their own level as they enter. If physical activity is the means by which the child has learned to negotiate his environment, then it must be utilized as a skill rather than suppressed. If the child's attention span is limited, then this may need to be an area of special training. If tempo and language styles of poor children are widely variant from middle-class norms, then teachers must be prepared to start by accepting what a child has and stimulating his interest in acquiring new and strange language skills. The incredulity and dismay, the total rejection of his small arsenal of abilities and modes, with which the average middle-class teacher initiates the poor child into the school system could hardly be better calculated to stultify inquiry and pride in learning. The work of Sylvia Ashton-Warner (1963) has special relevance—a model of what it is possible to do with children of special backgrounds.

However welcome such changes in the approach of the school system might be, this is still begging the issue. Although the schools might be less defeat-ridden, the basic point is that, given society as it is evolving and lacking the negotiable skill necessary to enter it, poor youth still face ultimate defeat. There is increasingly less opportunity for them to enter viable society from the public secondary school.

PUBLIC WORKS

Other proposals calling for structural change to meet the problems of the poor include an expanded public works program and a revival of youth training camps in conservation, forestry and the like. Although the results of such programs might benefit society as a whole by the creation of schools, roads, parks, and renewed urban areas, the problems facing the poor would remain constant. Public works projects will tend to enforce relative inequality. The poor and unskilled will dig the ditches, while the planners and engineers for the programs will come from the affluent sectors of society; meanwhile, over the horizon lurks the shadow of the automatic ditchdigger, ready to displace the unskilled yet again.

NEW CAREERS

In addition to examining and criticizing various current theories and programs in aid of the poor, this chapter intends to advance an alternative proposal and draw attention to a pilot experimental intervention established to implement it.

BACKGROUND FOR THE PROPOSAL

A basic tenet of this proposal is the necessity for providing the poor with a chance for life careers as opposed to the dwindling supply of menial, dead-end niches which are their current lot. The poor need jobs which offer some avenues for personal realization, dignity and improvement of skills and status—careers which would give them a stake in the system. It is important, initially, to recognize where the opportunities lie. As previously stated, the private sector of the economy is committed to increased efficiency of production, which results in more automation and increasingly fewer opportunities for the entrance of untrained personnel.

In the past five years rates of employment growth have slowed or declined in the various industries of the private sector. Trade, manufacturing, construction, mining, and transportation have shown actual decreases in employment. The public sector claimed 64 per cent of the job growth between 1947 and 1962, with the greatest increases occurring in the fields of health, education and sanitation in local and state governments (U.S. Department of Labor, 1963). These activities, influenced greatly by an expanding population and relatively unaffected by automation, provide a means by which millions of poor can be put to work. Details of how this can be done can be found in Pearl and Riessman (1965).

In brief, however, the argument is: (1) there are more jobs than people in the helping professions (education, welfare, health, etc.); (2) these professions contain functions which require little formal training; (3) these functions can be performed by the poor.

Placing the poor in low-paying jobs must be regarded only as a first step of *inducting* the poor into the labor market. Such a program by itself would hardly be expected to affect the life styles of the poor. If life station is to be improved, then training must be provided *after* the poor are placed on jobs. The pay-off of the training would be eligibility for a series of intermediate positions created between initial function and professional duties. Thus, the insoluble aspect of the problem can be obviated by hiring first, training afterward, and making possible access to full professional status by negotiable steps. Only when both entrance jobs and opportunities for advancement exist is there true career potential for the poor.

Many factors must be considered if "new careers" are to be an integral part of American economic life. These include:

1. *Establishment of self-sustaining training groups among the young people starting new careers*—The function of such groups would be to develop morale and goal identification, to discuss and seek solutions for problems arising in the course of work and training, and to render mutual assistance among group members.

2. *Development of multi-level training programs to be utilized while on the job*—These would include remedial courses in basic learning skills, self-study courses in academic and technical subjects, extension classroom courses in community colleges and universities, and on-the-job sessions with professional supervisors. Negotiations with accredited educational institutions should arrange to give academic credit for' experience and knowledge gained on the job as verified by examinations and work records.

3. *Training professionals to maximize the utilization of the new personnel at their disposal*—The professional, whose duties would include more training, consultation, administration, and supervision functions, must be provided with skills to better perform an altered responsibility.

4. *Rapid change in policy and form of governmental agencies*—Such metastasis will not come easily. There is need to encounter every bureaucratic control. New positions must be approved and budgeted. Civil service merit systems must be considered, since there is no assurance that, with current practice, many of the poor would survive entrance tests. Many of the youth will have a history of extra-legal activities, and social agencies have shown a disinclination to hire persons with delinquency records.

There is obvious risk in any new undertaking. Agency heads, for a variety of understandable reasons, do not relish risks. Established procedures have been tempered and improved by continual trial and reappraisal. They will not readily succumb to change.

5. *Use of demonstration for agency change*—Sponsoring innovative programs as a demonstration is the responsibility of some government agencies and private foundations. Unfortunately, insufficient attention is given to the use of demonstration for establishing agency change. Independent entities are, in fact, formed to sponsor demonstration to by-pass the tedious regulations of the appropriate agency. Demonstration of new careers must include a strategy for increasing the commitment of the

agency. Initially expense may be borne by outside funds, but agency investment must be phased in and continually increased until fully absorbed as an integral part of agency operation.

CAN THE POOR DO THE JOBS?

What has been proposed as a solution to a chronic problem is placing the poor where jobs are most plentiful. One basic issue must be considered—do the poor have sufficient capacity to perform even the low-level entry jobs? Or phrased differently, can society afford the luxury of entrusting the education and the health of the nation, even in subordinate roles, to the nation's poor? There is some evidence that there is potential, even among those with the least achievements.

In Flint, Michigan, a group of fourth grade pupils with reading problems were assigned to the tutelage of sixth grade pupils who were also experiencing reading difficulties. While the fourth graders made significant progress, the sixth graders also learned from the experience (Hawkinshire, 1963). This is in accord with what Frank Riessman (1964) has called "the helper principle." Persons who are given a stake or concern in a system tend to become committed to the task in a way that brings about meaningful development of their own abilities.

In Chicago, gang leaders have been employed as directors of lower-class youth in recreational and social facilities. Their talents for leadership and ability to identify with young people of their own class and background make them especially useful (Hubbard, 1963).

The New York State Division for Youth employed a number of delinquents on a research team which conducted interviews of other delinquents. Unanticipated benefits were realized from their employment. When graduate students conducted the tape-recorded interviews, they confirmed the usual conclusion that lower-class youth were inarticulate. But when lower-class interviewers canvassed the same persons, responses were entirely different. The subjects were animated and highly verbal.

Mobilization for Youth has demonstrated that women from welfare rolls can be used as "homemakers" aiding other women receiving welfare (Goldberg, 1965). The California Department of Corrections has employed inmates and former inmates in a variety of treatment and research roles (Ballard, 1963; Briggs, 1963).

In education the employment of the poor has particular significance. As previously described, schools are usually an alien imposition in poor neighborhoods, having all the elements of colonialism. Education takes place in a charged atmosphere. Surrounded by fear and distrust, there is little in the way of a true community base for education. The system "belongs" to the non-residents.

If community residents are offered a stake in the system by way of the employment of indigenous youth, the whole relationship between school and community should begin to change. Pupils will have models to identify with and aspire toward. The problems of poor children and their families would be interpreted by new careerists with a foot in both camps. The dynamics of the relationship between the community and the school should be profoundly affected by a program which obviously can *accept* something from the community.

A PILOT STUDY

At Howard University in Washington, D.C., ten young people from disadvantaged backgrounds were the subjects for a pilot study designed to test the feasibility of new career development.[1] The only qualifications for entrance into the program were that the youth could not have more than a high school education, could have no pending legal action which might remove them from the study, could pass a physical examination (which only really disqualified those with an active tuberculosis or venereal disease), and could fill out an entrance application form keyed to a fourth grade reading level.

The aims of the study were to determine if youth would volunteer for the program; persist in it; be trained to have usable skills in day care, recreation, and research; and, upon completion of training, be hired by agencies in the community.

The program had, in addition, the purpose of creating a group of ten to establish new norms of acceptable behavior; a group that would be responsible for sanctioning or proscribing behavior; a group that would have a sizable measure of self-determination.

Twenty-eight youth were referred to the program; these came primarily from a youth employment center. Of these, twenty-four appeared for an initial interview, and nineteen returned for the health examination, all but two passing the examination. Fourteen of the seventeen who remained were pair-matched according to age, sex, grade attained in school, employment history, and arrest record. One member of each pair was randomly assigned to the program, and the three without a matched pair were added to complete the team. The seven not selected constituted a contrast group to be used to obtain preliminary gross appraisal of the job experience that could have been expected had this program not been attempted.

All youth referred were Negro. Of the seventeen who survived the screening procedures, six were girls. The group ranged in age from sixteen to twenty, in school attainment from the eighth to the eleventh grade.

---

[1] The details of this project can be obtained from *The Community Apprentice Program*, 1964. (Monograph No. 1, Center for Youth and Community Studies, Howard University, Oct. 1964)

Six of the eleven boys had extensive arrest records; three of the six girls had children born out of wedlock. None of the youth had stable work histories.

The program began with all ten receiving a minimal orientation of three days in all of the job areas (recreation, day care, research). In research they were instructed in use of a desk calculator and a tape recorder, taught how to calculate percentages, how to interview, how to administer sociometric choice check lists, and how to observe and record processes and activities. In day care the youth were oriented to the organization of the day-care center; the basic principles of growth and development; the supervising technique with young children; and the particulars of specific games, arts, and crafts. In recreation they were advised about the administration and purposes of the center, recruitment of youth to the program, rules of various recreation pursuits, adolescent development, and supervision techniques to be used with older children and young adolescents.

At the end of the two weeks, the young people were given job assignments (although it was stressed that each had the responsibility of briefing the others on the details of their duties, since it was not at all clear in which categories job placements could be established). Four were assigned to a day care center (Friendship House); four to a Howard University Community Mental Health Center (Baker's Dozen) to be part of the recreation program there; and two to the research team at the Howard University Center for Youth and Community Studies.

Training was established as a group experience. The young people were given job assignments for half a day and assembled as a group of ten for half a day to discuss and critically review job performances. Lectures, motion pictures, trips, etc., were scheduled in the context of group discussion. (Fluidity in the organization of such instruction is crucial. Lectures, motion pictures, trips, etc., should be decided on by the youth themselves, and be part of group responsibility. The staff must be adaptable without losing sight of program goals. In the study described here, efforts to attain such disciplined flexibility were only partially successful.)

After four weeks the youth were placed full time on the job except for three-hour-a-week group meetings to discuss policy issues, *e.g.*, rules for excused absences or grievance procedures and disciplining practices. The group was encouraged to meet additionally on its own time. To add structure, a club was formed, dues collected, and a fund established to provide short-term loans to youth caught short between pay days.

During the first six weeks, youth were provided stipends of $20 per week; after the sixth week this was raised to $50 per week. During the first six weeks, there were no excusable absences or tardiness. For every fraction of an hour missed, fifty cents was deducted from the youth's pay. After the sixth week the group established a policy which allowed pay for some absences (prearranged appointments with doctor or welfare worker), and allowed some to be made up by overtime work (only if prearranged); on those occasions where no prearrangements and agreements with supervisors were made, absences and tardiness would result in loss of pay.

At the end of the tenth week, all ten of the youth were still in the program. They had demonstrated abilities to perform a variety of tasks; they had had no serious involvement with the law. They were increasingly responsible and prompt.

On the negative side, despite efforts to establish a group reference, these youth largely use the group only when presented with problems that they *must* solve. Cliques composed of the same youth who "ran" together prior to the program remain, and basic attitudes appear much the same; however, perception of self as one who helps others has been tenuously engendered.

GROUP RESPONSIBILITY—SOME ILLUSTRATIVE ANECDOTES

The new career was designed as a group experience in which much of the program responsibility would be referred to the group. The importance of group decision-making cannot be overemphasized. It must be understood that the poor are denied opportunity to express initiative and self-determination in formal structures and organizations. Their group values reflect the range of possibilities open to them. In the new career program the group was to provide a reference for a changed life situation. The group was explicitly told that staff members could not be norm determiners since relationships would have to be relatively distant and transient.

Group references and group identification need to be established because the youth are placed in an uncomfortable situation. On the one hand, they are asked to renounce, as non-functional, the ways of their erstwhile peers; but on the other hand, they do not possess the trappings, the style, or the credentials that would permit them entrance into the establishment.

It is to be anticipated that the group members will meet some unpleasantness and taxing challenges in attempting to gain a foothold in the pursuit of their new careers. Without a group to provide support, the probabilities of success would appear to be extremely small. Without the support of others in a similar situation, old friends and old ways would be extremely difficult to resist at times of discouragement.

However, merely announcing the necessity of a group function does not guarantee a functioning group. In fact, if great care is not taken, a program designed to develop initiative and self-determination could easily be corrupted into mere recapitulation of previous alienating encounters with welfare workers, school personnel, police, etc. The program starts with a handicap. It has been constructed by outsiders. It therefore bears a stamp of colonialism. The youth have no precommitment to the program. Not developed by them, the program is not perceived as being their own. They expect expertness in the staff; they expect direction from it. They expect that to earn their pay, they must do as they are told; and if the program demands that they change attitudes, they are prepared to state what they believe to be the appropriate sentiment. They shirk from responsibility for the program. They do not wish to be blamed for failure. They do not want to be held liable for the behavior of others. Lack of authoritarian posture of the staff is viewed with distrust; it might reflect weakness, an invitation to anarchy, an abdication of responsibility, or it might be some kind of trap.

The staff also views the group members with trepidation. If authority is renounced, how can order be re-established? It is possible that group members vying for leadership, unless given a role model, could turn the program against the staff. These youths have turned to violence before; without firm adult leadership it could happen again.

The staff is not completely comfortable with group meetings. Three to four hours can be a fearfully long time. Sometimes the group "grits it out" (refuses to discuss anything). Sometimes the group turns unmercifully upon one of its marginal members, to the discomfort of the staff member. Most of the time the group appears to be bored. Sometimes the staff member wonders whether he isn't more involved in trying to convince the group that he is a "good guy" than he is in trying to present issues for deliberation and policy determination. Most of the time there do not appear to be any issues which require deliberation.

The staff sometimes becomes overly solicitous. They undermine group responsibility by overidentifying with particular individuals. They are overwhelmed by apparent pathology and overtly express shock at peer callousness and brutality. However, despite staff intrusion, the group did make decisions.

During the third week of the program, a girl assigned to research was given a tape recorder and asked to interview one of the other youth. She was given a "hard way to go" by the interviewee and, taking the tape recorder home, she did not return to the program for three days. Staff then offered these alternatives to the group: (1) the police could be called and the girl charged with theft; (2) staff could go visit her and at least get the tape recorder back; (3) the group could assume responsibility for the situation. The group accepted the challenge and, in teams, visited the girl's residence, found her, and convinced her to return to the program.

Establishing policy for excusable absence presented the biggest challenge to the youth. They were conflicted by two diverse impulses. On the one hand, many had been "docked" during the first weeks of the program and wanted others to have a similar fate. On the other hand, the group was tempted to let everyone get away with as much as he could. Superimposed on these options was the desire to reward friends and punish those not in the dominant clique. Ultimately, after much discussion and insistence upon an operational policy, the youth did come up with a workable formula.

Probably the most important decision the youth were asked to make was assignment to jobs. Contrary to the expectations and desires of staff, the group assigned the boys with the most serious delinquency backgrounds to day care; assigned a girl with seemingly no propensity for athletics to recreation; and assigned, according to the director of the day care agency, the youth best suited for day care to research.

The director of the day care center, with misgivings and after some wrangling, acceded to the decision of the group. The two boys in question made remarkable contributions to the day care center.

The choice made by the group in this instance is important because it contrasted sharply with staff preferences. Complying with the group decision might not only have been best for establishing group responsibility, but also best for recruitment of staff for the day care center. Day care is a female-dominated field. It needs men for a variety of reasons, not the least of which is that many of the children are from broken homes and have little contact with adult males. Yet, had staff made the decision, the boys would have been rejected. Part of the staff problem was a fear of alienating the boys by assigning them to "girls' work." This instance accentuates, given the current state of knowledge, the danger of prejudgment.

All but one of the group were in favor of the assignments—the one exception was a boy who opted for research but was given a recreation assignment. The reasons offered by the group members for the choices give some insight into their thought processes. They had made their decision that the youths with delinquent backgrounds would go to day care because during the orientation period these two boys had been most active with little children. Unlike the others, who stood around and watched, they had participated in activities with the children. When asked about their decision to do "women's work" rather than recreation, they replied that they had appreciated the children's enthusiastic response. One of the two pointed out that recreation presented a problem. He would return to the playgrounds where he had earned a "rep" as a troublemaker and would have to confront his friends. Inevitably, his friends would engage in disruptive activities, and he would be placed in a position where he could either violate a deeply ingrained code and "drop the dime" (call the police); or he could ignore the disruption and thereby jeopardize his job; or he could attempt to establish control through the use of physical force (and thereby also jeopardize his job).

He felt he could maintain control with three- to five-year-olds without such conflicts.

The other youth asserted that he felt the children truly needed him, and that this was the dominant reason for his choice.

DISCUSSION—SOME CONCEPTUAL ISSUES

There has been an attempt, in this chapter, to demonstrate the need for structural change in our society if the poor are to play a more viable role. It must be stressed, however, that mere creation of employment possibilities does not guarantee a change in the values or even the life style of the poor. Any change in structure must also bring with it dignity for the individual. Dignity and status and concept of self are determined by group standards. The group values are guided by reality and limited by setting.

It has been stated here that group values of poor youth emerge in response to attempts to solve the insoluble. Merely raising them to the status of middle-class youth is no solution. To a lesser degree all adolescents are denied meaningful function and self-respect in our society. As Friedenberg points out: "Adolescents lack reserves of self-esteem to sustain them under humiliating conditions." (Friedenberg, 1959, pp. 107-108) Although Friedenberg stresses the school as an agency of humiliation, his observations hold true for other institutions. He argues that the classroom situation, the guidance office, and the extracurricular activities of the school intrude upon the adolescent with the goal of exacting conformity rather than stimulating growth.

A further failure of the school is the denial of development of a youth culture that has continuity with adult responsibility. To obtain a measure of dignity, youth must develop peer groupings which are not under the control of adult authority.

The growth in middle-class delinquency also reflects the adolescent's reaction to a difficult problem—a problem described by Friedenberg to be "the terrifying emptiness of the world he must deal with, which gives him no hint of any reason why people might be valuable." (Friedenberg, 1959, p. 24)

There has been recognition of the chronicity and severity of youth problems. However, there is too much reliance on standard measures without reflection on their utility. Too often proposed solutions only add to the magnitude of the problem. Often the "solution" serves only to add to an institutional empire (Miller, 1964).

Almost all proposed solutions to youth problems carry with them further adult interventions. Improved school programs call for more and better trained teachers, preschool training for poor children, more modern plants and more efficient administration, and a better diagnostic system for selecting the educable. In employment programs it is proposed that more trained counselors be retained to help the youth find nonexistent jobs. Similarly, it is argued that poor youth need more correctional officers, more social workers, more police, more recreational specialists, and more psychiatrists and psychologists. All these suggestions, unless offered with markedly new features, militate against youth.

It is not suggested here that all the above services are not needed or that there should be less of an economic investment in youth. Rather, youth should be permitted a say in their own destiny, and further, the roles which they play should be of sufficient importance to command payment. The adult role should be more humble, more compassionate, less tyrannical.

Low-income youth suffer more humiliation from society's institutions than do middle-income youth and have less reason to accept the affront. The middle-class youth must only have patience, for he is on a path to a functioning future. The same is not true for poor adolescents. There is no pay-off to them if they grit their teeth under oppressive conditions. They react more outrageously than middle-class youth because they are more outraged. Although an understanding of the conditions precipitating antisocial behavior does not condone it, such understanding does provide a solid basis for improving the situation.

One of the reasons that the solutions suggested here are not more widely accepted is that youth, to protect themselves, go through elaborate deceptions. Goffman (1959) describes the self-preserving mechanisms employed by persons in unequal power positions as "fronts" that youth must present to the establishment as a posture of acceptance of the system. They are given no other choice. If need be, youth are prepared to seem deferential, respectful, apologetic, contrite, dedicated, sincere, loyal, obsequious, and trustworthy. The performance of these roles can reflect self-interest but not commitment. In the confines of their own group, youth are prepared to scoff at all of the above. In the confines of their own groups, in the polarized situation between adolescents and adult authority, the fronts take on a coloration of extreme rebelliousness. Often youth are placed in an intolerable position, a role conflict which happens when the audience contains both peers and adults.

It is in the self-interest of poor youth to pretend to be non-assertive, passive, and dumb, since any other role would disrupt an accepted image. Unfortunately, social scientists accept these attributes to be general traits and, through acceptance, tend to reinforce them without recognizing the relationship of role behavior to power structure.

While youth must submit to overwhelming force, they do this at great cost to self. It seems inevitable that capitulation will bring with it tension that can be resolved only in the interplay of peer groupings. Certainly some of the unsocial and antisocial norms established by adolescent groups stem from lack of opportunity for "pro-social acting out" (Fishman and Solomon, 1963) and by adult insistence upon fronts of conformity to adult authority.

GROUPS AS AGENTS OF CHANGE

A variety of group techniques have been used in rehabilitation and education programs. A detailed analysis of the range and the impact of these interventions transcends the scope of this chapter. It is sufficient to state that there is both empirical evidence and anecdotal suggestion of desirable change occurring as a result of group intervention (Jones, 1953; McCorkle, Elias and Bixby, 1958; Epstein and Slavson, 1962). Much of the change may be illusory, the creation of new fronts for new power structures. Often the change is short-lived and only demonstrable within an institution. But despite limitations, the ability to use the group to change the individual is sound in theory and workable in practice. The issue really is not whether groups can be an effective force but how to maximize the return from group influence.

The most difficult barrier is artificiality. Sherif and Sherif (1964) point out the difficulty in maintaining natural group functioning even when the only outsider present is a non-participant observer. Groups that have been contrived by adults for youth are much more vulnerable. The intrusion is greater and more deliberate. The aim of the group is to produce change. As long as the outside influence is maintained, change can be effected in a predictable manner (Sherif, Harvey, White, Hood, Sherif, 1961), but such groups are not self-sustaining—they depend upon the adult members and institutions to supply the mucilage.

Natural groupings of youth exist. They exercise an influence on members. These groups take certain forms because other alternatives are nonexistent. In a closed society, the group becomes extremely important to the individual, and as Sherif and Sherif point out: "The greater the importance to an individual member of a natural group . . . the more binding for him is participation in activities initiated by the group. . . . By 'binding for him' is meant the experience of feeling that participation and regulation of his behavior is a necessity." (Sherif and Sherif, 1964, p. 91) The trouble with natural youth groups is that they are irrelevant to future functioning and often tend to prevent development of marketable skills. All too often participation in natural youth groups leads to involvements causing long-range consequences of stigma and forced exclusion from functioning society.

A model has been presented in this chapter for the creation of youth groups which do have a self-perpetuating capacity and also offer continuity to a life career. In a sense, the adult role is to organize and establish a setting and a climate in which youth-run groups can emerge. If the adult can tolerate groping and refrain from intruding when youth make "wrong" decisions, and if the group has viability for future existence, a natural group can emerge from artifical creation.

In essence, youth in lower-class settings need to be provided an opportunity to form groups which have a link to the future; which permit them to develop marketable competence; and in which they have the right to be wrong, the right to correct wrongs, and mostly, the right to belong.

REFERENCES

Ashton-Warner, Sylvia, 1963. *Teacher*. (New York: Simon and Schuster.)

Ballard, K. B., 1963. Offender roles in research. *Experiment in culture expansion* (State of California, Dept. of Corrections), 77-82.

Briggs, D. L., 1963. Convicted felons as innovators in a social development project. *Experiment in culture expansion* (State of California, Dept. of Corrections), 83-90.

Cohen, A. K., and M. Hodges, Jr., 1963. Characteristics of the lower-blue-collar-class. *Soc. Probs.*, 10, No. 4, 303-334.

Deutsch, M., 1963a. The disadvantaged child and the learning process: some social, psychological and developmental considerations. In A. H. Passow (ed.), *Education in Depressed Areas* (New York: Teachers College Bureau of Publications, Columbia University), 163-179.

———, 1963b. Minority group and class status as related to social and personality factors in scholastic achievement. In Grossack (ed.), *Mental Health and Segregation*. (New York: Springer.)

Empey, L. T., and J. Rabow, 1961. The Provo experiment in delinquency rehabilitation. *Amer. sociol. Review*, 26, No. 5, 679-696.

Epstein, M., and S. R. Slavson, 1962. Breakthrough in group treatment of hardened delinquent adolescent boys. *Internat. J. group Psychotherapy*, 12, No. 2, 199-210.

Fishman, J. R., and F. Solomon, 1963. Youth and social action perspectives of the student sit-in movement. *Amer. J. of Orthopsychiatry*, 30, No. 5, 872-882.

Friedenberg, E. A., 1959. *The Vanishing Adolescent*. (New York: Dell Publishing.)

Galbraith, J. K., 1964. "An Attack on Poverty." *Harper's Magazine*, March, 1964, 16-26.

Goffman, E., 1959. *The Presentation of Self in Everyday Life*. (New York: Doubleday, Anchor Books.)

Goldberg, Gertrude, 1965. Untrained neighborhood workers in a social work program. In A. Pearl and F. Riessman, *New Careers For the Poor*. (New York: Free Press of Glencoe.)

Harlow, H. F., and Margaret K. Harlow, 1962. Social deprivation in monkeys. *Scientific American*, Nov., 1962, 136-146.

Harrington, M., 1962. *The Other America*. (New York: Macmillan.)

Hawkinshire, F. B. W., 1963. Training needs for offenders working in community treatment programs. *Experiment in culture expansion* (State of California, Dept. of Corrections), 27-36.

Hollingshead, A. B., and F. C. Redlich, 1958. *Social Class and Mental Illness.* (New York: Wiley.)

Hubbard, F. B., 1963. The youth consultant project of the program for detached workers, Young Men's Christian Association of Metropolitan Chicago. *Experiment in culture expansion* (State of California, Dept. of Corrections), 65-72.

Hunt, J. McV., 1964. How children develop intellectually. *Children,* May-June, 83-91.

Jones, M., 1953. *The Therapeutic Community.* (New York: Basic Books.)

Lewin, K., 1951. *Field Theory in Social Science.* (New York: Harper.)

Lewis, O., 1961. *The Children of Sanchez.* (New York: Random House.)

McCorkle, L. W., A. Elias, and F. L. Bixby, 1958. *The Highfields Study: A unique experiment in the treatment of juvenile delinquency.* (New York: Henry Holt.)

Miller, S. M., 1964. Stupidity and power. *Trans-action,* 1, No. 4, 7.

Miller, W. B., 1958. Lower-class culture as a generating milieu of gang delinquency. *J. soc. Issues,* 14, No. 3, 5-19.

Mowrer, O. H., and P. Viek, 1948. An experimental analogue of fear from a sense of helplessness. *J. abnorm. soc. Psychol.,* 43, 193-200.

New York State Division for Youth, 1963. *The school dropout: Rochester,* Part II.

Pearl, A., and F. Riessman, 1965. *New Careers for the Poor.* (New York: Free Press of Glencoe.)

Riesen, A. H., 1947. The development of visual perception in man and chimpanzee. *Science,* 107-108.

Riessman, F., 1962. *The Culturally Deprived Child.* (New York: Harper.)

————, 1964. *New Approaches to Mental Health Treatment for Labor and Low-income Groups.* (New York: National Institute of Labor Education.)

Sherif, M., O. J. Harvey, B. J. White, W. R. Hood, and Carolyn W. Sherif, 1961. *Intergroup conflict and cooperation: The Robbers Cave experiment.* (Norman, Okla.: University of Oklahoma Book Exchange.)

Sherif, M., and Carolyn W. Sherif, 1964. *Reference Groups.* (New York: Harper, Row.)

Snyder, J. I., Jr., 1964. The myths of automation. *American Child,* 46, No. 1, 1-5.

U.S. Dept. of Labor, 1963. *Manpower report of the president and a report on manpower, requirements, resources, utilization and training.* (Washington, D.C.: U.S. Govt. Printing Office.)

SIX

PSYCHOLOGICAL ACCULTURATION
IN MODERN MAORI YOUTH
David P. Ausubel

To anyone concerned with cross-cultural and dynamic aspects of adolescent personality development, modern Maori culture offers almost unlimited research opportunities. In western culture, children at adolescence are expected to strive more for *primary status* based on their own efforts, competence, and performance ability and to strive less for *derived status* predicated on their personal qualities and their dependent relationship to and intrinsic acceptance by parents, relatives, and peers. Concomitantly, in support of this shift in the relative importance and availability of primary and derived status, adolescents are expected to be less dependent than children on the approval of their elders, to play a more active role in formulating their own goals, and to relate more intimately to peers than to parents. They are also under greater pressure to persevere in goal striving despite serious setbacks, to postpone immediate hedonistic gratification in favor of achieving long-range objectives, and to exercise more initiative, foresight, executive independence, responsibility, and self-discipline (Ausubel, 1954).

But what happens to adolescent development in cultures such as the Maori where the importance of derived status is not so de-emphasized during and after adolescence as in western civilization, and where youth and adults alike continue to obtain a substantial portion of their self-esteem from a broad-based system of mutual psychological support, emotional interdependence, and reciprocal obligations? (Beaglehole and Beaglehole, 1946; Ritchie, 1956) What course does adolescent personality development take when the culture is less concerned than ours with personal ambition, self-enhancing achievement, and other self-aggrandizing features of primary status, and when it places greater stress on task-oriented motivation, kinship obligations, the enhancement of group welfare and prestige, and the social values of working cooperatively toward common objectives? (Beaglehole and Beaglehole, 1946) Do traits important for implementing achievement goals (*e.g.*, persistence, self-denial) develop when the attainment of vocational success is considered less important as either a reason for living or a criterion of status in the community? (Beaglehole and Beaglehole, 1946)

Are personality outcomes markedly different when peers rather than parents are the principal socializing agents and sources of derived status prior to adolescence? (Ritchie, 1956) Or when rapprochement with parents and the adult world occurs during adolescence, instead of abrupt emancipation from the home and general alienation from the adult community? (Mulligan, 1956; Ritchie, 1956) Or when adolescents assume the role of junior adults instead of living in a separate world of peripheral status (school and peer group) as in our society? (Ritchie, 1956)

To add further interest to the problem of modern Maori adolescence, the above description by the Beagleholes is more typical of an earlier period in the post-withdrawal[1] phase of Maori acculturation, while Ritchie's and Mulligan's accounts describe the current scene in an isolated and relatively backward rural Maori community. The present-day Maori in more progressive rural areas and in urban centers are generally much more acculturated. Although the perpetuative device of extreme physical, social and psychological withdrawal, which preserved an attenuated version of traditional Maori culture in the face of external pressures to change, is still a factor to be reckoned with, it is a less vigorous social reality today than a decade ago. In the struggle to dominate orientations and emotional identification of the coming generation of Maori adults, adolescence constitutes the major psychological battleground for the conflicting claims of two contrasting cultures. The Maori adolescent is still caught midway between two worlds, but in most districts of New Zealand he is considerably closer to the *pakeha*[2] side than previous investigators have pictured him.

PROBLEM AND RESEARCH DESIGN

The present study presented in this chapter was concerned with the psychological mechanisms of this cultural tug-of-war and its influences on the outcome of Maori adolescence. The study sought to identify

[1] The Maori, a Polynesian people, migrated to New Zealand about A.D. 1350, probably from the Society Islands. Initial contact with the Europeans, beginning in 1769, was largely characterized by the incorporation of selected aspects of European goods and technical processes into traditional Maori social and economic organization without any fundamental changes in the value system. Threatened, however, by massive European colonization and coercive alienation of their land, contrary to treaty guarantees, the Maori were forced into war with the British colonists. Catastrophically defeated but not annihilated after a dozen years of bitter conflict (1860-1872), they withdrew, resentful and disillusioned, into reservation-like areas and villages. Emergence from this withdrawal and entrance into the mainstream of New Zealand life first began in earnest with the onset of World War II and is still continuing, despite growing indications of color prejudice and discrimination.

[2] *pakeha*—a person of predominantly European descent in the context of New Zealand race relations, *i.e.*, a non-Maori.

culturally determined uniformities and differences in the personality structure and development of Maori and *pakeha* adolescents and how they are transmitted to the developing individual. More specifically, it sought (1) to identify Maori-*pakeha* uniformities and differences in expressed and internalized levels of academic and vocational aspiration and in the motivations underlying these aspirations; (2) to identify Maori-*pakeha* uniformities and differences in supportive personality traits important for the realization of achievement goals; and (3) to relate these motivational and other personality differences to cultural and interpersonal factors and mechanisms that account for their transmission from one generation to the next.

Another focus of research concern was on urban-rural differences in aspirational patterns among Maori adolescents and on the relative magnitude of Maori-*pakeha* differences in urban and rural areas. An attempt was also made to assess the relative magnitude and significance of Maori-*pakeha* differences by comparing them to urban-rural differences.

In addition to their theoretical significance for general problems of adolescent personality development (*e.g.*, cross-cultural uniformities and differences; the impact of acculturation), findings such as these obviously have important practical implications in the direction and organization of education and vocational guidance for Maori youth. The data have particular relevance to the serious problems of keeping Maori youth in school beyond the age of fifteen and of increasing Maori representation in the professions and skilled trades.

The general plan was to utilize one rural and one urban group of Maori male adolescents and comparable groups of *pakeha* adolescents from the same localities. Partly because subjects would be more easily accessible, and partly because one focus of inquiry was on academic aspirations, only young adolescents attending school were studied. Fifty Maori and fifty *pakeha* subjects in each sample (urban and rural) were drawn from the same secondary schools and were matched individually on the basis of form, course, ability group and father's occupation. The purpose of using matched groups of Maori and *pakeha* pupils and both urban and rural samples was to distinguish distinctively Maori personality traits from those assimilated from *pakeha* culture; and to isolate the effects of Maori culture on personality from the effects induced by the inequalities in such factors as occupation, social class status, urban-rural residence and academic aptitude on Maori and *pakeha* populations. Because of generally higher *pakeha* than Maori I.Q.'s in the same ability groupings, and the unavailability of sufficient subjects, it was not possible to match subjects on the basis of I.Q. Separate matchings were conducted for the Maori-*pakeha* and the urban-rural comparisons.

The procedures and instruments used in this study included: structured academic and vocational interviews with pupils; Test of Occupational Prestige Needs; Achievement Imagery Test (McLelland, *et al.*, 1953); Vocational Tenacity Test (Ausubel, *et al.*, 1953); Responsiveness to Prestige Incentives Test (Ausubel, 1951); Teachers' Ratings of motivational and aspirational traits; and participant observation at community functions (tribal committee and tribal executive meetings, *huis, tangis*,[3] weddings, sports meetings, birthday parties, etc.), and informal interviews with parents, teachers, Vocational Guidance Officers, Maori Welfare Officers, community leaders and clergymen.

There is no such thing as a "typical" Maori community, and no attempt was made in this study to use a stratified sample representative of the Maori population in New Zealand. These findings may be properly generalized only to Maori communities similar to those described here, *i.e.*, to urban provincial centers, and to relatively prosperous Maori rural districts with roughly equal numbers of Maori and *pakeha* inhabitants and with better than average race relations. Implications from these findings for the educational and vocational achievement of Maori youth *as a whole* are only tentative and suggestive, and would have to be confirmed by research on a more representative sample of Maori adolescents (*i.e.*, drawn from the various main types of Maori districts) before they could be generalized more widely.

THE FINDINGS

Matched groups of Maori and *pakeha* secondary school pupils exhibited a striking measure of over-all similarity in educational and vocational aspirations, underlying motivations for achievement, supportive traits, and perceptions of both prevailing opportunities and family and peer group pressures for achievement. This finding supports the view that many (but by no means all) of the traits commonly regarded as typically Maori largely reflect low occupational and social class status, predominantly rural residence, and environmentally stunted verbal intelligence. Some Maori-*pakeha* differences may have been obscured in part either because of insufficient sensitivity of the measuring instruments or because of their transparency to the subjects. This possibility, however, is discounted both by the adequate range of variability obtained for the various instruments, and by the substantial degree of intercultural uniformity found with those measures where transparency was impossible. In fact, obtained Maori-*pakeha* differences are probably overestimates of true differences since the *pakeha* sample was favored by several factors that could not be controlled by matching.

The major finding of this study was that there was much greater similarity between Maori and *pakeha* pupils in their *expressed* educational and vocational aspirations than there was in those factors necessary

---

[3] *hui*—a large Maori gathering; *tangi*—ceremonial Maori mourning rites.

to internalize and implement these aspirations; namely, underlying needs and motivations for achievement, supportive traits, and perceived pressures and opportunities for academic and occupational success. In terms of over-all magnitude and prestige of academic and vocational aspirations, Maori and *pakeha* samples were not significantly different. Even though the stated aspirations of Maori pupils are not later internalized and implemented to the same extent as those of *pakeha* pupils—because of the absence of suitable cultural, family, and peer group pressures and supports—there was no reason to believe that they were insincere or did not correspond to genuine intentions at the time they were reported. Maori aspirations were especially expansive in relation to more remote goals (*i.e.*, School Certificate, university, hypothetical vocational ambitions) unconstrained by current reality considerations, and were more restrained in relation to less distant goals (*i.e.*, end-of-the-year marks, improvement of scholastic standing in the class).

Maori pupils' assimilation of *pakeha* academic and vocation aspirations—despite inadequate later internalization and implementation—is a datum of tremendous cultural and psychological significance. It constitutes an all-important first step in the taking-over of *pakeha* achievement patterns, and is indicative of a degree of acculturation that undoubtedly was not present twenty or even ten years ago. Maori acculturation has evidently proceeded to the point where it can sustain the *generation*, if not the *implementation*, of European educational and occupational ambitions. The development of these aspirations during late childhood and early adolescence is facilitated by considerable contact with the school and with the wider *pakeha* culture, and by relatively poor communication with parents and the Maori adult community. As this communication improves and as Maori adolescents begin to perceive more accurately the lack of strong cultural and family pressures for educational and vocational achievement, their ambitions not only fall far short of realization but are also drastically lowered.

Pakeha pupils had higher occupational prestige needs than Maori pupils and considered vocational achievement a more important life goal.[4] They also gave higher ratings to such factors as prestige, wealth, and advancement as reasons for seeking occupational and academic success. Maori pupils, on the other hand, were more highly motivated by task-oriented ("interest in studies," "liking job") and group welfare ("to help others") considerations. Urban *pakeha* pupils were more highly rated by teachers than were their Maori counterparts on such supportive traits as persistence, attentiveness, conscientiousness, planning, and initiation of activity; and in the rural school, *pakeha* pupils did more studying for examinations.

[4] All differences reported in this paper were significant at the .05 level of confidence or better.

Because of poor parent-child communication in our Maori sample, obtained Maori-*pakeha* differences in *perceived* family pressures and opportunities for educational and vocational achievement were less striking than those that actually prevail, which were noted in the course of participant observation and informal interviews. Nevertheless, *pakeha* parents were still perceived as demanding higher school marks and as prodding more about homework than Maori parents. *Pakeha* pupils were more optimistic than their Maori age-mates about the chances of achieving occupational success; they saw fewer obstacles in their path. Another indication of defective Maori parent-child communication was the fact that only about one-quarter of the Maori pupils had any insight into the existence of blatant anti-Maori discriminatory practices in employment.

As predicted, Maori-*pakeha* differences were greater in the urban than in the rural environment. Despite being more highly acculturated than rural Maoris, urban Maoris have not yet assimilated the urban *pakeha* pattern as completely as rural Maoris have assimilated the rural *pakeha* pattern. This, of course, is largely because of the recency of Maori migration to the cities. Not only is rural life much closer than urban to his indigenous pre-*pakeha* culture, but the Maori has had at least a hundred years more time to accustom himself to it.

With progressive urbanization of the Maori population, urban-rural differences among Maori adolescent pupils are becoming increasingly more important, even though these differences in aspirational and motivational traits are currently less conspicuous than corresponding uniformities. Many factors undoubtedly contributed to the finding that Maori pupils in our urban sample were closer to *pakeha* norms in these traits than were rural Maori pupils. These factors include the selective migration to the city of vocationally more ambitious youth, the greater acculturation of longstanding urban residents, the difficulty of practicing Maori cultural values in the city, and the lack of exposure to the traditional practices and influence of Maori elders and of the Maori peer group.

Differences between urban and rural Maori pupils were most marked in their expressed educational and vocational aspirations, prestige motivation, desire for occupational success, and supportive traits. Urban pupils strove more for top marks and for higher class standing, had higher occupational prestige needs, made higher scores on the Achievement Imagery Test, and valued occupational achievement more highly. They also spent more time on homework and in studying for examinations. Although they saw more obstacles in their path they were more hopeful of eventually achieving vocational success. On the other hand, consistent urban-rural differences were not found in relation to task-oriented and group welfare motivation and perceived family pressures for achievement. It seems, therefore, that urban surroundings may encourage *pakeha* aspirations, motivations and supportive traits without immediately weakening Maori motivations. Since Maori parents were only recent arrivals to the city, they apparently did not play an important role in transmitting *pakeha* achievement patterns to their children; urban children did not perceive that their parents demanded any higher educational and vocational achievement than did the parents of rural pupils. Urban parents, however, seemed to be less authoritarian than their rural counterparts, and to have less contact with and control over their children; they generally played a less important role in determining their children's choice of career.

Contrary to our hypothesis, urban-rural differences were slightly greater in the Maori than in the *pakeha* sample. The original prediction was based on the assumption that because they were relatively recent urban residents, the Maori population would have assimilated the urban pattern of achievement less completely than their *pakeha* countrymen. Although this factor was undoubtedly operative, it was apparently more than offset by the tremendous change—and hence the great impact—involved when a Maori moved to the city.

With the progressive advance of Maori acculturation and migration to urban centers, the increase in urban-rural differences among the Maori people has been paralleled by a corresponding decrease in the magnitude of Maori-*pakeha* differences. A credible hypothesis supported by our data would be that Maori acculturation with respect to aspirational patterns has proceeded to the point where, in rural areas, Maori and *pakeha* pupils are more similar to each other than are urban and rural Maori adolescents. In the city, however, Maori youth are, *relatively speaking*, not quite so far along on the acculturation continuum. Maori and *pakeha* pupils are still more different from each other than are matched urban and rural pupils within the Maori population.

FACTORS AFFECTING MAORI VOCATIONAL ACHIEVEMENT

PARENTAL INFLUENCES

Maori parents are less sophisticated than their *pakeha* counterparts about vocational matters, and are accordingly less capable of assisting their children with appropriate information, advice and guidance. Even if they were more capable in these respects, however, they would still be handicapped in transmitting helpful insights from their own life experiences because of the conspicuous estrangement and lack of adequate communication existing between them and their children, especially in urban centers. Because of their smaller incomes and larger families, Maori parents are also more reluctant to commit themselves to supporting plans requiring long-term vocational preparation. Many are greatly confused about the standards of behavior they should properly expect and demand from their adolescent children, and others are ambivalent about letting the latter leave home in search of better vocational opportunities.

Maori parents tend to be more permissive and laissez-faire than *pakeha* parents about their children's vocational careers. Despite occasional and inconsistent displays of authoritarianism in this regard, they are usually content to let them drift. They apply fewer coercive pressures, but also give less support and encouragement to the long-term occupational ambitions of their children. Their own values concerning vocational achievement—and the example they set their children—also tend to encourage the adoption of a short-term view. In practice they seldom demand the deferment of immediate hedonistic satisfactions or the internalization of supportive traits consistent with high academic and occupational attainment. It is small wonder, therefore, that Maori adolescents are unable to resist the lure of immediate "big money" in unskilled laboring jobs. Although in early adolescence they tend to lack adequate insight into their parents' lack of genuine commitment to educational and vocational achievement, Maori pupils in our sample perceived fewer family pressures regarding these matters than did *pakeha* pupils.

PEER GROUP INFLUENCES

Maori pupils also receive less encouragement from their peers than *pakeha* pupils do to strive for vocational achievement. Not only is occupational success less highly valued in the Maori peer culture, but the greater availability of *derived status*—based solely on membership in and intrinsic acceptance by the group—also removes much of the incentive for seeking *primary status* based on individual competence and performance. In districts where community morale is low and *bodgieism*[5] flourishes, vocational achievement tends to be deprecated.

CULTURAL INFLUENCES

Maori culture characteristically places greater emphasis on derived than on primary status, and on the task-oriented and group welfare features of primary status, rather than its self-aggrandizing aspects. Less concerned with achieving occupational prestige, the Maori is also less willing than the *pakeha* to internalize traits important for implementing achievement goals, *i.e.*, to develop initiative, foresight, self-denial and self-discipline, to persevere in the face of adversity, and to defer immediate pleasure in favor of remote vocational goals. He values personal relationships, derived status, and kinship ties above material possessions and occupational prestige; in his eyes, helpfulness, generosity, hos-

---

[5] A form of adolescent cultism in New Zealand and Australia comparable to the former American *zoot-suit* movement.

pitality, and sociability count for more than punctuality, thrift, and methodicalness.

Many Maori attitudes towards work, which stem both from his indigenous and current value system and from his pre-*pakeha* organization of economic life, impede his vocational adjustment. In the first place, he is less accustomed than the *pakeha* to regular and steady employment, and he finds dull, monotonous labor less congenial than the *pakeha* does. The concept of thrift for vocational or economic purposes is foreign to him. He has greater ties of kinship and sentiment to the locality of his birth and is less eager to migrate to other districts. He does not value work as an end in itself, as a badge of respectability, or as a means of getting on in the world. Lastly, he is more dependent than the *pakeha* on the psychological support of an intimate group in his work environment.

Another factor limiting the vocational achievement of Maori youth is the relatively low occupational status and morale of Maori adults. Young people lack the encouragement of a tradition and a high current standard of vocational accomplishment. They are also denied the practical benefits of guidance and financial backing that would follow from the existence of such a standard and tradition. Moreover, they are discouraged by the marginal economic position of their elders, by social demoralization (*i.e.,* wretched housing and sanitation, alcoholism, apathy, neglect of children) in many communities, and by the institutionalization of a period of occupational drifting during late adolescent and early adult life. Compounding this situation are the overly casual, "She'll be right" attitude that is generally rampant in New Zealand, and the absence of sufficient incentive for a young person to acquire a trade or profession. This is largely a function of an undifferentiated national wage scale which places a tremendous premium on unskilled manual labor.

RACIAL PREJUDICE

Finally, discriminatory employment practices deriving from color prejudice and from the popular stereotype of the Maori as lazy, undependable, and capable of only rough, manual labor, tend to bar Maoris from many higher status occupations in banks, commercial establishments, private offices, shops, and skilled trades. Maori boys desiring apprenticeships usually must migrate to urban centers where they face further discrimination in obtaining suitable board and lodging. The denial of equal occupational opportunity to Maori youth constitutes the most serious and prognostically least hopeful factor impeding Maori vocational achievement—color prejudice is not only deeply ingrained and increasing in the *pakeha* population, but its existence is also categorically denied by both the people and government of New Zealand.

FACTORS AFFECTING MAORI EDUCATIONAL ACHIEVEMENT

HOME INFLUENCES

Despite their high educational aspirations, incomparably fewer Maori than *pakeha* pupils take or pass the School Certificate Examination, enter the upper forms of post-primary school, attend the university, or obtain a university degree. Home factors are largely responsible for this situation. Many Maori parents have had little schooling themselves, and hence are unable to appreciate its value or see much point in it. Although they accept the necessity for post-primary education, they do not give active, wholehearted support for high level academic performance, by demanding conscientious study and regular attendance from their children.

Maori pupils tend to lead two discrete lives—one at school, and one at home in the *pa.*[6] There is little carryover from school to home, but probably much more in the other direction. Conflict between home and school standards exists until middle adolescence and is resolved into a dichotomy of behavior: each standard prevails in its own setting. Thereafter, parental values, reinforced by increased contact with the Maori adult community, tend to predominate over the influence exerted by the school and the wider *pakeha* culture.

Maori parents are less vitally concerned with their children's educational achievement than are *pakeha* parents, and they are also less capable of helping them with their lessons. Because of their larger families they seldom even have time to do so. Living more frequently in outlying rural areas, they are less able to consult with headmaster and teachers. Divided responsibility for children, because of the common Maori practice of adoption and the greater informality and irregularity of marital arrangements, further compounds this situation.

Keeping a large family of children in secondary school constitutes a heavy economic burden on Maori parents in view of their low per capita income and the substantial hidden costs of "free" education. Maori pupils have more onerous household, dairying, and gardening chores to perform than their *pakeha* classmates, and seldom have a quiet place in which to do their homework. Their parents may take them to another district during the sheep-shearing season. They are further handicapped by inadequate lighting and late hour social activities in the home, and frequently by serious malnutrition.

CULTURAL INFLUENCES

Maori cultural values regarding achievement have had a less adverse effect on the educational than on the vocational accomplishments of Maori youth. In the first place, acculturative progress has been greater

[6] *pa*—Maori village.

in the educational sphere. Secondly, since motivations for educational achievement are referable to the less remote future, they are influenced less by the values of the peer group and of the adult Maori community. But although Maori intellectual traditions and traditional respect for learning have been seriously eroded, the loss has not been adequately compensated for by a corresponding acquisition of European intellectual values and pursuits. The modern Maori tends to be distrustful of book learning, intellectuals, and higher education. This attitude is, in part, a reflection of residual disenchantment with *pakeha* education, stemming from the Maori Wars and subsequent withdrawal.

Other limiting factors in the current cultural situation of the Maori include the relatively low educational attainment of most Maori adults, the absence of a strong academic tradition, residence in remote areas where there are only district high schools or no post-primary facilities whatsoever, and serious staffing problems in most Maori district high schools. But since the percentage of Maoris attending secondary schools is progressively increasing, many of these problems will gradually disappear.

ADJUSTIVE DIFFICULTIES

Coming as they frequently do from small rural schools where they are in the majority, know all their fellow pupils, and enjoy intimate personal relationships with their teachers, Maori pupils experience considerable difficulties in adjusting to the new secondary school environment. Less well prepared academically for post-primary studies, and less accustomed to impersonal and authoritarian teacher attitudes, they often develop serious feelings of personal inadequacy. In many secondary schools also, teachers adopt covertly antagonistic and overtly patronizing attitudes towards Maori pupils. They accept them on sufferance only, feeling that it is a waste of time, effort, and money to educate Maoris since they "only go back to the mat" (revert to Maori ways of behavior). Hence, they offer the latter little encouragement to remain in school beyond the minimal leaving age. Some university lecturers also manifest similar intolerant and unsympathetic attitudes. Maori students at the universities encounter color prejudice in seeking board and lodging and must often contend with patronizing treatment and social aloofness from their fellow students.

STUNTING OF VERBAL INTELLIGENCE

Maori pupils are undoubtedly handicapped in academic achievement by a lower average level of intellectual functioning than is characteristic of comparable *pakeha* pupils. In both our urban and rural samples, particularly the latter, Maori pupils had significantly lower Otis I.Q.'s than their *pakeha* classmates. They were also retarded in arithmetic, English usage, and ability to handle abstract concepts. This retardation is attributable to two main factors: (1) the status of the Maori people as a generally underprivileged lower-class minority group with unusually large families; and (2) special disabilities associated with problems of acculturation. Pointing to an environmental, not a genic, origin for these differences are the facts that urban I.Q.'s were higher than rural I.Q.'s in both Maori and *pakeha* samples, and that the Maori-*pakeha* difference was significantly lower in the urban than in the rural sample. The extreme intellectual impoverishment of the Maori home *over and above* its rural or lower social class status comes from the poor standard of both Maori and English spoken in the home and the general lack of books, magazines, and stimulating conversation.

The low average level of intellectual functioning among Maori pupils cannot be dismissed simply as a function of test bias or of "language difficulty." The inability to handle verbal concepts that leads to low intelligence test scores is undoubtedly of environmental origin; nevertheless, the individuals are still no more competent to handle analogous verbal materials in educational and vocational situations than if it were hereditary.

BILINGUALISM

The widely held view that the bilingualism of the Maori child causes his educational retardation is not adequately supported by research data. Competent observers have failed to note any negative relationship between bilingualism, on the one hand, and school marks or passes on School Certificate English, on the other. Cook Islanders, Fijians, and Samoans tend to be more bilingual than Maoris, and yet are academically more successful in New Zealand secondary schools and universities. Although rigorous research is urgently needed in this area, it may be tentatively concluded that the language retardation of Maori secondary school pupils is attributable to the poor standard of English spoken in the home and to the generally impoverished intellectual environment in Maori rural districts, rather than to bilingualism itself. When Maori children grow up in the intellectually more stimulating urban environment, mental and language retardation are markedly reduced.

ACCULTURATIVE HISTORY AND PERSONALITY DEVELOPMENT

ACCULTURATIVE HISTORY

The source of current Maori values regarding educational and vocational achievement lies in the pre-*pakeha* Maori culture and in the distinctive features of Maori acculturative history since contact with Europeans was established by Captain Cook in 1769. In the early phases of Maori acculturation, *pakeha* goods and technical processes were simply incorporated into the traditional Maori system of social and economic organization. The Maori sought to retain as far as possible his land, his social institutions, and his distinctive way of life, while at the same time acquiring all the benefits of European technology. But in accepting colonization and British sovereignty he naively placed his trust in treaty guarantees and failed to reckon realistically with the predatory designs of the colonists, who were determined to obtain the most desirable land in New Zealand and to establish the supremacy of their own economic and political system. When no more land could be obtained by sharp practices, or questionable, coercive or frankly illegal means, the colonists finally resorted to war and confiscation, and after a dozen years of bitter conflict eventually gained their ends.

The war and the confiscations left bitterness, disillusionment, and resentment in the Maori camp. The Maori lost confidence in himself and in the *pakeha*. European motives, values, customs, education, and religion became suspect. The Maori withdrew from contact with the *pakeha* and surrendered to apathy, despondency, demoralization, and stagnation. He lived in isolated villages and reverted to a subsistence type of agricultural economy supplemented by land clearing and seasonal labor for *pakeha* farmers and for the railways and public works departments. Various messianic, superstitious and nationalistic "adjustment cults" flourished during this period of withdrawal. Although the old communal system of common ownership, cooperative labor organized under the direction of chief and *tohunga*,[7] and sharing of the harvest among the kinship group was largely abondoned, much of Maori social organization and cultural values tended to remain intact.

The perpetuation of Maori culture during this period (1872-1939) was possible because of the vigor and adaptive qualities of indigenous cultural institutions; strong needs, nourished by smoldering bitterness and resentment, to reject *pakeha* ways of life arbitrarily; organized efforts to preserve as far as possible the central values and institutions of pre-*pakeha* culture; and semi-complete physical, social and psychological withdrawal, in reservation-like areas, from erosive contact with European culture. This is the classical pattern of *resistive acculturation* in post-defeat withdrawal situations, contrasting sharply with *assimilative acculturation*, such as has taken place in Hawaii. Between these two extremes is *adaptive acculturation*, that is, incorporation of material and ideational elements of the new culture into the existing social and ideological structure (*e.g.*, Fiji, Western Samoa).

Emergence from withdrawal was facilitated by the convergence of several factors—the gradual weakening of bitterness, resentment, and suspicion of the *pakeha*, the paternalistic policies of the New Zealand government, the desire of the better educated younger generation to obtain *pakeha*-type jobs, overseas experience during World War II, and

---

[7] *tohunga*—in former times a priest or expert craftsman, in more recent times a practitioner of Maori folk medicine and magic.

the effect of new highways, schools, automobiles, telephones, and the wireless in reducing the isolation of the Maori village. The phenomenally rapid growth of the Maori population and the shrinking of Maori land resources had also created a serious problem of unemployment in rural areas. Thus, when attractive new jobs opened up in the cities during World War II, young Maoris were ready to enter the mainstream of New Zealand life.

Yet, neither the emergence-from-withdrawal process nor the reversal of seventy years of experience in actively resisting *pakeha* culture were phenomena that could be accomplished overnight. A strong residuum of traditional values, ingrained mechanisms of resistance to acculturation, and deep-seated tendencies to reject *pakeha* values indiscriminately still remained among the older generation. Thus, even though young Maori adolescents are currently able to assimilate the *pakeha* pattern of educational and vocational aspiration, they still fail to internalize and implement it adequately, largely because of insufficient support and pressures from their parents, older siblings and peers, and the adult Maori community.

The post-withdrawal phase of Maori acculturation has been characterized by the following major developments stemming from the reestablishment of contact with the *pakeha*: (1) gradual disintegration of Maori village life and social organization as isolation decreased and the young people migrated to the cities; (2) the growth of a youthful urban proletariat and of serious youth and social problems (crime, juvenile delinquency, bodgieism) associated with excessively abrupt urban acculturation; (3) the revival of latent anti-Maori racial prejudice in the *pakeha* population as a result of suddenly increased interracial contact under unfavorable conditions; (4) the growth of supra-tribal racial nationalism as a manifestation of national self-consciousness, as a reaction against color prejudice, and as a compensation for the weakening of tribal loyalties and of traditional cultural practices; (5) notable advancement along many social and economic fronts, *i.e.*, income, health, education, entrance into industrial and skilled occupations and into some professions; and (6) the establishment of self-government at a community level.

Regarding the future, only two alternatives seem credible: gradual cultural assimilation of the Maori to the *pakeha* way of life without appreciable racial mixture; or the establishment of the Maori people as a highly and progressively more acculturated ethnic community within the larger framework of New Zealand social, political, and economic life, enjoying a certain measure of cultural autonomy and separateness even in the status of underprivileged, second-class citizens. To the writer the latter alternative seems the more likely possibility in view of the residual vigor of various Maori psychological traits, the growing problem of color prejudice, and the development of Maori supra-tribal nationalism. Perpetuation of the indigenous value system hardly seems likely now, since village life is decaying and withdrawal is no longer possible, rapid urbanization is taking place, and youth is becoming disinvolved from traditional practices. Overt expressions of *Maoritanga*[8] will become less important as ends in themselves and more important as tangible expressions of racial nationalism.

SOURCES OF MAORI MOTIVATIONAL TRAITS

The ultimate source of Maori-*pakeha* differences in adolescent personality development may be attributed to two core aspects of traditional Maori value structure dealing with the basis of self-esteem: greater emphasis on *derived status* throughout the entire life cycle of the individual; and less emphasis on the self-aggrandizing aspects and greater emphasis on task- and group-oriented aspects of *primary status*. The Maori of old valued primary status highly as a proper source of self-esteem, and fostered achievement motivation in youth by encouraging appropriate supportive traits. But the self-aggrandizing features of primary status (*i.e.*, personal ambition, individualism, competitiveness, compulsive need to work, relentless anxiety-driven drives to succeed), although not unknown, were not so highly emphasized as in *pakeha* society. Greater stress was laid on mastery of skills for their socioeconomic importance, pride of craftsmanship, and the personal satisfactions of meritorious accomplishment; on kinship obligations, the enhancement of group welfare and prestige, the personal-social values of cooperative effort towards a common goal, and *inter*-tribal competition; and on the satisfactions associated with working together in an intimate, personal context of reciprocal psychological support. These characteristics of primary status and the continued importance of derived status engendered and made valuable the traits of mutual helpfulness and cooperative effort in bearing economic burdens, and of generosity, hospitality, and concern for the welfare of kinsmen.

This cultural orientation towards status and self-esteem was modified by the Maori's subsequent acculturative history. Several factors militated against acceptance of the *pakeha* achievement pattern. In the first place, lingering resentment towards the *pakeha* and disillusionment with their values, motives and practices fostered an attitude of rejecting *pakeha* ways simply because they were *pakeha*. Secondly, it was difficult for the task- and group-oriented Maori to accept the self-aggrandizing aspects of *pakeha* primary status and the supportive traits that went with it, and to grow accustomed to *pakeha* working conditions. Thirdly, he was handicapped in utilizing *pakeha* channels to primary status by his lack of education and training for *pakeha* jobs, by lack of familial indoctrination in *pakeha* values, by general unfamiliarity with *pakeha* vocational opportu-

---

[8] "Maorihood" or Maori way of life.

nities, and by discriminatory attitudes on the part of many *pakehas*. Lastly, the residual vitality of the traditional Maori value system created basic needs and provided basic satisfactions for those needs which the *pakeha* pattern could not easily gratify.

On the other hand, traditional channels for implementing the Maori pattern of primary status, and its associated social organization and leadership devices, were no longer functional. Any type of constructive achievement was greatly hampered by the widespread demoralization, lassitude, and feelings of hopelessness and impending cultural obliteration that gripped the Maori people in the first three decades following the civil wars. Hence, the easiest solution for most Maoris seemed to lie in de-emphasizing the importance of *all kinds* of primary status and achievement motivation and in making exaggerated use of the psychological support offered by derived status.

Distinctive cultural expectations with respect to primary and derived status also influenced indirectly the nature of adolescent aspirational patterns. The kinds of childhood and adolescent role and status experiences available to children were determined parallel with these expectations. These factors were relevant: Maoris were used to getting the major portion of derived status from group rather than from parental sources, and so tended to greater dependence on and conformity to the group. Peers and siblings were the major socializing agents during childhood, with a resulting tradition of more equalitarian relationships and reciprocal obligations. Since early satellizing relationships to parents were weak or nonexistent, there was no need for resatellization to peers during adolescence. There was less pressure to repudiate derived status and to strive for a great amount and self-aggrandizing form of primary status, and in general less discontinuity between childhood and adolescence. The direct influence of the cultural ideology on the types of aspirations adolescents internalized was thus reinforced by actual experience with particular kinds of status satisfactions and equalitarian relationships in the peer group—experience that was consonant with the cultural value system and therefore sanctioned by it.

The aspirational and motivational traits of Maori adolescents are undoubtedly influenced by the fact that Maoris are predominantly members of lower social class groups. By using matching procedures that controlled for social class, however, it was possible to eliminate the effects of relative social class status on our Maori-*pakeha* differences. Intelligence is another variable that is significantly related to educational and occupational aspirations, but the small Maori enrollment in our two schools precluded the possibility of matching pupils on this basis. It is extremely unlikely, however, that our Maori-*pakeha* differences in aspirational traits would have been materially reduced if it had been possible to adopt this procedure.

CONCLUSION: TRANSMISSION OF MAORI
ASPIRATIONAL AND MOTIVATIONAL TRAITS

In accounting for the transmission of the distinctive Maori pattern of aspirational, motivational, and supportive traits from one generation to the next, our logical point of departure must lie with the heritage of pervasive and interlocking cultural values regarding primary and derived status that functioned in the pre-*pakeha* Maori culture and was subsequently modified by acculturation. The cumulative effects of (1) recurrent exposure to these values and observation of culturally stereotyped role models, and (2) actual participation during childhood and adolescence in analogous types of role and status experience, are that this ideology is gradually internalized by the developing individual. This occurs through the operation of these mechanisms: primacy and exclusiveness of exposure; prerational identification on the basis of personal and group loyalties; implicit and explicit indoctrination; the development of particular needs and the experience of particular satisfactions (canalization); incidental learning; prestige suggestion; the pressure of group expectations and demands; and the application of internal and external sanctions (reward and punishment, shame and guilt, disapproval, threat of exclusion, induced anxiety).

From our data it was clear that young Maori adolescents in our urban and rural samples had for the most part successfully assimilated the *pakeha* pattern of educational and vocational aspiration. These aspirations reflected the prevailing *pakeha* achievement ideology which they encountered in school and in the wider culture, as well as the expressed but superficial desires of their parents. Parents, however, basically identified with the Maori orientation towards primary and derived status and generally had no deep emotional commitment to *pakeha* achievement values. They did not *really* encourage the implementation of these aspirations by voicing appropriate expectations, making unequivocal demands, dispensing suitable rewards and punishments, and insisting on the development of the necessary supportive traits. However, because of poor communication between parents and children, this situation was not clearly perceived by Maori secondary school pupils. Thus, during early adolescence, although they frequently revert to parental standards in the home environment, the influence of the school and of *pakeha* culture generally tends to predominate in developing educational and vocational aspirations and conforming to *pakeha* work standards.

Later on, however, as relationships and communication with parents and the adult community improve, the influence of Maori cultural values, as mediated through parents and peers, begins to prevail. Educational and vocational aspirations, achievement motivation, and essential supportive traits fail to become adequately internalized. Eventually, as the possibility of implementation progressively recedes, the aspirations are either lowered or abandoned. Concomitantly, Maori adolescents also become progressively more aware of the actual obstacles standing in the way of their vocational success because of *pakeha* prejudice and discrimination. This perception of the relative unavailability of the promised rewards of self-denial and striving also tends to make them abandon or modify their earlier aspirations. Other important factors that contribute to the lack of internalization and implementation of educational and occupational aspirations include traditional Maori attitudes towards work, acute social demoralization in some Maori communities, and the absence of adequate guidance and traditions of high scholastic and vocational accomplishment in most Maori families.

On the basis of our data it appears likely that significant Maori-*pakeha* differences in achievement orientation may be reasonably anticipated for at least another generation. They will be gradually obliterated, however, by the increasing urbanization of the Maori people, and by progressive improvement in both the cultural level of the Maori home and the parents' concern for their children's educational and vocational advancement. The next generation of Maori parents will probably be able to sustain the internalization and implementation along with the instigation of *pakeha* aspirations for achievement. Racial discrimination will undoubtedly make it more difficult for Maoris to implement their aspirations; but depending on the magnitude of the handicap imposed, this situation may either stimulate greater striving, as in the case of the Jews and Greeks in the United States (Rosen, 1959), or may promote an attitude of apathy and hopelessness, as is partly true in the case of the American Negro, who often perceives the cards as so overwhelmingly stacked against him that striving seems futile. In any event, the achievement ideology of the Maori will certainly reflect his predominantly lower social class status, becoming in time more and more similar to that of the lower-class *pakeha*.

REFERENCES

Ausubel, D. P., 1951. Prestige motivation of gifted children. *Genet. Psychol. Monogr.*, 43, 53-117.

————, 1954. *Theory and Problems of Adolescent Development.* (New York: Grune and Stratton.)

Ausubel, D. P., H. M. Schiff, and Marjorie P. Zeleny, 1953. Real-life measures of academic and vocational aspirations in adolescents: relation to laboratory measures and adjustments. *Child Devel.*, 24, 155-168.

Beaglehole, E., and Pearl Beaglehole, 1946. *Some Modern Maoris.* (Wellington, New Zealand: Council for Educational Research.)

McLelland, D. C., J. W. Atkinson, R. A. Clark, and E. L. Lowell, 1953. *The Achievement Motive.* (New York: Appleton-Century-Crofts.)

Mulligan, D. G., 1957. *Maori Adolescence in Rakau.* (Wellington, New Zealand: Dept. of Psychology, Victoria University of Wellington.)

Ritchie, J. E., 1956. *Basic Personality in Rakau.* (Wellington, New Zealand: Dept. of Psychology, Victoria University of Wellington.)

Rosen, B. C., 1959. Race, ethnicity and the achievement syndrome. *Amer. sociol. Rev.,* 24, 47-60

SOCIOCULTURAL AND PSYCHODYNAMIC PROCESSES IN ADOLESCENT TRANSITION AND MENTAL HEALTH

Rogelio Diaz-Guerrero

BACKGROUND OF AN INTELLECTUAL DILEMMA

It was what I would like to call the golden age of psychoanalysis and its psychodynamics. True, Karen Horney had already started the "cultural rebellion" substituting environmental security for the semibiological libido and thanatos. It was a case, however, of exchanging one concept for another in the play of psychodynamic forces. While Jung had preferred a metaphysical concept, Adler had done something very similar to Karen Horney by favoring an interpersonal concept of power which was decidedly environmental, although far from being only a human concept. All in all, however, the mechanisms through which all of these concepts worked their way in order to lead, or not to lead, to neurosis were the "psychodynamic mechanisms." There is no need for our purposes to try to establish to what extent the word "psychodynamics" referred to the same kinds of processes for each of these authors.

At this time, we were all aware, I believe, that socioculture was a powerful factor. We felt, however, that it militated *against* the best interests of mental health. Furthermore, socioculture was primitive, traditional, and static; and psychodynamics were very dynamic. Sometime in this era, about 1949, I found in a sample of residents of Mexico City that, on the average, one out of every three people above eighteen years of age answered affirmatively to questions such as these: "Do you consider yourself a nervous person?" "Do you feel very depressed frequently?" "Do you find it difficult to concentrate?" They answered negatively to questions such as, "Do you think life is worth living?" "Do you like your type of work?" "Do you believe in trusting people?" Concurrently, I found that almost three out of every four persons answered affirmatively to these questions: "Is the mother for you, the dearest person in existence?" "Do you believe the place for woman is in the home?" "Do you believe that men should wear the pants in the family?" "Do you believe that men are more intelligent than women?" "Do you believe that the stricter the parents the better the children?" "Do you think that most married men have lovers?"

Then I wrote, "Traditions, like old maps, may very well not represent within their frame the many and new territories gained and lead necessarily to frustration and conflict and hence to unhappiness and ill mental health." (Diaz-Guerrero, 1952)

Later, in a bolder fashion I predicated: "The Mexican family is founded upon two fundamental propositions: (1) The unquestioned and absolute supremacy of the father; and (2) The necessary and absolute self-sacrifice of the mother." (Diaz-Guerrero, 1952) The mother's role is "abnegation," which means the denial of any and all possible selfish aims.

From this I derived a tightly logical and quite meaningful description of the behavior patterns and of the roles expected to be filled by each of the members of the Mexican family in each of the stages of development from childhood to adulthood.

But then I derived from all of this nothing less than the main psychodynamics, the main neurotic conflicts and, to some extent, the main neurosis to be found in the Mexican culture. It was implicit but so implicit that I was not aware I had implied that the main sociocultural premises were to blame—or, to be less judgmental, were the cause—for neurosis in Mexico.

Later, and perhaps more elegantly, this was said:

In many of the male Mexican patients that I have seen there is, to one degree or another, prominent in the picture a battle of "super-ego" and "id," the former representing the mother set of values and the latter the father set. This is Freudian metapsychology à la Mexicain. (Diaz-Guerrero, 1955)

Caramba! In my enthusiasm for psychodynamics, I had blamed socioculture for producing neurosis and gone so overboard that I ended by taking away the etiological explanation of neurosis from psychodynamics and its constructs.

Let us see specifically what I did: In the first place, I had used sociocultural data to substantiate a series of psychoanalytic (psychodynamic) hypotheses. To psychoanalysts this should have been a very spurious and unnecessary demonstration, since it is in the vicissitudes of the libido and of thanatos that one should look for the origin of neurosis. In the second place, neurosis resulted from the inadequacy and conflict of the premises embodied in a given culture. If not right, at least I seem to have been quite intense about this. I said: "From this vantage point one could say that many of the neurosis-provoking conflicts in the Mexican are inner conflicts, that is, provoked more by clashes of values rather than by clashes of the individual with reality." (Diaz-Guerrero, 1955) Luckily for me, the theoretical confusion apparently was neither discovered nor unacceptable. Psychoanalysts, as well as social psychiatrists, anthropologists and even psychologists, congratulated me, asked for reprints, and in general appeared to accept the theoretical frame. I assume that this was so because the general frame was dissonant neither to psychoanalytic nor to cultural-anthropological or other frames of reference.

Whatever the value and the errors of the approach, I was not alone. The company could not be, I assure you, any more distinguished. Freud, with the great disadvantage of time, had done just the reverse. He had very decidedly tried his hand at reducing culture to psychoanalytical psychodynamics. You know the examples, but I just cannot keep from joining into the game. Following Freud's tenets, groups that stress cleanliness would have a developed reaction formation to the pleasure of playing with feces. Should we want to draw a logical conclusion from this, and express an operational hypothesis, we might state, for instance, that average Americans must have played with feces either more excitedly or, at least, more often than Mexicans. In this context, this is of course not an insult, but a compliment; it means that, on the average, Americans are cleaner people than are the Mexicans.

More recently, Erich Fromm was willing to say, "By social character I refer to the nucleus of the character structure which is shared by most members of the same culture." (Fromm, 1949, p. 4) He, however, immediately gets in all kinds of unrelated difficulties by trying to explain that this is not a statistical concept and trying to relate his statement to (as Muzafer Sherif called it then) a recast Freudian concept. Fromm states the following in one of his clearest examples: "In our discussion of the meaning of work for modern man we have dealt with an illustration of this point. We saw that the intense desire for unceasing activity was rooted in aloneness and anxiety." (Fromm, 1941, p. 282) Only two pages later, he says: "Let us take up once more the example of work. Our modern industrial system requires that most of our energy be channeled in the direction of work." And all of this is the case, says Fromm, because, "The social character internalizes external necessities and thus harnesses human energy for the task of a given economic and social system." (p. 284)

On this basis, Fromm also predicts the impossibility of making certain people in certain societies work:

Thus for instance the idea of work and success as the main aims of life were to become powerful and appealing to modern man on the basis of his aloneness and doubt, but propaganda for the idea of ceaseless effort and striving for success addressed to the Pueblo Indians or to Mexican peasants would fall completely flat. (Fromm, 1941, p. 280)

Thus, a sort of compromise is reached between psychoanalytic and a species of socio-psychological interpretation. In the case described, man is conveniently driven to work by both psychodynamic and socio-psychological forces. Still, the relationship of the two motivations never becomes clear enough to state it in operational terms.

EXPLORING SOCIOCULTURAL PREMISES

About two years after the publication of my paper (1955) on "Neurosis and the Mexican Family Structure," referred to above, Drs. Maldonado Sierra, Fernandez Marina, and Trent of the Puerto Rican Institute of Psychiatry became interested in determining to what extent the description of and the sociocultural premises utilized for the Mexican family would apply to the Puerto Rican family. Doctor Trent worked on my original questionnaire, extending it to 123 items. He went through several stages, including the development of 195 items, revision of questions, pretesting of all items, use of judges to assess the face validity, eliminating ambiguous items, etc. They applied the questionnaire to 494 University of Puerto Rico students; and the results indicated that Puerto Ricans held, in striking resemblance, the same beliefs that the Mexican sample had shown. Later with the help of twenty students, I had the Trent–Diaz-Guerrero questionnaire applied to 472 high school students from seventeen high schools in Mexico City, selected to represent both areas of the city and socioeconomic levels. Seven were all male (M) high schools; six, mixed sexes (MM and MF) high schools; and four, all female (F) high schools. Ten of the 127 items are presented in Table 2, to show what we call sociocultural premises (S.C.P.'s), the type of sociocultural premises developed in this case, and the amount of agreement between the original study and the two replications.

Next on the agenda of the Puerto Rican investigators came an ambitious study. Since Puerto Ricans held to the same sociocultural premises as the Mexicans, and since alliance to such beliefs was considered by Diaz-Guerrero to lead into some neurotic disturbances, was it possible to develop an experimental design to test the hypothesis?

With the same painstaking care, these investigators went about obtaining sixteen young neurotic subjects and thirty-two non-neurotic ones (after testing and screening 750 non-neurotic students). At the end the non-neurotic matched the neurotic subjects in eleven variables: sex, age, marital status, family size, religion, church attendance, parents' marital status, home ownership, value of homes, annual income of subject's father, and subject's occupational orientation. Also, for both groups it was determined that the father belonged within the category of the upwardly mobile.

Going beyond the psychiatric definition of neurotic and non-neurotic, the authors developed a list of self-descriptive adjectives and found significant differences between the two groups, showing the neurotic group to use self-descriptions of maladjustment far more frequently than the non-neurotic group. As a last step, they selected from the 127 items a scale of thirty-two aimed specifically at determining the subject's expressed acceptance of the traditional Latin American beliefs. This subscale, referred to as the "traditional subscale," was applied to both the neurotic and the non-neurotic subjects. Split-half reliability for this subscale was found to be .81 (p = .01); each item was studied for validity as determined by face validity and by the discriminatory power of each item. Although both neurotics and non-neurotics held quite highly to the Latin American pattern of belief, the mean score of the non-neurotics was significantly *higher* than the mean score for the

TABLE 2

Comparison of Sociocultural Premises from Three Studies

	N-294 Original Study		N-494 Puerto Rican			N-472 Second Mexican			
	Male (percentage agreeing)	Female	M (percentage agreeing)	F	M	MM (percentage agreeing)	MF	F	
1. To me the mother is the dearest person in existence.	95	86	84	89	90	90	95	88	
2. The place for women is in the home.	91	90	81	77	84	87	90	74	
3. Men should wear the pants in the family.	85	78	81	65	84	69	63	72	
4. The stricter the parents, the better the child.	41	40	12	6	59	58	51	44	
5. A person should always obey his parents.	°		48	56	69	65	75	62	
6. A boy should always obey his parents.	°		65	75	88	89	87	83	
7. A father's word should never be questioned.	°		45	55	84	72	75	74	
8. Men are more intelligent than women.	44	23	64	16	45	32	19	9	
9. Men are natural superiors to women.	°		55	35	56	44	47	31	
10. Most married men have lovers.	51	63	36	42	30	36	52	26	
11. A good wife never questions the behavior of her husband.	°		71	51	80	77	74	83	

° These items were not included in the original study, but were added for the Puerto Rican study. They were used subsequently in the second Mexican study.

neurotics. That is, neurotics were rebelling more than non-neurotics against the traditional family beliefs; or, to say it another way, non-neurotics held more closely to the sociocultural premises of the group.

It was at least clear, therefore, that although both neurotics and non-neurotics held quite strongly to the Latin sociocultural premises, the non-neurotics on the average held them more consistently. Among other things, this might mean that (1) the extension of the concept of sociocultural premises to explain neurotic phenomena etiologically was inadequate; and (2) there was the possibility of an opposite explanation for cultures in transition, like that in Puerto Rico. This challenging possibility was that holding to sociocultural premises could have some sort of protective value. I became interested in the second possibility and changed my focus of attention to investigate further this phenomenon of the sociocultural premises. It was at least proven that they were held strongly in both Mexico and Puerto Rico, and they could have an interesting and complex relationship with what we have called neurosis in psychoanalytic and psychiatric tradition.

Searching for some important aspects in this regard and having a fairly good understanding of both the American and the Mexican cultures, I started a trial to compare the two cultures theoretically in regard to certain aspects. Dr. Abraham Maslow and I, discussing our observations on both cultures, finally decided to write a paper (Maslow and Diaz-Guerrero, 1960). This pointed out a series of outcomes which, it was felt, had to do with the present beneficial effects that the Mexican culture had on child and adolescent behavior and with the apparent protection that values in a culture provide in the prevention of juvenile delinquency.

Later in 1959, a kind invitation from Dr. Wayne H. Holtzman and the psychology department of the University of Texas brought me to teach a seminar on culture and personality. At this time, Dr. Robert F. Peck and the writer decided to start a joint research project that was partially backed by The Hogg Foundation for Mental Health. We found that we were both interested in values and decided to explore a series of concepts felt to have a high evaluative loading cross-culturally. Convinced that a concept crucial to interpersonal relations in everyday life was a case in point, we decided to start with the concept of *respect*. Here was a concept with the same Latin root in both Spanish and English, referring to a very important interaction among human beings.

A few comparisons of notes made us realize that there should, however, be a great deal of difference in the actual operational meaning of this concept for the two cultures. For its study we used a simple questionnaire technique. It had three sections. In the first one, we told the subjects that the word *respect* had several important meanings and that not everybody used the word in the same way. We were going to present them with twenty-one possible connotations of the word and wanted them to mark those connotations that, according to them, implied a good use of the word *respect*. The second part of the questionnaire presented the subjects with sixty characteristics, roles, or occupations of people. Some stimuli in the questionnaire were: "mother," "father," "brother," "sister," "older sister," "younger brother," "older children," "younger children," "physician," "lawyer," "philosopher," "artist," "low class people," "middle class people," "rich people," "poor people," "worker," "servant," "beggar," "priest," etc. In the third section we had a semantic differential scale applied to the statement "a respected person."

Unwittingly, and using a questionnaire, we were trying to cover two of the criteria that Sherif and Sherif consider important in the study of groups: (1) the study of their norms in regard to respect; and (2) the structure or organization of the relative status or the distribution of power given to the members in a group regarding respect (Sherif and Sherif, 1963).

The results indicated not only that there were significant differences in the meaning of the word *respect* in nineteen of the twenty-one statements for the first questionnaire and in forty of the sixty stimuli for the second, but also that there was a kind of core-culture pattern for the meaning of *respect* for the Mexican and a different one for the American. The study was carried out on students of the Mexican *preparatorias* and first year junior college students in the States who were matched for age, sex, and education.

Specifically, the study was carried out in Mexico City, Monterrey, Edinburg, Texas (on the other side of the Mexican-American border) and Austin, Texas. There were 1,814 subjects all told. In Table 3, taken from the Peck and Diaz-Guerrero (1963) study, we see not only the core-culture patterns in Mexico and in Texas but also the diffusion of values across the border. The meaning of the word *respect*, a very traditional concept used in cultures for many centuries without perhaps much change, has taken on a very different meaning within the United States, as you see. In Mexico it is possible to see both the "positive" aspects of the traditional culture pattern in such items as affection, interdependency of protection, and love; the ambivalent aspects such as the need for obedience; and the more "negative" such as awe and fear.[1]

In Table 4 the objects of respect in Mexico and the United States are compared, each column representing a qualitative category (age-sex, family, friends, etc.). Immediately following the list of objects, there are four columns, two columns for Mexico and two columns for the U.S. The first column under Mexico compares the level of respect in Mexico with that in the U.S. When there is a +, that particular stimulus was signifi-

---

[1] This ambivalence and "negativity" are clearest in the perception of heterosexual love as shown in Peck and Diaz-Guerrero (1963).

cantly more respected in Mexico than in the United States. For example, there is significantly higher respect for old men in Mexico than in the U.S. The next column under Mexico refers to whether, within the Mexican culture, the stimulus received High Respect, Medium Respect or Low Respect. For instance old men get significantly higher respect (HR) within Mexico, young men receive medium respect (MR), and boys receive low respect (LR) within Mexico. (In numerical terms, HR means that significantly more than fifty per cent of the subjects marked old men as individuals deserving respect. LR indicates that significantly less than fifty per cent of the subjects marked boys as individuals deserving respect). The two columns under U.S. signify exactly the same as the two previous ones, that is, + or − indicates more or less respect in the U.S. than in Mexico for the individuals in the list, and HR, LR and MR

TABLE 3

The Cultural Diffusion of Values: Provisional Evidence

I. Mexico
  a) "Culture-typed" Values
    7. Affection
    9. Expect protection from
    13. Avoid trespassing on rights } Mexican—in Mexico and U.S.
    15. Have to obey, like it or not
    16. Duty to obey

  b) "Diffused" Values
    4. To love
    11. Protective toward
    20. Avoid interfering in
       their life

Mexican—but also shared by Edinburg "Anglos," who are perhaps acculturated to the Mexican pattern in these points.

II. United States
  a) "National" Values
    5. Treat as equal
    6. Give someone a chance
    8. Feel admiration
    12. (Not) dislike
    17. Consider feelings
    18. Consider ideas

United States—including Mexican-Americans in Edinburg, who are perhaps acculturated to U.S. pattern on these points.

  b) "Diffused" Values
    1. Look up with admiration

United States—but shared by Monterrey people, who are possibly acculturated to the U.S. view on this point.

III. "Border" Effect
    2. Look up with awe

Monterrey (especially women), not U.S. or Mexico City.

    3. Fear
    10. Expect punishment from
    14. Like to obey

Edinburg and Monterrey but not U.S. or Mexico City.

TABLE 4

Cross-Cultural Comparison of Objects of Respect
(Male Liberal Arts Students in Mexico and in U.S.)

AGE-SEX:

	Mexico	U.S.
Old men	+ HR	− HR
Young men	− MR	+ HR
Boys	+ LR	− LR
Baby boys	+ LR	− LR
Young women	+ HR	− HR
Young girls	+ HR	− MR
Girls	+ HR	− LR
Baby girls	+ MR	− LR

IMMEDIATE FAMILY:

	Mexico	U.S.
Older brothers	+ HR	− HR
Older sisters	+ HR	− HR
Younger sisters	+ HR	− HR

COLLATERAL FAMILY:

	Mexico	U.S.
Grandfathers	+ HR	− HR
Uncles	+ HR	− HR
Aunts	+ HR	− HR
Younger female cousins	+ HR	− MR

FRIENDS:

	Mexico	U.S.
Older male friends	− HR	+ HR

OCCUPATION:

	Mexico	U.S.
Laborers	+ HR	− MR
Servants	+ HR	− MR
Ministers	− HR	+ HR

ECONOMIC:

	Mexico	U.S.
Middle class people	+ HR	− HR
Low class people	+ HR	
Poor people	+ HR	− MR
Wealthy people	+ MR	− MR
Beggars	+ HR	− LR

MISCELLANEOUS:

	Mexico	U.S.
The Constitution	+ HR	− HR
Your equals	− HR	+ HR

KEY TO SYMBOLS:

Comparison between cultures: + = more respect
− = less respect

Degree of respect *within* the given culture:
HR = High Respect
MR = Medium Respect
LR = Low Respect

A significant difference to the Chi Square Test above 50 per cent gives HR.
A significant difference below 50 per cent gives LR.

Note: All differences in this table are significant beyond 0.05 using the Chi Square Test.

Source: Diaz-Guerrero and Peck, 1963

have exactly the same statistical meaning within the U.S. as that explained for the Mexican culture.

It was striking to find that in the United States respect was allotted for achievement, individual merit, youth, middle class people, etc., and that in Mexico respect was given to femaleness, old age, childhood, poor people, low class people, rich people, and beggars. In general, there was a defined socioeconomic determination of respect in the U.S. and a defined sociocultural determination for respect in Mexico. In other words, we said, "This type of respect that we have been studying appears to be given to productive or active and successful individuals in the U.S. and in Mexico is given following the premises of the culture." (Diaz-Guerrero and Peck, 1963)

Dr. Noel McGinn, teaching at the Instituto Tecnologico y de Estudios Superiores de Occidente in Guadalajara, apparently also became fascinated by the obvious personality differences between Americans and Mexicans and by the number of theoretical statements made by psychoanalysts and writers in Mexico about the personality of the Mexican. He has recently tried to test several of these hypotheses. He utilized a modification by Harburg of the semantic differential of Osgood, Suci and Tannenbaum. His subjects were 174 University of Michigan students and 174 Guadalajara University students. The subjects were asked to report how they would feel and react under the following circumstances: (1) Their best friend liked a person the subject disliked strongly. (2) Their best friend refused to write a letter of recommendation for the subject. (3) A mildly disliked person criticized the subject's performance in a well-liked activity.

McGinn, Harburg, and Ginsburg (1963a) indicate that, "The Mexican students reported being more upset as a result of the disagreement with their friend and a tendency to break the friendship as a result"; and that, "Michigan students were more upset by criticism of their abilities by a disliked person." The authors conclude, "Results were tentatively interpreted to say that Mexican students value friendship more than do American students." The results could, of course, be interpreted either in terms of Diaz-Guerrero's search for the positive in the Mexican culture or in those of a psychoanalytic interpretation such as one offered by Santiago Ramirez, a Mexican psychoanalyst. Santiago Ramirez feels that Mexicans, far more than Americans, use the defense mechanism of negation and that in this fashion they would protect themselves from disagreeable realities by denying their existence. In another study (1959), I indicated that Mexicans value interpersonal relationships very highly, perhaps above all, and that because of this, to them, reality in interpersonal relations could be defined as follows: "The degree of reality of an interpersonal situation lies in the frequency, quality and warmth of the interpersonal reactions that can be achieved in a given period of time."

This is an excellent example of the tendency that both sociocultural and psychodynamic approaches may have to meet head on and try to explain, beyond the hermeneutic capacity of their concepts, what is going on in human behavior.

Recently, McGinn, Harburg and Ginsburg (1963b) presented another relevant paper. An attempt was made to test several of the hypotheses presented in the Maslow–Diaz-Guerrero paper cited previously. To measure the perceptions that subjects had in their relations with their parents, the authors used a modified form of a semantic differential—the parent-image differential used previously by Harburg and McGinn. Also they utilized an attitude questionnaire.

The results were summarized as follows:

Perceptions of their middle-class parents which Guadalajara students have differed from those of Michigan students in that the Guadalajara parents are seen as more strict and demanding of obedience, as more arbitrary, but at the same time more affectionate and sure in their treatment of the child. Significantly, this type of treatment is not associated with resentment in the child but rather with an even greater respect and admiration for his parents. As a result the child is more likely to adopt his parents' values, as indicated by the high agreement among Guadalajara students that authority is to be obeyed without question. It was argued that this kind of parent is likely to generate in his child a strong motivation to seek and maintain friendship with the parent and, assuming that this kind of motivation generalizes outside of the family, to value friendship more than would children of other kinds of parents. (McGinn, Harburg and Ginsburg, 1963b)

Also relevant is the series of studies by the Andersons on the relationship of children with their peers, parents, and teachers (1956, 1957, 1959, 1961). These were carried out in several different countries, including traditional and highly industrialized sociocultures. I have had the privilege of seeing both the published and unpublished data and have been able to look into the results both with a cross-cultural eye and with the attitude of searching for any possibly traditional values.

From the very beginning, I was fascinated by the differential results that were obtained with the Andersons' technique in countries with an authoritarian philosophy and in those with a democratic philosophy. But I was even more fascinated by the fact that there were several differences between German authoritarian philosophy and the traditional Mexican, perhaps Latin American, sort of authoritarian philosophy. I would naturally feel that the differences between the Mexican and the German children, for instance, would be due precisely to the kind of relationship that Maslow–Diaz-Guerrero postulated and that McGinn and Ginsburg have begun to substantiate. We hope that the intervention of the specific sociocultural premise (see the next section of this chapter) will help greatly in understanding these results of the Andersons' and in several of the results that we have thus far tried to summarize. The Andersons' contribution is complex, and its interpretation would require a chapter in itself.

TOWARD AN ADEQUATE APPROACH

These theoretical and cross-cultural explorations, together with the testimony of everyday living that people actually adhere to many of the positive counterparts of the Mexican sociocultural premises, had led me to believe that neither the psychodynamic approach nor the sociocultural approach was sufficient, in isolation, to explain the complexities of human behavior. But the concerns were too many, and they were not about to form a meaningful pattern by themselves. In the first place, how could some meaningful and generalized ways be developed of differentiating the Mexican from the American culture? How could a theoretical approach be developed that would make sense on both sides of the border? How could all of these ill-organized doubts be reduced into some kind of an operational definition of these concerns? What in the world was the relationship between socioculture and psychodynamics?

Finally, one day, at least a fraction of a complex solution appeared. When it arrived, it not only provided an anchorage point to compare the American and the Mexican culture but it also strongly involved a concept reeking with the essence of psychodynamics and appeared to identify one of the "good points" of the Mexican socioculture. What was found was, indeed, a sociocultural premise that appeared to control the ways in which the members of the two groups were assumed, expected, and almost commanded to deal with stress.

In what follows let us try to (1) see how sociocultural premises (S.C.P.'s) in general function; (2) specify how they are different from defense mechanisms; (3) describe the specific S.C.P. that embodies sociocultural and psychodynamic attributes; (4) use it to clarify further the relationship of S.C.P.'s to defense mechanisms; and (5) present examples of the construct in action.

A definite step toward a solution to the first problem above had been taken from the time that it was felt that a socioculture produces its action upon its members through the construct that we called the sociocultural premise—the S.C.P. (When I gave a paper in Washington at the International Congress of Psychology, people who arrived late and heard this term were asking each other in great confusion, "What are those 'recipes' that guy is talking about?") The S.C.P.'s behave like any other premises in logic. The mechanism for their function is syllogistic logic, fundamentally as described by Aristotle.[2] They also function, and

---

[2] Even Aristotelian logic gets people in trouble, as general semanticists have clearly shown. But at the present, probably 99 per cent of the population in the world relies on Aristotelian logic even though it may be improperly applied. This last, alone, is likely to be the source of much human confusion.

can be modified, or exert their effects within the individual mind by processes (akin to those enumerated by Charles Osgood) manifested in the limited and consistent number of automatic evaluations that man possesses. Finally, they also work in accordance with principles similar to that which Osgood has summarized in stating his principle of congruity.[3] These mechanisms were evidently different from what we may call the less rational, or (if you so desire) non-cognitive, or (if you insist) more primitive mechanisms known as the defense mechanisms.

To make the differences between the processes clear diametrically, let us give some examples. If I agreed with the statement that the authority of my father is indisputable, I would also tend to agree with the statement that all children should obey their father. On the other hand, if I were stingy and I could not accept this fact, I would tend to see stinginess in most other people. I believe that the difference is striking. To take another example, at the sociocultural level I may feel that the mother is the most abnegative creature on earth, and I may automatically evaluate this as good and hold the view that the mother is the dearest being in existence. On the other hand, I may not want to talk so that I cannot go and talk with my mother-in-law, and I will develop aphonia. Or, if I am answering a questionnaire, and I respond with "yes" to the statement, "Children should always respect their parents," and I am a Mexican, I would tend to answer "yes" also to the statement, "Children should always obey their parents." On the other hand, I may want to hit my boss, but since he can fire me, I go and hit my wife—well, or kick the dog. If one insisted on an analysis of some psychodynamic phenomena, one might be able to find some purer kind of reason or logic further in the background, but let us be content with indicating that the mechanisms by which sociocultural processes and psychodynamic processes function are quite different.

Now, let us return to the concept for the cross-cultural comparison of cultural beliefs and psychodynamic styles. In order to understand it better, let us enumerate some of the assumptions that should be considered to develop such a concept. The first is that, in spite of deceptive appearances such as those implied in the vision of a South Sea island paradise, all humans in all cultures have to deal with a multitude of life stresses. The second is that, in all cultures and at all times, men are interested basically in the problem of how best to deal with stress, and that in their development all cultures have finally arrived at what they consider workable ways of dealing with these omnipresent life stresses.

It is felt that cultures have ended their search for a major S.C.P. that would handle this problem by making one of these assertions: (1)

---

[3] Osgood has made a brilliant effort to demonstrate that attitudes are the significant mediating links between stimulus and response. Thus, his views fit with a behavioristic theory. We feel that premises may be so considered but want to make clear that, besides mediating between S and R, premises have a life of their own.

The best way to deal with the stresses of life is by enduring them (facing them) actively; or (2) the best way of dealing with life stresses is by enduring them (accepting them) passively. Because of better knowledge and the data collected about them, the American and the Mexican cultures were selected as representatives of these dichotomous ways of dealing with stress. In a recent paper (Diaz-Guerrero, 1963), it was pointed out that, to the Mexican, to endure stress passively is not only the best, but also the virtuous way. Abnegation in the mother, obedience in the children, self-sacrifice in all, submission, dependence, politeness, courtesy, *el aguante* (there is not such a word in English, but it means the ability to hold well even in the face of abuse) were either Mexican sociocultural virtues, or realistic (or, at least, *approved*) ways of coping with the stresses of life. It was further indicated that the prevalent religion and the pre-Cortesian agreed that "this is a valley of tears" and that there is a prevalent easy adjustment of the Mexican to tragedy, even to death. The same can be said about a chronic illness or deformity. There is, also, a widespread use of the expression *ni modo*, which is said with a gigantic shrug of the shoulders and which means, "What can anyone do? There is no way." The widespread use of proverbs, stories, and jokes of a quasi-stoic philosophy as well as the strong fatalistic attitudes are all very clear examples of a well-integrated and well-learned philosophy indicating that the very best way, the fair way to others and to oneself, the righteous and the virtuous way to deal with stress is passively.

On the other hand, the prevalent American philosophy makes a virtue of dealing with stress actively and considers this the best possible way to face reality. For the American, life is best lived in constant activity. Here is a culture where self-esteem decays if you are idle, as demonstrated by the studies of Lazarsfeld and Isenberg. But since the best way, the virtuous way, the righteous way, even the fair way in dealing with others is to face stress actively, Americans would have a difficult time dealing with death, chronic illness, deformity, poverty, beggars, etc. In a cross-cultural research project (Diaz-Guerrero, 1963), which we are in the process of carrying out under a grant from the Foundations' Fund for Research in Psychiatry and in collaboration with Dr. Wayne H. Holtzman of the University of Texas, the plan has been to include a series of Thematic Apperception Test pictures showing some of the situations that we feel will demonstrate the extent of the cross-cultural dichotomy.

Within the American culture there seems to be a definite trend to make *activity* synonymous with *efficiency* and with *healthy*. This appears to be so prevalent that passive coping will often be considered wishy-washy at the least and more often as cheating or as downright unhealthy. It is no wonder that in Mexico the active *stravaganzas* of Americans may often be considered also inadequate, unfair, somewhat crazy (*esos gringos locos*, "those crazy Americans"), and even unhealthy and psychopathic. It is very difficult for me to forget the reactions of a delightful, friendly, and efficient American secretary who was typing for me the items of a test in which children were portrayed *as coping with stress* either actively or passively. I cannot forget her quite consistent reactions as she typed. To the active coping with stress, she would exclaim, "That is Johnny, that is my boy!" To the passive coping, she would exclaim just as enthusiastically, "Oh! He is cheating, that Gaspar is cheating!"

Thus the American problem is to find meaningful and admirable ways of being passive, above and beyond whiskey, tranquilizers, and L.S.D.; while the Mexican, and the "underdeveloped" countries', problem is to find meaningful and admirable ways of being active above and beyond talk about doing, love-making, the *fiestas* and the *parrandas*. There is, apparently, in Mexico City and other urban centers, a defined beginning of activity associated with pride in Mexico and its progress.

There is no need to go into further examples of these modal ways of dealing with stress in the two societies. What is important, since the accent of this particular sociocultural premise falls upon dealing with stress, is to observe to what extent and in what ways this particular S.C.P. allows us to get a closer view of the connection between psychodynamic and sociocultural processes. This relationship is not easy to establish in spite of the fact that I may have convinced you that sociocultural processes make use of different mechanisms than psychodynamic processes. The evidence is the fact that very modern approaches to understanding psychodynamics, which have discovered the dichotomy of coping[4] and defense, still appear to insist on understanding both defending and coping through the frame of reference of psychodynamic concepts and mechanisms. This subsuming of coping into the classical psychodynamic mechanisms has been made possible by the generalized trend toward an ego psychology rather than the original id-ego, super-ego approach and by the final acceptance that man is not always just defending himself from problems but that he is also able to handle such problems constructively. Thus, in a recent, interesting and important monograph by Norma Haan (1963), there is a distinction made between the classical defense mechanisms, which, as she says, "seem primarily concerned with impulse economics" and are termed displacement, reaction formation and repression, and the defense mechanisms that seem primarily to involve cognitive activity. This interesting distinction I would like to see as another inadequate extension of the psychodynamic frame of reference leading to a confusion of processes. (Perhaps it is justifiable because it helps develop a fairly complete classification of defense mechanisms and coping processes from a psychodynamic point of view.)

In our view, coping would "always" utilize the processes that serve

---

[4] Coping has been best defined and illustrated by Lois Murphy (1962). Her admirable and probably more realistic and valid attitude of not "pre-judging" leads her to state that *defense mechanisms* may partially intervene in the over-all coping effort and process.

for the sociocultural premises, and defense would consistently make use of "lesser" or "poorer" logical processes. Thus, when rational processes are supposed to be defensive, as in rationalization, there is always the terrible danger that a series of syllogistic or congruent statements may be considered a rationalization merely because they do not agree with the premises of the hearer, but that they will be called logical and rational analysis if the listener agrees with the premises from which the reasoning started. In this use of "rational processes" as defense, a very defined subjective judgment is passed in at least two respects: (1) on the formal logical validity, and (2) on the validity of the premises from which the statements depart.[5]

To make a very long story short, let us try to make essentially the same characterization of the difference between "reason" and psychodynamics in two different ways:

1. The psychodynamic mechanism: This "lower form of logic" (irrational processes, Freud would say) enters into action whenever the stress goes beyond the individual's limits of acceptability or limits of possibility of doing something about the situation. These limits are established by his specific S.C.P.'s; his specific socioeconomic premises, "S.E.P.'s"; group premises, "G.P.'s" (such as those demonstrated in Sherif and Sherif's research); by his personal premises, "P.P.'s" (somehow my use of symbolism is deteriorating); and his interpersonal premises, "I.P.P.'s."

2. Coping fails not only as a function of the degree of complexity of difficulty of the situation faced, not only as a function of the ability and capacity of the coper (ego strength?), and not even only as a function of his cognitive control systems (as understood by the constitutional-developmental cognitive hypothesis)—coping fails fundamentally as a function of the degree of meaningfulness that the situation will have in function of the person's S.C.P.'s, S.E.P.'s, G.P.'s, I.P.P.'s, and all the other P.'s. The limits of meaningfulness and the evaluation of the whole situation is usually made in terms similar to the following: just or unjust, valid or invalid, good or bad, or even okay or not okay, important-unimportant, senseless-sensible, possible-impossible, "the limit," etc.

We should make a note that this "within the limit or beyond the limit" and "just or unjust," etc., are very important categorical evaluative processes, used, we feel, just before the individual utilizes either coping or defense. Because of their critical importance in regard to how stress

[5] The importance of this second criterion cross-culturally is underlined by Benjamin Paul (1953): "Our rationalistic bias leads us to classify people as 'reasonable' or 'unreasonable.' But people are neither reasonable nor unreasonable in the abstract. By their own cultural standards their behavior and beliefs are reasonable, by the standards of others they are unreasonable."

is handled, they should be studied better. They may have not appeared as a factor independent from evaluation in Osgood's (1957) monumental work because the demand to fit adjectives to nouns was not beyond the limits of endurance of the subjects.

In summary, coping fails, that is to say, we do not use the "rational processes" described for the S.C.P.'s, when (1) the situation we are trying to handle does not make sense or sufficient sense to a sufficient number of our premises; and (2) it makes sense but is beyond the limits we have set for ourselves in regard to justice and our own realistic or unrealistic impression of our physiological, psychological, interpersonal, social, etc., capacity and abilities.

An analysis of the relationship of the S.C.P.'s of a given group to its modal fashion of handling stress will further show the fallacy of trying to interpret rational processes (at least those involved in the S.C.P.'s) through a purely psychodynamic approach. In order to pinpoint these contradictions, let us see the criteria that Haan (1963) has developed as the properties of defense mechanism:

Properties of a defense mechanism:

1. Behavior is rigid, automatized, and stimulus bound.

2. Behavior is pushed from the past, and the past compels the needs of the present.

3. Behavior is essentially distorting of the present situation.

4. Behavior involves a greater quantity of primary process thinking, partakes of unconscious elements, and is thus undifferentiated in response.

5. Behavior operates with the assumption that it is possible to remove disturbing affects magically.

6. Behavior allows impulse gratification by subterfuge.

In a passive culture, major portions of properties 1, 2, and 5 may be considered as criteria descriptive of passive coping. Let us work with the hardest, Number 1. In effect, very often the behavior in a passive culture is set, rigid, automatized and stimulus bound, quite predictable indeed from the S.C.P.'s of the group—and still, and because of this, it is coping.[6] Thus, for instance, if a Mexican child were asked to do something, the child would obey much more easily and frequently than would an American child. But in Mexico the child is coping, using his logical and rational armament to resolve a situation where it is "rational" and "meaningful" to obey. He should be thinking something like this: "In Mexico, everyone, particularly all 'grown-ups,' appear to agree that children should obey their parents. I am a child, my father commands, I should obey."[7] Thus, here formal, logical deduction or some other sort of

---

[6] That coping can be different in different cultures has been shown in terms congenial to those used here—by Coelho, *et al.* (1964).

[7] In time this behavior may become very automatized.

"rational" mechanism is being used. Besides, the premise from which the reasoning begins is acceptable to all and apparently to him also and he obeys. This is just what McGinn and Ginsburg have found.

Coping, in this context, is defined then by the following:

1. The individual is coping if he employs the proper use of formal logic or at least of congruence in general.

2. If the behavior is coping, a valid premise from which to depart is utilized. *It is, of course, the problem of psychologists and other social scientists to find out the best and most valid premises in terms of a methodologically reliable and valid appraisal of what man is and can become; of what interpersonal relations are and can become; and what group, national, and international relations are and can become.* However, in the meantime we can judge coping and defense only in terms of the premises valid to the individual and to the group or culture to which he belongs. Therefore, the child of the example is coping also because the premise from which he departs is highly acceptable to his group.

3. A person is coping if, as a result of his behavior, he gains something in terms of self-development or mental development. Does obedience help the development of a person? Americans say "no"; Mexicans would probably say "yes." Americans are thinking in terms of specific individual achievement, Mexicans in terms of improving interpersonal and social relations. Americans might feel that an individual's potentialities cannot flourish because he is simply doing what someone else wants him to do, and so he does not learn to create. Mexicans might argue that the individual learns greater emotional control; that in the way he obeys his father, he obeys himself; and that creativity, particularly where much stress has to be endured, requires a great deal of "obedience" to one's own ideals and goals.

4. If the behavior is coping, no defense mechanism will appear (Haan's impulse control mechanisms), no symptom complex, or neurosis or delinquency or psychosis will appear as a result, immediately or at a later date.

5. The thinking or behavior is coping if, as a result of handling the situation, the individual learns something that will help him better handle the same situation or other problems later on.

6. The individual is coping if, as a result of the experience, he increases his productivity, constructivity, and creativity, immediately after or at a later date.

7. Finally, the individual is coping if the original meaning of the situation dealt with is not distorted. This may be enough for the criteria of coping as inspired by the cross-cultural comparison.

Defense will participate if the opposite characteristics are found, that is:

1. It will bring about the use of mechanisms other than the syllogistic, evaluative, and congruent as described.

2. It will depart from premises in conflict with the S.C.P.'s, S.E.P.'s, G.P.'s, and all the other P.'s.

3. It will use the "lower logic" or "defense mechanisms," for example, converting something into its opposite.

4. It will provoke symptoms, complexes, etc.

5. It will not allow the later development of potentialities; it will not increase the ability to deal with the same or other later problems.

6. It will decrease the productivity, constructivity, and creativity.

7. It will distort the meaning of the situation. Let us use Osgood's example of a phobia: A person is not originally afraid of closed spaces. If later he is afraid of them, the person has distorted the original meaning of closed spaces.

PSYCHODYNAMIC PROCESSES AND LOGICAL PREMISES

Adolescent transition is indeed an extremely challenging and complex problem with multiple facets. The variety covered by the chapters of this book is indeed a good verification of the statement.

Let me start the last section of this chapter with two statements from Sherif and Sherif. In the first one, they say:

In short, what is called "behavioral" and what is called "institutional" or "organizational" in the social sciences can cease to be antithetical in concept or in research practice through research designs for the study of part-processes in terms of their appropriate levels of interaction. (Sherif and Sherif, 1963, p. 24)

In the second one:

Categorizations are not ordinarily arrived at inductively through "rational" evaluation of direct experience in social life. Everything we know about human culture, and language in particular, informs us that our reference groups have ready-made categories for us which color even our direct experiences and trial-and-error encounters with the social world around us. The needed research must link thought process and categorical mentality with problems of group reference and values. It is hardly begun. We are still plagued by the arbitrary historical dichotomy between "rational" and "irrational" thinking, and too frequently the "irrational" is a label for thinking which leads to conclusions we do not like. (Sherif and Sherif, 1963, p. 26)

I would like to propose something terribly obvious, that irrationality begins only when rationality fails. On the basis of this proposal, with what has been said previously, and with the statements of Sherif and Sherif, I want to present a somewhat simple outline of the relationships of the different processes *that enter into the making of the kind of deci-*

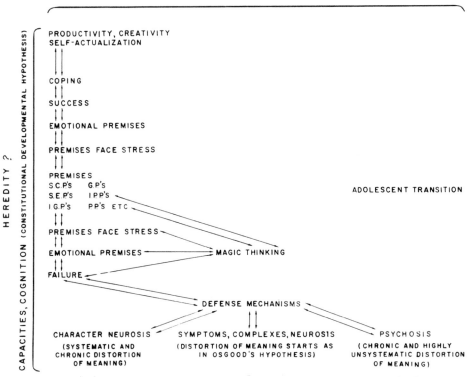

FIGURE 5. Relationship between Sociocultural Premises and Psychodynamic
          Processes

sions that we call healthy or unhealthy with their consequences thereof.
Figure 5 is nothing but an extension of the previously explained relationship of S.C.P.'s to psychodynamic processes. But the entire constellation
will be adequately understood only if there can be more research designs
like those indicated by the Sherifs in the first quotation and if we find
answers to the questions raised in the second.[8]

In the outline, you see at the center the word *premises* and under it
most of the possible ways in which man can make assertions from which

_____

[8] Sherif and Sherif's *Reference Groups* (1964) and their presentation in this
book (Chapters 12 and 13) are extremely important documents: theoretically, methodologically, and factually. The richness of the data collected will be difficult to equal.
From my vantage point there is here a mine of socioeconomic, group, interpersonal
and personal premises of adolescents in gangs. They, interestingly, call "sociocultural"
what I would call "socioeconomic." To me, the first refers to differences in S.C.P.'s
between nations, etc. At any rate, their contribution fulfills the expectation raised
in their working papers and cannot be pigeonholed here.

we deduct or infer other assertions or actions or feelings. An example has been given of a sociocultural premise and its interrelationship with psychodynamic processes. We would like to give an example of a socioeconomic premise from the work of Sherif and Sherif (1959). In one of their papers, they point out that lower socioeconomic class Mexican-Americans and upper socioeconomic class Mexican-Americans in San Antonio differ in regard to what they consider to be "really well off." For the first group, it is earning about $82 a week; for the second group, it is earning about $332 a week. I should expect that these premises will also function like the sociocultural premises that I have referred to before; that is, they will utilize in their functioning syllogistic logic, automatic evaluations, the principle of congruity, etc.

But how do observations of socioeconomic conditions become premises, or how does any kind of observation become a premise? In the Sherifs' quotation above there is a reference to the problem. In their superordinate goal example, the inference is of the scientist but accounts for the changed behavior of the two groups and is an intergroup premise of high order. In normal conditions we will have to assume that grown-ups, like the scientist, arrive at their various premises inferentially-inductively from observations. However, here again they will have to do this, as Sherif and Sherif suggest, on the basis of their previous norms and organizations; that is, on the basis of S.C.P.'s and G.P.'s and all the other P.'s. Again, this problem requires much exploration. We know reasonably well how defense mechanisms work. We know something about how the rational processes function. But we know short of nothing about how the premises, including the S.C.P.'s and the P.P.'s,[9] are gained and how they interact in specific problems.

At any rate, when premises face stress, we feel that the premise becomes further colored with emotion. Following down in the diagram, if the emotional premise meets with failure, then we expect the defense mechanisms to come into action. The defense mechanisms will lead into symptoms, complexes, neurosis, character neurosis, or psychosis, depending on many factors that cannot be considered here, though many of them have been worked through by psychodynamicists. Naturally, it is here where, besides the purely psychodynamic processes, the constitutional nature of the individual, his capacities and his perhaps congenital cognitive controls, will direct much of the specific processes and will lead into the different types of mental conditions. We have placed "magic thinking" to the right, somewhat independently from the defense mechanisms, because, although magic thinking partakes of the somewhat irrational characteristics of the defense mechanisms, it may be indulged in very early in the process of facing stress or even before. Within certain

---

[9] This is in spite of the fact that "self" psychologists have made important contributions in this area.

limits it may be protective, at least in the sense that it will not require the use of defense mechanisms in the solution of certain problems.[10]

Upward in the diagram, we see the premises facing against stress and becoming emotional premises as they become further colored with emotions. But here, they find success and we have, therefore, coping, which utilizes the rational processes that we have so many times enumerated. When this is obtained, the individuals learn better techniques of handling problems; they are prone to self-actualize in the terms of Goldstein and Maslow; and productivity, creativity, and self-development will be the results.

At the bottom, there is made an additional statement regarding the nature of neurosis, character neurosis, and psychosis. Here we are following Osgood's hypothesis in regard to the fact that in an operational fashion it is possible to determine at least the distortions of the meaning of a number of concepts and premises in neurotics, even if not the nature of neurosis. We assume that this can be extended to the meaning systems of psychotics, etc.

Finally, at the center, we have placed adolescent transition. Here we have an extremely complex problem: adolescence is transition enough all by itself without any help from the environment. In adolescence there is anatomical, physiological, and psychological developmental transition, etc. But, when the environment itself is in rapid transition, and even the basic sociocultural premises (and socioeconomic, group, and interpersonal premises) are in constant evolution, then almost anything goes. One would be willing to hypothesize that for the adolescent to remain fairly stable, there must be at least a minimum of congruency between the different sets of premises and a minimum of efficiency of this congruent result in the daily facing-of-life stresses.

It is in the hands of the social scientists to try to determine more closely, utilizing all the avenues and approaches that will give us objective knowledge, what each of the set of premises that we have talked about is and should become in order to develop some kind of rational approach, or, at least, some kind of effective approach to help with the extreme deviations which may fall upon the adolescent in transition. In the meantime, "Adolescent Transition" is left at the center of the figure to await further contributions, such as *Reference Groups* (Sherif and Sherif, 1964). Such contributions will help in establishing its connections to the diagram and—hopefully—to reality.

---

[10] Says Benjamin Paul (1953): "So long as men must face emergencies beyond their capacity to control they will seek 'solutions' that are magical or mystical or in some other way 'unreasonable.'"

REFERENCES

Anderson, H. H., and G. L. Anderson, 1956. Cultural reactions to conflict: A study of adolescent children in seven countries. In G. M. Gilbert (ed.), *Psychological Approaches to Intergroup and International Understanding*. The Hogg Foundation for Mental Hygiene, Austin, University of Texas, 27-32.

————, 1957. A cross-national study of teacher-child relations as reported by adolescent children. (Mimeographed.)

————, 1961. Image of the teacher by adolescent children in seven countries. *Amer. J. Orthopsychiatry*, 31, 3.

Anderson, H. H., G. L. Anderson, I. H. Cohen, and F. D. Nutt, 1959. Image of the teacher by adolescent children in four countries: Germany, England, Mexico, United States. *J. soc. Psychol.*, 50, 47-55:

Coelho, G. V., and A. G. Steinbert, with the collaboration of E. Maldonado Sierra, and R. Fernandez Marina, 1964. A cross-cultural assessment of coping behavior: student TAT responses of competent adolescents in Maryland and Puerto Rico. (Mimeographed.)

Diaz-Guerrero, R., 1955. Neurosis and the Mexican family structure. *Amer. J. Psychiatry*, 112, 6, 411-417.

————, La socio-culture mexicana. Unpublished monograph.

————, 1959. Mexican assumptions about interpersonal relations. A *review of general semantics*, 16, No. 2.

————, 1963. Discussion. *Amer. J. Orthopsychiatry*, 31, No. 3.

————, 1963. Socio-cultural premises, attitudes and cross cultural research. (Mimeographed.)

————, 1963. Personality development of Mexican school children. A research proposal submitted to the Foundations' Fund for Research in Psychiatry. (Mimeographed.)

Diaz-Guerrero, R., and R. R. Peck, 1963. Respeto y posicion social en dos culturas. In Sociedad Interamericana de Psicologia, *VII Congreso Interamericano de Psicologia* (Mexico, D. F.), No. 62, 116-137.

Fromm, E., 1941. *Escape from Freedom*. (New York: Rinehart.)

————, 1949. Psychoanalytical characterology and its application to the understanding of culture. In S. S. Sargent and H. W. Smith (eds.), *Culture and Personality*. (New York: Viking Fund.)

Haan, Norma, 1963. Proposed model of age functioning: Coping and defense mechanism in relationship to IQ change. *Psychol. Monogr.*, 77 (8 Whole No. 571), 1-23.

Maldonado Sierra, E. D., R. D. Trent and R. Fernandez Marina, 1958. Three basic themes in Mexican and Puerto Rican family values. *J. soc. Psychol.*, 48, 167.

————, 1960. Neurosis and traditional family beliefs in Puerto Rico. *Internat. J. soc. Psychiatry*, 6, 237-246.

Maslow, A. H., and R. Diaz-Guerrero, 1960. Delinquency as a value disturbance. In J. G. Peatman and E. L. Hartley (eds.), *Festschrift for Gardner Murphy*. (New York: Harper.)

McGinn, B. N., E. Harburg and G. Ginsburg, 1963a. Differencias entre mexicanos y norteamericanos en su reaccion a conflicto interpersonal. *Revista Mexicana de Psicologia*, 1, No. 2, 109-122.

————, 1963b. Perceptions of middle class Mexican and American males about parent-child and interpersonal relations. (Mimeographed.)

Murphy, Lois B., 1962. *The Widening World of Childhood*. (New York: Basic Books.)

Osgood, C. E., G. J. Suci, and P. H. Tannenbaum, 1957. *The Measurement of Meaning*. (Urbana, Ill.: University of Illinois Press.)

Paul, B. D., 1953. Respect for cultural differences. *Community development Bull.*, London, 4, 3.

Peck, R. F., and R. Diaz-Guerrero, 1963. Two core-culture patterns and the diffusion of values across their border. In Sociedad Interamericana de Psicologia (ed.), *VII Congreso Interamericano de Psicologia* (Mexico, D. F.), 107-115.

————, no date. The meaning of love in Mexico and the U.S. (Mimeographed.)

Sherif, M., and Carolyn W. Sherif, 1959. Operational report to the Hogg Foundation for Mental Health. (Mimeographed.)

————, 1963. Research on intergroup relations. Theoretical and research reports (mimeographed). (Norman, Oklahoma: Institute of Group Relations).

————, 1964. *Reference Groups*. (New York: Harper and Row.)

PART III

YOUTH
IN TROUBLE

EIGHT

SOCIAL STRUCTURE AND GROUP PROCESSES
IN EXPLANATION OF GANG DELINQUENCY

James F. Short, Jr.

Early in *Reference Groups,* the opinion is expressed that "the conception of gangs as unique formations in a class of their own makes advance in the analysis of their formation and the behavioral consequences of membership well-nigh impossible." (Sherif and Sherif, 1964, p. 48) The misconception to which the Sherifs refer is, to some extent I suppose, a regrettable by-product of Thrasher's classic survey of gangs in Chicago, and of the enthusiasm of the old Chicago school for studying the phenomena of the inner city. (Anderson, 1923; Thrasher, 1927; Shonle, 1928; Wirth, 1928; Landesco, 1929; Zorbaugh, 1929; Shaw, 1929, 1930; Shaw and McKay, 1931, 1942; Cressey, 1932; Frazier, 1932; Reckless, 1933; Hayner, 1936) So many interesting problems were found to be concentrated in the slum that the impression was perhaps inevitable that these problems were unique to the slum and causally related primarily to one another rather than to more general social processes. The fact that this was not the intention of the Chicago school was offset by the descriptive, as contrasted with theoretical, interests of most of its adherents, and by their failure to incorporate in study design the principles of comparative study. The confusion is compounded by the fact that persons whose primary interests are in amelioration of social ills find it easier to focus on the slum as a physical and social entity and to deal with its immediate problems rather than facing the conceptually more realistic, but operationally more difficult task of identifying and working with general social

Research reported in this chapter, and the time to prepare it, are supported by grants from the Behavior Science Study Section of the National Institute of Mental Health (M-3301 and MH-07158); a curriculum development grant from the Office of Juvenile Delinquency and Youth Development, Welfare Administration, U.S. Department of Health, Education and Welfare in cooperation with the President's Committee on Juvenile Delinquency and Youth Crime (62220); the Ford Foundation, and the Research Committee of Washington State University. I am grateful for this support and for the aid and encouragement of staff members and collaborators at the University of Chicago, Washington State University, and the Program for Detached Workers of the YMCA of Metropolitan Chicago, whose wholehearted cooperation has made possible and fruitful the entire enterprise.

processes related to the behavior with which they are concerned, and with realities of social structure which concentrate so many social problems in the slum.

This chapter deals with the relation of different levels of behavior explanation to one another, and specifically to the manner in which they become "translated" into behavior. The levels of explanation to which I refer are *social structure, culture* (or the currently more popular *subculture*), *group process,* and *individual personality.* I shall be concerned with the behavior of members of groups comprised largely of adolescent boys and referred to commonly as "delinquent gangs," although, as we shall see, the groups to which I refer do not by and large conform to the popular stereotype of gangs. The term "gang" is unnecessary, and its popular connotation is inappropriate to the theoretical resolution I shall suggest.

To those who have followed the monumental work of the Sherifs and their associates over the past several years, it will be clear that in many respects we have been pursuing the same objectives—too much in isolation from one another, I regret to say. This very isolation makes similarities of findings more impressive, however, and differences provide grist for the theoretical mill and for more direct empirical tests in the future.

The chapter draws heavily on the work of others, both theoretical and empirical. I shall be most concerned, however, with data from an ongoing study of delinquent gangs in Chicago with which I have been associated since the fall of 1958 (Short and Strodtbeck, 1965). At that time, the YMCA of Metropolitan Chicago and the department of sociology at the University of Chicago brought together four academicians (Albert Cohen, Lloyd Ohlin, Walter Miller, and myself) whose substantive research interests in the phenomena of gang delinquency meshed well with Philip Hauser's interests in human ecology and social organization and Fred Strodtbeck's social-psychological interests. Lay and professional leaders of the YMCA met with us also and made important contributions and commitments to the action-research collaboration which emerged. At that meeting the academicians were encouraged to present and argue about alternative theoretical positions and their implications for research design and for possibilities of working with the new Y program. The others doubtless were curious to know what research and theory had to say about problems which they considered most pressing, and whether, after all, academicians might have some contribution to make to action problems. That conference was the springboard for an action-research program of considerable proportions, with very generous foundation, university, and YMCA support. En route to discussion of research strategies and findings from this program, I should like to discuss the notion of delinquent subcultures, their nature, and their generality. In the process, perhaps some notion can be gained as to whether the concept is helpful in the scientific enterprise, and how it relates to other levels of explanation.

DELINQUENT SUBCULTURES

The sociology of subcultures is not well developed theoretically. A subculture generally is understood to be a "way of life" that has become traditional among members of a particular category or subgroup of individuals within a larger society which shares a common culture. Subcultures commonly are distinguished by specialized argots and behavior expectations of participants (oftentimes by others as well as by participants themselves), as well as by special training of those who are carriers of the culture (as in the case of members of professions and learned disciplines), or physical or social characteristics such as race, class, and ethnicity. These characteristics do not define subcultures, and their possession does not make one automatically a carrier of a particular subculture. A person may be, and quite likely is, a carrier of more than one subculture, with varying degrees of commitment to the values and the customs of each, depending upon such factors as amount and type of interaction with other carriers, personal experience with the problems to which subcultures are a collective solution, etc.

Though "hard data" on the matter are extremely rare, enough evidence and informed opinion exist to suggest that some type of delinquent subculture is to be found in communities that vary widely in size, population, composition, and regional location. Even in the metropolis, however, except in relatively rare instances, these do not appear to take the highly specialized forms described in the literature as *conflict, criminal,* or *retreatist* (Cohen and Short, 1958; Cloward and Ohlin, 1960; Yablonsky, 1962). The behavioral versatility of most "delinquent gangs" is attested to by virtually every empirical effort which has been directed to the problem, from Thrasher's classic survey to current studies (Thrasher, 1927; Bloch and Niederhoffer, 1958; Short, Tennyosn, and Howard, 1963). It is against this background of versatility, I believe, that the emergence of more specialized varieties of delinquent subcultures must be understood. Let us look, therefore, at the characteristics of the more common and diffuse varieties which have been reported.

In describing the community setting of the Provo Experiment in Delinquency Rehabilitation, Empey and Rabow comment as follows concerning delinquents in the "string of small cities . . . ranging in size from four to forty thousand" from which the experiment was drawn:

> Despite the fact that Utah County is not a highly urbanized area, when compared to large metropolitan centers, the concept of a "parent" delinquent subculture has real meaning for it. While there are no clear-cut gangs, *per se,* it is surprising to observe the extent to which delinquent boys from the

entire county, who have never met, know each other by reputation, go with the same girls, use the same language, or can seek each other out when they change high schools. About half of them are permanently out of school, do not participate in any regular institutional activities, and are reliant almost entirely upon the delinquent system for social acceptance and participation. (Empey and Rabow, 1961)

Similar reports have been received from other western cities, with occasional and usually short-lived gangs being reported. More recently, the Lane County Youth Project, on the basis of early returns, appears to be discovering a similar phenomenon in rural Oregon, as well as in smaller towns and cities (Polk, 1963).

Across the continent, in Vermont's idyllic Green Mountain Town and in Mountain City, where delinquents are hard to come by, Himelhoch reports that "There is evidence in both communities that the delinquents share a subculture which distinguishes them from the conformists who participate in an opposite subculture. The delinquent subculture comprises . . . a cluster of anti-moralistic attitudes which support and encourage law violation, usually of a minor or moderate nature." He concludes further that "the typical rural and small city convicted youthful offender in Northeast State belongs to a loosely organized, non-exclusive, sporadically delinquent group. The shifting membership of this group draws upon a larger population of youth who are mostly, but not always, of lower class backgrounds." (Himelhoch, 1964)

From the midwest, Elmtown and John Clark's samples, and from Reiss and Rhodes in Nashville, come similar reports (Hollingshead, 1949; Reiss and Rhodes, 1961; Clark and Wenninger, 1962). I have emphasized these reports from rural and smaller urban areas because most of the literature has concentrated on the highly urban slum as the locus for gangs and for delinquent subcultures (Crawford, Malamud and Dumpson, 1950; Glane, 1950; Bloch and Niederhoffer, 1958; Yablonsky, 1962). This was Thrasher's great emphasis, and it has tended to characterize virtually all the research and speculation since. Even in Thrasher's day, however, there was recognition of the generality of youth groups referred to as gangs beyond city boundaries. In his Editor's Preface to the first edition of *The Gang*, Robert E. Park remarked that "Village gangs, because they are less hemmed about by physical structures and social inhibitions of an urban environment, ordinarily do not become a social problem, certainly not a problem of the dimensions and significance of those which constitute so obvious and so obdurate a feature of city life." (P. ix in abridged edition.)

Albert Cohen and I coined the phrase, "parent delinquent subculture," in the course of an investigation into varieties of subcultures which seemed to characterize delinquent groups in various cities (Cohen and Short, 1958). These groups—*e.g.*, "bopping" gangs in New York City, drug-using "cats" in Chicago, and semiprofessional "hoods" engaged in theft for profit in several places, seemed not to fit *the* delinquent subculture described earlier by Cohen (1955). So, we set out, by literature search and by correspondence with police and others in dozens of places, to delineate variations on Cohen's earlier theme. Very early in the process we were impressed by the absence of reports of highly specialized gangs, even from large cities such as Detroit and San Francisco. This, plus such notions as the "natural history" of delinquent careers and "differential association," provided by our mentors, Clifford Shaw and Edwin Sutherland, and our own research, led us to the concept of a parent delinquent subculture from which variations were thought to emerge by processes we hoped to discover. Thus, drug users in both Chicago and New York emerged from the ubiquitous street corner groups found in those cities, only later forming or joining associations which were the carriers of distinct subcultures. The latter appeared to be characterized by very loose group ties, but strong attachment to subcultural norms and values. Youngsters who stole for profit came from similar initial groups, developing their theft patterns only after earlier and repeated delinquencies, including minor thefts not of a profit nature. Bopping gangs started out in similar fashion, adopting their bellicose posture, it appeared, in response to common cultural values such as "toughness" and local opportunities, not the least important of which were the availability of rival groups.

At the time of our initial speculations we had no very clear ideas as to just how varieties of delinquent subcultures emerged from what we were calling the parent delinquent subculture, but we were convinced of the relevance of Kobrin's notions concerning the relative integration of the carriers of criminal and conventional values in lower class communities. We did not know of Cloward's brilliant addition to the theory of "Social Structure and Anomie," having to do with the differential availability of illegitimate means to success goals; and only later (at the Chicago conference) did we learn that he and Ohlin were engaged in writing *Delinquency and Opportunity*. We were perhaps not sensitive enough to the characteristic gradual isolation of drug users from their more "conventionally delinquent" groups, described by Chein and his associates in New York (Kobrin, 1951a; Chein and Rosenfeld, 1957; Cloward, 1959; Cloward and Ohlin, 1960); or of the extent to which these boys were therefore thrown on their own resources, and the implications this appears to have for formation of the "society of cats" described by Finestone (1957). In retrospect it seems also we did not fully appreciate the implications of our own data on semiprofessional stealing, which we described as appearing "to be more of a differentiation of emphasis within a more diversified climate of delinquency than an autonomous subculture independently organized." Certainly we were not aware of the extent to which even elaborately organized conflict gangs with cherished names and a strong sense of corporate identity were loosely organized and shifting in membership and "attendance" on the corner or at other hangouts. Nor were we aware of the forces motivating conflict among these gangs.

The notion of varieties of delinquent subcultures provided the basis for the design of the Chicago research concerning "street corner groups and patterns of delinquency." (Short, 1963) Theoretical focus was derived from Cohen's *Delinquent Boys*, from *Delinquency and Opportunity*, from Walter Miller's thesis (1958) of lower class culture as the "Generating Milieu of Gang Delinquency," and from our own determination, at first only vaguely formulated, to keep a window open on the gangs in order to bring to bear data on group processes and later to study both characteristics of individual gang members and the cultural and social structural data implied by the other theories. I will summarize our research procedures and findings rather than present detailed data on these myriad matters. The synthesis which I shall attempt must be seen as an approximation, based on data at hand, from our own work and from the work of others; it is subject, of course, to revision in the process of coming closer to reality, which is the hallmark of the scientific endeavor.

I will bring to bear findings from a considerable variety of data generation procedures, including field observation by members of the research team and by detached workers, ratings on the basis of such observation, interviews with gang boys, workers, and local community adults, paper and pencil instruments, and carefully controlled laboratory assessments of gang boys. For comparative purposes, data (except for field observations) were gathered on non-gang boys from the gang neighborhoods and on middle class youngsters as well as gang boys. We have studied Negro and white boys in each of these categories. Our basic research design thus permits comparisons by race, social class, and gang status, as well as comparisons among the different groups under observation.

FROM SOCIAL STRUCTURE TO GANG DELINQUENCY:
AN INTERPRETATION

In the interest of clarity, I will first summarize some notions about the classes of variables and the nature of their relation to one another, which, on the basis of our research, appear to be involved in the "translation" of social structure into gang delinquency (and at least some other forms of "deviant" behavior).

Realities of social structure, such as class and ethnic differentiation and the operation of ecological processes, place severe limitations on the realization of certain cultural universals—for example, the high value placed on material wealth and status achievement in the contexts of important institutions such as school and the world of work. For many lower class and ethnically disadvantaged persons, failure to achieve these goals begins early in life due to socialization practices which are defective in meeting the criteria for achievement of the larger society. This process is complicated by the existence of subcultures with distinctive ethnic and lower class characteristics, and by youth subcultures, some of which are delinquent in a variety of ways. These subcultures have both historical and contemporary roots. They serve both to insulate their adherents from experiences which might make possible achievement of many "respectable" goals in terms of "respectable" criteria, and to compensate in some measure for failure, or the likelihood of failure, in these areas. Indeed, compensation appears to be one of the chief functions of peer group participation in every strata of society and at every age.

Important *goals* of the larger society are quite successfully communicated, as Merton suggests (1957). So, also, are values concerning legitimate means for their achievement. Evidence from a variety of sources, *e.g.*, the Flint Youth Study and our own, suggests that disadvantaged youngsters do not become alienated, that even the gang ethic is not one of "reaction formation" *against* widely shared values in society (Gold, 1963).

Peer groups in the lower class often come to serve important *status functions* for youngsters who are disadvantaged according to the success criteria of the larger society's institutions (schools, churches, places of business, etc.). Peer groups become the most salient status universe of such youngsters. Group norms and values come to stress means of achievement not prescribed by conventional norms and values, which in effect provide alternative means of achievement for group members. Delinquency arises sometimes as a by-product and sometimes as a direct product of peer group activity.

The groups and institutions which are the primary carriers of lower class, ethnic, and delinquent subcultures are marked in many cases by instability and by a high incidence of physical objects and social situations which combine to create a high risk of involvement in delinquency. One thinks of elements such as the public nature of drinking and "party" behavior, shifting sexual and economic liaisons, widespread possession of guns, and the acceptance of violence as a means of settling disputes.

There is evidence that the gang offers less solidarity and less satisfaction to its participants than nostalgic accounts of "that old gang of mine" would suggest. There is evidence, too, that the "lack of social assurance" which Whyte attributed to his corner boys is especially aggravated among these seriously delinquent youngsters, and that they are characterized by other social disabilities which contribute to delinquency-producing status threats within and outside the gang (Whyte, 1955; Gordon and Short, 1962).

Though evidence from our own study is incompletely analyzed, such measures as we have been able to obtain of social structural variables (such as race, class, and gang status; some, but not all, measures of "position discontent"; and perceptions of opportunity structures) and of individual social disabilities (such as negative self-concept and low intelligence) are found to *order* the groups by race, by class, or by gang status in much the same way as their delinquency rates. The same measures, however, are not highly correlated with individual behavior in the group context. That is, these variables generally are not predictive of behavioral variations of individual gang members. In accounting for this finding, it is insufficient simply to regard the group as a catalyst that releases potentials for delinquency not readily apparent in known characteristics of its individual members. To further specify the relation between the group and the behavior of its members, we have looked for specific group processes and mechanisms which are involved in delinquency episodes. Three of these have been suggested in our recent work:

(1) REACTIONS TO STATUS THREATS
When gang boys perceive threats to some valued status, delinquency often follows (Short and Strodtbeck, 1963). This mechanism has been found to operate in response to perceived threats to status as a leader, as male, as a member of a particular gang, or as an aspiring adult. It may operate individually or collectively, though the delinquent solution characteristically involves other members of the group. Why status threats should produce delinquency episodes doubtless is a very complex matter, but we have observed several characteristics of gang boys and their social worlds that are apparently related to this mechanism.

There is, first of all, the lack among gangs of a formal structure supporting group continuity and stability. There is further the lack of institutionalized support in adversity, in contrast to more formal organizations such as voluntary associations, schools, churches, businesses, and governments. At a more individual level, leaders can control few resources of crucial value to the group, so that their own ability to dominate the group by internally directed aggression is severely restricted. Gang members tend to lack social skills which might permit them to meet status threats in more creative, less delinquent ways. At the group level, delinquent actions often are acceptable, if not generally prescribed, by group norms. They constitute a sort of "least common denominator" around which members can rally. Finally, externally directed delinquency, particularly of an aggressive nature, serves to unify these loosely structured groups in common cause. Indeed, the latter appears to operate not only in conjunction with status threats, but independently, as a basic mechanism accounting for delinquency involvement by these youngsters (Gordon and Short, 1962). This point will be further developed later in the chapter.

(2) THE GAMBLE OF STATUS GAIN VERSUS PUNISHMENT RISK

In the calculus of decision making, status *rewards* within the group often tip the scales toward "joining the action," and therefore becoming involved in delinquency. The chief *risk* in such behavior appears to be the probability of punishment at the hands of a society which seems disinterested in one's personal fate (Strodtbeck and Short, 1964). Episodes which on the surface seem to reflect simply a hedonistic orientation to life thus may actually involve a rational assessment of probabilities resulting in a decision to risk the consequences of joining the action, going along with the boys, etc. The decision is understandable in view of the low risk of serious consequences associated with most delinquency episodes, and the somewhat higher probability of associated group rewards consequent to joining the action—affirmation of friendship bonds, status accruals from performance in an episode, personal satisfaction derived from demonstration of toughness, masculinity, etc.

(3) THE DISCHARGE OF GROUP ROLE OBLIGATIONS

As obvious examples, a leader may be *required* to "join the action," or even to precipitate it if the situation involves *group threat*. A "War Counselor" is required to perform when gang conflict appears imminent or is engaged. Centrality in the group, or striving toward this goal, exposes one to involvement in situations with a high "delinquency potential," by means of the previously discussed mechanisms, including those associated with specific roles in the group. Thus, an apparent paradox in our self-concept data may be resolved. As reported earlier, boys who describe themselves in "scoutlike" terms (loyal, polite, helpful, religious, obedient) are *more* involved in conflict behavior than are boys who describe themselves as "cool aggressives" (mean, tough, troublesome, and cool) (Short and Strodtbeck, 1965). Our interpretation rests upon the connotation of *responsibility* in personal relations and recognition of their implied obligations, which are characteristic of the "scout" terms. The "cool aggressive" terms, by contrast, carry overtones of disruption or disregard of obligations to associates or to convention, and of a type of detachment which is the antithesis of reciprocity in personal relations. The scouts, we believe, facilitate cohesive relations and reduce interpersonal tensions in these loosely structured groups, becoming more central in the group. They then find themselves in situations in which role expectations, status threats, and potential rewards associated with joining the action make their involvement in episodes of aggression more likely.

SOCIAL STRUCTURE: POSITION DISCONTENT AND
PERCEIVED OPPORTUNITIES

Having sketched major conclusions concerning the topic of this chapter, some of the evidence upon which they are based seems in order. I will begin, like most recent sociological treatises on the subject, with social structure. The "Social Structure and Anomie" paradigm and related theoretical efforts say, in effect, that pressures toward deviance are greatest among those persons who have accepted culturally defined success goals but who find culturally approved means to achieve them unavailable (Cohen, 1955; Merton, 1957; Cloward and Ohlin, 1960). The discrepancy between goals and means is commonly expressed as "position discontent," which in turn is hypothesized as a principal component of pressures toward deviant behavior. But, how are we to measure position discontent, and likewise, pressures toward deviance? We have tried several ways. For the moment we will ignore differences between gangs and concentrate on comparing our highly delinquent gang boys with their non-gang counterparts, both lower and middle class. Consistent with the stress that anomie theory puts on the "success theme" as a universal in our culture, we find that both gang and non-gang boys aspire to occupational levels considerably above their fathers. This finding was based on Duncan's modification of the NORC—North-Hatt scale of occupational prestige as shown in column 1 of Table 5 (Duncan and Reiss, 1961; Gold, 1963; Rivera, 1964; Sherif and Sherif, 1964; Short, 1964).

This criterion orders our six groups quite differently from the two measures of delinquency involvement—mean number of offenses known to the police per boy (column 4) and a measure of self-reported delinquency (column 5). (Differences between gang and non-gang boys are highly statistically significant on both of these behavior measures.) Negro boys, especially the less delinquent non-gang boys, both aspire (column 1) and expect (column 2) to achieve far beyond their fathers' levels. White boys, whose fathers have achieved higher occupational levels, have less lofty ambitions than do any of the Negro boys. So, by the criterion of column 2, white gang (WG) boys should be least delinquent of the lot; and by those in columns 1 and 2, Negroes, both middle class (NMC) and lower class non-gang boys (NLC), should be most delinquent. Although these discrepancies probably reflect pressures to succeed, they do not generate pressures toward deviance in the manner that anomie theory predicts. This may be because they do not indicate the same type of position discontent that the theories discuss; one of the great difficulties with the theory is that it is not specific in this regard. Column 3 offers yet another index of position discontent; this time, within race, the groups rank in the same order as they do according to police contacts and self-reported "corner boy" delinquency. For both Negroes

TABLE 5

Indexes of Position Discontent and Delinquency Involvement, Ranked for Six Population Groups*

1	2	3	4	5
Mean Discrepancy between Fathers' Occupational Levels and Boys' Aspirations°	Mean Discrepancy between Fathers' Occupational Levels and Boys' Expectations°	Mean Discrepancy between Boys' Occupational Aspirations and Expectations°	Mean Number of Offenses Known to the Police per Boy	Self-Reported Delinquency Factor (Corner Boy Delinquency)†
NLC 16.6	NMC 14.4	NG 7.1	NG 3.14	WG 15.8
NMC 15.2	NLC 12.1	NLC 5.8	WG 2.73	NG 17.3
NG 13.8	NG 7.3	WG 5.7	NLC .47	WLC 21.0
WLC 11.4	WLC 6.8	WLC 4.6	WLC .31	NLC 22.7
WG 9.2	WMC 4.9	WMC 1.2	NMC .06	NMC 23.8
WMC 6.1	WG 3.7	NMC .8	WMC .02	WMC 27.9

°N's for each column are as follows:	1	2	3	4	5
NG = Negro gang boys	204	205	194	350	153
WG = White gang boys	88	87	88	100	55
NLC = Negro lower class, non-gang boys	89	89	82	117	111
WLC = White lower class, non-gang boys	74	74	74	91	71
NMC = Negro middle class boys	26	26	26	34	29
WMC = White middle class boys	53	53	53	51	50

† *Lower Scores Indicate More Delinquency.* Scores range from 7, representing "every day" involvement in seven activities, to 35, representing no involvement. The activities, extracted from factor analysis of 22 behaviors of 469 boys, are *gambling* (playing cards or pool for money, shooting dice, penny pitching); *signifying or playing the dozens; hanging* (being with the boys on the street); *drinking* beer, wine, whiskey; *riding in cars; fighting* (humbug or rumble); *making money* (bread) *illegally.*

and whites, class differences in this index are greater than gang–non-gang differences.[1]

To support the theory, it might be argued that the discrepancy between an individual's occupational aspirations and expectations is the index most directly relevant to his own feelings of disjuncture between goals and aspirations. On the other hand, discrepancy between class of origin (father's occupation) and class of orientation (one's own ambitions and/or expectations) seems likely to reflect a more objective disjuncture in terms of its consequences for the individual. Certainly we can assume that, viewed objectively, opportunities are more restricted for Negroes

[1] The situation is more complex with respect to self-reported behavior, where class differences are slightly greater among whites, gang status among Negroes. In both instances, there is less "spread" among Negro populations than among whites. Analysis of the data and more extended discussion are presented in Short and Strodtbeck (1965).

than for whites, and for lower class than for middle class boys. If it could be shown that *gang membership* itself restricts occupational achievement, and/or that gang members are less able to achieve than non-gang youngsters (from the same class of origin), an important advance would have been made; this effect would add factors to the subjective disjuncture shown in column 3.

Some leverage on this question is provided by the fact that school adjustment of the non-gang boys is more successful than that of the gang boys (Freedman and Rivera, 1962), and that their mean intelligence level is higher (Howard, Hendrickson and Cartwright, 1962). Estimates of the latter were obtained with a "culture free" test, as well as a standardized arithmetic test, and vocabulary, memory, and information tests designed especially to avoid "middle class" biases which would disadvantage lower class and gang subjects. Nearly one-half of the gang boys (46.8 per cent of the Negroes; 42.7 per cent of whites) were judged to be unsuccessful in school adjustment on the basis of a composite objective index derived from their interview responses; only about one-quarter of the lower class non-gang boys and virtually none of the middle class boys were judged unsuccessful. Among gang boys, those with poor school adjustment have, as expected, higher delinquency rates. But those who also have high educational aspirations are "protected" to an extent against delinquency involvement (in the sense that their delinquency rates are lower than those of boys with lower aspirations). I have suggested elsewhere that high educational aspirations indicate an identification with norms of the larger social order concerning legitimate means, and hence they operate to restrain involvement in delinquency, despite blocked opportunities in the form of poor educational adjustment (Short, 1964). This "protection," however, is too limited to explain a great deal of the variance in the behavior of the boys.

Another way of looking at social structural variables that possibly influence our youngsters concerns their own evaluation of their "areas" in terms of legitimate and illegitimate opportunities following Cloward and Ohlin (1960). Boys were asked whether or not a series of twenty-six statements applied to the area where their group hung out. The statements concerned educational and occupational opportunities, integration of the carriers of criminal and noncriminal values, opportunities for learning crime, the visibility of criminal careers and of criminal elites, and general perceptions of the power of adults and their helpfulness to teenagers. Mean summary scores of boys in each sample are presented in Table 6 (Short, Rivera and Tennyson, 1965). Here the groups rank the same in both perception of legitimate opportunities (column 1) and perception of adult power and helpfulness (column 3) as they do in the official delinquency rate. This is consistent with Cloward and Ohlin's reference to illegitimate opportunities as intervening for lower class

TABLE 6

Perception of Opportunities and Offenses Known to the Police, by Six Populations

Legitimate Educational and Occupational Opportunities	Perception of Illegitimate Opportunities (less inclusive)	Perception of Adult Power and Helpfulness	Total Opportunities Score*	Mean Number of Offenses Known to Police, Per Boy
(low to high) (0 to 22)	(high to low) (0 to 18)	(low to high) (0 to 8)	(low to high) (− 18 to 30)	(high to low)
NG (9.0)	NG (11.4)	NG (4.5)	NG (2.1)	NG (3.14)
WG (9.3)	NLC (9.5)	WG (4.7)	WG (5.0)	WG (2.73)
NLC (11.0)	WG (9.0)	NLC (5.6)	NLC (7.1)	NLC (0.47)
WLC (13.7)	NMC (8.2)	WLC (5.6)	WLC (12.6)	WLC (0.31)
NMC (15.6)	WLC (6.7)	NMC (6.2)	NMC (13.6)	NMC (0.06)
WMC (20.2)	WMC (3.5)	WMC (7.4)	WMC (24.1)	WMC (0.02)

* Total Opportunities Score is designed to reflect both legitimate and illegitimate pressures toward delinquency, and is obtained by adding together legitimate educational and occupational opportunities and adult power and helpfulness scores, and from this sum subtracting illegitimate opportunity scores. Hence it is expected to be negatively correlated with delinquency.

youngsters *following* assessment of legitimate opportunities. Our data support the notion that legitimate achievement tends to be the universal standard against which alternatives are weighed. However, illegitimate opportunities do exist and provide an avenue to financial success; and, within race, perception of these illegitimate opportunities (column 2) places the boys in the same order as their official delinquency rates.

We may comment briefly on the relatively high "illegitimate opportunity" scores of the Negro boys. Despite white hoodlums' generally acknowledged domination of organized crime in Chicago (and, one suspects, in part because of it), much large-scale, organized vice flourishes in Negro communities (e.g., prostitution, heroin, and "the numbers"). There is more independent entrepreneurship in the form of street-walking prostitutes, marijuana peddling, pool sharks, professional burglars and robbers, smaller policy wheels, etc., than in lower class white communities. Intercorrelations of illegitimate opportunities with the measure of adult "clout," furthermore, indicate that the white areas are more "integrated," in the Cloward and Ohlin sense, than are the Negro areas. Finally, perceptive analyses by Drake and Cayton, and Frazier indicate the extent to which criminal and "shady" elements penetrate Negro social structure from bottom to top, providing a type of pervasive influence, but one less powerful than that found in some white communities (Drake and Cayton, 1962; Frazier, 1962).

BEHAVIOR PATTERNS: SUBCULTURES?

Returning now to behavioral variation *among* gang boys, we may assess its patterning in terms of various suggested delinquent subcultures. From the beginning of the study we had been impressed by the lack of "purity" of the hypothesized types, even though our selection of gangs, with the full cooperation of the YMCA detached workers, was oriented toward obtaining the best possible representatives of the three most discussed types in the literature—conflict, criminal, and retreatist. Negro conflict gangs were plentiful, but they were also involved in a great deal of stealing; we were unable to locate a real criminal gang, despite a determined and prolonged effort to do so. We did find occasional cliques or other subunits within larger gangs, which engaged in special criminal activities, *e.g.*, systematic theft or strong-arming. In one group there was a clique of "winos," and several had "singing" cliques. After a full year of investigation we located what appeared to be a genuine retreatist group. Thus it became clear that the subcultural emphases specified in the literature were not as exclusive as their descriptions suggested. Our factor analysis of ratings by detached workers isolated a conflict pattern; and a combination of drug use, homosexuality, common-law marriage, attempted suicide, and pimping which we could label as retreatist, but not a criminal factor. Neither conflict nor retreatism characterized exclusively any one gang under study. Other activities also emerged as factors and blended into the behavior patterning of these boys; *e.g.*, stable corner-boy activities, heterosexual behavior, and an "authority protest" factor involving chiefly auto theft, truancy, running away from home, vandalism, and creating public disturbance (Short, Tennyson and Howard, 1963). The described *simplicity* of subcultural patterns clearly was challenged by these data, if not their hypothesized etiology.

Field observation, coupled with systematic measures of the boys' values according to a semantic differential, indicated that gang boys' commitment to delinquent norms was quite tenuous (Short, Strodtbeck, and Cartwright, 1962). Indeed, commitment was virtually nonexistent except in specific types of situations involving the group, such as a threat from another gang, or, in some instances, threats to the status of boys individually. Analysis of behavior patterns and self-concept measures suggested that the gangs contained considerable numbers of "stable corner boys" and even a few "college boys"; there were "scouts" as well as "cool aggressives" within the same gang. This led us to question both the homogeneity of gangs and the degree of normative commitment which they place on their members (Gordon, Short, Cartwright, and Strodtbeck, 1963).

Yet there was, within each of these gangs, a shared perspective, which was often shared with members of other groups as well. For some gangs, conflict with other gangs was a major focus of group activity, and the source of considerable status within the gang. These gangs more often than others engaged in a variety of violent episodes in addition to gang conflict. These gangs were *invested* in their reputation for fighting, though the "boundaries" of their concern for such a "rep" are not clear. We know it includes other fighting gangs, but there is evidence, also, that it includes a much broader public. Members of such gangs often evidenced great pride when the mass media noticed their activities, even though the notices often were derogatory. A prominent member of one such gang compiled a scrapbook filled with newspaper articles featuring his gang. Newsmen looking for a story found that gang boys would be suspicious and ambivalent at first, but to the best of my knowledge reporters never experienced prolonged difficulty, and always found willing informants.

Conflict gangs also created roles expressive of their conflict orientation, thus differing in structure from other gangs. Such positions as "war counselor" and "armorer" were jealously guarded, even though the duties and privileges of office were rarely defined in a formal way. These roles served as a focus of ceremonial deference within the group, and they provided still another basis for individual status and for group identity. The nature of typical "guerrilla warfare" and its function for the participants is dramatically portrayed by a detached worker's report of a minor skirmish between the Knights and the Vice Kings, two groups which had been feuding for some months:

[I] was sitting there talking to the Knights . . . re-emphasizing my stand on guns, because they told me that they had collected quite a few and were waiting for the Vice Kings to come down and start some trouble . . . I told them flatly that it was better that I got the gun rather than the police, and though they agreed with me, they repeated their stand that they were tired of running from the Vice Kings and that if they gave them trouble, from now on they were fighting back.

. . . While I was sitting there in the car talking to William (the remaining guys have gotten out of the car in pursuit of some girls around the corner), William told me that a couple of Vice Kings were approaching. I looked out of the window and noticed two Vice Kings and two girls walking down the street by the car. . . . William then turned around and made the observation that there were about fifteen or twenty Vice Kings across the street in the alley and wandering up the street in ones and twos.

At this point, I heard three shots go off. I don't know who fired these shots, and no one else seemed to know, because the Vice Kings at this point had encountered Commando, Jones, and a couple of other Knights who were coming from around the corner talking to the girls. The Vice Kings yelled across the street to Commando and his boys, and Commando yelled back. They traded insults and challenges, Commando being the leader of the Knights and a guy named Bear being the leader of the Vice Kings. . . . I got out of the car to try to cool Commando down, inasmuch as he was half-way across the street hurling insults across the street and daring them to do something about it, and they were doing the same thing to him. I grabbed Commando and began to pull him back across the street.

By this time the Vice Kings had worked themselves into a rage, and three of them came across the street yelling that they were mighty Vice Kings and to attack Commando and the Knights. In trying to break this up, I was not too successful. I didn't know the Vice Kings involved, and they were really determined to swing on the Knights, so we had a little scuffle around there. . . . At this point, along the street comes Henry Brown, with a revolver, shooting at the Vice Kings. Everybody ducked and the Vice Kings ran, and Henry Brown ran around the corner. When he ran around the corner I began to throw Knights into my car because I knew that the area was "hot," and I was trying to get them out of there. Henry Brown came back around the corner and leaped into my car also. I asked him if he had the gun, and he told me that he did not, and since I was in a hurry, I pulled off in the car and took him and the rest of the boys with me.

. . . In the car Commando and the other boys were extremely elated. There were expressions like: "Baby, did you see the way I swung on that kid"; "I really let that one kid have it"; "Did you see them take off when I leveled my gun on them"; "You were great, Baby. And did you see the way I . . . ," etc. It was just like we used to feel when we got back from a patrol where everything went just right [the worker had been a paratrooper in the Korean conflict]. The tension was relieved, we had performed well and could be proud. (Short and Strodtbeck, 1965)

Our comment on this is in Chapter 9 of the *Group Process* book (Short and Strodtbeck, 1965):

Here the status function of the conflict subculture is seen in bold relief. No doubt the Vice Kings, too, felt the thrill of the conflict. They had faced great danger and had a perfect alibi for not winning an unequivocal victory, viz., the fact that the opposition had a gun—and so, of course, did the Knights, for the worker intervened to prevent them from following up their advantage. Thus, participants on both sides of such a conflict can share the elation and the status-conferring glow of an encounter such as this. It is, in effect, *not* a "zero-sum game" in the sense that points won by a party to the conflict are not necessarily lost by his adversary. No one need necessarily be defeated; behavior in conformity with the norms of the subculture takes place and is rewarded, and law and order are restored. In this way society, too, shares in this non-zero-sum game. Lest we be accused of too sanguine a view of gang behavior, we note that boys may be defeated, individually and collectively, and much injury and property damage may and often does result from this "game."

We know from studying numerous incidents that not all members of conflict gangs participated in such skirmishes even though they may have been on the scene. We do not fully understand why this is the case. In part, it is because much of the analysis so far has not concerned inter-gang differences; and analyses which have studied these differences have focused on hypothesis formation rather than testing, and on illustration rather than demonstration. Our suspicion, however, is that boys who are involved at any one time are those who are most heavily committed to the gang at the moment, usually gang leaders or other boys who aspire to prominence in the gang. Outstanding performance on such occasions is one of the few available avenues to achieving real prominence in gangs such as these, for reasons which we shall note presently.

So much for conflict. What of retreatism? The contrast between our one group of retreatists and all other gangs under observation was striking. I quote from the same book's earlier description of these young men:

The basis of camaraderie among the drug users was their common interest in kicks. Past and present exploits concerned experiences while high, and "crazy" behavior rather than bravery or toughness. Use of pills and other drugs seemed virtually a way of life with these boys, interspersed with other kicks such as sex, alcohol, and "way out" experiences which distinguished them, individually and collectively. After several observations of this group in their area, a member of the research team reported:

The guys make continual references to dope. They talk about it much as a group of drinkers might talk about liquor. It comes up freely, easily in the conversation, a couple of remarks are made about it, who's taken it recently, how it affected this or that person, etc., and then it is dropped only to come up again before long. Today the guys made comments about dope and baseball. (You get the feeling that whatever the activity of the moment, the guys will talk about it in relation to dope—how taking dope affects their participation in the activity.) A commonly expressed notion was that so and so played baseball better when he was "high" than at any other time. Whether they believed this was hard to tell. It sounded much like oft heard remarks that "I play poker better when I'm half drunk or high" (i.e., remarks made in the community at large). . . . The guys like to talk about their "highs," how much they have taken, how high they were, what they did while high, etc. . . . Perhaps one attitude is implicitly expressed, though, in these remarks; the attitude of acceptance.

Five months later this same observer reported on a hanging session in which the group related "tales about some of the crazy and humorous things" in which various of the drug users had been involved.

The relating of these tales was greeted by laughter from all. Often the worker or observer would mention an incident and Butch would fill us in or correct us on details. Some of the incidents mentioned:

(1) The time Willie was so high he walked off a roof and fell a story or two and broke his nose . . . . Butch said it was over a week before he went to the doctor . . . . Harry said he walked around the hospital in a crazy looking green coat whenever the guys went to visit him.

(2) The time Snooks, Baby, and Jerry climbed on a roof to wake

Elizabeth. One of the guys reached through the window and grabbed what he thought was Elizabeth's leg and shook it to wake her up. It turned out to be her old man's leg and it woke him up.

(3) The more recent incident in which Sonny leaped over the counter to rob a Chinaman who proceeded to beat him badly. When the police came, Sonny asked that they arrest this man for having beaten him so. He was doped out of his mind and didn't know what was happening.

(4) Walter got into an argument with a woman over whose car it was they were standing by. He insisted they call the police, and waited confidently until the police showed and took him away.

(5) Sonny tried to break into a building and was ripping off a door when the police found him.

(6) Some of the guys slept out in a car and woke the next morning to find the car was being pulled away. They asked the tower to stop just long enough so they could get out.

(7) One of the guys broke into a car and just about tore the door off doing so—this was a car with all the windows broken out—he was too high to notice.

(8) One of the boys tried to start a car but just could not manage it. The car had no motor.

All laughed at these true tales. Butch even noted that he had been with the guy who broke into the car with no windows.

[The observer then remarked] "These tales may be in the process of becoming legendary within the group. They are so characteristic of this group and describe it so well."

Though several of these boys had "grown up" together, they were not bound to each other by feelings of loyalty. Virtually their only common bond appeared to be use of drugs and the type of experiences which are recounted above. They did not really *share* drugs. Every boy was expected to "cop" (purchase drugs) on his own. In a peculiar way this was functional to the group, for although all the boys who were financially and otherwise able to do so would get high, seldom were more than a few heavily under the influence of drugs at any one time. They liked to get high together, but boys who were not high appeared to enjoy the antics of others who were. They were really quite individualistic in their pursuit of kicks. Often the worker would find a boy off by himself, or with a girl friend or perhaps one other member. But these were not stable friendships. The group served the function of a sounding board for their common but individualistic interests—of moral support for a way of life. (Short and Strodtbeck, 1965)

Finally, we may describe briefly the most clearly criminal group of boys we were able to locate—a clique of eight boys from a number of loosely related "hanging groups," that coalesced sporadically and in widely varying numbers for activities such as drinking, athletic contests, occasional drug use, driving around in cars, general "roughnecking" and "hell raising," and once in a great while, a fight of major proportions.

According to the leader of the criminal clique, these boys had joined to-gether specifically and exclusively for the purpose of promoting theft activities.

They were engaged in extensive auto stripping, burglary, and shop-lifting—no "heavy stuff" such as strong-arming, robbery, or shakedown. The boys hung on the corner with the larger group, and when they did so were in no way distinguishable from this larger group. They were a clique only when they met away from the larger group, usually in each other's homes, to discuss and plan their theft activities. According to the worker assigned to these boys, "Bobby and his guys talk about what they are doing in one room, while Bobby's old man, who used to be some sort of wheel in the syndicate, talks to his friends about the 'old days' in the next room." The boys made it a point not to "clique-up" visibly on the street, and apparently their chief motivation for association with one another was the success of their predatory activities. In this way they were quite successful for a period of approximately two years. There is testimony that Bobby, in particular, enjoyed a considerable degree of police immunity.

In each of these instances, representing extremes of "specialization" in delinquency orientation, I believe the term "delinquent subculture" (or some variant) is appropriate, but not sufficient to explain the behavior of the members of the groups. Similarly, I believe the behavior of less specialized but highly involved groups is more easily understood in terms of subcultural participation. Norms are generated by the group; many shared activities and perspectives among participants are, so far as group members are concerned, unique to the carriers of a particular subculture, though the boundaries of participation often transcend a particular group. Characteristically, the group effectively constrains individual members from expressing conventional "middle class" values by deriding what-ever attempts are made, and by espousing alternative (rather than "anti") values such as toughness, sexual prowess, being "sharp" or "cool," etc. Specific examples from our data include the merciless kidding of young-sters who attempt serious discussion of matters such as responsible family relations and future aspirations regarding the family (Short, Strodtbeck and Cartwright, 1962), or occupational and educational hopes and problems (Short and Strodtbeck, 1965). Yet these boys remain troubled and ambivalent about many of these problems, and their men-tion does not always meet with derisive or invidious comment relative to other goals and activities. Even when serious comment is entertained, however, it is not likely to be helpful, because the boys' experiences, in-dividually and in common, can rarely provide any basis for solutions or realistic hopes. Delinquent subcultures do not minister directly to these concerns, but deal with alternative means of finding gratification through association and status in many dimensions. In some measure, we believe, this compensates for rebuffs in more conventional institutional contexts and perhaps for relatively poor prospects of future achievement in the conventional world.

I do not believe these, and perhaps other, characteristics of gangs can be portrayed adequately without the subculture concept. Yet these characteristics are not adequate to explain the boys' behavior unless the notion of subcultures can include other processes, chief among them the characteristics of individual gang boys, group mechanisms such as are discussed above, and the nature of lower class "institutions." The next section examines these "institutions" briefly.

LOWER CLASS INSTITUTIONS AS A GENERATING MILIEU OF GANG DELINQUENCY

In thus paraphrasing the title of Walter Miller's rich and provocative treatment (1958) of lower class culture in relation to delinquency, we intend to focus on organizational forms of association within lower class communities and how they are related to delinquency causation. The nature of this relation goes beyond, but is intimately related to, gang delinquency.

William Foote Whyte's brilliant depiction (first published in 1943) of significant features of *organization* in the slum he called Cornerville dispelled many false notions that blighted areas lacked organization. From Doc and the Nortons, through the police and the racket, politics, the church, and "old country" ties, Whyte demonstrated that Cornerville was organized into "a hierarchy of personal relations based upon a system of reciprocal obligations." (Whyte, 1955, p. 272)[2]

We will focus here on organizational forms that are even less formally structured and less "conventional" in orientation than those suggested by Whyte. Even in Cornerville it was clear that social organization was conducive to some types of behavior considered "deviant" by conventional standards—police and political corruption, gambling and exploitation of sexually available girls. The "institutions" to which I shall direct attention appear to lack the commitment to ethnic values and community welfare which characterized Cornerville, as well as the constraining features of such commitments. They appear to be motivated instead by more "elemental," personal and immediate goals, perhaps in part because the future holds little more promise than the bleak present. The rewards they provide are in many cases short lived but concrete, unstable but compelling and available. The contrast with Whyte's classic treatment is important, for I will be discussing institutions characteristic of a different ethnic subculture (I will focus on lower class Negro communities) and of persons deeper in poverty than the residents of Corner-

---

2 Whyte was not the first to call attention to these forms of organization. See, for example, the volumes by McKay, 1941, and Shaw and McKay, 1942.

ville. As in Cornerville, however, these forms of association are recurrent, they have structure, and they function in a variety of ways to their clientele. The variety of their functions provides an added dimension to youth problems, inasmuch as both youth and adults often are involved. Although the literature contains no systematic treatment of lower class institutions, as such, some descriptions of various lower class ethnic communities are rich and suggestive in this regard (Drake and Cayton, 1962). Since our concern is with juvenile delinquency, we will not discuss institutions in which the clientele is primarily adult, such as store-front churches.

The type of institution with which we are primarily concerned is cogently revealed by the response of a detached worker to a question posed by the director of the YMCA program with which the Chicago study of "Street Corner Groups and Patterns of Delinquency" was associated. The director, R. W. Boone, posed this question to the staff: "What are the most significant institutions for your boys?" (Meaning members of gangs with which the program was in contact.) He had explained briefly the concept of institutions as recurrent forms of association which satisfy important needs of participants and which have recognizable structure. The detached worker who first answered the question deliberated briefly, then said slowly:

"I guess I'd have to say the gang, the hangouts, drinking, parties in the area, and the police."

The other workers nodded assent, though a few thought they might want to add the boys' families. Certainly this list is not definitive, but it is instructive. The only reference to a conventional institution is the police, and this was clearly a negative association, an antagonistic link with the conventional world of social control associated with political and economic institutions. No reference was made to the school or the church, and the family received only half-hearted acknowledgment. The "institutions" listed, with the exception of the police, have much in common, for adults as well as adolescents. They call to mind Drake and Cayton's description (1962) of "The World of the Lower Class:"

> Lower-class people will publicly drink and play cards in places where people of higher status would lose their "reputations"—in the rear of poolrooms, in the backrooms of taverns, in "buffet-flats," and sometimes on street corners and in alleys. They will "dance on the dime" and "grind" around the juke-box in taverns and joints, or "cut a rug" at the larger public dance halls. They will "clown" on a street corner or in public parks.

It is in such settings that much illicit behavior is encouraged:

> These centers of lower-class congregation and festivity often become points of contact between the purveyors of pleasure "on the illegit" and their clientele—casual prostitutes, bootleggers, reefer peddlers, "pimps," and "freaks."

Some of these places are merely "fronts" and "blinds" for the organized under-world.

However, the relation between institutions of this sort and delinquent behavior goes much beyond the contact they afford between illegitimate "purveyors of pleasure" and their potential clientele. In such settings much behavior occurs that is disruptive to both the larger social order and the local community because of its threat to basic values of life and property. Of particular concern are episodes of violence which result in serious injury, death, or property destruction, and which are a constant threat in situations ranging from the shifting liaisons of common-law marriage to the more elaborate but even less formally structured quarter parties, pool halls and street corners. Drake and Cayton provide an apt example of the former in their portrayal of the trials and tribulations of Baby Chile and Ben, which gave these authors an ideal vehicle for contrasting styles of life among lower and middle (professional) class Negroes in *Black Metropolis* (1962).

The more informally structured situations are the subject of more extended treatment in the *Group Process* book (Short and Strodtbeck, 1965). Here I will examine only the "quarter parties," as revealed by detached workers from the Chicago project. These case materials are particularly instructive about the structure and functions of such gatherings in a lower class Negro community, home of the King Rattlers, a tough Negro group known throughout the city for their prowess as gang fighters, strong-armers, and purse snatchers. "Quarter parties" are regular events in this and in many other such communities. Although they vary in format and participants, they all have common objectives. Typically, an adult will hold a party in his or her (usually her) home for adults and teens, usually some of both. The objective of the hostess is to make money. (In Seattle, I am told, such gatherings are called "rent parties.") Party-goers pay a quarter to get into the party, and a quarter per drink after they are in. The parties are boisterous, loud and crowded. Fights are not unusual—often they involve members of rival gangs. Two examples, one of "body punching," which is common among these groups, and one of relations with girls, illustrate how these gatherings may precipitate serious gang conflict. In both instances, intervention by a detached worker appears to have averted serious consequences.

A. This teenage party that was held at the girl's house on 10th and Harwood. Her mother and father were there, although they stayed out of the way. There was friction. The Rattlers were there, and there were some boys from the projects just west of the area [members of a rival gang known as Navahoes]. They weren't in the Rattlers. David and Donald, Duke's brother, took me down. It was a pay-at-the-door party. Pay a quarter at the door. Right away when I got in I knew there was friction because there was this one group of boys in one room and another group in another. I saw several bumpings as they came through the door and looks, "Stay out of my way." They were trying to see how much each group would take. They had three rooms occupied. Living room, dining room, and kitchen. I was in the dining room around 10:00, I guess. I heard this noise in the living room. Right away everyone started running for the living room. There's a fight out there. I started out and tried to get through the crowd to get into the living room, and just as I was fighting my way through the crowd I saw one of my boys, Bill, he's 16—very big though for his age. . . . He and this other fellow from the projects—it started out as these things usually do—they had started out boxing at a party. Bill had hit the other fellow a little too hard and he had hit back, and it led to that. This other fellow was much smaller than Bill but he was older, and he hit Bill and knocked him into this huge window, and *plang*, the window went out. By this time I saw my way through the crowd and I stopped them. . . . David helped me break it up. They respected him . . . . He grabbed the other fellow. Nobody bothers him. I just got between them and told Bill to stop. Bill said, okay . . . He was coming back for the boy, though, after he broke the window, and he's a big boy. The other fellow stopped right away.

Q. Party go on?

A. No, the lady said this was it. But I thought there might be a little trouble 'cause some of the other boys from the projects were waiting outside, so I told Bill to stick close to me and we would leave together. Bill, myself, David, and Donald. This we did. The other boys were standing outside. They made a few remarks but they didn't do anything.

Two weeks later this same worker provided a more elaborate picture of a similar party in which adults played a major role. Here the objectives of various classes of partygoers is commented on:

This woman who is called "Ma" was giving the party. . . . There was a lot of drinking—inside, outside, in the cars, in the alleys, everywhere. There were Rattlers and a bunch of boys from the [housing] projects. They had two rooms, neither of them very large. There was some friction going on when I got there—boys bumping each other, and stuff like this.

There were a lot of girls there. Must have been about 50 to 75 people in these two rooms, plus another 20 or 25 outside. There were some older fellows there, too—mainly to try and grab one of these younger girls. The girls were doing a lot of drinking—young girls, 12- and 13-year-olds. This one girl, shortly after I got there, had passed out. I took her home. Nobody there, but two of the other girls stayed with her.

The age group in this party amazed me—must have been from about 11 to the 30's. There were girls there as young as 11, but no boys younger than about 15. The girls are there as a sex attraction, and with the older boys and men around, you know the younger boys aren't going to do any good.

We had one real fight. One of David's sisters was talking to one of these boys from the projects—a good sized boy, bigger than me. I guess she promised to go out to the car with him. . . . To get outside you had to go out this door and down this hall, and then out on the porch and down the stairs. She went as far as the porch. As she got out there, I guess she changed her mind. By this time the guy wasn't standing for any "changing the mind" business, and he started to pull on her—to try and get her in the car. She yelled for David, and he came running out. All he could see was his sister and a guy he didn't know was pulling on her. David plowed right into the guy. I guess he hit him about 15 times and knocked him down and across the street, and by the time I got there the guy was lying in the gutter. David was just about to level a foot at him. I yelled at David to stop and he did. I took him off to the side and told Gary to get the guy out of there.

The worker walked down the street with David, trying to cool him down. What happened next very nearly precipitated a major gang conflict:

Duke, Red, and Mac were standing eight or ten feet away, sort of watching these project boys. This one boy goes up the street on the other side and comes up *behind* David and me. We didn't see him. All of a sudden Duke runs right past me. I was wondering what's going on and he plows into this guy—crashed the side of his mouth and the guy fell flat. Duke was about to really work the guy over . . . .

Duke said, "Well look, man, the guy was sneaking up behind you and I wasn't gonna have him hit you from behind! I did it to protect you."

I got the guy up and he said, "I wasn't going to hit you—I just wanted to see what was going on," and this bit.

By now, Duke says, "Well, the heck with it. Let's run all these project guys out."

They banded together and were ready to move, but I talked them out of it. I said, "Look, don't you think you've done enough? The police aren't here yet, but if you start anything else they'll be here. Somebody is bound to call them. The party is still going on so why don't we all just go back inside. No sense in breaking up a good thing—you paid your quarter."

I finally got them all back inside, but Duke says, "We've been laying off fighting for the last year or so. Looks like we'll have to start again." (Dillard, 1961)

Other examples could be given explicitly involving many forms of behavior considered delinquent by the larger society, such as fighting, extensive property damage, excessive drinking, illicit sex (violent and nonviolent), drug use, disturbing the peace, and at times various forms of theft. Other settings, such as pool halls and the street itself, could be similarly described, but perhaps the point is sufficiently made.

I must also comment briefly concerning community level differences between our Negro and white lower class youngsters. Conventional ecological data indicate clearly that the white areas were less disadvantaged economically than the Negro areas. Occupational prestige data indicate that the mean decile rank of the fathers' occupations was, for Negro gang boys, 3.6, or the level of a laborer in metals industry, cook, or waiter; for white gang boys this figure was 5.0, or, say, an auto mechanic or bartender. In the white areas our observers and workers reported the distinct impression that life tended to revolve around more conventional institutions such as the Catholic Church, local political and "improvement" associations, ethnic and extended kinship organizations, unions, and such formally organized recreational patterns as bowling leagues, and social and athletic clubs. The research of Kobrin and his associates in largely white communities in Chicago is particularly instructive in this regard (Kobrin, 1961; Kobrin, Puntil and Peluso, 1963).

Finally, with regard to community-level problems, our data suggest that relations with adults differ for gang and for non-gang boys. Although gang boys gave various local adult incumbents more credit for having an interest in teenagers and being "right guys" than would be expected from "reaction formation" or "adolescent protest" theories, non-gang boys tend to rate these adults still higher (Short, Rivera and Marshall, 1964). Non-gang boys also report more contact with these adults, and among Negroes, the non-gang youngsters report that the adults have more "clout." When the boys were asked to nominate adults with whom they have the most contact (they were probed for four names), gang boys gave fewer names than the other boys (Negro = 3.2; white = 2.5), and their nominees had significantly lower occupations than the nominees of the non-gang boys. In sample interviews with these "high contact" adults, far more of those named by non-gang boys reported that they had been consulted about school problems than did the gang nominees. In other respects, non-gang nominees appeared more "middle class" in their aspirations for their nominators, their attitudes toward juvenile misbehavior, and their conceptions of "a good life" for these youngsters (Short, Marshall and Rivera, 1964). Contrary to expectations based on the Cloward and Ohlin position on the difference between adult-adolescent relations in "integrated" and "unintegrated" communities and its impact on adolescent behavior, nominees from a conflict gang area agreed as much about such behavior as did those from an area characterized by a high degree of "integration" of the carriers of criminal and non-criminal values (Marshall, 1964). Negro lower class boys, both gang and non-gang, had more multiple nominees than did their white counterparts. The conception that conflict gang boys' relations with adults are especially "weak" appears to call for some revision on the basis of findings such as these.

SOCIAL DISABILITY AND GANG DELINQUENCY

We have seen, and inferred further, the nature of group influences on expression of individually held values consistent with "responsible" goals, and of efforts toward their realization. In this final section I should like to give some of the evidence concerning individual characteristics of the boys which appear to be related to the nature of their behavior in the group context. In so doing I will draw heavily from earlier work with

Gordon and with Strodtbeck (Gordon and Short, 1962; Short and Strodtbeck, 1965).

A "lack of social assurance" among the gang boys, more serious in its
implications for their social adjustment than that seen by Whyte in his
corner boys, was apparent almost from the beginning of our contact; and
as with so many types of observations, it was especially aggravated among
Negro gang boys. Workers reported frequently that their boys did not
feel comfortable outside "the area" and that they were ill at ease in most
social situations outside the gang context. However, some surprising
semantic differential data from these boys directed our attention to their
apparent lack of gratification even in gang membership and interaction.
We moved then to a hypothesis about a fundamental lack of social skills
which seems even more crucial in understanding gang boys' behavior than
does lack of social assurance.

Gang boys were found to rate "someone who sticks with his buddies
in a fight" less highly than "someone who stays cool and keeps to himself,"
while both lower class and middle class non-gang boys (Negro and
white) reversed these ratings. Gang boys evaluated *themselves* higher
than they did *fellow gang members*, while the other boys' evaluations
were more nearly equal, and white middle class boys even rated their
friends as "better" than themselves. Further evidence of ambivalence with
respect to peer associations was found in a motivational opinionaire administered to the boys. Gang boys were more likely to endorse such
statements as "Friends are generally more trouble than they are worth,"
and "Time spent with the guys is time wasted." And they agreed less
often with the statement, "A guy should spend as much time with friends
as he possibly can." Yet they also agreed *more often* than the other boys
that "You can only be really alive when you are with friends," and *less
often* that "People can have too many friends for their own good." We
believe there is an implication here of dissatisfaction with present associates and perhaps an expression of things as they might be more ideally.

The range of Negro gang boys' physical movements is especially
restricted, only to a minor degree by fear of infringing on a rival gang's
territory. More importantly, both Negro and white gang boys are reluctant to expose themselves to situations demanding skills which they
lack and so their development of role-playing abilities and sensitivities,
and their sensitivity to normative requirements of varying situations is
further retarded (Goffman, 1963).

There is evidence that even in activities which are inherently gratifying, and for which the gang provides the chance to achieve such gratifications, such as sexual intercourse, gang boys (and girls) come off with
less than satisfying experiences, particularly in terms of interpersonal relations. It is true that our gang youngsters were a good deal more sexually
active than their non-gang counterparts, either lower or middle class, but

most of these boys and girls are neither knowledgeable nor skilled in sexual matters or in interpersonal relations (Salisbury, 1958; and Rice, 1963, pp. 153 ff). Relations with persons of the opposite sex tend to be characterized by the same sorts of aggressive expression as do many other interpersonal relations. For males the norm is sexual exploitation of females, and for females the economic exploitation of males, which combine to produce a situation with a high potential for tension and frustration, and very little likelihood of mutual and lasting gratification.

The gangs we have studied lack stability in membership and in attendance; hence the rate of social interaction is lower than was the case with the Nortons (Whyte, 1955). Mutual obligations tend to be tenuous among most gang members and in many instances, as with the requirements of group norms, to be specific to the situation. Hence, according to the argument, group cohesion is low. It seems likely, however, that gang boys are dependent upon one another for a large measure of interpersonal gratification, so that the gang has a high relative value for the boys. According to this interpretation, the gang gives its members a reasonably realistic solution to their problems—problems which derive in part from the fact that these boys are adolescents, and in part from the peculiar situations in which they find themselves. Given the gratifications of gang membership and the lack of apparent available alternatives, it seems likely that the gang will be highly valued, especially by those boys who have experienced the most gratification and/or those whose interpersonal skills and perhaps other abilities are most impaired. When a boy is caught up in the group process, however, he may become involved in delinquency, regardless of his personal skills or even of the amount of gratification which he derives from gang membership.

Jansyn's research in Chicago is relevant at this point (Jansyn, 1960; see also Sherif and Sherif, 1964). He recorded daily the "attendance" and time spent with the group of members of a white gang with whom he was in contact for more than a year. A "solidarity index" constructed on the basis of these data was related to measures of individual and group behavior during this period. Delinquent acts, by individuals or by group members, and non-delinquent group activities, were found to occur most frequently following low points of the index of group solidarity. The index characteristically rose following these acts. Jansyn's interpretation was that the boys were responding to low solidarity by creating situations which would bring the gang together, thus raising group solidarity. This was done, he believes, because solidarity of the gang was a primary value for these youngsters.

Our interpretation is similar. Symbols such as group names and individual nicknames, styles of dress and other behavioral affectation provide a basis for group identity. But why delinquency? Aside from certain inherent gratifications, delinquent activities provide opportunities for the expression of dependency needs, and they create instrumental problems demanding cooperative enterprise (Homans, 1950; Allport, 1962). This, for youngsters lacking in basic social skills, can be very important. Expressing dependency needs is likely to be hard for lower class youngsters because of the persistent concern with toughness (Miller, 1958). The problem is aggravated for gang boys whose experiences in conventional institutional contexts are less than satisfactory in this respect, and whose gang norms interpret dependency, except under special circumstances, as weakness. (Among the excepted circumstances are protecting and caring for one another when under attack or taking care of a buddy who may be in danger from too much alcohol or drugs.) In effect, such delinquent activities represent contrived opportunities to realize important gang functions.

Our hypothesis, therefore, is that social disabilities contribute both to group norms and to group processes which involve these norms. The hypothesis is important, for by extension it provides a possible linkage between early family socialization, later experience, and gang behavior. Space does not permit this extension except to suggest that important elements involved are identity problems in early childhood, the inculcation of role-playing abilities, along with flexibility in this regard, and the cultivation of sensitivity to situational requirements for behavior. The aggressive posture and rigidity of response found among many gang youngsters cannot be explained by cultural themes alone. Observations from Strodtbeck's experimental nursery school for lower class Negro children in Chicago are appropriate. Strodtbeck and his associates find that at the age of four and one-half these children are less able to maintain nonaggressive close physical contact with their age mates than are children from middle class homes. The early development of these children appears to be produced by a combination of harsh socialization practices, frequent cautions about a threatening environment, and little cognitive development or verbal skill. The latter seems attributable in some measure to an almost complete absence of stimulation from reading materials or from any type of constructive play opportunities (Strodtbeck, 1963). Data from our own personality testing program indicate that gang boys are more reactive to false signals than the non-gang control group; they are less self-assertive (in this conventional testlike situation), they are slightly more anxious, neurotic, and narcissistic, and less gregarious. As we have noted elsewhere, "the possible cumulative effect of these differences is more impressive than are the individual findings, for they add up to boys who have less self-assurance and fewer of the qualities which engender confidence and nurturant relations with others." (Short and Strodtbeck, 1965)

The social disability hypothesis is important also because it differs from "all for one, one for all" explanations of gang behavior, which rest on

group solidarity and rigid conformity to group norms as the chief determinants of the behavior of gang members. The carefree image of "that old
gang of mine" is hardly recognizable. Its functions and imperatives are
seen quite differently.

The Sherifs (1964) offer the hypothesis that "the adolescent living in
a setting where opportunities for peer contacts are available, either formally or informally, turns more and more to others caught up in similar
dilemmas—to his age mates who can really understand him." But the
"social disability" and "status threats" hypotheses suggest that one of the
major problems of our gang youngsters is that "understanding" of their
problems by fellow gang members occurs at a very superficial level—
extending little beyond freedom to participate in "adult" activities, such
as sexual intercourse and drinking, and support for the achievement of
freedom from adult control. The gang gives scant attention to adult goals,
and in some instances deters the expression of interest in and achievement of these stable goals involved, for example, in employment, family
life, and civic participation; the gang may also hinder the expression of
dependency needs. Gang experience is hardly conducive to stable adjustment in terms of the "virtues" of modern industrial society—punctuality,
discipline, and consistency on the job, the acceptance of authority relations, dependability concerning organizational commitments and interpersonal relations. It seems unlikely that gang experience, with its
constant challenge to prove oneself tough, adept with the girls, "smart,"
"cool," "sharp," etc., alleviates status insecurities or related social disabilities except for the few who are most successful in the gang, and even
then chiefly in terms of ability to respond to gang challenges. The extent
to which these skills enhance one's prospects for status or achievement
outside the gang is questionable at best.

I would suggest that the gang's failure to deal satisfactorily with
these very real concerns and problems of its members contributes to the
instability of most gangs. It contributes also to the fact that the direct
influence of gang norms on gang boys' behavior appears to be limited to
situations directly involving other gang boys. That is, to paraphrase the
Sherifs' recent work, "the attitudes (stands) the individual upholds and
cherishes, the rules that he considers binding for regulating his behavior,"
are those defined by the gang only in special circumstances when other
gang boys are directly involved. When in instances *not* involving other
gang boys they still behave as gang boys, I suggest it is not due to gang
norms, but to other features of the situation and of their abilities to cope
with it. Much latitude is given individual boys even when they are with
other gang boys, sometimes under circumstances most provocative of
aggression and other forms of delinquent behavior. It seems a good
hypothesis that the degree of such latitude for a given boy depends upon
his own investment in the gang, his role in the gang and in the situation,

and the importance of the situation to the gang. We can cite instances in which each of these elements seem clearly related to behavior of boys in a given situation.

CONCLUSION

The authors of the various chapters in this book are engaged in common cause. We have sought to describe and understand reality, and more than this, to explain it by general theoretical statements. In terms of the latter criterion, the work reported in this chapter is largely exploratory, tending to generate hypotheses rather than test them. Our *data* are drawn chiefly from Negro gangs, and the implications of the social disability hypothesis, in particular, appear to be more characteristic of the Negro gangs we have studied than of the white. Preliminary observations from a study of Negro gangs in Los Angeles suggest that social disabilities of these boys are a good deal less serious than those of our boys.[3] The area in which these Los Angeles boys live looks very much like the community settings of our Negro *middle* class, not our lower class. The institutional setting in the Los Angeles communities is more conventional and less like the lower class varieties we have described.

If the hypothesis is to be theoretically significant, however, it must be the case that *to the extent* that a group is characterized by social disabilities such as those to which we have drawn attention, it will be characterized by attempts by its members, individually and collectively, to create symbols and situations which will allow for—perhaps even demand —the expression of dependency needs and the achievement of interpersonal gratifications. Friendships and loyalties which derive from this process are no less real, and may prove to be quite as binding and lasting as any. But if they must continue to exist in an unstable gang context, which serves as an arena for playing out the consequences of status threats, they are likely to be undermined and, therefore, shorter lived and less binding. Certainly it cannot be denied that friendships exist among our gangs and that their gratifications are an important source of stability and continuity. Indeed, the ability of some—but not all—of our gangs to survive without support from conventional institutions, and often with considerable pressure against their continued existence, is remarkable. Derivation of the social disability and status threats hypotheses from our material should not obscure these facts. It has been our intention to draw attention to processes which might account for the specifically delinquent behavior among our gangs. We have attempted, on the one hand, to account for the delinquent content of group norms; and on the other, to

[3] The study is under the direction of Malcolm W. Klein, Youth Studies Center, University of Southern California. Helen E. Shimota is Senior Research Associate for the study.

discover the circumstances under which delinquent norms are invoked. Perhaps empirical differences of this nature between the groups studied by the Sherifs and those to which we have had access in Chicago may account for differences in interpretation of the two studies. If so, it should be possible to resolve our differences by further empirical inquiry and theoretical synthesis.

In his summary (1959) of problems and prospects concerning "Personality and Social Structure," Inkeles argues strongly that the translation of social structural variables into behavior must include an explicit theory of human personality. Thus, to the sociological S–R (State of society–Rate of behavior) proposition should be added P (Personality). "The simplest formula (S) $(P) = R$, although probably far from adequate, would be greatly superior to the S–R formula, since it provides for the simultaneous effect of two elements influencing action." (Inkeles, 1959, p. 255) The social disability hypothesis is hardly a theory of personality, but it is a step in this direction. It represents the introduction of a personality level variable which may provide an important link between social structure, early and later socialization, and behavior. If our observations concerning institutional relations, subcultural participation, and group process are correct, the equation may be further refined and a significant variable added. Experiences in conventional institutions and in lower class, ethnic, and peer group "institutional" or subcultural patterns of association may be viewed as refinements of S (social structure), or more specifically, the state of society so far as a particular individual is concerned. Group process, on the other hand, represents yet another *level* of variable in the equation, in addition to S, P, and R. It should be clear that no simple linear relation exists between these variables. P, social disability in our terms, interacts with institutional and subcultural experience and with group process; and each of these acts in turn with the others. It seems likely that social disability is a factor both in selection for gang membership and in participation within the gang, and therefore in group process involvement. The precise nature of these relationships, and of other parameters and other variables, is not well established, either theoretically or empirically. In their specification may lie the resolution of fundamental differences in perspective among and within disciplines.

REFERENCES

Allport, F. H., 1962. A structuronomic conception of behavior: individual and collective. I. Structural theory and the master problem of social psychology. *J. abnorm. soc. Psychol.*, 64, No. 1, 1-30.

Anderson, N., 1923. *The Hobo.* (Chicago: University of Chicago Press.)

Bloch, H. A., and A. Niederhoffer, 1958. *The Gang.* (New York: Philosophical Library.)

Cavan, Ruth S., 1928. *Suicide.* (Chicago: University of Chicago Press.)

Chein, I., and Eva Rosenfeld, 1957. Juvenile narcotics use. *Law and Contemp. Probs.,* 22, 52-68.

Clark, J. P., and E. P. Wenninger, 1962. Socio-economic class and area as correlates of illegal behavior among juveniles. *Amer. sociol. Rev.,* 27, Dec., 826-834.

Cloward, R. A., 1959. Illegitimate means, anomie, and deviant behavior. *Amer. sociol. Rev.,* 24, April, 164-176.

Cloward, R. A., and L. E. Ohlin, 1960. *Delinquency and Opportunity.* (New York: Free Press of Glencoe.)

Cohen, A. K., 1955. *Delinquent Boys: the culture of the gang.* (New York: Free Press of Glencoe.)

Cohen, A. K., and J. F. Short, Jr., 1958. Research in delinquent subcultures. *J. Soc. Issues,* 14, No. 3, 20-37.

Crawford, P. L., D. I. Malamud, and J. R. Dumpson, 1950. *Working with Teenage Gangs.* (New York: Welfare Council of New York City.)

Cressey, P. G., 1932. *The Taxi-dance Hall.* (Chicago: University of Chicago Press.)

Dillard, L., 1961. Personal interviews, Jan. 31, Feb. 16.

Drake, St. C., and H. R. Cayton, 1962. *Black Metropolis: a study of Negro life in a northern city.* Vol. II (rev. and enlarged ed.). (New York: Harper and Row.)

Duncan, O. D., 1961. Chapters V and VI in A. J. Reiss, Jr., *Occupations and Social Status.* (New York: Free Press of Glencoe.)

Empey, L. T., and J. Rabow, 1961. The Provo experiment in delinquency prevention. *Amer. sociol. Rev.,* 26, Oct., 679-695.

Finestone, H., 1957. Cats, kicks and color. *Soc. Probs.,* 5, 3-13.

Frazier, E. F., 1932. *The Negro Family in Chicago.* (Chicago: University of Chicago Press.)

————, 1962. *Black Bourgeoisie.* (New York: Collier Books.)

Freedman, J., and R. Rivera, 1962. Education, social class and patterns of delinquency. (Paper at annual meeting, American Sociological Association.)

Glane, S., 1950. Juvenile gangs in east side of Los Angeles. *Focus,* 29, Sept., 136-141.

Goffman, E., 1963. *Behavior in Public Places.* (New York: Free Press of Glencoe.)

Gold, M., 1963. *Status Forces in Delinquent Boys.* (Ann Arbor, Mich.: Institute for Social Research.)

Gordon, R. A., and J. F. Short, Jr., 1962. Social level, social disability, and gang interaction. (Unpublished manuscript.)

Gordon, R. A., J. F. Short, Jr., D. S. Cartwright, and F. L. Strodtbeck, 1963. Values and gang delinquency: A study of street-corner groups. *Amer. J. Sociol.,* 69, Sept., 109-28.

Hayner, N., 1936. *Hotel Life.* (Chapel Hill: University of North Carolina Press.)

Himelhoch, J., 1964. Socioeconomic status and delinquency in rural New

England. (Paper prepared for annual meeting of American Sociological Association.)

Hollingshead, A. B., 1949. *Elmtown's Youth: The impact of social classes on adolescents.* (New York: Wiley.)

Homans, G. C., 1950. *The Human Group.* (New York: Harcourt, Brace.)

Howard, K. E., A. E. Hendrickson, and D. S. Cartwright, 1962. Psychological assessment of street corner youth: intelligence. (Unpublished manuscript, Youth Studies Program, University of Chicago.)

Inkeles, A., 1959. Personality and social structure. In R. K. Merton, L. Broom, and L. S. Cottrell (eds.), *Sociology Today.* (New York: Basic Books.)

Jansyn, L., 1960. Solidarity and delinquency in a street corner group: a study of the relationship between changes in specified aspects of group structure and variations in the frequency of delinquent activity. (Unpublished M. A. thesis, University of Chicago.)

Kobrin, S., 1951. The conflict of values in delinquency areas. *Amer. sociol. Rev.,* 16, Oct., 653-661.

————, 1961. Sociological aspects of the development of a street corner group: an exploratory study. *Amer. J. Orthopsychiatry,* Oct., 685-702.

Kobrin, S., J. Puntil and E. Peluso, 1963. Criteria of status among street gangs. (Paper at annual meeting, American Sociological Association.)

Landesco, J., 1929. Organized crime in Chicago. Part III of *Illinois Crime Survey,* Illinois.

Marshall, H., 1964. Slum community organization: analysis of a concept. (Unpublished M. A. thesis, Washington State University.)

McKay, H. D., 1941. The neighborhood and child conduct. *Annals,* 261, 32-41.

Merton, R. K., 1957. *Social Theory and Social Structure* (rev. ed.). (New York: Free Press of Glencoe.)

Miller, W. B., 1958. Lower class culture as a generating milieu of gang delinquency. *J. soc. issues,* 24, No. 3., 5-19.

Polk, K., 1963. An exploration of rural juvenile delinquency. (Mimeographed, unpublished paper from Lane County Youth Study Project, Sept. 1963.)

Reckless, W. C., 1933. *Vice in Chicago.* (Chicago: University of Chicago Press.)

Reiss, A. J., Jr., and A. L. Rhodes, 1961. Delinquency and social class structure. *Amer. sociol. Rev.,* 26, Oct., 720-732.

Rice, R., 1963. "The Persian Queens." *The New Yorker,* Oct. 19, 1963.

Rivera, R., 1964. Occupational goals: a comparative analysis. (Unpublished M. A. thesis, University of Chicago.)

Salisbury, H. E., 1958. *The Shook-up Generation.* (New York: Harper and Row.)

Shaw, C. R., 1929. *Delinquency Areas.* (Chicago: University of Chicago Press.)

————, 1930. *The Jack-roller.* (Chicago: University of Chicago Press.)

Shaw, C. R., and H. D. McKay, 1931. *Social factors in juvenile delinquency, report on the causes of crime for the national commission on law observance and enforcement,* Vol. II. (Washington, D.C.: U.S. Government Printing Office.)

————, 1942. *Juvenile Delinquency and Urban Areas*. (Chicago: University of Chicago Press.)

Sherif, M., and Carolyn W. Sherif, 1964. *Reference groups: exploration into conformity and deviation of adolescents*. (New York: Harper and Row.)

Short, J. F., Jr., 1963. Street corner groups and patterns of delinquency: a progress report. *Amer. Catholic sociol. Rev.*, 24, 13-32.

————, 1964. Gang delinquency and anomie. In M. B. Clinard (ed.), *Anomie and Deviant Behavior*. (New York: Free Press of Glencoe.)

Short, J. F., Jr., H. Marshall, and R. Rivera, 1964. Significant adults and adolescent adjustment. (Mimeographed.) (Revision of paper read at annual meeting, Pacific Sociological Association.)

Short, J. F., Jr., R. Rivera, and H. Marshall, 1964. Adult-adolescent relations and gang delinquency. *Pacif. sociol. Rev.*, Fall, 59-65.

Short, J. F., Jr., R. Rivera, and R. A. Tennyson, 1965. Perceived opportunities, gang membership and delinquency. *Amer. sociol. Rev.*, 30, Feb., 56-67.

Short, J. F., Jr., and F. L. Strodtbeck, 1963. The response of gang leaders to status threats: an observation on group process and delinquent behavior. *Amer. J. Soc.*, 68, March, 571-579.

————, 1965. *Group Process and Gang Delinquency*. (Chicago: University of Chicago Press.)

Short, J. F., Jr., F. L. Strodtbeck, and D. S. Cartwright, 1962. A strategy for utilizing research dilemmas: a case from the study of parenthood in a street corner gang. *Sociol. Inquiry*, 32, Spring, 185-202.

Short, J. F., Jr., R. A. Tennyson, and K. I. Howard, 1963. Behavior dimensions of gang delinquency. *Amer. sociol. Rev.*, 28, June, 412-428.

Strodtbeck, F. L., 1963. The reading readiness nursery: short-term social intervention technique. Progress report to Social Security Administration (Project 124, The Social Psychology Laboratory, University of Chicago), Aug. 1963.

Strodtbeck, F. L., and J. F. Short, Jr., 1964. Aleatory risks v. short-run hedonism in explanation of gang action. *Soc. Probs.*, 12, Fall, 127-140.

Thrasher, F. M., 1927. *The Gang*. (Chicago: University of Chicago Press.)

Wirth, L., 1928. *The Ghetto*. (Chicago: University of Chicago Press.)

Whyte, W. F., 1955. *Street Corner Society: The social structure of an Italian slum* (enlarged ed.). (Chicago: University of Chicago Press.)

Yablonsky, L., 1962. *The Violent Gang*. (New York: Macmillan.)

Zorbaugh, H. W., 1929. *The Gold Coast and the Slum*. (Chicago: University of Chicago Press.)

NINE

THE STRUCTURE AND FUNCTIONS
OF ADULT-YOUTH SYSTEMS

Howard W. Polsky and Daniel S. Claster

Nothing we ever do is, in the strict scientific literalness, wiped out. Of course, this has its good side as well as its bad one. As we become permanent drunkards by so many separate drinks, so we become saints in the moral, and authorities and experts in the practical and scientific spheres, by so many separate acts and hours of work. (James, 1964, p. 132)

In the last few decades behavioral science has been profoundly influenced by structural-functional theory (Barber, 1956, p. 131; Nagel, 1956; Buckley, 1957; Hempel, 1959; Polsky, 1962a; and Fallding, 1963). Unfortunately, not all are agreed upon the precise denotations of these concepts. By *structure* we refer to a set of relatively stable and patterned relationships of individuals and groups; *function,* we define as the consequences of the social activity for the adaptation or maintenance of the structure and its components. Structure refers to relatively enduring patterns, and function to shorter-range processes growing out of and creating the social structure.

Structural-functional theory is the native-born son of gestalt theory (Kurtz, 1956). It dominates behavioral science today because social scientists require a theoretical orientation that is adequate for analyzing the transactions of individuals in social systems. Structural-functional theory seeks to overcome the perspective of atomistic, unidimensional interaction by emphasizing the impact of environment upon individuals through social systems in which they are actors.

Structural-functional theory is used increasingly as an orientation for analyzing transactions within and between systems in equilibrium, but it is equally useful in studying deviant behavior and social disorganization. Within the theory, it is possible to consider American society as a comprehensive system and focus on the worlds of the adult and the adolescent as subsystems. We can look then at both functional and dysfunc-

This chapter is based on a demonstration project supported by the National Institute of Mental Health, MH-993.

189

tional consequences of the transactions between adolescents and adults in terms of the socialization function of the larger system (Merton, 1961).

In our fast-changing society, many adolescents are not lagging behind. James Coleman, who has conducted intensive research into adolescent societies, has commented on their increasing social sophistication, their discontent with a passive role, and their passionate involvement in activities which they can call their *own* (Coleman, 1961, pp. 311-329).

Much of what adults see as the problem of "lagging adolescents," however, comes from their lack of concern and involvement in activities which adults believe would be most beneficial for their development and functioning as responsible citizens in society; for example, the lack of passionate devotion to scholarly work. In fact, the norms of the adolescent community often counterpose such activities. It has been pointed out many times that organized athletics represents one area for positive action by adolescents which carries its own rigorous discipline. Undoubtedly, athletics absorbs energy which would be directed against society in violence and other forms of deviancy.

We find missing in contemporary studies of adolescents any probing analysis of the interpersonal structure of adult-youth systems. The central issue is how the structure of adult-youth relationships frees, inhibits, or frustrates, the abundant potential energy that adolescents could release for furthering both society's interests and their own. What do we know about the structure of adult-youth relationships which we can use to reinforce, rather than impede, the fulfillment of constructive and creative aims?

Getzels and Jackson (1960) compared students high in scores on creativity tests, but not especially high in I.Q. scores, with students high in I.Q., but not especially high in creativity. Both groups performed nearly identically on standardized achievement tests. They differed markedly, however, in their attitudes and relationships with the teachers. The highly creative were far less concerned with conforming to teachers' demands and much more imaginative and wide-ranging in their interests. The personal traits they preferred were negatively correlated with what they felt the teachers preferred. The teachers preferred the high I.Q. students to the highly creative ones.

What underlies this implication that the teacher's role inhibits and under-selects creativity? To answer this complex problem, we can move toward conceptualizing the teacher-student transaction as a *system*, with its interrelated institutional and societal contexts. A British exchange teacher, who spent a year in New York City's Bronx High School of Science, probably put his finger on the central problem. He had high praise for both the students' obvious liveliness and intelligence and the superbly equipped physical facilities, but he made this shrewd negative criticism:

It was after I returned to New York from an Easter vacation spent with friends who teach at colleges that I suddenly realized how much of the depression I had been suffering . . . was due to one thing. I had been beginning to see myself in the way New York's educational administrators apparently want their teachers to see themselves: over-burdened by officialdom, left little or no say in the planning of curricula and examinations, and even barely trustworthy enough to do an honest day's work without constant checks and supervision. (*New York Times*, 1964)

A full discussion of the adult-youth transaction in any social system requires an analysis of all the critical social systems in which the adult functions, since they impinge upon his relationship with the younger generation. Excellent examples of how the press within the economic sphere can reverberate through the family system are given in *Five Families* (Lewis, 1962) and *Family Worlds* (Hess and Handel, 1959):

The Littleton family is scarcely in a position to organize time to serve the group's needs or to assist the family in its pursuit of overt individual or group objectives. The emotional separateness of the members is augmented by the daily routine that they have established for themselves. A summary of these routines is provided as each member described the activities of an average day:

Mr. Littleton: "Work, work, work from five until two every day; five until three on Saturdays, home, bed, and up."

Interviewer: "Can you tell me generally what the family usually does on other days?"

Mr. Littleton: "I couldn't tell you. I know what they do and where they go, but I don't know just when they have the activities. Now Bobby is beginning Cub Scouts." (Hess and Handel, 1959, p. 141)

In this chapter, we hope to make clear the multiple roles adults attend to in the superordinate-subordinate relationships formed with adolescents in diverse social systems. We will then exemplify the conceptual framework with a current research project on transactions between child care workers and residents in a residential treatment center for emotionally disturbed and delinquent adolescents.

A CONCEPTUAL FRAMEWORK FOR ADULT-YOUTH TRANSACTIONS

Our main task is to formulate a practical middle-range scheme for analyzing adult-youth systems. "Social system" here implies an interdependence of parts so that a change in one part will have repercussions for the entire system. The concept of social system emphasizes the relations between units rather than the individual characteristics of the actors. The social system is open and in active interchange with the larger organization in which it is embedded.

Generally, a system is conceptualized by boundarying the amount of energy transacted within it. The internal parts are in close and dense interaction with each other; together they form a functional relationship with the environment.

In the social system model we place the adult and youth together within it, to examine independently the problems of joint adaptation and goal attainment in the external system, and those of group support and integration in the internal system. This model is simply diagramed in Figure 6.

The social system approach derives from the functional imperatives that flow from the nature of the system. This type of analysis was pioneered by Robert Bales at Harvard (Parson, Bales and Shils, 1953; Bales and Slater, 1955; Bales, 1956; Bales, 1953). Over many years of laboratory experiments, he observed the emergence of *system roles* in a variety of groups confronted with problems to work out together.

The *instrumental* role called for taking initiative and leadership in

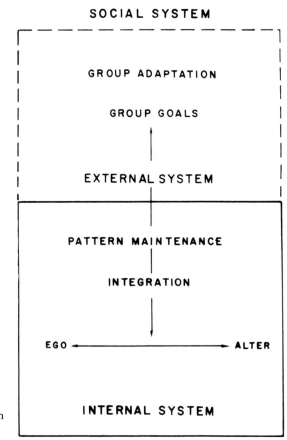

FIGURE 6. Diagram of Adult and Youth in Social System Model

formulating goals and coordinating tasks presented to the group; the instrumental leader was frequently not the best-liked person in the group. Another person, the *expressive* leader, excelled in supporting individual members and mediating intragroup tensions and differences. This role was not directly important in the task or instrumental sphere, but it was critical in building group morale. These two system roles, the instrumental and expressive, underlie all social system theory. Their discovery is important because they indicate that group achievement and gratification from group relationships depend largely on how these specific functions are carried out.

In agencies this distinction is between the executive, the instrumental leader, and the expressive "key man"; the latter, often high in the hierarchy, is accessible to the rank and file and serves as an important outlet for differences among the members in the organization. The same distinction can be seen in the system roles performed by adults in interaction with adolescents. The example to be given later from our current research in a total institution for youths perhaps reflects the differentiation most cogently because the system is circumscribed by time, space, and function; but the distinction should also be generalizable for less boundaried systems in communities.

The other major distinction among functional roles, according to our adaptation of system theory, can be visualized from Figure 6 by crisscrossing the internal and external axis with the instrumental-consummatory (expressive) axis. The individual and the group are conceived as purposive, *i.e.*, organisms which formulate goals and experiment with diverse means for attaining them. This results in the fourfold paradigm of social roles, functions and phases shown in Figure 7 (Parsons, 1959).

This paradigm can be used for adult-youth interaction conceptualized as a system with foci ranging from the teacher-student relationship to the transaction between child care worker and resident. In the adult-youth relationship, four key functions are derived that the adult assumes at various stages. We call these functions *role segments*, and they are related to the system imperatives as shown in the following chart:

System Function	*Role Segment*
adaptation	protector-custodian
goal attainment	advisor-counselor
pattern maintenance	consoler-nurturer
integration	friend-judge

The *custodial* role indicates an orientation by the adult toward the youth's adapting to the regulations of the agency or society in which the transaction is enacted. Goal attainment reflects not mere adaptation to externally imposed standards but formulation and attainment of goals which emanate from the youth's needs and which are at the same time

	INSTRUMENTAL	CONSUMMATORY (EXPRESSIVE)
EXTERNAL	ADAPTATION	GOAL ATTAINMENT
INTERNAL	PATTERN MAINTENANCE AND TENSION MANAGEMENT	INTEGRATION

FIGURE 7. Paradigm of Social Roles, Functions, Phases

compatible with the value system of the adults and the society. In the *counselor* role, the superordinate helps the subordinate to formulate and attain such goals.

Correspondingly, two functions contribute to the maintenance of the internal system. *Nurturer* characterizes the supporting role of the adult, in which he enables youths who are immobilized (*e.g.*, psychologically disturbed) to function at an adequate level within the system. Finally, the integrative function is fulfilled by assuming the role of *friend, judge,* or *monitor;* here the adult evaluates the youth's activity vis-a-vis peers (Weber, 1962).

The analytical breakdown of these various functions enables us to analyze more effectively the total function of various socializing agencies in our society. The mother-infant transaction is essentially one of nurturance; the counselor role is institutionalized by the teacher in our society; the integrative role is assumed in an extreme degree by the judge, especially at a time when the youngster has violated the rules of society; finally, the custodial function is assumed in its purest form by the policeman or guard in a reformatory.

We would argue, however, that in each of these institutionalized roles, the superordinate in the adult-youth relationship performs each of the four role segments at various stages. Now the most important implication of conceptualizing the adult-youth relationship as part of a larger social system is that it sensitizes us to the constraint which the larger system exercises on interpersonal transactions. In other words, the larger, more powerful organization determines which function should be stressed and how it should be performed. This results in an intermediate or emergent adult-youth structure that directly determines the on-going interaction between adult and youth.

How the agency structures the function of its workers can be briefly illustrated by the changing role of the probation officer (Ohlin, 1958). Initially, he was a "punitive officer," a custodian who supervised the parolee and made sure he adapted to society and did not violate the law. Next, the parole officer became a protective officer, who balanced the community's need for protection and the youngster's protection from the community. He assumed a judge-like role in which he balanced the welfare of the community with a knowledge of the client and his life history. A third stage evolved when the parole officer took a more active role in rehabilitating the parolee, counseling him in getting work, in recreation, and in his general social adjustment to family and society. Finally, with increased education and gradual adoption of social work philosophy, the parole officer increased his attention to psychological and emotional factors influencing the client's behavior and was much more sensitive to giving reassurance and support (the nurturance role).

Our main point is that the superordinate socializing agent performs effectively to the extent that he utilizes all four role segments of his central function. He must decide on the appropriate role segment for the immediate situation and then adopt a specific pattern of behavior within the rubric of that role segment. He may choose to enact one role segment at a time or several simultaneously; conduct within each may be rigidly or diffusely defined. All of this must be seen in the context of the relevant social system. In the example of the parole officer's changing role, it is important to emphasize that the legal agency alone is not chiefly responsible for modification. This change of role is not a one-way street coming only from the courts, but one which is actively influenced by recruitment practices, social work schools, the stature of the profession, and the community.

The adult and youth should be thought of as forming a system wherever they are connected. Four indispensable functions can be derived from thus conceptualizing their relationship as a social system. But this is only a point of departure. We want to use the above framework now to analyze the diverse structures that emerge from the interaction of adult and youth as their system functioning is related to the larger field in which it is embedded.

Total institutions and repressive authoritarian reformatories are undergoing a transformation from custody to therapy. However, custodial functions still remain; and the dilemmas, contradictions, and conflicts inherent within each role segment, as well as how they impinge upon each other, are critical theoretical and research problems, which must be probed in depth to increase adults' potential for effectively socializing youngsters. We turn now to a comparison of adult-youth systems in the cottages of a progressive, psychotherapeutically-oriented residential treatment center.

THE COTTAGE SYSTEM IN THE RESIDENTIAL INSTITUTION

Each cottage in the center is a separate building occupied by nineteen youngsters and four staff members (two are normally on duty at a time). Our focus is on the recurrent internal patterns of three senior cottages (boys' ages from 15 to 18) and on their interchanges with the institution. The cottage staff is given a set of implicit prescriptions of how the cottage should function. Staff have some autonomy within this structure to develop their own procedures—in effect, to evolve distinctive subcultures. In this treatment center the cottage staffs receive much less attention and prestige than the psychiatrists and psychiatric case workers, who see individual youngsters throughout the week in a clinic removed from the cottage.

The chief function worked out in detail for cottage workers is custodial: as supervisors of the cottage, they maintain constant track of the children. They wake them in the morning and put them to bed at night. Their numerous responsibilities include preparing snacks during the evening, mending and laundering clothes, and supervising the canteen and allowances.

To manage the cottage, the staff evolves a structure superimposed on the routines and sanctions prescribed by the institution. However, we would be seriously abridging the total functioning of the cottage system by concentrating solely on the custodial or adaptive function. We have adopted a fourfold functional sphere for the manifold activities differentially performed by staff with youngsters in the three cottages. This is pictured in Figure 8.

The activities that the cottage performs in what Homans calls the "external system" may be classed as adaptation and goal attainment. Adaptation refers to all activities and routines incumbent upon the cottages by virtue of membership in the institution: cleaning-up, wearing appropriate dress, adherence to the time schedules, general conformity with institutional regulations. We also include in this category the punishment or deprivation of youngsters who have violated institution rules.

The cottage, however, does not merely respond to institutional rules. In addition to all the adaptive adjustments to the institution, there are many activities which emanate from youngsters and cottage staff. All activities not directly sponsored by the institution which are generated from within the cottage we place in the goal-attainment sphere. This includes activities such as ping-pong and chess, a singing group, an auction, a camera club, card-playing, record groups, etc. Needless to say, the cottages vary in the kind and complexity of group activities and autonomous goals which are formulated, participated in, and attained.

In addition to the two external functions (adaptation and goal attainment) are two internal functions. Pattern maintenance (tension management and latency) is any activity in which the staff member gives

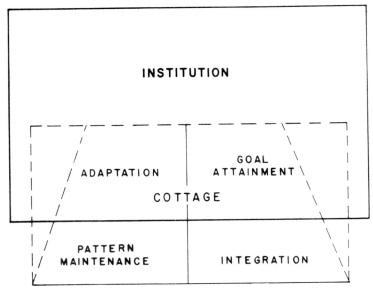

FIGURE 8. Diagram of Staff Activities in Cottages

direct emotional or psychological support to a youngster or group. This ranges from expressing sympathy for a youngster with a sprain to holding structured individualized, private sessions, as is done in two cottages by the two professional head counselors. By pattern maintenance we mean direct assistance and "bucking up" given to the individual. Mostly, it is directed to youngsters who are in a temporary state of depression, rebellion, or general confusion.

The final function we concentrate upon is the integrative: the informal staff-youth relationships which are not especially goal-oriented, related to fulfilling an adaptive task, or directly psychologically supportive. By integrative function we mean the informal interplay of staff and youngsters in general conversations and bull sessions. We call this *integrative* because we think that the major function of this kind of interchange is cementing internal relationships along specific values and themes (Murray, *et al.*, 1938; Opler, 1945; Hess and Handel, 1959, pp. 11 *ff*).

Before presenting concrete examples of how each of these four functions is performed, a word about methodology.[1] Three senior cottages have been intensely observed by three members of the research team.

---

[1] For a full discussion of theoretical orientation, methodology and findings of the research summarized below, see Howard W. Polsky and Daniel S. Claster, *A Comparative Analysis of Three Cottage Systems*, Hawthorne Cedar Knolls School, Hawthorne, N. Y., mimeographed.

Systematic observation consists of half-hour time samples during which the observer sees at close range a staff member's interaction with a resident. These transactions are rated on a precoded observation schedule. General observation consists of one-hour contact with the youngsters. All observation is based upon operationalism of the functional spheres outlined above.

As a part of our research-demonstration project on cottage systems, two of the three senior cottages under study are directly headed by two professional counselors. Cottage 1 is headed by an educator who stresses stable, orderly routines; cottage 2 is directed by an old-line nonprofessional who is concerned about orderly routine but, in addition, has developed an easy-going, joking relationship based upon an implicit understanding that the cottage will have "no trouble"; cottage 3 is headed by a professional social group worker who has considerable influence with the administration. In order to simplify the analysis of each cottage system, we will focus at first on the head counselor in each cottage and later advance tentative propositions of how they are supported by their assistants.

COTTAGE 1

In cottage 1 the head counselor is preoccupied with the cottage routines, which he supervises in prep school fashion. During regular checkups, he may run his finger across cabinet edges and behind radiators to see that every bit of dust is collected. Once, seeing that a bed was loosely made, he pulled out the covers and stripped off its blankets and sheets. These activities seem to be going on not only during the specific time alloted for general room-cleanup but pervade the cottage during the entire week. The head counselor's assistant also has assumed this supervisory custodial role; both undertake joint inspections to rate the youngster's cleanup according to a merit scheme.

The other major activity the head counselor-educator performs is private sessions with individuals in his office. These last from ten to twenty minutes and cover different subjects but are mostly concerned with the current upset of the youngster in the cottage. Only the head counselor carries out this activity in cottage 1. In addition, he plays games with the youngsters but always to win; he plays hard and generally beats all the boys in ping-pong and in chess. This is the general level of complexity of goal attainment in the cottage, although recently there has been an attempt to form a committee of boys to plan a party. Finally, we find relatively little integration. This head counselor initiates relatively little informal integrative activity with groups of youngsters. Representing the cottage to the institution, maintaining stable, orderly routines and conducting individual sessions leave little time for informal lengthy interpersonal contacts with the youngsters.

COTTAGE 2

In contrast to the "prep school" atmosphere in cottage 1, cottage 2 gives the classic accommodation picture between old-line nonprofessional staff and youngsters which was described in detail in *Cottage Six* (Polsky, 1962b). In contrast to that study, however, cottage 2 has less open physical aggression among the youngsters. The head counselor carries out the adaptive function in an arbitrary, dictatorial manner. If a youngster has a job to do and falls down on it, the counselor will yell at him until he does it right. However, the counselor is not too sticky about how thoroughly the job is done. He wants it to conform to institutional expectations but, unlike the counselor in cottage 1, does not demand more than this.

The head counselor in cottage 2 also holds general bull sessions with the youngsters; often these have an undertone of delinquency. The counselor initiates discussions of past exploits such as the boys' excessive drinking of diluted wine during the last Passover holiday. He discussed in detail a boy's attempt to go AWOL. The other negative feature of his extensive informal contact with the youngsters is his denigration of their ambitions. One boy is intent on attending college and has been poring over college catalogues; he is the butt of considerable wry joking by the counselor, who casts great doubt upon his ability to achieve this important goal. Much of this informal transaction seems to be good fun, but its denigrating repetition has the earmarks of considerable hostility. The counselor apparently gains superiority by belittling both the boys' ambitions and their accomplishments, especially in the intellectual sphere. In this cottage there is little "alter-therapy" performed by the counselor in any formal sense and relatively less informal personal support of the youngsters. Finally, the counselor does little to help the youngsters plan and execute autonomous goals. A singing group receives scant attention. This cottage has little purposeful autonomous group activity.

The other nonprofessional counselors in this cottage take their cues from the head counselor and support his orientation and prevailing mode of operation. Communication among the counselors is centered about practical problems and routines. The female staff person is new and is taking over some of the nurturing aspects of staff work, but it is too early yet to clearly delineate her role in the total emergent staff pattern.

COTTAGE 3

In cottage 3, headed by a skilled group worker, the prevailing atmosphere is quite different from that in cottages 1 and 2. First of all, the adaptive sphere is unusually self-regulating with much less active staff direction than in the other two cottages. The boys take care of their various daily tasks routinely without much prompting by the staff, especially the group worker. He operates in a unique way. Often he will suggest to boys standing around that they take advantage of the time to get some cottage task completed. After a discussion with the youngsters, he generally leaves it up to them to decide if they want to do it now or later. This is in marked contrast to the head counselors' persistent need-ling in cottages 1 and 2.

The nonprofessional assistants in cottage 3 are somewhat more in-sistent on pressing the youngsters to do the adaptive tasks adequately, but the head counselor does not spend much time with this functional sphere. His preoccupation is with enabling the youngsters to formulate and exe-cute cottage goals. They have had overnight hikes and dinners at restau-rants; they have planned a huge auction sale, and remodeled each bedroom after a college with its pennant, picture, and colors. The cottage is a buzz of activity; at this writing, almost all the boys are intensely involved in painting and repairing items for the planned auction.

Another important role the head counselor plays in this cottage is alter-therapist. He conducts group therapy sessions with the youngsters, as well as talking to them individually in closed sessions in his office. This counselor has little informal interaction with the youngsters; much of his general contact seems to be organized around enabling the young-sters to formulate and attain the cottage goals discussed above. However, his two female assistants do spend a considerable amount of time in in-formal, integrative transactions. The counselor has so organized his staff, however, that they have also participated increasingly in enabling the youngsters to execute various cottage goals.

In cottages 1 (the prep school headed by the educator) and 2 (the old-line nonprofessional), we find most activity directed toward adaptive routines. These routines are pursued throughout the day and week rather than limited to specific time periods. The important difference between cottages 1 and 2 lies in the other functional spheres. Cottage 1 in addition has developed an elaborate alter-therapy system whereby individual youngsters are counseled in the office of the head counselor. A peculiar conflict emerges in cottage 1 where the educator is both "therapist" and chief custodian. We quote from our general observation log:

Two boys burst into the cottage in a high vocal state of elation. The head counselor immediately challenged them pointedly about their leaving the cot-tage when he had told them not to. One boy said: "I told you I was going. I had an appointment with the social worker and you can't keep me from seeing my social worker when I was supposed to go."

The counselor repeated that they were not supposed to go anywhere un-less they had his permission. The upshot was a vehement argument between the boys and the counselor. During the dialogue the counselor stressed that the boy had first obligations to the cottage and to him as his cottage parent irrespective of obligations elsewhere.

During the discussion the boy insisted that he wanted to see his social worker because the head director had denied him a "session." The counselor's retort was that he would have to give it at a time when he had time.

This is a conflict between the head counselor in his custodial-disciplinarian role and his alter-therapist role. This role conflict rarely occurs in cottage 2 where individuals and groups are addressed privately only when they have violated institutional regulations. The head counselor in cottage 2 reinforces his authoritarian adaptational procedures with a great deal of kidding and joking in bull sessions, much of which has a delinquent flavor. In contrast, in cottage 3 we find the adaptive routines are limited to specific time periods. The group worker uses himself and the other staff people to develop multiple group activities. The "basic work," *i.e.*, the routine, has been worked out to the extent where the cottage is much more peer-regulated without intensive staff supervision. In cottages 1 and 2 the staff are used primarily to back-stop supervising cottage routines. The educator's assistants take "orders" from him in carrying out custodial functions. The other staff participate in games with the youngsters but do not help them organize complex group goals. In cottage 2 the head counselor gives very little direction to the other staff, all of whom work together in a laissez-faire fashion. In cottage 3 the group worker-director has consciously assigned manifold functions to his counselors. Each of them has a task to do in the custodial sphere, but is also assigned a group activity which is carried out with his guidance.

Among the most important differences among the three staff directors is that the group worker in cottage 3 has considerable influence with the administration. In addition to his group work skills, and a group-process perspective for utilizing his staff, he, more than the others, develops in the external environment opportunities which his youngsters can exploit. As for internal regulation, the staff work as if a minimum of dictated routines is best for everyone. In fact, the group worker joined a cottage that was already very stable in carrying out routines; a female housekeeper remained in the cottage after the group worker entered and continued to be chiefly responsible for cottage routines.

THE EMERGENT COTTAGE STRUCTURE

The cottage staff role, especially that of the head counselor, is one of dovetailing institutional administrative tasks with the needs and social order of the residents. Like the foreman, his marginal position subjects him to varying pressures which are at the juxtaposition of an authoritarian structure with a group of rebellious youngsters. Just as a foreman carries the essential function of bridging the gap between management and the worker, so the head counselor is crucial in connecting the administrative structure with a developmental program in the cottage.

The primary point of departure for comparing the different adjustment patterns of cottage systems is how each counselor conceives his custodial role, that is, how he handles problems imposed by the institutional structure. Our case materials point to three emergent structural patterns. The head counselors' centers of gravity in the cottage system can be best summarized in the diagrams shown in Figure 9. These give an impressionistic estimate of time and effort directed by the counselors at four functional spheres: (A) adaptation, (G) goal attainment, (L) latency and pattern maintenance, and (I) integration.

In cottage 1 the educator has gone far beyond the institutional requirements for maintaining clean and orderly routines in the cottage. He is also developing a growing opposition among the youngsters, who see his emphasis on this sphere as unduly extreme. The educator meets this opposition by many individual sessions with the youngsters. He realizes that he must develop more fully autonomous goals but has not been able to acquire staff to carry out this function.

In cottage 2 an extreme split prevails between two major functions carried out by the head counselor. He is very dominant and dictatorial in supervising the boys' fulfillment of cottage and institutional tasks. However, he moderates this role with an attempt to be a "buddy" of the boys and enters into considerable horseplay with them, much of which has a semi-delinquent flavor. He is not trained to help the youngsters attain autonomous goals, and he does not use much of his time for individual alter-therapy sessions. He is able to mediate the extreme custodial role with his joking relationship.

In cottage 3 the center of gravity is in marked contrast to cottages 1 and 2. The attainment of autonomous goals has become the head counselor's main preoccupation, and the youngsters and the other staff are caught up in a considerable amount of autonomous planning, coordinating and executing of goals. Individual boys gain prestige by their ability to perform maintenance tasks: plumbing, electrical repairing, painting, gardening, etc. A "big brother-apprentice" system has been established; new boys are attached to the more skilled youngsters and are slated to take over their jobs when they leave the institution. Thus, in the third cottage, the activity around attaining goals sharply conditions how all the other functions in the cottage are performed.

The counselors in the first two cottages are not challenging the institutional structure. In cottage 1 the heavy emphasis is on identification with administrative superiors and on going even further in institutionalizing rigid adaptive routines. This strategy carries the danger of increasing the opposition of the residents to the cottage staff. In cottage 2, the administration is conciliated by impressing the youngsters with the need to conform to the regulations of the institution. This is tempered with an easy-going, semi-delinquent orientation to the youngsters, in which the impression is conveyed that together they must see to it that there is little trouble and maximum conformity.

The old-line counselor in the second cottage uses himself to allay

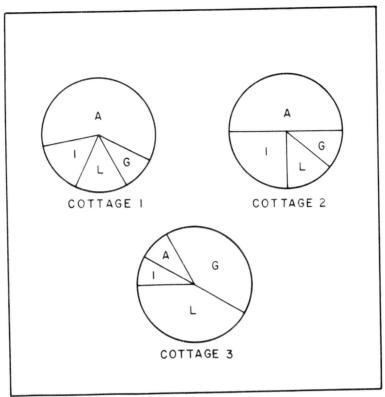

FIGURE 9. Functional Spheres of Three Head Counselors

the tension that arises from adaptation to institutional regulations. Instead of communication toward the institution, the counselor and the resident build up a cumulative joint suspicion of it. There is joint resentment at administrative rules. Staff popularity with the youngsters is purchased at the cost of united opposition to administrative rigidity or ignorance.

Our multiple functional analysis shows that the cottage care worker's role and the emergent social structure are crucial to the potential autonomous goals that can develop among the residents. We must give close attention to how functions are originally carried out and how they cause a particular type of cottage social organization. Effective counseling cannot be expected from a staff surrounded by pressures which undermine their counselor function. In order to inaugurate resident programs and goals, the social forces to which the counselor and the residents must adapt have to be carefully engineered.

In cottage 1, for example, the feedback to the staff is qualitatively different from that in the group worker's cottage 3. If the head counselor-educator is not present, his assistants have their hands full maintaining order in the cottage in the way he does. A staff member will not give a boy canteen privileges until he has finished his job; he will check closely on whether the job has been completed. This often results in a struggle over how well the job has been done. When it is not done to his satisfaction, the counselor will not give the canteen privilege, and hence a bitter struggle emerges between the residents and the staff. One counselor has, in effect, become an "enforcer," forcing his will on the boys when they are not conforming. The whole cottage seems to be struggling around the attempt to fulfill cottage tasks according to the high standards established by the head counselor. Not only the residents, but the staff, too, have their hands full in regulating the cottage according to this prep school mode; and the residents come to look on staff members as "power hungry." Staff-resident integration is on a quid-pro-quo basis, so that canteen privileges are traded for the boys' conformity to the adaptive tasks of the cottage and institution.

Here it seems pertinent to review recent analyses of attitude and behavior change as related to the exchange structure of superordinate and subordinate.

Herbert C. Kelman (1961) has isolated three structures of social influence: compliance, identification, and internalization. He focuses on the nature of the exchange structure as related to the meaning of the superordinate's influence upon the subordinate.

Compliance is the acceptance of influence by the subordinate because he hopes for a favorable reaction from the other person. He is concerned with attaining specific rewards or in avoiding punishment that the superordinate controls. The critical factor is the superordinate's authority, which induces the subordinate to behave and evince attitudes that he knows the other wants.

Identification, in contrast, is the acceptance of new behavior by the subordinate because the relationship is of a satisfying self-defining character. The subordinate's role vis-à-vis the superordinate is an important part of his self-image, and he accepts influence because he wants to maintain the relationship to the superordinate person. The subordinate adopts new behavior and attitudes not because he is compelled to, but because of a genuine liking and comfortableness in wanting to be with the superordinate person and to be liked by him. This is close to identification in the classical psychoanalytical sense.

Internalization is influence accepted by the subordinate because it is congruent with his own value system. It is intrinsically rewarding, and he adopts it because he finds it useful for solving a problem in a way that is congenial to his orientation or demanded by his value perspective. In internalization the subordinate perceives new attitudes and behavior as inherently conducive to the maximization of his own goals and values. The influencing agent plays an important role in internalization, but the crucial dimension is the partner's credibility, *i.e.*, his influence is regarded by the subordinate as intimately tied-in with his own goals.

Kelman has carefully analyzed the antecedent, intervening, and consequent characteristics of each structure of influence. Effective work with youngsters may very well go through these processes in stages. However, our research indicates that by stressing certain functions in his transactions with the youngsters, the superordinate can create a structure in which one of these influences will predominate.

In cottages 1 and 2 the head counselor has adopted an extreme custodial position in order to induce the youngsters to carry out cottage and institutional tasks. The functioning of this role segment conflicts with the counselor's ability to carry out his other functions effectively. This is quite in contrast to cottage 3, where the adaptive sphere is of considerably less importance because the head counselor has defined his primary role as counselor: the planning and development of autonomous cottage goals. Thus he uses himself to induce the youngsters to promote for themselves group goals and methodologies compatible with their needs.

The cottage care worker's role as a man-in-the-middle is analogous to the factory foreman described in sociological literature. A typology of "middle-man" roles that the village level worker plays in India has been described by Dubey and Sutton (1962). In their study they found four types of accommodation to the conflicting pressures from the powerful administrative hierarchy and the villagers whose needs they are presumed to serve. These constellations are (1) the link pattern, (2) the block pawn, (3) the village idol, and (4) escape.

The link pattern describes a man who can work with both the village and the "block" (next higher administrative unit) in such a way that he can accomplish his basic function of effectively communicating administrative policy to the village and village needs to the administration. The block pawn identifies primarily with his administrative superiors and becomes enmeshed in the bureaucratic organization to an extent which keeps him from being sensitive to the welfare of the village for whose needs he is responsible. The village idol takes sides with the villagers and is suspicious and even resistant to the administrative program. Finally, the escapist either resigns or escapes psychologically by acting minimally on behalf of either the block or the village.

These ideal types provide a framework in which to view the counselors in the three senior cottages. The educationally oriented head counselor in cottage 1, who imposes a set of requirements on the boys and devotes a great deal of energy to enforcing them, approaches the concept of the block pawn described above in that his major identification is with the upper administrative echelon. This counselor is a model of identification by the boys; he has built up his image with individual talks with the residents—and by relating to them by playing ping-pong, etc. His goal in forming these attachments is secondary to the achievement of greater control; his expressive patterns of relationships are directed toward the ultimate goal of meeting the demands of superior authorities in the institution.

In cottage 2 the nonprofessional head counselor is a combination of the village idol and escapist. On the one hand, he does relate to the boys on the basis of many delinquent values; on the other, he appears not really to side with either the boys or the institution but rather aims toward a mutual adjustment. He is not idolized by the boys nor, on the other hand, is he awarded much recognition by his administrative superiors. He has been able to work out a pattern of not rocking the boat, which is not so unsatisfactory as to cause him to be completely rejected either by the administration or by the boys.

The counselor in cottage 3 has been known to capture the boys by virtue of his demonstration of skills with which they identify—athletic skills, knowledge of jazz, etc. In addition, the boys are aware that because of his connection with the higher administration he can fulfill their needs for physical and other resources.

THE NEXT STAGE OF DEVELOPMENT IN INSTITUTIONS

The total institution constitutes a network of subsystems designed to bring about effective collaboration among the staff and rehabilitation of the youngsters. Contemporary efforts to design a therapeutic milieu today are focused on the role of the cottage care worker. Paradoxically, for many years, he was the forgotten man in the institution. But he is the only adult in day-to-day direct contact with the youngsters, and his functioning conditions the boys' total living situation. The cottage care worker is crucial in bridging the distance between the institution and the youngsters.

The main definition of the cottage care worker's role comes from the institutional structure. For many years he was thought of as a custodian who had a special skill for regulating a controlled integrated life but also had a "feel" for children. The amount of specific training designed for the cottage care worker varied among institutions, but in most is still unsystematic. He is often "trained" by professionals who have no intimate contact with cottage life. Since the cottage care worker is directly dependent upon administrative superiors, the pressures stemming from the administration for controlling the youngsters are of crucial importance.

Today, his role is conceived as multifunctional. He must perform the custodial dimension. He must be sensitive to the emotional disturbances of individual youngsters. He is now becoming trained to develop the atmosphere in the cottage which will be most conducive to enabling the youngsters to formulate goals, to become motivated toward attaining them, and to helping them coordinate their efforts to achieve them. Any efforts designed to help the cottage attain autonomous goals must flow from his understanding of the felt needs and interests of the residents. Needless to say, he can help the cottage achieve goals only by having ample "back-stopping" from other personnel. The most important tendency he must overcome both within himself and among the residents is to expect that the institution will provide everything and that the residents are essentially passive, conforming dependents.

How can the institution imbue the cottage care workers with goals and grass-roots methods of working with residents? His low subordinate status in the administrative hierarchy is geared toward an emphasis on control. A widespread acceptance of the multifunctional definition of his role may facilitate his effort to organize his tasks within a more coherent and effective pattern. Thus, he must learn how to implement his function within the cottage of helping it attain autonomous goals by more effective communication upward to administrators in the institution.

He must think through the following issues: How does he resolve difficulties of enabling the group to attain goals within the rigid structure in which the cottage must function? How does he work out a balance among his multiple functions? How does he resolve the conflict in influencing the cottage toward autonomous goals and changing the expectations of the institution?

It is clear in our analysis of the different adjustment patterns of cottage care workers that the emphasis in each derives from the strengths the head counselor develops to handle the adaptive and goal problems imposed by his marginal position. The cottage worker must strive to match the level of interest, motivation, and resources in the cottage with opportunities to exploit new patterns in the institution. This involves calculated risks. In the Appendix to this chapter is a document from our files which illustrates the ambition of a small group of senior boys to extend radically their areas of decision-making in the institution.

The next stage of institutional development is toward developing a perspective of residential treatment in which the resident groups are offered an opportunity to plan and execute goals stemming from their own interests and needs. In several total institution settings, this program is being advanced. Two outstanding examples are Jones' therapeutic milieu (Jones, 1953) and the program of sociotherapy initiated by Paul Daniel Sivadon in France (Sivadon, 1957). The latter is especially perceptive about the need to promote autonomous goals by resident groups.

Sivadon asserts that one of the main problems of residents in institutions is the great amount of time that lies heavily on their hands. Furthermore, there are always gripes and complaints that the residents have about the restrictions on their freedom and their ability to plan and attain goals. The basic need to overcome passivity within the controlled authoritarian environment is met by provoking the residents into meeting their gripes with positive and constructive group activity. Sivadon has asserted, in fact, that the most important function of the resident-counselor is to incite the residents to work out their complaints in positive programs of group action. If institutional life is boring for the residents, they should be helped to voice their complaints but also encouraged to take the next step in planning a program which can overcome the ennui. This has the advantage of using group process not only for developing programs but also for enabling the residents to work more effectively with each other. Through these activities they learn from their own errors and, instead of projecting their impotency onto the institution and into enervating intra-institutional conflict, they are forced to look more at their own individual and joint functioning, to locate their inadequacies, and to develop strategies for overcoming them.

Sivadon's program essentially informs the group worker's activity in cottage 3. He is very familiar with Sivadon's work and spends most of his time thinking through programs on which he and his assistants can help the youngsters follow through.

Cottages 1 and 2 cannot attain new orbits because they are stuck in the adaptational sphere. Imposing the carrying out of cottage tasks on the youngsters influences the entire social functioning of the cottage system. There is an overemphasis on the institutional value of maintaining a stable and orderly cottage and a corresponding de-emphasis of the counselor role that would enable the youngsters to promote autonomous goals.

The crystallization of the adaptive function results in a spiraling effect in which imposition on the youngsters results in resentment which further rigidifies the counselor's attempts to make the youngsters conform. The primary emphasis on adaptive tasks results in the cottage orbiting about the problem of maintaining order. In one cottage they try to offset this through an informal easy-going, joking relationship with semi-delinquent overtones, and in the other, with individual alter-therapy sessions. What is overlooked in these two cottages is the possibility of enabling the youngsters to formulate and carry through on autonomous cottage and subgroup goals which are related to their individual and collective needs. Thus, each head counselor institutes a regime which has a multiplier effect on certain kinds of investments. The growth and crystallization of a significant function is the degree to which that activity is channelled from the receivers, the residents, back to the formulators, the counselors. But in cottage 3 the process has been reversed. Instead of the counselors imposing the execution of cottage tasks on the youngsters, the youngsters themselves are urged to formulate and carry through goals, and the counselors use themselves to enable the youngsters to meet these goals.

The differences in the cottages are revealed in how the counselor's assistants are deployed. In cottages 1 and 2 the difficulties emerging around maintaining a stable cottage have so grown and multiplied that the assistants are also utilized to maintain this basic order. This only increases the feeling of constraint that the youngsters have and the attitude of being surrounded, controlled, and/or attacked by the counselors. In cottage 3, on the other hand, the assistants have been increasingly used as assistant group workers who enable the youngsters to adopt more positive values and behavior. This is in line with a conclusion stated by Sherif after extensive research with adolescent groups:

> The crux of the matter for effective policy and action is not the busy-work as such, not the programmed activities *as such,* or even the end-products of training to exhibit for public display. The cardinal point is to insure throughout (whatever the activities) the youth's feeling of having a *function* in their initiation, development, and execution.
>
> What we do not take part in initiating and developing and producing, what we engage in without our own choosing and aspiring, is not felt as ours. What we do not feel as ours lacks in the experience of inner-urgency and in sense of responsibility. The important thing to actualize at the very start is not immediate technical proficiency, but the feeling of participation, the feeling that we have indispensable roles with others in things that all feel should be done. (Sherif and Sherif, 1964, pp. 314-15)

Thus we see that in the third pattern of adjustment, the social group worker's main function is to link the youth's needs with a dynamic reciprocal impact upon the institution. This means that his function is not merely to make the cottage adapt to institutional regulations, but to create, with the youths, goals that they can attain within the authoritarian setting. This means that the worker must have influence with the administration to carry on, within and outside the cottage, a variety of goals that are primarily planned and executed by the youngsters for themselves.

APPENDIX

HOLLYMEDE RESISTANCE SOCIETY

Aims and Purposes:

Our primary purpose is, simply, the resistance of authority.

We will resist authority whenever and wherever we feel that power to be abused.

We will publish articles and other thought pieces aimed at stimulating thought and debate among our fellow H.R.S. students.

Our Aims and Purposes:

An end to compulsory religious observance.

Greater freedom to achieve intellectual stimulation, *i.e.*, access to books, lectures, theatre, etc.

An end to compulsory education.

An end to the school-cottage conflict, which leaves students little or no time for academic pursuits.

An end to the unnatural separation of males and females.

An end to student pressure on other students and the molestation of aforesaid students.

An end to campus fighting and instigating.

An end to regimentation and unfair group punishment.

An end to all student discrimination.

The allowance of students to dress and comport themselves according to the limitations of society, not the unnatural regulations imposed by Hollymede.

In order to facilitate the accomplishment of these ends, we purpose to establish a forum for student discussion of common problems and ideas to be reviewed by staff. We also intend to nominate and support an H.R.S. candidate in the next student council election.

REFERENCES

Bales, R. F., 1953. The equilibrium problem in small groups. In T. Parsons, R. F. Bales, and E. A. Shils, *Working Papers in the Theory of Action.* (Glencoe, Ill.: Free Press.)

————, 1956. Task status and likeability as a function of talking and listening in decision-making groups. In L. D. Whyte (ed.), *The State of the Social Sciences.* (Chicago: University of Chicago Press.)

Bales, R. F., and P. E. Slater, 1955. Role differentiation in small decision-making groups. In T. Parsons and R. F. Bales, *Family, Socialization and Interaction Process.* (Glencoe, Ill.: Free Press.)

Barber, B., 1956. Structural-functional analysis: problems of misunderstanding. *Amer. sociol. Rev.*, 21, No. 2, April.

Buckley, W., 1957. Structural-functional analysis in modern sociology. In H. Becker and A. Boskoff (eds.), *Modern Sociological Theory.* (New York: Dryden Press.)

Coleman, J. S., 1961. *The Adolescent Society.* (New York: Free Press of Glencoe.)

Dubey, D. C., and W. A. Sutton, Jr., 1962. A rural man-in-the-middle: The Indian village level worker in community development. (Paper at meeting of Rural Sociological Society, Aug. 1962.)

Fallding, H., 1963. Functional analysis in sociology. *Amer. sociol. Rev.*, 28, No. 1, Feb.

Getzels, J. W., and P. W. Jackson, 1960. The study of giftedness: a multidimensional approach. *The Gifted Student.* Coop. res. Monog. No. 2, U.S. Department of Health, Education, and Welfare (Washington, D.C.: U.S. Government Printing Office), 1-18.

Hemple, C. G., 1959. The logic of functional analysis. In L. Gross (ed.), *Symposium on Sociological Theory* (Evanston, Ill.: Row, Peterson), 271-311.

Hess, R. D., and G. Handel, 1959. *Family Worlds.* (Chicago: University of Chicago Press.)

James, W., 1964. *The Principles of Psychology.* Quoted in B. Berelson and G. A. Steiner, *Human Behavior.* (New York: Harcourt, Brace and World.)

Jones, M., 1953. *The Therapeutic Community.* (New York: Basic Books.)

Kelman, H. C., 1961. Processes of opinion change. *Public opinion Quar.*, 25, Spring, 57-78.

Kurtz, P. W., 1956. Human nature, homeostatis and value. *Philos. and phenomenol. Res.*, 17, No. 1, Sept., 36-55.

Lewis, O., 1962. *Five Families.* (New York: Science Editions.)

Merton, R. K., 1961. Social problems and sociological theory. In Ŕ. K. Merton and R. A. Nisbet, *Contemporary Social Problems.* (New York: Harcourt, Brace and World.)

Murray, H. A., et al., 1938. *Explorations in Personality.* (New York: Oxford University Press.)

Nagel, E., 1956. *Logic Without Metaphysics.* (Glencoe, Ill.: Free Press.)

New York Times, 1964. "The News of the Week in Review," April 5, 1964.

Ohlin, L. E., H. Pevin, and D. M. Pappenfort, 1958. Major dilemmas of the social worker in probation and parole. In H. D. Stein and R. A. Cloward (eds.), *Social Perspectives on Behavior.* (New York: Free Press of Glencoe.)

Opler, M., 1945. Themes as dynamic forces in culture. *Amer. J. Sociol.*, 51, No. 3, Nov., 198-206.

Parsons, T., 1959. General theory in sociology. In R. K. Merton, L. Broom, and L. S. Cottrell (eds.), *Sociology Today.* (New York: Basic Books.)

Parsons, T., R. F. Bales, and E. A. Shils, 1953. *Working Papers in the Theory of Action.* (Glencoe, Ill.: Free Press.)

Polsky, H. W., 1962a. Structural-functional theory: guide line to group work. (Paper at Group Work Section meetings, New York City Chapter, Natl. Assoc. Social Workers.)

———, 1962b. *Cottage Six.* (New York: Russell Sage Foundation.)

———, 1964. Three models of transaction for social work. (Mimeographed.) Paper at meeting of Field Supervisor Conference, Columbia University School of Social Work, March, 1964.

———, 1965. A social system approach to residential treatment. In H. Maier (ed.), *Group Work as Part of Residential Treatment.* (New York: National Assoc. of Social Workers.)

Sherif, M., and Carolyn W. Sherif, 1964. *Reference Groups.* (New York: Harper and Row.)

Sivadon, P. D., 1957. Techniques of sociotherapy. *Psychiatry*, 20, No. 3, Aug.

Weber, G. H., 1962. *A Theoretical Study of the Cottage Parent Position and Cottage Work Situations*, U.S. Department of Health, Education, and Welfare, Social Security Administration Children's Bureau. (Washington, D.C.: U.S. Government Printing Office.)

TEN

GROUP ORGANIZATION THEORY
AND THE ADOLESCENT INPATIENT UNIT

Frank T. Rafferty

Concepts are like optical instruments. If one looks through a microscope, or a telescope, or a magnifying glass, the appearance of the object examined will be strikingly, even startlingly, different. So it is in the behavioral sciences. Behavioral phenomena are strikingly different when examined through different concepts. Unfortunately, it is easy in the interactional excitement of behavior to forget that we are observing the phenomena through conceptual abstractions. This is compounded when the concepts are built into the general culture or into the specific subculture of a professional discipline. A corrective device is the deliberate replacement and alternative use of one conceptual instrument with another. Then, there is also the uncertainty that the same phenomena are being examined. For example in the various chapters in this book, many of the authors have examined the processes in a normative society, while as a psychiatrist, I will be looking at a special segment in this chapter— those adolescent individuals who have failed to make a minimum adjustment to the normative society.

The purpose of this chapter is to examine a psychiatric inpatient unit for adolescents in a state hospital through the medium of group organization theory. In doing this, the usual psychiatric concepts of individual psychopathology are forsaken along with the characteristic attitude of describing patients and their problems in a different language from that used in describing staff personnel. Several targets of the study can be outlined. First, the behavior of adolescents in an inpatient setting has been quite difficult to comprehend with only the traditional concepts from individual psychology, so there is the need to enlarge the theoretical range. Second, the behavior of staff personnel in such units is often of great concern to the administration, and a theory to encompass such behavior is needed. Third, the best studies of the methods and means

The original study for this chapter was supported in part by Special Project Grant No. OM-104, National Institute of Mental Health. Subsequent study was supported by Crownsville State Hospital, Crownsville, Maryland.

whereby actions, values, attitudes and judgments are controlled or influenced by social situations have been carefully controlled experiments or normative field operations. So the complex, disorderly, and uncontrolled behavior in a psychiatric unit for adolescents is a worthy challenge for group theory. Fourth, a discussion of the adolescent unit furnished the opportunity to develop further a modification of group theory introduced several years ago in a more controlled study of social structure with disturbed adolescents.

CONCEPTS OF GROUP AND MODIFICATIONS

Adolescence has been of interest as a point in individual development where the concepts of social psychology and individual psychology are obviously interrelated. The literature on adolescents has concentrated on the effect of peer group on the adolescent and on the problem of transition from the family to the larger social group. In 1957, a special program was designed as a clinical laboratory to study the power of the group in the treatment of seriously disturbed adolescents. Radical alteration of the usual treatment structure was planned. The goal was to develop a unified, cohesive, stable group that would become a primary object of identification and reference for the children and the major source of their values.

Sherif has indicated that as individuals become members of a group in the process of interaction, the differential effects of this process on the members becomes more pronounced and predictable (Sherif and Sherif, 1956, p. 181). The definition of a group was: A group consists of two or more individuals interacting in relationship to a common motive; manifesting differential effects on the participants; resulting in the formation of an organization consisting of roles and hierarchical statuses; a demarcation from nonmembers; and the development of values or norms which regulate relationships and activities of consequence to the group (Sherif and Sherif, 1956, pp. 151, 152). It soon became obvious that this was a strict and demanding definition. Following my opening analogy with optical instruments, I would describe it as a concept with tremendous resolving power in that it differentiates sharply between group and non-group behavior. A quick comparison to another definition of *group* will demonstrate this quality: A group is "two or more people who bear an explicit psychological relationship to one another." (Krech and Crutchfield, 1948, p. 18)

In any event, the treatment program quickly became a study of the various regular non-group phenomena and has been reported in previous papers (Rafferty, 1961, 1962, 1963). Subsequently, the lessons learned were transferred to a more standard treatment setting, which is the subject here.

Several important differences between the two situations should be noted. In the previous study, there was a unique laboratory social structure that provided an opportunity for observation and control not available in an operating psychiatric service. The crucial factor manipulated was the control over the social organization by the adult staff. The ten to twelve children and four staff were allowed to interact 900 hours in five-hour intervals, with a minimum of conformity pressure from the adults. This process would be impossible to duplicate in the psychiatric unit. The reasons for this may be of some interest. The process of self-determination that could be followed strictly with ten children and four staff is impractical with thirty children and twenty staff. In the special project, the process of organization with the ten children was initiated and terminated by criteria related to the development of a group, whereas in a hospital, the admission and discharge of each child is determined primarily by either individual or family considerations. Only occasionally will a child be admitted or discharged from the ward because of group organization criteria. Also, the special project was set up in such a manner that it was almost free of the impact of other institutions. But the adolescent service described here is a part of an 1,800-bed hospital, which is part of a large department of mental hygiene which has been assigned the tasks of custody, treatment, and protection of the mentally ill. The effect of the larger organizational structure on the adolescent unit is primarily on the staff. A major result of this is the greater need to procure conforming behavior from the children. The practical result is a fairly tightly structured, 24-hour program that is staff-determined.

Three principles of social organization were differentiated. The first of these is that of *group*, as defined earlier. The function of the other two principles is to organize the non-group behavior that was so predominant a feature of the treatment program studied. An anecdote may be helpful to introduce the terms used. Initially, an anthropologist had been invited to observe and to collaborate in the project, since it was expected that cultural concepts could help describe the interaction and interdependence of group and individual dynamics. After a period of observation, the anthropologist made the cogent remark that there was nothing for him to do since there was no culture present. Instead, there was a collection of primates who were in constant motion, picking, pulling, shoving, fighting, and jabbering at one another and communicating practically nothing of any cultural significance.

Concepts from other social sciences seemed equally inappropriate, but the literature on social behavior in animals did offer the useful and frequently studied concepts of territory (Carpenter, 1955) and dominance (Scott, 1958, pp. 158-188). These concepts are far from fully explored or understood, but they have been thoroughly studied in many biological species, from fish to primates. However, they have not been systematically applied to humans. To some extent, the phenomenon of dominance has been described under the aegis of status. But status is intimately related to the concept of role, *i.e.*, functionally differentiated behavior with respect to a common conceptualized task. There seemed to be value in looking at dominance separately, as an operating principle of organization that has different results and significance from status hierarchy. Dominance is a more primitive form of organization, which distributes the resources of survival and is not task-oriented in the conceptual sense. Its significance can be better appreciated when there is absence of task-oriented groups. Sometimes in a normative society, the absence of a common goal is obscured by language conventions.

The concept of territory has been less explored in human behavior than dominance, although individual psychological concepts such as attitudes, self, ego, ego boundaries, and ego involvement can be understood as manifestations of territoriality. These concepts are in considerable use in the practical fields of politics and law. A scholarly tracing of the various forms of these ideas from antiquity to the present is desirable, but unfortunately not available. Suffice it to say that law has been much concerned with the ramification of private property, property rights, and personal rights. Politics and political science have thoroughly studied the use of power in the area of government and international relations. Studies of administrative structure have also defined concepts of "line of authority" and "areas of responsibility," which are readily understood as dominance and territory (Simon, 1960).

The use of dominance and territory seemed to serve the following purposes: (1) organized behavior not adequately covered by the concept of "group"; (2) provided a bridge from the study of small groups to the study of larger communities and societies; (3) provided a transitional concept from sociology and social psychology to law, politics, and administration; (4) facilitated the use of small group theory in the practical operation of institutions, such as hospitals and prisons. An analogy to individual psychology is illustrative. For centuries we dealt with a basic concept of man as a rational animal. The philosophers who publicized this view were perhaps the most rational of men and generalized their crowning cerebral achievements of rationality to all men at all times. Faced with such influential testimony, generations were unprepared to deal with the overwhelming evidence that men behaved quite irrationally in a majority of situations. If rationality is defined as "the deliberate intentional choice of a course of action or thought from all alternative courses with a full and adequate knowledge of the results and ramifications of each alternative" (Simon, 1960), then it is apparent that we achieve a relative rationality some of the time after much preparation and great effort. Social psychology and psychoanalysis have been quite influential in revealing the sources of influence on our individual judgments. In social psychology, "the group" is comparable to rationality. The group seems to be the most flexible, democratic, creative, and effective problem-solving organization. In a sense it represents the zenith of man's social organization skills. Unfortunately, it is achieved relatively rarely. Territory and dominance help to explain the conflictive and inefficient problem-solving behavior found in so many clubs, boards, committees, departments, etc. An example would be a curriculum committee spending hours in repeated, unfruitful meetings laden with emotional conflict, while shared goals and values still elude definition. Much of the shock and dismay related to disturbed psychological and social behavior can be dissipated when the nostalgia for rationality and groupness can be modified.

Working definitions of dominance and territory are required. The following are offered as tentative descriptive definitions. *Dominance* is a pattern of regular social behavior in which one individual is able to do something to another which cannot be done in return, resulting in more favorable access to specific necessities or privileges. The establishment and acceptance of a dominance relationship is accompanied by a reduction of tension and conflict. Conversely, non-acceptance of a dominance relationship is manifested by overt conflict or escape. In lower animals, physical dominance is a primary form; when it is established, actual physical conflict is replaced by a sign or show of some type that makes full-scale fighting unnecessary. The pecking of hens is an example. In humans, physical dominance is still a very real factor of existence in all cultures. But as the culture becomes more complex, more subtle but equally definite symbols of dominance, such as age, sex, academic degree, tenure, seniority, title, date of rank, etc., replace or supplement physical dominance. A characteristic of dominance in administrative structures is that the decision of one man becomes an environmental fact for another (Simon, 1960). It will be noted that there is no necessary presumption that the dominant one is making the rational, the correct, or the best decision. In effect, the process allows a decision to be made out of a maelstrom of uncertainty and irrationality.

Territory is more difficult to define, since it is a more primitive form of social organization found in all species. Territorial style is specific to a species. Originally the concept was limited to a geographical or spatial relationship. An individual animal, a pair, or a tribe defines an area by some specific behavior. Fighting behavior is elicited when the territory is transgressed. An important phenomenon is observed in the relative reversal of dominance within a territory. That is, a weaker animal within its own territory is frequently able to withstand the attack of the stronger.

Another kind of territorial relationship can exist between two animals. In such a relationship the animals will return to each other as to a spatial territory, will fight for each other, and will be "depressed" if separated (Lorenz, 1959, p. 181). In humans the concept is essentially the same but with many subtle and symbolic variations. There is the fundamental territorial experience with a geographical space, *i.e.,* our private home. There is also the possessive territorial relationships with other individuals—our wife, our children, our friends. Furthermore, in humans there is the extension to abstract ideas. As a rule of thumb, territoriality in humans may be defined as applying to any person, place, thing, idea, or relationship about which one would characteristically use a possessive pronoun. In humans territory is frequently marked by devices such as fences, wedding bands, ankle bracelets, fraternity pins, or customs houses. But although many territorial relationships are not visibly marked, the boundaries will be defined by the emotional and behavioral response of the possessor. In the event of a transgression, the possessor will feel in danger, threatened, or angry, depending to some extent on the dominance of the transgressor. Fighting behavior will follow—sometimes physically, more frequently verbally, and occasionally legally. Self-esteem and a feeling of well-being are the signs of a secure territory. If an individual's territory has been usurped by some more powerful individual, he will be depressed. It is important to note that the emotional and behavioral response is in the possessor. The transgressor is capable of transgressing without any clear sign of his own. An analogy may be made to the theatergoer who makes his way among the crowded seats unknowingly stepping on many toes. He is unknowing, but the possessor of the toe will be acutely aware of the action; only through an act of empathy will the latecomer (the transgressor) be able to exercise special care. A current example is the statement of an integrationist leader that the oppressed must fight and demand their freedom.

Territoriality in humans provides an integrating concept between theories of individual behavior and theories of social behavior. Psychology, psychiatry, medicine, psychoanalysis, and social work have espoused the individual. Sociology and anthropology have been more interested in the social organization, institution, or culture. Social psychology has bridged the gap by studying the effect of groups on individual behavior and, to a lesser extent, the effect of individual behavior on groups. Territoriality is manifested by the basic and elementary relationship of an individual to another object. By inference, it also is a psycho-physiological state within the individual.

Semantically, we distinguish between inanimate and animate objects and abstract ideas. This distinction is reflected in some of our sciences and more frequently in our attitudes. For example, in psychiatry we are likely to think of a depression as caused by the loss of a love object. If we are not careful, the love object will be unwittingly thought of as being another person, when in fact it may well be an inanimate object or an abstract concept of self. Territoriality defines the quality of a relationship of an individual to an object—inanimate, animate, or abstract, e.g., my car, my wife, or my idea.

It is important to delineate the distinctions between and the interdependencies of *group, dominance,* and *territoriality* as principles of organization. Territoriality is the most elementary, the most primitive, the most rigid, the most limiting, the most emotionally oriented, and the most survival oriented. A decisive advantage for territoriality in the complex human individual is its ability to transcend time and distance. As a concept, it helps explain why I could present my ideas before a meeting of strangers with only a moderate amount of anxiety. As a result of interaction of myself and a variety of animate, inanimate, and abstract objects over a period of years, I have acquired a concept of my territory that can roughly be summarized in the phrase, "my identity." Fortunately, an individual's identity is mobile and goes with him at all times to provide some measure of security.

However, territory is not necessarily inviolate, absolute or rational. My car may be stolen, my wife's affection may be alienated by a more attractive man, and my ideas may be refuted. The dominance principle of organization provides another dimension. Dominance may distribute territory, or give one the opportunity to acquire territory, or deprive one of territory, or determine an order of access to a particular privilege or territory. A dominance order provides an organization for a larger number of individuals and has thus greater manpower potential. In certain situations, it provides more efficiency and flexibility than simple territoriality, as in the overlapping areas of responsibility that are represented in the usual organization chart of a large department or corporation. Its limitations are derived from the one-way communication patterns developed, the tendency for the dominant to transgress on the subordinate, the constant threat of change in the dominance order, and the continuous need to reaffirm dominance by symbol, action, and frequently overt aggression. Again it should be emphasized that nostalgia for rationality, logic, fairness, and democracy should not blind us to the reality of dominance as a principle of social organization. The Ph.D. is not necessarily more intelligent or more competent than one with the Master's degree; the professor is frequently not the most capable, creative, or productive man in the department; the principal of the school is not necessarily the best trained teacher. The corporation president may frequently be much less expert or informed than many others. The man with inherited wealth may be morally indefensible. But if scientific concern is for the reality of social organization, never overlook the real power and influence that is inherent in the dominant position.

Group would appear to be the highest form of social behavior, available only to humans and requiring the conceptual level of intellectual functioning with an elaborate symbolic communication process. Group does not imply that territory and dominance are excluded. Rather it seems to be a higher level of organization, which requires prior establishment of territory and dominance. In the development of a group, the conceptual choice of a common motivating task seems crucial. The task requires a differentiation of function, *i.e.*, roles. The complexity of the role skills varies with the difficulty of the motivating tasks; and the hierarchy is related to role requirements rather than to more primitive tests of power.

GROUP THEORY AND THE COLLECTION OF PATIENTS

The adolescent unit under observation consists of thirty patients between the ages of twelve and sixteen. The selection process that brings a particular group of youngsters into the state hospital is a complex one, but not exclusive nor exhaustive, in that many more youngsters with the same characteristics are presumably out of the hospital. Children from all socioeconomic classes are represented, but with fewer from wealthy homes. Typically, they have a long history of chronic symptomatology covering the range of neurotic, psychosomatic and disordered behavior. Relatively infrequently are there gross psychotic symptoms or disorganization. If there were such symptoms on admission, they would rather quickly subside. Presumptive evidence of minimal brain dysfunction is present in about one out of four patients. Usually the child is a chronic school problem, several years behind grade level, with a history of truancy, school phobia, belligerence, lack of motivation, incorrigibility, etc. The family will be marked by several of the stigmata of dysfunction, such as severe marital conflict, emotional divorce, absence of father, unemployment, welfare placement, mental illness, or erratic behavior in one or both parents, etc. Most frequently the immediate reason for hospitalization would be an act or series of acts of aggression toward self, school, or parents, or some antisocial acts flagrantly violating the mores of the community.

What does the history of a patient look like through the abstract conceptualization—the group? First, one is struck by the relative absence of membership in groups. The average early teenager can point to a series of formal and informal group memberships—Scouts, Brownies, the neighborhood play group, the athletic team, the classroom, the camp, and, very significantly, the family. The typical patient has been at best only a nominal or marginal member of such groups. One is impressed, for instance, with the forces extruding him from participation in the classroom, the rejection, rather than any sustained performance as a member. The family has been dignified with the phrase "primary group." Our patient will have had an extended period of time living in a "family," but an examination of his family with the strict definition will reveal few of the qualities of a group. It will be evident that the members of the family have a spatial relationship over extended time and have important psychological significance to one another. But in terms of organizational essentials, the term *group* can only be applied through the greatest stretch of the imagination, by courtesy, or by failure to analyze the actual social functioning of the family. Only at the most primitive level of survival will common goals be apparent. There may well be a primitive differentiation of function between husband and wife in that one goes to work and one stays home. But this is less a differentiation of function related to a common task than it is a division of responsibility on a territorial basis.

In evaluating the group membership history of an individual, it is necessary to consider the complexity of the group task and the requirements of functional roles. The average patient has the following problems: His parents are severely limited in group skills; while, very significantly, the role skills they do possess are usually occupational skills which are not visible to the child in the family. Instead, the adolescent patient has been exposed to years of parental jockeying for position and interfamilial conflict about responsibilities and values. Here is involved a concept about performance in groups that seems well established and well defined to the developmentally oriented psychiatrist, but is not always clear in group theory literature. An individual is not prepared for effective role performance in groups simply by virtue of being a normally intelligent human nor even necessarily by possessing the technical skill required by a specific role. Experience in functioning, successful groups throughout childhood seems necessary for an individual to have group skills. At this point the dichotomy of group and individual psychology theory comes full circle. An individual achieves a large measure of fulfillment through successful participation in groups, and this successful participation in groups is dependent on his individual history of experience in groups.

Two other frequent family situations need comment on from a group point of view. One is the family that is apparently the opposite of the one described above. Both parents may be successful individuals, and the family a tight organization prepared to tackle a number of tasks with a clear set of sharply defined roles and values. Unfortunately, for a variety of reasons, a given child may not be able to live according to the values prescribed as conditions for membership in the family. A frequent example is the child who does not achieve at the academic level required. Usually this child is not obviously retarded, but is characterized by a style of psychological and social functioning different from the academically oriented child. Reasons for this are not germane to this discussion, but usually they are beyond the comprehension or intuitive knowledge of the parents. The significance here is that over a period of years this child will be constantly subjected to criticism, negative evaluation, and punitive sanctions. Frequently the child will rebel vigorously against the family values and become an active member of a peer social organization that embraces a less demanding set of values. Sometimes if the level of resentment is high and shared by the peer group, vandalistic activity becomes the unifying purpose of the peer group.

A more subtle situation is the child who has been a member in good standing of an intact, successful family group, but who becomes disorganized suddenly and apparently without warning. Looking at this situation, one usually finds that this disorganization occurs at a time when the child is expected to enter and perform in another group, usually peer type, while at the same time maintaining family membership. Close examination will usually reveal a serious value conflict between the two groups; while further analysis will demonstrate that the child has such an exclusive, cohesive relationship with one parent that autonomous performance in other groups is virtually impossible. In fact, psychological existence for the child as an individual distinct from the parent is lacking.

In the hospital, the adolescent will live in intimate spatial relations with others with the same preparation. There are fifteen boys and fifteen girls with separate dormitory accommodations, but with common dining, educational, recreational and treatment facilities. There is very little privacy, no escape from relating to one another, and considerable pressure from hospital staff to relate. Remember that the selection procedure for this collection of young people procured those individuals who had failed at membership in practically every type of group situation. Yet groups become cohesive, with a strong sense of positive membership morale, when the goal of the organization is well defined, accepted, and within reach of the group's efforts. With this in mind how does the collection of patients look? Despite the high incidence of voluntary admissions, it is improbable that an adolescent will enter the ward with any real understanding or acceptance of the reason for his admission. In fact, it is rather disheartening to view the variety of goals that significant people will have toward admission.

The child may come with no perception at all of the mission of the unit, but only an awareness of his rejection from some other organization, such as family or school. He may perceive the ward as a relief from some previous unpleasant circumstance, *e.g.*, an angry father, principal, or policeman, or the threat of reform school. Parents may expect some act of psychiatric surgery that will rend their child acceptable to themselves and their society. Staff goals are most often verbalized as the manipulation of some internal abstract concept—*e.g.*, ego strength, male identification, trust—that the child or parent doesn't even know exists.

So we have a collection of thirty youngsters selected for their lack of group success, motivated by a diverse set of pressures unrelated to the intimate social experience that they will undergo. One other variable must be identified since it is perhaps a distinguishing factor of this social structure from others such as the neighborhood delinquent subculture or the long-term residential institution. A relatively short period of confinement will be a necessity. Some of the youngsters, invariably the better organized, will be discharged within six months of their admission. A few will remain as long as eighteen months. This results in a constant shifting of the patterns of social interaction. Stability is never achieved. If a youngster does understand the significance of his hospitalization and begins to direct his energy toward treatment goals, he will quickly be discharged to pursue such worthy efforts in more favorable circumstances.

By this time it should be obvious that the social organization achieved by this collection of youngsters has little if any resemblance to a group as defined. But regular patterns of interaction between individuals are observable, and these are assumed to be the criteria of some kind of social organization. The staff-determined schedule of the unit provides a matrix of the basic tasks of eating, sleeping, bathing, playing, and going to school. The majority of the children move through this schedule most of the time. It is very evident, though, that the organizing principle is the dominance relationship of the staff. This is an unpopular and undesirable insight for the professional staff, who are intellectually committed to "treatment goals." These goals require the child to be aware of and to share the value connotation of the reasons why he was admitted, to be free of emotional commitments to other ways of life, and to have the role skills to participate in the staff group activity. The professional staff associates the dominance relationship with the presumed primitive structure of the training school, not with their own functions. The nonprofessional staff, on the other hand, are intuitively aware of the dominance principle and frequently work on a "let him know who's boss" level. In fact, they are so aware of it that it is a constant administrative effort to keep the attendant staff from descending to the level of struggling for physical dominance rather than using the more subtle symbolic and structural dominance.

There are brief periods when a small number of children may participate in what can be called a group by the strict definition. This happens most frequently in school, in group psychotherapy, in athletic events, and in the occasional special recreational event—such as a play, fashion show, or party. However, even in these situations the strong dominant influence of the staff person is necessary, or the activity will degenerate into a disorganized mess of scattered individual actions or, even worse, a chaos of aggressive destructiveness.

One of the constantly disturbing activities in a unit is the almost continuous testing and shifting of dominance relationships among the youngsters. The aggressive interaction that marks this kind of activity will occur overtly or covertly, depending on staff's reaction to it. The constant changing population prevents a well-settled structure from developing (Polsky, 1962, p. 193). A new boy with appropriate dominance equipment can move up the scale and in a matter of a few weeks be challenging the leader. A new girl or a shift in a girl's loyalty will set off a series of changes up and down the ladder. The struggle for dominance at the top of the children's organization flows directly over onto the staff. The two or three boys struggling for the number one position will use open challenges to staff as a means of competition. They will usually succeed in acquiring a dominance relationship over a number of staff until they overreach and provoke the staff as a group to make some show of dominance, usually through a disciplinary move.

But the challenging or resisting of staff dominance is not by any means limited to the children's leaders. Scott has described three kinds of aggression—fighting, escape, and passivity (Scott, 1958, p. 58). Overt aggression signals the absence of acceptance of dominance, and occurs in practically all the children at some phase of their hospitalization. Passivity is a favorite technique, and escape is easy. In a relatively tight geographical space with a reasonable staff-patient ratio, it is always a surprise to realize how much behavior is beyond the influence of staff. The literature on total institutions, especially prisons, has emphasized the informal organization of inmates which may have totally different goals than the stated ones of the institution. Such a fully developed split of formal and informal organization usually does not form in the hospital for a variety of reasons, but one can visualize a continuum of dominance relationships from top of staff to bottom of patient population, with some escape and resistance throughout the entire scale.

Looking through the social organization concepts, the serious dissociative or depressive pathology of mental illness appears much like resistance to dominance or escape from dominance into territorial space beyond the influence of the dominant ones. No special brief will be made for this as truth, but illness in the adolescent disappears to a great extent when he is able to act out in the dominance structure. The passivity and escape maneuvers enable the patient to involve relatively little of his behavior in the social organization. It is possible that this explains the relative inefficiency of dominance social structures as change agents, *e.g.*, prisons, training schools, etc.

Fortunately for treatment purposes, the dominance principle is not the only mode of social organization. Territoriality is pervasive and exerts the most positive influence. An unanswered question is, "What are the factors that elicit a territorial response between two strangers?" The only answer available at the moment is, "Direct interaction over a period of time." The next query is, "What kind of direct interaction, and how does it differ from the direct interaction of members of a group?" The resolving power of the strict definition of *group* is again helpful. An effective, functioning group has to have a common goal that is appreciated and known by the group members. The efficiency and cohesiveness of a group are enhanced and maintained by sharply, clearly and frequently defining the goal. Territorial interaction will be based on unself-conscious motives at a more primitive biological level; I might even resort to "instinctual" as a descriptive term. Such motives would be sexual, care giving, care receiving, aggressive, nutritional, protective, imitative, inquisitive, etc. The operational motive apparently varies among individuals. Sex, age, physique, previous experience, previous territorial relationships—all seem important.

There is nothing specific about territorial relationships. Anybody is eligible if the motivational interaction fits, and therein lies the lottery of treatment success or failure. As soon as a child is admitted, there are a number of potential territories offered to him. "This is your dormitory and your bed." "This is your doctor, your nurse, your group leader, your group therapist, your group, your class, your teacher, your recreational worker." At the same time other children are making themselves available for interaction, and they have even greater availability for territorial relationships. The staff are severely handicapped by who they are and by the fact that they are usually (hopefully and rightfully so) involved in territorial relationships with other people. You will notice that in the quoted introductions, the relationships offered are "your doctor," "your nurse," "your teacher," etc. Each one specifies a complex role relationship which is meaningful to the staff, but, more often than not, meaningless to the patient for a long time. The children offer themselves as direct undifferentiated interactors.

For example, in a ward of adolescents, sexual interaction is always a prime motivator of territorial attachments. The kids can always flirt, tease, hold hands, "neck," "make out," etc., to the extent that the dominant staff permits or cannot prevent. Staff is severely handicapped in sexual interaction with patients by a variety of social, legal and professional taboos. In private hospitals or in outpatient practice with higher socioeconomic patients, some sexual interaction can take place at the verbal level. This is relatively infrequent in the state hospital. If there are young staff members at the nonprofessional level, there will be frequent sexual interaction. However, if this gets past the flirting stage, the staff member, especially a man, will usually be subject to disciplinary action.

The most available interaction for a territorial relationship between patient and staff is a dependency or care-receiving need on the part of the child. Reviewing the role relationships offered to the new patient, you will notice that practically all include an element of "taking care of." For example, the child can respond to the taking-care aspect of the nurse without any appreciation of the complex role that the nurse is trained to play. By and large, the most successful patients from the treatment point of view will be those who can mobilize their dependency needs and establish territorial relationships with staff. The staff can then guide them through the complexities of the dominance structure and often lead them into acquiring role skills. Unfortunately, the adolescent is usually trying to deny dependency needs, and he may not be readily available for interaction. The denial of dependency is closely related to the rejection of subordination in the dominance hierarchy. Aggressive interaction is again much more common among the peer groups, and so the significant territorial relationship that can develop will be with a peer. However, with considerable regularity, one does observe the phenomenon of a child's fixing a staff member with a determined, aggressive challenge of dominance. If this is followed by decisive establishment of dominance in a nondestructive manner by the staff members, a strong territorial relationship will follow.

Imitative behavior is another motive for establishment of territory. This motive is extremely influential in normal children and leads to quick relationships in such areas as athletics, Scouts, hobbies, etc. However, the youngster in a state hospital ward is so poverty-stricken in game and hobby skills that imitation is limited to more primitive behavior. Even in playing pool, table tennis, basketball, etc., his sensitivity to, and fear and rejection of dominance will interfere with imitation and the development of a territorial relationship. Instead the children imitate the aggressive teasing, the obscene language and gestures, the horseplay, and general destructiveness that Redl referred to as the contagion of behavior in the ego damaged child (Redl and Wineman, 1951).

The psychotherapist and group psychotherapist have the best opportunities for exploring, seeking, and trying to make themselves available for territorial relationships. But to move a territorial relationship—"my therapist, my patient"—into the role-differentiated structure of successful psychotherapy is often a major frustrating task.

GROUP THEORY AND STAFF ORGANIZATION

It has long been considered that children's inpatient units are especially difficult to administer and present unusual stress to the personnel. Of children's residential units, the adolescent service is perhaps the most difficult and threatening. The experience of organizing a staff to deal with a difficult, perhaps impossible, continuously threatening task in an atmosphere of critical surveillance and high expectancy without adequate scientific knowhow is an education that should be shared.

The staff consists of ten attendants, four practical nurses, one graduate nurse, a social worker, a clinical psychologist, a mental health counselor (Rioch's Rangers), four teachers, and a psychiatrist. All of these people have been chosen for their jobs as carefully as the personnel facts of life allow. Presumably the organizing task is to develop a group with a clearly defined goal of treatment of the children, functionally differentiated roles, and organizational norms. The goals and values are easy to verbalize. The roles seem built into the professional disciplines involved. The hierarchy should be easy to form. On paper a magnificent organization can be described. A training period prior to actual work with the children can establish a marvelous esprit de corps. Given any kind of a break with the task to be accomplished, a well-functioning group should jell in a relatively brief time.

Here we have an interesting observation. The work on development of small group structure has emphasized the process of developing a group, the differentiation of roles, hierarchy, etc., as a result of direct interaction over time (Sherif and Sherif, 1956, p. 82). Sociology describes the institutionalized roles, so that we have some expectation of the doctor, the nurse, the social worker, etc. There are prolonged periods of training to inculcate role skills in appropriate individuals. If we hire people with good training and experience in these institutionalized roles we expect a harmony of reciprocity. Go into any hospital emergency room and watch the smooth coordination of practicing roles; watch the surgical team in the operating room. I once joined an army evacuation hospital with approximately thirty doctors, forty-five nurses, two hundred-odd corpsmen, and assorted administrative officers, all drawn abruptly from different areas of the country. Within a matter of a few months, there was a smoothly functioning hospital of four hundred beds. Obviously previous training in role skills can lead to reciprocal relationships in a formal organization very rapidly with complex tasks. But even in these situations there must be a time period of interaction before the togetherness situation becomes a group (Sherif and Sherif, 1956, p. 227). It is amazing how frequently this is forgotten in practice; and the assumption is made that training in a role, and designation by the role title will in effect bring about a functioning role in an organization.

But what of the influence of the task? Tasks may be characterized by their degree of complexity; by the adequacy of related knowledge; by the definiteness of the task structure; by the degree of difficulty in achieving; and by the significance they may have to members of the organization. The task of treating seriously disturbed, acting out adolescents in a state hospital is highly complex, poorly understood, extremely difficult to structure, frequently unsuccessful, and roughly analogous to a projective test for members of the organization. In other words, the task of treating adolescents is one which is most cleverly contrived to prevent a number of highly skilled individuals from moving from a togetherness situation to a group. No experimenter would dare try to inflict such a task on a research group. But given the opportunity of such a wonderful natural experiment, it certainly should be used to study the details of the process of a number of individuals moving from a point of no organizational structure to some approximation of a group. The natural history of the program would include a detailed, elaborate plan of space, staffing patterns and operation. The paper organization would specify roles, hierarchy of authority, etc. Then the paper organization would be filled with real people. A training period would be successfully completed with a fine staff morale and every manifestation of groupness. But then what happens with confrontation with the actual task? The most interesting observation is that the highly trained and successful staff will manifest all the principles of more primitive organization described earlier for the psychologically sick, primitive, unsuccessful children. Their actual behavior may be a more subtle manifestation of the same principles of territory and dominance, but frequently even the same behavior will be apparent. It seems significant that the organizational phenomena that follow the deterioration of a group are the same as those observed in the development of a group.

The effectively functioning group has a hierarchy of roles. As an individual works in his role, he assumes a responsibility for the conduct of his role. There is an aura of confidence in his role skill, an expectation of success, an expectation of the respect of others, and a relationship to the leader that assumes the delegation of authority and responsibility in that area of action. When the task is one like treating disturbed adolescents, this type of group operation is difficult to maintain. The individual members feel uncertain of their skill and anxious about success. They expect criticism from authority and attempt to relieve themselves of decision-making responsibility. In this context decision-making is not used in the meaning of policy decisions, but simply in terms of the multitude of alternative behaviors that are available to everyone from minute to minute in the daily operation of such a unit. They will continually attempt to turn to some authority person for direction of their actions down to the minutest detail. This may be disguised as turning to "someone who will know what to do." But in reality the psychiatrist-authority will probably not have available a rational answer.

The group thus is replaced by an organization in which dominance is the prevailing principle. This is a far less flexible structure, but it does preserve a structure in times of stress. An organization structured by the dominance principle can be very efficient and can accomplish certain tasks effectively. However, the perception of the task must be simplified. For instance, the treatment of adolescents will be simplified to the control of the adolescents. The goals of the program will be predominantly to keep the patient behavior within certain definite bounds, and a system of rewards and punishments will be instituted. In other words, there will be a continuum of dominance relationship from the director down through staff and patients. This is the predominant type of organization in most prisons and training schools. Also this is the kind of organization that is suggested in most community drives to reduce delinquency. In effect, the more primitive, non-group behavior of the adolescents forces the group-oriented adult to participate in a dominance structure.

There are at least three general disadvantages to this structure. First, the psychological problem to be treated or changed is a far more complex situation than can be attacked with this method. The problem is related to the complexity of ego structure as described in the psychoanalytic literature, or to the better defined concept of ego involvement of Sherif, or to the concept of territory as described earlier in this chapter.

The second disadvantage to the dominance structure is that it ultimately depends on strength or power in some degree, and there is always a reciprocal relationship to territory. In other words, there is a spatial relationship to power—for example, a dean has authority only in his own school. In a hierarchy of dominance, subordinates are continuously in a process of carving out territorial fiefs that are unknown to the dominant one because the flow of communication in the dominance structure is downward. Since in a dominance structure there is also the tacit understanding that the order of dominance will shift when strength shifts, there is a constant testing of strength and maneuvering for power. This is the reason for some token sign of the dominance relationship in such an organization, e.g., pecking in hens, the salute in the military, the uniform in prison. In the adolescent psychiatric service, few professionals are willing to behave in the manner required. This presents a staff recruitment problem which is probably related to the dearth of adolescent services, to their mortality, and also to the fact that prisons, training schools, etc., are predominantly staffed by nonprofessionals. (Obviously, there are many other reasons, such as finances, numbers, etc.) In the nonprofessional staff of these institutions the dominance efforts of the lower nonprofessional staff can become very crude and might be termed sadistic in another frame of reference.

A third disadvantage to the dominance structure is that it is self-perpetuating from one generation to another. Studying the manifestations of a dominance organization, it has become evident that it is against the commonly held ideological principles of our society. There is considerable reluctance to deal intentionally and consciously with the idea. There is a sense of guilt in the violation of the ideological concepts of the rights and dignity of the individual. We deal with it by euphemistic ideas such as "authority" and "discipline," and characteristically cloak its manifestations with an aura of rationality. Although most everyone really knows better, there is an unspoken expectation that people in authority are the best prepared, wisest, etc., and so there is a constant process of disillusionment. Fortunately, power and wisdom do coincide frequently. Although it seems impossible to eradicate dominance as a principle of social organization, there does seem to be an assortment of styles in using it. If the individual rights of man are included under the term territory, then crude dominance can be modified by territory. Territoriality obviously favors the weak and to a limited extent reverses dominance. That is, the dominant individual, if in the clearly defined territory of a subordinate one, behaves in a way which respects the territorial rights of the weaker. This is observed in animals, and presents contrasting styles of authority for humans. The person in authority can act without consideration for the rights, needs, feelings, etc., of the subordinate one. This is characteristically called authoritarian. On the other hand, the dominant one can act with a constant awareness of the territorial rights of the subordinate ones. A quick familiar example would be the different lots of the teacher with the authoritarian principal and the teacher with a so-called democratic principal. The authoritarian administrator will never move his social organization from the dominance structure to a structure more closely resembling a group. The democratic administrator, on the other hand, can use his dominance relationship to bring his organization closer to being a true group.

At the moment, the strict concept of *group* seems to limit the membership number to approximately eight. This seems the maximum number that can directly interact around a task, maintaining individuality, and keeping intact the necessary communication network. When more than this number are part of the organization, then subgrouping necessarily occurs. A staff of twenty-five does not seem large, but it naturally breaks down into subdivisions. The inherent difficulties of the task magnify this subdividing, which is likely to follow territorial lines. The significant territories may be related to professional disciplines such as nursing, social work, child care aides, teachers, etc., or to the day shift, evening shift, and night shift. Or the territorial relationships between individuals may determine the subdivision.

These may be between staff; for instance, a psychiatrist might align himself with nurses against teachers. Or, more frequently than is appreciated, a staff person will have a territorial relationship with one or several youngsters; the most obvious example is the individual therapist with a patient. This form of organization can appear under a variety of circumstances. In this hospital setting, it occurs sometimes when the individuals are poorly trained in the roles required and seek security in their territorial identity. Or the impossible, poorly structured, inadequately understood task may force anxiety in the best trained of individuals. Territorial organization will appear if an authoritarian structure is not forthcoming.

This likewise results in a false simplification of task. For example, if the individual therapist deserts the group organization and enters the territorial relationship with a patient, they will concentrate on mutual needs to the exclusion of the over-all goal. Specifically, a therapist and patient may be satisfying their mutual dependencies rather than moving the patient toward independent performance out of the hospital.

Equally destructive are the professional discipline territories. A specific treatment goal may well have vastly different significance to different disciplines. Loose use of the word *role* frequently identifies the concept of role with a professional discipline, so that we speak of the "nursing role" or "social work role." There is a justification for this in that professional training is designed to indicate role skills. However, an individual is not truly in a functionally differentiated role unless he is operating within a group. The existence of a role skill in an individual and the common feeling shared by a number of individuals with this skill is more appropriately thought of as a territory. A large state hospital will have a number of such territories—medical service, social work, nursing, occupational therapy, maintenance, dietary, etc. These departments are necessitated by the size of the organization, the communication network, etc.; they are usually organized on a hospital-wide basis, and departmental goals set at some point remote from the locus of patient care.

Even in professional departments there is potential for conflict. Although this may look like a conflict of goals and values, it most frequently is related to a dominance struggle. A frequent example would be a hospital director of nursing attempting to maintain authoritarian control over the head nurse of a ward. This mixture of professional territoriality and a dominance pattern prevents the nurse from entering into a reciprocal role relationship with the other disciplines represented in the ward treatment team. On the other hand, if the hospital director of nurses operates in the democratic tradition of authority, she will allow the ward head nurse a high degree of territoriality, which can in turn be appropriately maneuvered into a group structure at the ward level.

The ultimate example of territoriality as a potential interference with ward functioning is the individual member of the staff who has idiosyncratic characteristics that prevent him from relating to other members of the staff. These may very well prevent him from accepting the authority structure of the unit or from identifying and accepting as his own the values of the staff group. Some examples of this are the teacher who is so thoroughly committed to a curriculum orientation that he cannot accept the child-problem orientation of the staff; an attendant who is concerned about satisfying his sexual needs by establishing a territorial relationship with a patient; or the status-driven staff member who can neither accept the hierarchy of his role nor the dominance structure of the staff. It is interesting that these individuals' behavior becomes indistinguishable from the patients'. In fact, if they remain for any period of time on the staff, they will frequently be designated as sick and referred for treatment or fired as psychopathic.

SUMMARY

This has been an effort to use group theory to look systematically at phenomena that would be impossible to study experimentally. Natural history accounts have described various parts of the picture, and participant observers have made a few studies to code some aspects of the informal social structure in adolescent treatment centers. This attempt differs in that the author has had a different vantage point in observing the phenomena and has had the opportunity to use the concepts operationally at the same time.

As a result of the latter, the concept of *group* was not found adequate to include all the behavioral phenomena that needed to be understood and controlled. Two additional concepts of territoriality and dominance were introduced and defined. These are far from new concepts. They have been thoroughly studied by the animal behaviorists and under different names are familiar to social scientists. Their significance is derived from Sherif's position:

> In the course of repeated interaction over a time span among individuals with common motives or problems, togetherness situations become group situations. The appearance of a group is marked by the formation of structure (organization) and a set of norms. As individuals become group members in this process, differential effects of the interaction process become more pronounced and more predictable in direction and degree.

Behavior that defies predictability and understanding is the crux of mental illness. The interaction of the adolescents under observation does not lead to a smooth, harmonious development of a group, but to tortured, straining, primitive way stations on the way from togetherness to groupness. These way stations are so frequent, last so long, and produce such different results that it seems wise to conceptualize them as different principles of organization, or as evolutionary stages in the development of groups. They are more easily observed in adolescent patients, but once identified appear ubiquitous. Explanatory value is found in administrative problems, conflictual social situations, intergroup frictions, and families. Such concepts may be a bridge between the individual problem of mental illness and the problems of social organization, or they may help clarify the kind of social structure required to deal with mental illness. Experience indicates that mental illness can be described in terms of non-organization, of lack of role skills, of lack of potential for groupness, of primitive forms of organization that are the way stations in all social individuals. Unfortunately, experience also indicates that mentally ill individuals can disrupt the organizational structure of their presumed normal brethren and elicit behavior of equally primitive nature.

REFERENCES

Carpenter, C. R., 1955. Territoriality: A review of concepts and problems. In Anne Roe and G. G. Simpson (eds.), *Behavior and Evolution.* (New Haven: Yale University Press.)

Krech, D., and R. S. Crutchfield, 1948. *Theory and Problems of Social Psychology.* (New York: McGraw-Hill.)

Lorenz, K. Z., 1959. The role of aggression in group formation. In Bertram Schaffner (ed.), *Group Processes.* (New York: Jonah Marz Jr. Foundation.)

Polsky, H. W., 1962. *Cottage Six: The social system of delinquent boys in residential treatment.* (New York: Russell Sage Foundation.)

Rafferty, F. T., 1961. Day treatment structure for adolescents. In Jules Masserman (ed.), *Current Psychiatric Therapies.* (New York: Grune & Stratton.)

———, 1962. Development of social structure in treatment institutions. *J. nerv. ment. Dis.,* 134, 263-267.

———, 1963. Gang formation in vitro. *J. nerv. ment. Dis.,* 137, 76-81.

Redl, F., and D. Wineman, 1951. *Children Who Hate.* (Glencoe, Ill.: Free Press.)

Scott, J. P., 1958. *Animal Behavior.* (Chicago: University of Chicago Press.)

Sherif, M., and Carolyn W. Sherif, 1956. *An Outline of Social Psychology.* (New York: Harper and Row.)

Simon, H. A., 1960. *Administrative Behavior.* (New York: Macmillan.)

PART IV

AGE-MATE
REFERENCE SETS WITHIN
DIFFERENTIATED
NEIGHBORHOODS

ELEVEN

URBAN NEIGHBORHOODS AND INDIVIDUAL BEHAVIOR

Wendell Bell

It is a matter of everyday observation that metropolitan areas are subdivided into different sections, each exhibiting certain distinctive features. There are manufacturing, warehouse, theater, financial, department store, used car lot, residential, and many other districts in most modern American cities. The residential areas themselves are further differentiated with respect to many additional characteristics. Some are inhabited predominantly by Negroes, Chinese, Japanese, Puerto Ricans, Italians, Germans, Poles, Swedes, Mexicans, or some other racial or nationality group. Some districts are set apart from others because Jews, Catholics, or the members of a particular Protestant denomination live there in relatively large numbers.

Some districts are characterized by old, dilapidated dwellings, or by large apartment houses, or by access to such desirable places as lake fronts, beaches, or river views, and still others by prominence of concrete, steel, asphalt, or general neglect. All urban areas have sections where the "rich people" live; others where the "poor people" live; and most urban subcommunities contain residents representing the many gradations in amount of wealth or income between these two extremes. Some neighborhood communities are marked by the presence of older persons, renters instead of home owners, more women than men, or certain occupations such as proprietors, professionals, managers, and officials. Others contain unskilled or semiskilled workers, or many unrelated individuals, or many persons living together in family units.

Recognizing this diversity in the social characters of urban subcommunities, Louis Wirth (1938) described the city as "a mosaic of social worlds" and emphasized that the different sections of the city can be thought of as separate worlds, with the transition between them often

I am indebted to the Center for Advanced Study in the Behavioral Sciences for a fellowship during 1963-64 which enabled me to prepare this review of research, bringing up to date an earlier review published under the title "Social Areas: Typology of Urban Neighborhoods" (Bell, 1959) with permission of the publisher.

very abrupt, reflecting their different populations, subcultures, ways of life, and social organizations.

The casual observer usually is aware of these neighborhood community differences; yet he may consider them more as a crazy quilt than as a neat, orderly, and systematic pattern. On a superficial level, he is often correct, since the various neighborhoods are of miscellaneous sizes and shapes. But various economists, geographers, sociologists, and other social scientists studying the city have located and traced various kinds of orderly patterns underlying the apparently unsystematic nature, growth, and change of neighborhoods. The study of human ecology, for example, has resulted in many generalizations concerning the spatial distribution of different kinds of people and of various functions and activities. Such works as those of Hawley (1950) and Quinn (1950) attest that the body of knowledge created with ecological concepts and techniques of analysis has been productive and fruitful. Generalizations concerning the orderly patterns of city growth and spatial structure include the concentric zone theory of Burgess (1929), Hoyt's sector theory (1939), and Harris and Ullman's multiple nuclei theory (1945). These generalizations are to be found in most recent textbooks in introductory sociology and urban sociology published in this country.

Recently, new methods for the systematic analysis of population differences between urban subcommunities have been proposed; and sufficient work has been done with the methods by enough different research workers that a sizable body of information is beginning to emerge. One of these methods, first presented by Shevky and Williams (1949) and later modified by Shevky and Bell (1955), will be discussed in some detail in this chapter along with some of the work of other persons within the Shevky framework. Occasional reference will be made to a similar method constructed by Tryon (1955). In general, these methods can be referred to as *social area analysis*, although the particular techniques by which neighborhoods are combined into social areas differ somewhat in each case.

The purposes of this chapter are to review the method of social area analysis and some of the research that has resulted from its use, and to evaluate the method in the light of recent work. In particular, the utility of the social area method for the design and analysis of urban subarea field studies will be explored: Specifically, does social area analysis of census tract statistics for a metropolitan area provide a useful frame in which to design and execute detailed investigations of the behavior of individuals and groups in different subcommunities? If so, what is the function of social area analysis for such studies?

Since a logical place to begin is with the basic data that the method utilizes, a discussion of the nature of census tract statistics precedes a description of the social area typology.

CENSUS TRACT STATISTICS

The basic unit of analysis used in the construction of social areas is the census tract.[1] Census tracts are relatively small geographical areas into which certain cities and often their adjacent areas have been subdivided. They are larger than blocks and usually contain between 3,000 and 6,000 persons. In 1950, a metropolitan area the size of Chicago was divided into approximately 1,000 of these small units; the San Francisco-Oakland area about 244; San Jose, California, as few as 59; and smaller areas into even fewer tracts. Data collected in connection with the regular decennial census of the United States are published in a form that allows study of population and housing characteristics of these tracts or subareas.

The census tract program is a relatively recent development. New York City and seven other cities having populations over 500,000 were divided into census tracts in 1910, and census data were tabulated by tracts within these cities for the first time. The purpose was to obtain detailed population data for sufficiently small areas within the city so that neighborhood communities could be studied. In 1920, tract data were again tabulated for the same eight cities, and in 1930 this number was increased to 18. By 1940 tract data were available for 60 urban places. By 1950 as many as 69 urban places in the United States and its territories had been divided into census tracts. By 1960, the program had expanded to include published reports for 180 tracted areas, three of which were in Puerto Rico (see U.S. Bureau of Census, 1958, 1960). Comparative studies of urban neighborhoods with a scope and adequacy never before possible can now be made.

Some of the information contained in the census tract bulletins represented a complete count of all the persons in the census tracts. Additional information was presented which was obtained from a 20 per cent sample of persons in the tracts. The information given for each census tract for 1950 is listed below:

Total population	Type of structure
Race	Condition and plumbing facilities
Sex	Year structure was built
Nativity	Number of all occupied dwelling
Married couples	units
Families or unrelated individuals	Number of persons in dwelling unit
Number of dwelling units	Number of households
Owner- or renter-occupied dwelling	Population per household
units	Population in households

[1] Other units of analysis can be and, to some extent, have been used, such as the county, the state, countries as a whole, etc. The chief use of the social area typology to date, however, has been in connection with the census tract; thus, for simplicity this discussion will deal only with research related to the use of census tracts.

Institutional population   Women in the labor force
Years of school completed   Persons per room
Residence in 1949   Type of heating fuel
Income in 1949   Refrigeration equipment
Age   Television
Marital status   Contract monthly rent
Employment status   Value of one-dwelling-unit structures
Major occupational group   Spanish surnames (for certain areas only)

The above list, of course, greatly underestimates the total number of useful measures contained in the tract bulletins, since many combinations and permutations are possible. For example, an investigator can use data on age and sex to compute a fertility ratio for a tract by taking the number of women from age 15 to age 44, dividing that sum into the number of children under age 5, and then multiplying by 1,000. Thus, the fertility ratios of tract populations can be compared. Many other such permutations of the above variables giving important information about a tract population can be made.

If one wishes to get a coherent and easily understandable picture of the character of a tract population, however, it is cumbersome and inefficient to deal separately with as many different variables (and their permutations) as are contained in the census bulletins. For example, if one tried to compare and contrast the 244 tracts in the San Francisco Bay area with respect to thirty or more variables simultaneously, each handled individually, the task would be exceedingly tedious and would result in complex patterns difficult to comprehend. Thus, some ordering or clustering of the variables should be made as a prior step in constructing a composite of a tract's social characteristics.

ORDERING OF CENSUS VARIABLES

Apart from the variables reflecting sheer size of the census tract, there appear to be three sets of general characteristics in the census tract bulletins: *socioeconomic, family,* and *ethnic* characteristics. There are, no doubt, other ways in which the census variables can be ordered. For example, there are variables which refer to housing and other variables which refer to population. But for the purposes of systematically analyzing the social features of urban neighborhood communities, the division of the variables into those which are socioeconomic or socioeconomic-related, those which indicate the presence or lack of families, and those which reflect the presence or absence of certain racial and nationality groups seemed most revealing to those of us engaged in the early work using the social area typology. Looking back over the census variables given above, one can easily group most of them into one of these three categories. This has been done below:

Socioeconomic Characteristics	Family Characteristics	Ethnic Characteristics
Condition and plumbing facilities	Sex	Race
Persons per room	Married couples	Nativity
Years of school completed	Families or unrelated individuals	Spanish surnames
Income in 1949	Owner- or renter-occupied dwelling units	
Employment status	Type of structure	
Major occupational group	Age	
Type of heating fuel	Marital status	
Refrigeration equipment	Women in the labor force	
Contract monthly rent	Lack of institutional population	
Value of one-dwelling-unit structures		

The census variables were first grouped this way in the development of social area analysis by Shevky and Williams (1949). The author verified the classification by using 1940 census data for the Los Angeles area and the San Francisco Bay area (Bell, 1955a). Tryon (1955), working independently, analyzed all the census variables for the San Francisco Bay area as of 1940 and reached practically the same classification. In addition, Walter C. Kaufman (1961) has found that this grouping of variables is, in general, valid for the San Francisco Bay and Chicago areas as of 1950 as well.

Some of the work of Van Arsdol, Camilleri, and Schmid (1957, 1958a) is important in this connection. They performed a factor analysis of selected variables from the 1950 census tract data for ten American cities—Akron, Ohio; Atlanta, Georgia; Birmingham, Alabama; Kansas City, Missouri; Louisville, Kentucky; Minneapolis, Minnesota; Portland, Oregon; Providence, Rhode Island; Rochester, New York; and Seattle, Washington. They concluded that this grouping of census variables is an adequate measure of socioeconomic, family, and ethnic characteristics in eight of these cities.

In general, the ordering of the census variables into three basic types has been strongly confirmed by much of the research designed to test it. But Van Arsdol, Camilleri, and Schmid's deviant cases, along with the recent research results of Anderson and Bean (1961), suggest that additional attention should be paid to the possibility of some alternative —perhaps more complicated—clustering of the basic census variables.

For example, Anderson and Bean conclude from a factorial analysis of 1950 census tract statistics for Toledo (Ohio) that two factors, rather than one, constitute a more adequate representation of the second set of variables listed above. They divide the variables into *housing characteristics* (which they are willing to call *urbanization* after Shevky's original label for this index) and *family characteristics*, which is consistent with the suggested re-interpretation of this same index, *familism*, made by the present writer (Shevky and Bell, 1955, p. 68). More will be said of this later.

INDEXES OF SOCIOECONOMIC STATUS, FAMILISM, AND ETHNICITY

All the census variables can be reduced to three more basic factors, although more different factors may prove necessary in the long run. Using these three basic factors, it is possible to construct a picture of the smaller social worlds into which an urban area is subdivided in terms of the socioeconomic, family, and ethnic characteristics of the tract populations. It is neither necessary nor efficient to include all the possible measures of the three factors in indexes for them. A few indicators of a factor are sufficient.

Of course, some census variables are better measures of their particular factor than others. Thus, certain census variables were selected, and their average value used as an index of the socioeconomic characteristics of a census tract. The index was named the *index of socioeconomic status*. Other variables were selected to be averaged as an indicator of the family characteristics of a tract population, and this was named the *index of familism*. Finally, the average of still other variables was made an indicator of the racial and nationality characteristics of a tract population and was named the *index of ethnicity*. The variables selected to measure the three factors were as follows:

Index of Socioeconomic Status	*Index of Familism*	*Index of Ethnicity*
Rent	Fertility ratio	Race
Education	Women not in	Nativity
Occupation	the labor force	Spanish surnames
	Single-family detached	(when available)
	dwellings	

The specific procedures for the computation of the indexes are given in the appendix to this chapter. There have been some changes in composition, and there may be more, as indicated above. For example, for technical reasons the measure of rent was dropped in computing the socioeconomic index after 1940. It suffices to say here that each census tract can be given three scores—for the indexes of socioeconomic status, familism, and ethnicity. These scores have been standardized to range from zero to 100 according to the extremes on each measure in the Los Angeles area as of 1940. Therefore, it is possible for tracts in other urban areas (or in Los Angeles in other years) to receive scores less than zero or somewhat greater than 100. Ideally, of course, the scores should be standardized to the range of all the census tracts in the entire United States—or even throughout the world, when small area statistics become available for the metropolitan areas in other countries—or to some extreme lower and upper limits which cannot in fact be quickly transcended by the data for any particular time and place.

In tracts with high scores on the index of socioeconomic status there are many persons with white-collar occupations, such as professionals, proprietors, managers, officials, salesmen, clerks; many persons have a higher education; and rents are high. In tracts with low scores, there are many persons with blue-collar occupations, such as craftsmen, foremen, operatives, and laborers; many persons have no more than a grade school education; and rents are low.

This index was originally labeled *social rank* by Shevky, and is so designated by some other researchers using the social area typology. Although I have been using the term *economic status*, for reasons which do not seem too important in hindsight, perhaps a good compromise would be *socioeconomic status* or *level*. No significant alteration in the conceptual interpretation was intended in any event. On the other hand, Anderson and Bean (1961, p. 123) argue that to call this dimension *social rank* (or *economic status* either, apparently) is inappropriate. They suggest that the underlying factor measured by the index be "classed a measure of the *prestige value* of the neighborhood." Only additional data, along with conceptual and theoretical analysis, can lead to an adequate resolution of their difference of opinion.

It is possible for tracts to vary in family characteristics regardless of their scores on the index of socioeconomic status. Tracts having high scores on the index of familism contain populations which have high fertility ratios (that is, many children under age 5 in relation to the number of women between the ages of 15 and 44); many women not in the labor force, but at home in the roles of housewives and mothers; and many single-family detached dwellings. Tracts with low fertility ratios, many women in the labor force, and many multiple dwellings achieve low scores on the index of familism.

Originally, Shevky called this index *urbanization* (high urbanization being equivalent in operational terms to low familism), but his designation contains conceptual elements inadequately measured by the items comprising the index. It is also true that additional marital and family characteristics probably should be added to the index if a better indicator of the *family life characteristics* of census tract populations is desired. Scott Greer (1956, 1960, 1962a, 1962b), Greer and Kube (1959), Greer and Orleans (1962), and Kaufman and Greer (1960), among others, have compromised, while creatively elaborating the concept and stressing the underlying agreement and similarity of the two designations as referring to differential life styles or choice patterns of urban residents. They prominently use *urbanism-familism*, which seems to be a good solution to this terminological problem at the present time. The factor analysis of

Anderson and Bean, mentioned above, which located two factors within the *urbanism-familism* index, as well as some recent work of the Sherifs (1964), should stimulate additional work on this question. The latter researchers have decided that low *urbanization*, rather than high *familism*, is a better term to describe the family characteristics of a sample of low socioeconomic, largely Spanish-speaking populations, since almost a quarter of the large families lacked a male breadwinner. These facts seemed congenial to the idea that these populations were low in their acculturation to an urban way of life, a notion better conveyed by *urbanization* than by *familism*. The low socioeconomic level of these tracts may modify the nature of the family life in them and explain the absence of male breadwinners, while the concentration of Spanish-speaking persons may explain the low level of acculturation. Nonetheless, one can agree that more experimentation with this and alternative indexes needs to be done.

One additional problem has arisen with the designation *index of family status*, which I have suggested before for the urbanism-familism dimension. Fortunately, it is merely a terminological and not a conceptual problem. The use of *status* in the label led some readers to believe that the referent was the economic status, the social rank, or the prestige of the families in the census tracts. Such is not the case. Thus, *familism* or *urbanism-familism* may be superior as labels on the simple grounds that they more clearly convey the meaning intended.

Tracts which contain many Negroes, persons of other non-white races, persons with Spanish surnames, and foreign-born whites from certain countries receive high scores; and tracts which contain mostly native-born whites receive low scores on the index of ethnicity. This index, of course, is negatively related to the index of socioeconomic status, since Negroes and many other American minority groups are most often located in urban neighborhoods of low socioeconomic status. However, it is possible to find some neighborhood communities in which generally subordinate minority groups have high socioeconomic status and to find others inhabited by native-born whites of low socioeconomic status. Moreover, socioeconomic status is not the same thing as race and nationality; that is, the social significance of these two types of variables is different even though they have often been confused. Consequently, in spite of the empirical relationship between the indexes of socioeconomic status and ethnicity, they should be kept conceptually distinct in any sociological analysis, including one of urban communities.

CONSTRUCTION OF THE SOCIAL AREA TYPOLOGY

Since the three indexes are to be utilized as *distinct* properties of urban subcommunities, they cannot be simply added together. Some method must be devised to use them simultaneously in the analysis. To do this, types or a typology must be constructed. The use of the concept of type here follows Lazarsfeld (1937) who said:

One is safe in saying that the concept of type is always used in referring to special compounds of attributes. In speaking of the Middle-western type of American, one may have in mind certain physical features, certain attitudes and habits, certain affiliations and talents attributed to the inhabitants of this region. In speaking of types of books or of types of governments, a special combination of attributes is thrown into relief.

The special "compound of attributes" used in social area analysis is that composed of economic, family, and ethnic characteristics. Instead of a "Middle-western type of American," "types of books," or "types of governments," the types are composed of urban neighborhoods. As shown in Figure 10, a social attribute space is constructed which is bounded by the indexes of socioeconomic status and familism. Census tract populations near to each other in the social area diagram would necessarily have similar configurations of scores on the two indexes. Such tracts are grouped together by the divisions which are made in the indexes, segmenting each into four parts.

The social space has been segmented by divisions passing through socioeconomic status scores of 25, 50, and 75, and through familism scores also of 25, 50, and 75. Thus, potentially, sixteen groupings of census tract populations are made, and these represent different social types of tract populations. These *types* are also called social areas.

Social areas so far, then, are composed of a tract or tracts with particular patterns of scores on the indexes of socioeconomic status and familism. They are called *social* in that the properties of neighborhood communities dealt with are social properties. The term *area* is employed because a geometric space frame is utilized. By similar reasoning the diagram shown in Figures 10 and 11 can be referred to as a "social space diagram."

A number and letter designation are given to each of the types as shown in Figure 10. Social area 1D, for example, contains tract populations with low socioeconomic status and low familism. Tract populations in social area 1A would have the same socioeconomic status as those contained in 1D, but the familism of tracts in 1A would be high instead of low. Likewise, social area 4D varies systematically from 1D, but in this case the familism (or conversely urbanism) of the two groups of census tracts is the same, while the socioeconomic status differs, social area 4D containing tract populations low on familism (or high on urbanism) but high on socioeconomic status. Thus, each type of social area delimits census tracts which have a particular configuration of scores with respect to

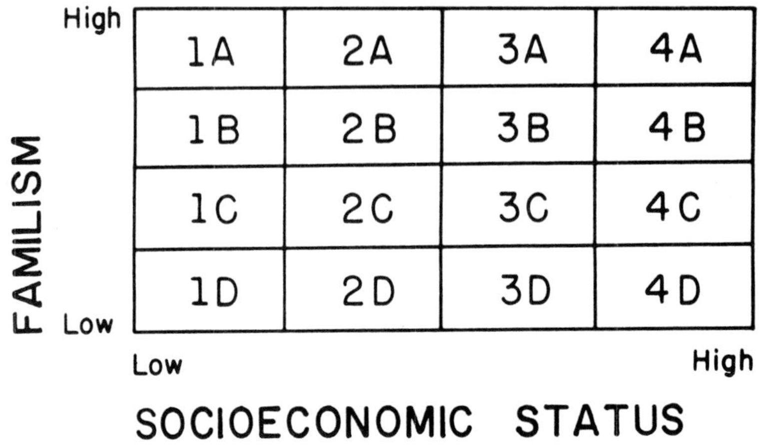

FIGURE 10. Social Area Key Based on Socioeconomic Status and Familism

economic and family characteristics (see Figure 10 for positions and designations of other social areas).

The third factor, ethnicity, adds to the typology so far constructed by distinguishing those census tracts which contain relatively many members of American racial and nationality minority groups. Tract populations having high indexes of ethnicity are given an "S" along with their social area designations as given in Figure 10. Tracts which have low indexes of ethnicity remain with only the designation as shown in Figure 10. Thus, there are thirty-two possible social areas or types of urban subcommunities: 1A, 1B . . . 4D and 1AS, 1BS . . . 4DS.[2]

Shevky called this index *segregation*, considering those tract populations which contained relatively more than average percentages of subordinate ethnic groups as segregated; and those which contained less than average as not segregated. This label created some confusion with another meaning of segregation used by Shevky as well as others (*e.g.,* Bell, 1954; Bell and Willis, 1957), namely the degree of residential segregation of a particular *group* summing across neighborhoods. Therefore, some of us began using the label *ethnic status* to refer to the racial and nationality composition of particular neighborhoods. This label, however, led to further lack of clarity, since *high* ethnic status designated tract populations with higher than average percentages of *subordinate* ethnic

---

[2] Tryon's method of constructing social areas differs somewhat from the Shevky method which is discussed here. However, the results are much the same; for instance, the social areas of the San Francisco Bay area as of 1940 and as established by the Tryon method are for all practical purposes the same as those achieved by the Shevky method (Eta = .82).

groups, groups generally having low rather than high status in the larger society. Thus, using *ethnic status* in this way flies in the face of common parlance by reversing general meaning. Again, this is simply a terminological problem, which several writers have solved by using the term *ethnicity* to refer to the ethnic composition of a census tract population, *high ethnicity* referring to a tract with relatively many members of subordinate ethnic groups.

SOME ILLUSTRATIONS OF THE USE OF SOCIAL AREA ANALYSIS

Since this chapter cannot discuss completely all the work using social area analysis, a selection of research executed in this framework will illustrate some of the uses and the nature of the findings. The census tracts of the San Francisco Bay area are plotted in the social space diagram in Figure 11 according to their scores on the three indexes for 1950. Included are 244 tracts with a total population of 1,509,678. The social position of each tract population can be seen in relation to all other tracts in the Bay area.

Notice on Figure 11 that there is little relationship between the indexes of familism and socioeconomic status, the correlation being —.13 between them. The correlation between the indexes of socioeconomic status and ethnicity is —.50, reflecting the fact that Negroes, Orientals, other non-whites, Mexican-Americans, and members of certain other foreign-born groups are most likely to live in neighborhoods characterized by low socioeconomic status. These groups are also increasingly likely to live in areas having little family life, as the socioeconomic levels of their neighborhoods increase.

Similar patterns of relationships have been noted for Los Angeles (Bell, 1955a) and Chicago (Kaufman, 1961). Whether the relations between the factors will vary markedly for other cities, or whether the stability of these patterns represents a generalization about the social structure of American cities at least for a particular time is a matter for future research. The Van Arsdol, Camilleri, and Schmid (1958a) research on the ten cities, which was mentioned earlier, suggests that this pattern of intercorrelations may be fairly general. But variation was reported for some of the cities, which may indicate the existence of differential patterns of social area distributions in cities of different regions, ages, economic bases, etc.

Orderly patterns have been found in the relationship between the sex ratio and the social areas in both Los Angeles and San Francisco. The sex ratio varies inversely with familism at low levels of socioeconomic status, and directly with familism at high levels of socioeconomic status; it varies inversely with socioeconomic status at all levels of familism. Thus, relatively more women than men are located in higher socioeco-

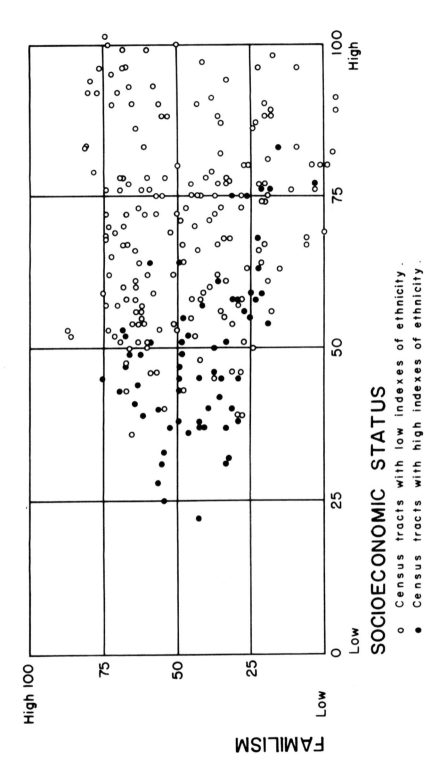

SOCIOECONOMIC STATUS

o   Census tracts with low indexes of ethnicity.

•   Census tracts with high indexes of ethnicity.

FIGURE 11. Distribution of the Census Tracts in the Social Areas of the San Francisco Bay Region, 1950

nomic status neighborhoods, with the greatest concentration of women in relation to men occurring in areas of expensive apartment houses, and the greatest concentration of men in relation to women occurring in the cheap rooming-house areas (Shevky and Williams, 1949; Bell, 1953; Shevky and Bell, 1955).

The age distributions of the persons in social areas also show systematic differences. In Los Angeles and San Francisco, the percentage of older persons increases with the socioeconomic status and decreases with the familism of a tract. The percentage of persons under fifteen years of age decreases with socioeconomic status and increases with familism. For example, social area 4D contains the largest percentage of older and the smallest percentage of younger persons. Although the pattern is less clear, the social area distribution of the middle-aged group tends to follow that of the older group.

STUDIES OF THE NATURE AND PATTERN OF SUBCOMMUNITIES

Once the census tracts of a metropolitan area have been given scores according to their socioeconomic, family, and ethnic characteristics, it becomes possible to execute systematically a variety of investigations into the nature of different urban subcommunities within the social area framework. For example, an examination of neighborhood place names used by the residents of a city allows a study of the relationship between subjective evaluations of urban neighborhoods and the social characteristics of the neighborhoods as determined by an analysis of census variables. Some named places in San Francisco are given below with their scores on the three indexes for 1950 (Shevky and Bell, 1955, pp. 61-63).

Identifying Place Name	Index of Socioeconomic Status	Index of Familism	Index of Ethnicity	Social Area
Nob Hill (A-12)	91	− 4	9	4D
Chinatown (A-15)	46	37	92	2CS
Sea Cliff (E-1)	93	58	10	4B
Potrero (L-1)	38	52	29	2BS
Diamond Heights (N-13)	52	71	11	3B

Studies could be designed to determine subjective evaluations of the social images of these named places. These evaluations could then be analyzed with respect to both the social characteristics of the named places and the social characteristics of the persons doing the evaluating.

Land use and topography, as might be expected, are related to social areas. Generally, in the San Francisco Bay area, neighborhoods of low socioeconomic status are located adjacent to the industrially occupied, low elevation areas of the inner Bay, while neighborhoods of high socioeconomic status are usually in areas of high elevation, farther from industrially occupied land. Neighborhoods of low familism are near commercial areas, especially near the downtown business district, while neighborhoods of high familism are located farther from the downtown commercial area, nearer to parks, lakes, or ocean beaches. The census tracts composing a social area, however, are not necessarily contiguous and continuous.

Additional studies of the spatial aspects of social area analysis have been made by Anderson and Egeland (1961) for four American cities between 200,000 and 500,000 population in 1950: Akron and Dayton, Ohio, Indianapolis, Indiana, and Syracuse, New York; by McElrath (1962) for Rome (Italy) using 1951 census data; and by McElrath and Barkey (no date) for Chicago in 1960.[3] These studies are of particular significance because they relate social areas to the well-known concentric zonal theory of Burgess and the sector theory of Hoyt.

Consistently, in every city, the familism-urbanism dimension is zonally distributed; it is also distributed sectorially in Rome and Chicago, but not in the four cities studied by Anderson and Egeland. Socioeconomic status (or social rank) is distributed differentially by zones in Chicago, Indianapolis, and Rome, but not in the three smallest U.S. cities studied. *However, in Chicago the high socioeconomic neighborhoods were located near the periphery of the metropolitan area, while in Rome they were located in the central districts.* Socioeconomic levels of neighborhood populations were clearly sectorial in all the cities except Chicago. Ethnicity was included in the analysis only in Chicago. There it was not distributed zonally, although there was a tendency for it to be distributed sectorially.

STUDIES OF PREVALENT ATTITUDES AND ACTIONS IN DIFFERENT AREAS

The social area typology has now been used in numerous studies as an analytic frame for the study of individual beliefs, attitudes, and behaviors. A review of a few of these studies will serve to further illustrate the analytic utility of the method.

Bell, Boat, and Force (1954) examined the Shevky social space diagram (see Figure 11) and selected four census tracts in San Francisco which had low scores on the index of ethnicity, but widely different scores in the indexes of socioeconomic status and familism. In these tracts, an investigation was made of the social isolation and participation of urbanites. The social space positions of the four subpopulations are shown in Figure 12 along with their census tract designations and their identifying neighborhood community names. From Figure 12 it can be noted that Mission, a low-rent rooming-house area, is characterized by low socioeconomic status and low familism. Pacific Heights, a high-rent

---

[3] Other work outside the United States includes Gagnon's study of Quebec (1960) and McElrath's study of Accra, Ghana (no date). Also, see Brody (1962) for a study of spatial aspects of social areas in ten additional American cities.

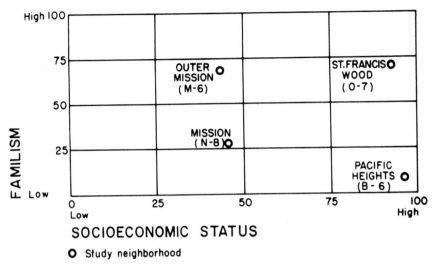

FIGURE 12. The Four San Francisco Study Tracts Located in the Social Space Diagram, 1950

apartment-house area, is high on socioeconomic status, but low on familism. Outer Mission, characterized by small single-family detached houses and residents of modest means, is low on socioeconomic status and high on familism. St. Francis Wood, an area of large single-family detached houses with residents who are fairly well off financially, is high in both economic and family characteristics.

After the selection of the study tracts, as described above, probability samples were drawn from a complete list of all the dwelling units within each tract. A total of 701 interviews was obtained with a response rate of more than 85 per cent, one randomly selected male over age 21 in each sample dwelling being interviewed.

The results of this study show different patterns of social participation in the different neighborhoods. Men living in high socioeconomic status neighborhoods (Pacific Heights and St. Francis Wood), when compared to those living in low socioeconomic status neighborhoods (Mission and Outer Mission), belong to a greater number of formal associations, attend formal association meetings more frequently, and are more likely to hold offices in formal associations (Bell and Force, 1956a). A greater percentage of their memberships are in general-interest types of associations (Bell and Force, 1956b); they interact with their co-workers away from work more frequently, have more informal contacts with friends who are not neighbors or relatives, rely more on their co-workers, are less likely to be calculating in their relationships with their neighbors (Bell and Boat, 1957), and are much more likely to achieve low anomia scores on the Srole Scale (Bell, 1957). Jews and, to a lesser extent, Protestants, are more likely to live in the areas of high socioeconomic status than in neighborhoods of low socioeconomic status. The reverse is true of Catholics (Bell and Force, 1957).

Men who live in high familism neighborhoods (St. Francis Wood and Outer Mission), when compared with those in neighborhoods low on familism (Pacific Heights and Mission), are somewhat less socially isolated from informal group participation, have more social contacts with neighbors and kin, and are more likely to have met their close personal friends in their neighborhoods (Bell and Boat, 1957). Of the men in the two high socioeconomic status neighborhoods, those in Pacific Heights belong to fewer formal associations, attend meetings less often, are less likely to hold office, and are more likely to belong to special in-dividual-interest types of formal associations than the men living in St. Francis Wood. Catholics are relatively more numerous in neighborhoods high in familism than they are in neighborhoods low in familism. "In-dependents," "agnostics," and "atheists" are most likely to live in areas low in familism.

It should be noted that the method and analysis in these studies were such that we can conclude that social participation or isolation variables are related to residency in these areas. Some work in social area analysis has used "ecological correlations," which contain pitfalls of in-correct interpretation made well known by Robinson (1950) in a now classic article. Such studies must be interpreted accordingly. The em-phasis here is upon the research value of social areas as "independent variables" for studying attitudes and life styles of particular subsets of the populations.

Using the social areas of Los Angeles, Scott Greer (1956; Greer and Kube, 1955, 1959) also selected four local areas in which to conduct a study of social participation in urban neighborhoods. His strategy, how-ever was to hold both economic and ethnic characteristics constant in his study tracts and to vary family characteristics widely. For 1950, Temple City had a score of 74 on the index of familism, Eagle Rock, 64, Silver Lake, 45, and Central Hollywood, 20. Each of these subcommunities had scores of about 70 on the index of socioeconomic status and scores of 6 or less on the index of ethnicity. From his interviews with persons in these four neighborhood communities, Greer concludes that the greater the amount of family life in a neighborhood, the more "neighboring," the more persons who have friends in their neighborhood, the more likely a person is to attend a cultural event in his neighborhood, the larger the percentage of persons who belong to formal organizations drawing mem-bers from the local area, the more husbands who belong to organizations meeting in the local area, and the more persons who could name at least one local leader.

Greer also found that persons living in high familism neighborhoods, as compared with residents of neighborhoods low on familism, are more likely to think of their local area as a "little community," like a "small town," where "people are friendly and neighborly." They are less likely to mention the convenience of their location in terms of its nearness to "downtown and everything." They are less likely to speak of their neighbors as "nice people who leave you alone and mind their own business"; but they are more committed to remaining in their neighborhoods, and more apt to have their friends (other than friends who are neighbors) in other high familism tracts.

McElrath (1955) and Williamson (1953, 1954) have used social area analysis in the design and analysis of sample surveys. Using the typology, they selected samples within neighborhoods in the Los Angeles metropolitan area. They reported, respectively, that the social areas were predictive of the prestige and esteem ratings for individuals and the degree of their marital adjustment (see also Sussman, 1959). Curtis (1957) has used the method as a sampling device in his study of the employability of aging workers in Buffalo, New York.

There are many other uses to which social area analysis has been put. Studying 1,107 petitioners for change of name in Los Angeles County, Broom, Beem, and Harris (1955) find that name changers were more likely than the general population to live in areas rated high in socioeconomic status, low in familism, and low in ethnicity. This suggests that name changers may be upwardly mobile persons, who have broken away from family ties and have been, or are being, assimilated into the larger society, and are moving away from membership in and identification with some particular ethnic group.

In another study Broom and Shevky (1949) demonstrated the utility of the typological framework for the differentiation of an ethnic group. They found Jewish neighborhoods in Los Angeles in the lower ranges of familism and in the full range of socioeconomic status. Tracts lacking Russian-born persons (which indicator was used for one segment of the Jewish population) tended to fall in the high ranges of familism, with a noticeable cluster at the lowest levels of socioeconomic status. Taking the members of four Jewish fraternities on the Los Angeles campus of the University of California, they found that the two rated by campus consensus as having high prestige had members from tract locations with significantly higher socioeconomic status than members of the two lower-prestige fraternities.

Studies of the incidence of suicide and juvenile delinquency have been made by Wendling (1954) and Polk (1958). Polk (1957, 1957-58), for example, found juvenile delinquency rates highest in those areas of San Diego in which minority group members live, and lowest in areas inhabited by native whites. Smaller correlations are reported for the other two indexes, but juvenile delinquency was negatively related to socioeconomic status and familism. The highest rates of juvenile delinquency occurred in neighborhoods with high indexes of ethnicity, with low levels of income, occupation, and education, and with little family life. The only significant correlation between suicide and any of the three indexes in Polk's San Diego study is a negative correlation between familism and suicide.

In his study of the social areas of Portland in 1960, Polk empirically demonstrates the need for a typological approach in relating delinquency rates to urban neighborhoods. He notes among other things that delinquency rates increase with socioeconomic status of the neighborhood at the lowest level of familism, but decrease with socioeconomic status generally.

The typology has been used to facilitate adequate social welfare planning for local areas in the San Francisco Bay area (Bange, *et al.*, 1953). The hypothesis was that each of the social areas had certain distinctive social welfare problems related to their differences in economic, family, and ethnic characteristics. This work does a great deal in suggesting one of the many possible practical applications of the social area typology.

Robert L. Wilson (1958) has used the social area typology for a comparative study of Episcopal, Methodist, Presbyterian, and United Lutheran churches in selected cities throughout the United States. He indicates that generalizations can be made regarding the relation of churches to social areas. Curtis, Avesing, and Klosek (1957) and Sullivan (1961) have related social areas to Catholic parishes.

Tryon and his associates have related social areas to additional variables such as political preference, voting participation, psychiatric hospitalization, and the probability of an individual's attending a university. There is insufficient space to elaborate with a detailed consideration of these findings. However, Tryon's findings and interpretations on the stability of social areas deserve further comment. Tryon (1955, p. 31) argued that:

It is difficult to believe that a social area, including a number of tracts of people having the same configuration of demographic and correlated psychosocial ways, would change much in a decade, or perhaps many decades. A change would be gradual. Individual persons may be born into the area, move out or die, but it should retain its subcultural homogeneity with considerable constancy, short of socially catastrophic events. Even those areas that undergo rapid growth through construction of new homes are likely to incorporate new groups of persons homogeneous with those already there.

Tryon (1955, p. 32) also concludes from his analysis of the homogeneity of his 1940 San Francisco social areas with respect to 1950 median rent that ". . . little change in homogeneity of the tracts composing the various areas has occurred in 10 years." He also reports a comparison between the 1940 vote for Roosevelt and the 1947 vote for the Democratic candidate for Congress, Havenner, a man identified with the Roosevelt-Truman program. The census tracts show practically the same rank order for Roosevelt as for Havenner, the correlation coefficient being .94.

Other evidence that social areas remain relatively constant is found in McElrath's Los Angeles study (1955). He reports that thirteen years after the collection of the data on which the social area scores were based, he achieved the anticipated results in his sample survey with respect to differences in economic, family, and ethnic characteristics in his study areas.

This is not to say that tracts never change their social area positions, but rather that most of them, short of catastrophe, can be expected to maintain consistent social patterns for relatively long periods of time. Still, the social area approach is most useful for analysis of current conditions when census data are up to date, close to census years. There is a need for techniques to keep social area analysis current in view of the high rates of change in certain parts of most American cities.

Tryon's comments are not to be construed to mean that the census tract populations need be homogeneous for the method to be valid. It is not inconsistent with the typology to find some urban neighborhoods that are typically characterized by heterogeneity in certain variables. Census tracts classified together in a social area, however, should have *about the same degree of heterogeneity* with respect to *the same set of variables*.

STUDIES OF SOCIAL ORGANIZATION IN DIFFERENT AREAS

Scott Greer and his associates (Greer, 1960, 1962a, 1962b; Kaufman and Greer, 1960; Greer and Orleans, 1962), in a 1957 study of the St. Louis metropolitan area, raise some serious doubts about the pessimistic view of the modern urban world which sees no structured force interposed between the massive power of large-scale organizations and the isolated (and therefore vulnerable) individual. (See Bollens, 1961, for a comprehensive report on the St. Louis survey.) In so doing, they both demonstrate the analytic utility of the social area typology and contribute to increasing confidence in the typology by showing its essential isomorphism with the realities of urban life. The city is not a single way of life, but many ways of life. The different ways are, for the most part, patterned and systematically variable. Greer and Orleans (1962, p. 645) wrote:

The theory of the mass society postulates an administrative state, a massified citizenry, and no mediating organizations between. We have discovered, in metropolitan St. Louis, that a widespread network of parapolitical organizations has consequences for the involvement and the competence of the citizenry with respect to local government.

In the St. Louis study, the strength of the parapolitical structure, the direction of the vote in presidential and local elections, a typology of local social participators, the amount of an individual's political participation, and the degree of individual political competence vary widely from one type of social area to another. In the discussion of their findings, Greer *et al.* make important elaborations of the theoretical bases of the social area types in terms of the *differential opportunity structures* they offer.

STUDIES OF AREAS AS VARIABLES IN REFERENCE GROUPS OF RESIDENTS

There is yet another way in which social area analysis can be utilized in connection with urban subcommunity field studies. This is in the analysis of the combined or independent effect of personal and unit characteristics on variables dependent on them. Lazarsfeld and Barton (1951) have discussed the difference between personal characteristics and unit characteristics:

Personal data characterize individuals. . . . Unit data characterize some aggregation of people. . . . Of course, people can be aggregated in many different ways, some of which imply social interaction and others only categorization by the observer. A "unit" in our sense will be any aggregation—an Army company, a neighborhood, an occupational category, a political party.

In the San Francisco study two subcommunities with high socioeconomic status and two with low were selected as study areas. In general, the men living in the high socioeconomic status neighborhoods had, as expected, higher educational levels than those in the low socioeconomic status neighborhoods; the median educational level for Pacific Heights and St. Francis Wood combined being "some college or more," and for men in Mission and Outer Mission being in the "some high school or less" category. This is a *neighborhood* or, as defined above, a *unit* characteristic, and can be assigned to all the men living in a particular neighborhood community as an attribute of their residence area. However, there are men living in Pacific Heights and St. Francis Wood who can be classified on the basis of their own educational level (a *personal* characteristic) as having only a grade school education or less (10.9 per cent so report). Likewise, some men in Mission and Outer Mission (9.6 per cent) report having some college or more. This raises an interesting question: Does the educational level of the neighborhood in which a person lives affect his attitudes and behavior, even when his individual educational level is controlled? The answer seems to be "yes" in many of the cases so far tested!

Table 7, for example, shows the percentage of men who attend formal association meetings frequently according to both the average educational level of the neighborhood and the respondent's own education. Comparing the percentages *within each neighborhood*, the general tendency is for the more frequent attenders to have completed more years of schooling. However, of particular interest here is the comparison of amount of formal association participation *between* neighborhoods for individuals with comparable personal education. In each of the individual education categories, men living in the neighborhoods with higher educational levels are more likely to be frequent attenders than the men in neighborhoods of lower educational levels. Considering that similar differences are found when personal measures of occupation and income are taken into account, it is suggested that the socioeconomic characteristics of a neighborhood population *as a unit* may be important indicators of the economic *reference group* of those living in the neighborhood; and that this reference group provides a set of expectations for the associational behavior of the residents.

TABLE 7

Percentage of Men Who Attend Formal Association Meetings Frequently by Neighborhood and Individual Educational Levels*

	Neighborhood Education	
Individual Education	*Low* (*Mission and Outer Mission*) (*percentage*)	*High* (*Pacific Heights and St. Francis Wood*) (*percentage*)
Some college or more	27.3 (33)†	46.4 (181)
Completed high school only	14.5 (83)	28.3 (92)
Some high school	17.3 (81)	30.4 (46)
Grade school or less	7.6 (144)	23.1 (39)

* Men were classified as "frequent attenders" if they attended meetings 37 or more times per year.
† The total number of cases on which the percentage is based is given in parentheses in each case.
Source: Adapted from Bell and Force (1956a, p. 31).

More recently, the Sherifs (1964), in a multi-faceted approach to the study of adolescent behavior in selected cities in the Southwest, have linked the study of behavior in small groups with the sociocultural settings in which such groups actually function. Oversimplifying, one can summarize their first report as including three major steps:

1. The selection of particular urban neighborhoods as study areas using social area analysis.

2. The assessment of the values and goals prevailing among representative adolescents in the study areas.

3. The intensive field observation of attitudes and behaviors of adolescents belonging to groups of their own choosing—that is, to "naturally-formed" groups whose members do not realize they are being studied—within the study areas.

The Sherifs' work is noteworthy in several ways—not the least of which is their determination to study *real* groups as they *actually* form and function. Of particular significance here is their methodological strategy of simultaneous, multi-level analysis in their focus on the *individual behavior–small group–neighborhood* (*i.e.,* setting) relationship. To them, the social areas are the physical, demographic, and normative settings within which the interaction process within the small groups takes place. It is clear from their major findings regarding the perceptions, social values, and goals of adolescents in different social areas that the social areas are real, not only in the sheer perceptual sense of being part of the maps of social reality carried about in individuals' heads, but also in the sense of providing individuals with significant reference groups for gauging their own behavior as well as the behavior of others. Furthermore, the sociological reality of the social areas as differential opportunity structures (cf. Greer and Orleans, 1962) is elaborated and made concrete in the detailed case histories of the lives of particular adolescents.

SUMMARY AND CONCLUSIONS

In this chapter on the nature of social area analysis and some of its uses, it has not been possible to discuss all the studies that have used this method of analysis. Nor has it been possible to discuss the underlying theory, methodological problems, and differing evaluations of its contribution to urban studies.[4]

Some of the procedural difficulties in a comparative study of American cities have been solved simply by the tracting of cities for the 1960 census. But there remain other difficulties stemming from the nature of census data, and still others from the specific techniques employed in the method. Nonetheless, as presently constructed, the typology has proved useful as an approach to the systematic study of the smaller social worlds which a city's neighborhood communities comprise.

In sum, the various uses to which social area analysis has been put are as follows:

1. *The delineation of subareas.* Through the application of these methods to data available for American cities, it is possible to delineate systematically urban neighborhood communities having different social characteristics. Such a delineation, with the precision with which it can be accomplished, has descriptive value to the social scientist and city planner alike.

---

[4] The interested reader can find these topics discussed in the following: Bell (1955b), Bell and Greer (1962), Bell and Moskos (1964), Beshers (1959, 1960), Buechley (1956), Carpenter (1955), Duncan (1955a, 1955b, 1956), Farber and Osoinach (1959), Hawley and Duncan (1957), Schnore (1962), Tiebout (1958), Udry (1964) and Van Arsdol, Camilleri, and Schmid (1958b, 1961, 1962).

2. *Comparative studies at one point in time.* Comparative studies of the social areas of different cities at one point in time can be made. The social areas of Los Angeles can be compared with the social areas of New York, Chicago, Philadelphia, San Francisco, Dallas, St. Louis, Miami, or other urban areas. Social area distribution of the neighborhoods in different cities can be compared to determine patterns differentiated by the regions in which the cities are located, the sizes of the cities, their chief economic functions, their relative ages, their topographies, their ethnic compositions, and their transportation bases.

3. *Comparative studies at two points in time.* Despite the relative stability of many social areas, some neighborhood communities within a given urban area are undergoing change. New neighborhoods appear, they grow and develop, they become old, and sometimes they change with respect to the condition of the buildings, the type of building structures, and the kinds of residents. Other neighborhood communities may maintain the same social character for generations, like Beacon Hill in Boston (Firey, 1945). The application of the social area typology can result in a systematic description and analysis of social changes in a neighborhood.

4. *A framework for the execution of other types of research.* In addition to the above uses, the social area method can also be utilized as a framework for analyzing the attitudes and behavior of individuals. As indicated by the research cited in this chapter, neighborhood populations differ not only in demographic features, but also in values and social structure, in life styles and differential opportunities. And variations *between* neighborhoods have important implications for variations in individual attitudes and behavior. Even from present formulations in sociological theory, it is possible to hypothesize many relationships between neighborhood differences and the attitudes and behavior of individual residents, ranging from suicide, voting behavior, religious preference, mental disorder, personal morale, and type of crimes, to such things as frequency and nature of participation in formal organizations, amount of close contact with neighbors, local community identification, extent of kinship ties, child-rearing practices, and patterns of courtship.

As a tool for urban subarea field studies, the typology serves a number of functions:

a. The typology can be used in the selection of neighborhoods for intensive study. In the examples given, census tracts were selected for particular economic, family, and ethnic characteristics. As an aid to sampling, the typology allows the research worker to select urban subcommunities for intensive study on the basis of informed judgment concerning the social positions of the subcommunities in the larger urban area.

b. The typology provides an integrative frame for urban subcom-

munity field studies by codifying a large mass of ordered data. In the
Bell and Greer studies, for example, relationships are specified between
particular census tracts and all other tracts in the same city with respect
to socioeconomic status, familism, and ethnicity. In addition, the analysis
of social participation and isolation between neighborhoods becomes possible in terms of variations in, or specific patterns of, economic, family,
and ethnic characteristics of the study neighborhoods.

c. The typology permits the investigation of the combined or independent effect of personal and unit characteristics on dependent variables.
The characteristics of a neighborhood may be related to the behavior and
the attitudes of individuals. In one example given, men living in high
socioeconomic status neighborhoods were more frequent attenders of
formal association meetings than men in low socioeconomic status neighborhoods, even though their personal socioeconomic characteristics were
held constant. It was suggested that the socioeconomic character of a
neighborhood population as a unit may be an important indicator of the
socioeconomic group with which those living in the neighborhood identify
themselves, and this may provide a set of expectations for the associational behavior of the residents. In another example, social areas were
shown to constitute reference groups for adolescents in a multi-level
analysis.

The relationship between neighborhood characteristics and individual behaviors and attitudes is clearly a promising subject for additional
research.

APPENDIX

COMPUTATION OF THE INDEXES OF SOCIOECONOMIC
STATUS, FAMILISM, AND ETHNICITY[5]

The procedures for the computation of the three indexes are given
in this section. The ratios for each variable are computed directly from
census tract statistics, and the standard scores for the variables from the
formulas given. All the variables composing the indexes of socioeconomic
status and familism have been standardized to their respective ranges
in Los Angeles as of 1940. A single scale is thus established for the
direct comparison of census tract scores on the respective indexes for
different cities at the same time or the same city at different times. The
range, lower limit, and conversion factor are given for each variable for
Los Angeles, 1940. The index of ethnicity, of course, is comparable from
place to place and time to time since it is a simple percentage.

A. The formula for standardization:

$$s = x(r - o)$$

[5] For manual computation, a table of standard scores is now available (see
Avesing, 1960). An IBM 709 computer program is available for machine computation (see Center for Metropolitan Studies, 1963).

where

> s = standardized score for a particular variable
> o = lower limit of the census tract ratio for a particular variable
> r = census tract ratio for a particular variable
> $$x = \frac{100}{\text{range of the ratio for a particular variable}}$$

B. For those variables (occupation, education, and women in the labor force) which have an inverse relation to the basic indexes for which they are computed, the formula is adjusted to read as follows:

$$s = 100 - [x(r - o)]$$

C. Index of Socioeconomic Status
   1. Compute the following ratios:
      a. Occupation ratio: the total number of craftsmen, operatives, and laborers per 1,000 employed persons.
      b. Education ratio: the number of persons who have completed no more than grade school per 1,000 persons 25 years old and over.
   2. Compute occupation and education standard scores using the formula given in B above and the conversion factors (x) given in F below.
   3. Compute a simple average of the occupation and education standard scores. The average is the Index of Socioeconomic Status for a census tract.

D. Index of Familism
   1. Compute the following ratios:
      a. Fertility ratio: the number of children under 5 years per 1,000 females age 15 through 44.
      b. Women in the labor force ratio: the number of females in the labor force per 1,000 females 14 years old and over.
      c. Single-family detached dwelling units ratio: the number of single-family dwelling units per 1,000 dwelling units of all types.
   2. Compute the fertility and single-family dwelling unit standard scores from the formula given in A above and the conversion factors (x) given in F below.
   3. Compute the women in the labor force standard score using formula given in B above and conversion factor (x) given in F below.
   4. Compute a simple average of the standard scores for fertility, women in the labor force, and single-family dwelling units. The average is the Index of Familism for a census tract.

E. Index of Ethnicity (categories for 1950 only; see Shevky and Bell, 1955)
   1. Add together the number of persons designated Negro; Other Races; and foreign-born white from Poland, Czechoslovakia, Hungary, Yugoslavia, U.S.S.R., Lithuania, Finland, Rumania, Greece, Italy, Other Europe, Asia, French Canada, Mexico, and Other America.

(Note: In this enumeration, include foreign-born white from Other
Europe *only* if the category contains mostly foreign-born white
from southern and eastern Europe. For urban areas in Arizona,
California, Colorado, New Mexico, and Texas, the number of white
persons with Spanish surnames can be used instead of the number
of foreign-born white from Mexico and Other America. A special
tabulation may have to be requested to obtain Spanish surname
data for each census tract. If "white persons with Spanish surnames"
is used, the figures given for *native whites* should be adjusted by
subtracting the number of *native whites with Spanish surnames*
from the total number of native whites in each tract.)

2. Divide the above sum by the total population in each tract.

3. Multiply the above quotient by 100 to obtain the Index of Ethnicity
for each census tract. Separate the census tracts into two groups on
the basis of their scores on the index of ethnicity. Select as the
cutting point the per cent of the total population of the *urban area*
represented by the *combined* racial and nationality groups listed.
Those tracts with more than the average proportion of the combined
racial and nationality groups are designated as being "high" in
ethnicity; those tracts with less than the average proportion of the
combined racial and nationality groups are designated as having
"low" ethnicity.

F. The range, the lower limit of the range, and the conversion factor (x)
for each of the ratios for the Los Angeles area, 1940, are as follows:

Ratio	Range	Lower Limit (o)	Conversion Factor (x)
Occupation	748	0	.1336898
Education	770	130	.1298701
Fertility	602	9	.1661130
Women in the labor force	458	86	.2183406
Single-family dwelling units	994	6	.1006441

REFERENCES

Anderson, T. R., and L. L. Bean, 1961. The Shevky-Bell social areas: con-
firmation of results and a reinterpretation. *Social Forces,* 40, 119-124.

Anderson, T. R., and J. A. Egeland, 1961. Spatial aspects of social area analysis.
Amer. sociol. Rev., 26, 392-398.

Avesing, F., 1960. *Table of Standard Scores for Social Area Analysis.* (New
York: Le Play Research, Inc.)

Bange, E., *et al.,* 1955. A Study of Selected Population Changes and Characteristics with Special Reference to Implications for Social Welfare. A group
research project submitted in partial fulfillment of requirements for the
Master of Social Welfare Degree. (Berkeley: University of California.)
(Mimeographed.)

Bell, W., 1953. The social areas of the San Francisco Bay Region. *Amer. soc. Rev.*, 18, 39-47.

————, 1954. A probability model for the measurement of ecological segregation. *Social Forces*, 32, 357-364.

————, 1955a. Economic, family, and ethnic status: An empirical test. *Amer. sociol. Rev.*, 20, 45-52.

————, 1955b. Comment on Duncan's review of "Social Area Analysis." *Amer. J. Sociol.*, 61, 260-261.

————, 1957. Anomie, social isolation, and the class structure. *Sociometry*, 20, 105-116.

————, 1958. The utility of the Shevky typology for the design of urban subarea field studies. *J. soc. Psychol.*, 47, 71-83.

————, 1959. Social areas: typology of urban neighborhoods. In M. Sussman (ed.), *Community Structure and Analysis* (New York: Crowell), 61-92.

Bell, W., in collaboration with M. D. Boat and M. T. Force, 1954. *People of the City.* (Mimeographed, Stanford University.)

Bell, W., and M. D. Boat, 1957. Urban neighborhoods and informal social relations. *Amer. J. Sociol.*, 62, 391-398.

Bell, W., and M. T. Force, 1956a. Urban neighborhood types and participation in formal associations. *Amer. sociol. Rev.*, 21, 25-34.

————, 1956b. Social structure and participation in different types of formal associations. *Social Forces*, 34, 345-350.

————, 1957. Religious preference, familism and the class structure. *Midwest Sociologist*, 19, 79-86.

Bell, W., and S. Greer, 1962. Social area analysis and its critics. *Pacific sociol. Rev.*, 5, 3-9.

Bell, W., and C. C. Moskos, Jr., 1964. A comment on Udry's "increasing scale and spatial differentiation." *Social Forces*, 42, 414-417.

Bell, W., and E. M. Willis, 1957. The segregation of Negroes in American cities. *Social and econ. Studies*, 6, 59-75.

Beshers, J. M., 1959. The construction of "social area" indices: an evaluation of procedures. Social Statistics Section, American Statistical Association, 65-70.

————, 1960. Statistical inferences from small area data. *Social Forces*, 38, 341-348.

Brody, S. A., 1962. Urban characteristics of centralization. *Sociol. and soc. Research*, 46, 326-331.

Broom, L., H. P. Beem, and V. Harris, 1955. *Amer. sociol. Rev.*, 20, 33-39.

Broom, L., and E. Shevky, 1949. The differentiation of an ethnic group. *Amer. sociol. Rev.*, 14, 476-481.

Bollens, J. C. (ed.), 1961. *Exploring the Metropolitan Community.* (Berkeley and Los Angeles: University of California Press.)

Buechley, R. W., 1956. Review of "Social Area Analysis." *J. Amer. statistical Assoc.*, 51, 195-197.

Burgess, E. W., 1929. Urban areas. In T. V. Smith and L. D. White (eds.), *Chicago, An Experiment in Social Science Research.* (Chicago: University of Chicago Press.)

Carpenter, D. B., 1955. Review of "Social Area Analysis." *Amer. sociol. Rev.*, 20, 497-498.

Center for Metropolitan Studies, 1963. *CENSAN: A 709 Program for the Computation of Social Area Analysis.* (Unpublished program description, Northwestern University.)

Curtis, J. H., 1957. The employability of aging workers in social areas of high urbanization and low social rank. (Unpublished paper read at the annual meetings of the American Sociological Association, Washington, D.C.)

Curtis, J. H., F. Avesing, and I. Klosek, 1957. Urban parishes as social areas. *Amer. Catholic sociol. Rev.,* 18, 1-7.

Duncan, O. D., 1955a. Review of "Social Area Analysis." *Amer. J. Sociol.,* 61, 84-85.

———, 1955b. Reply to Bell. *Amer. J. Sociol.,* 61, 261-262.

———, 1956. Review of "Identification of Social Areas by Cluster Analysis." *Amer. sociol. Rev.,* 21, 107-108.

Farber, B., and J. C. Osoinach, 1959. An index of socio-economic rank of census tracts in urban areas. *Amer. sociol. Rev.,* 24, 630-640.

Firey, W., 1945. Sentiment and symbolism as ecological variables. *Amer. sociol. Rev.,* 10, 140-148.

Gagnon, Gabriel, 1960. Les zones sociales de l'agglomeration de Quebec. *Recherches Sociographiques.*

Greer, S., 1956. Urbanism reconsidered: A comparative study of local areas in a metropolis. *Amer. sociol. Rev.,* 21, 19-25.

———, 1960. The social structure and political process of suburbia. *Amer. sociol. Rev.,* 25, 514-526.

———, 1962a. The social structure and political process of suburbia: empirical test. *Rural Sociology,* 27, 438-459.

———, 1962b. *The Emerging City.* (New York: The Free Press of Glencoe.)

Greer, S., and E. Kube, 1955. *Urban Worlds.* Laboratory in Urban Culture, Occidental College. (Mimeographed report.)

———, 1959. Urbanism and social structure: a Los Angeles study. In M. Sussman (ed.), *Community structure and analysis.* (New York: Crowell.)

Greer, S., and P. Orleans, 1962. The mass society and the parapolitical structure. *Amer. sociol. Rev.,* 27, 634-646.

Harris, C. D., and E. U. Ullman, 1945. The nature of cities. *Annals of the Amer. Acad. pol. soc. Science,* 242, 7-17.

Hawley, A. H., 1950. *Human Ecology.* (New York: Ronald.)

Hawley, A. H., and O. D. Duncan, 1957. Social area analysis: A critical appraisal. *Land Economics,* 33, 337-345.

Hoyt, H., 1939. *The structure and growth of residential neighborhoods in American cities.* (Washington, D.C.: Federal Housing Administration.)

Kaufman, W. C., 1961. A Factor-Analytic Test of Revisions in the Shevky-Bell Typology for Chicago and San Francisco, 1950. (Unpublished Ph.D. dissertation, Northwestern University.)

Kaufman, W. C., and S. Greer, 1960. Voting in a metropolitan community: an application of social area analysis. *Social Forces,* 38, 196-204.

Lazarsfeld, P. F., 1937. Some remarks on the typological procedures in social research. *Zeitschrift für Sozialforschung,* 6, 119-139.

Lazarsfeld, P. F., and A. H. Barton, 1951. Qualitative measurement in the social sciences: classification, typologies, and indexes. In D. Lerner and

H. D. Lasswell (eds.), *Policy Sciences*. (Stanford: Stanford University Press.)

McElrath, D. C., 1955. Prestige and esteem identification in selected urban areas. *Research Studies of the State College of Washington*, 23, 130-137.

———, 1962. The social areas of Rome: A comparative analysis. *Amer. sociol. Rev.*, 27, 376-391.

———, no date. The social differentiation of migrants in Accra, Ghana. (Unpublished paper, Center for Metropolitan Studies, Northwestern University.)

McElrath, D. C., and J. W. Barkey, no date. Social and physical space: Models of metropolitan differentiation. (Unpublished paper, Center for Metropolitan Studies, Northwestern University.)

Polk, K., 1957. The social areas of San Diego. (Unpublished M. A. thesis, Northwestern University.)

———, 1957-58. Juvenile delinquency and social areas. *Social Problems*, 5, 214-217.

———, no date. Urban social areas and delinquency. (Unpublished paper, Lane County Youth Project, University of Oregon.)

Quinn, J. A., 1950. *Human Ecology*. (New York: Prentice-Hall.)

Reeks, O., 1953. The social areas of New Orleans. (Unpublished M. A. thesis, University of California, Los Angeles.)

Robinson, W. S., 1950. Ecological correlations and the behavior of individuals. *Amer. sociol. Rev.*, 15, 351-357.

Schnore, Leo F., 1962. Another comment on social area analysis. *Pacific sociol. Rev.*, 5, 13-15.

Sherif, M., and Carolyn W. Sherif, 1964. *Reference Groups*. (New York: Harper and Row.)

Shevky, E., and W. Bell, 1955. *Social Area Analysis*. (Stanford: Stanford University Press.)

Shevky, E., and M. Williams, 1949. *The Social Areas of Los Angeles: Analysis and Typology*. (Berkeley and Los Angeles: University of California Press.)

Sullivan, T., 1961. The application of Shevky-Bell indices to parish analysis. *Amer. Catholic sociol. Rev.*

Sussman, M. B., 1959. The isolated nuclear famiiy: fact or fiction. *Social Problems*, 6, 333-340.

Tiebout, C. M., 1958. Hawley and Duncan on social area analysis: a comment. *Land Economics*, 34, 182-184.

Tryon, R. C., 1955. *Identification of Social Areas by Cluster Analysis*. (Berkeley and Los Angeles: University of California Press.)

U.S. Bureau of the Census, 1958. *Census Tract Manual* (2nd ed.). (Washington, D.C.: Government Printing Office.)

U.S. Bureau of the Census, 1960. *Census Tracts*, series PHC (1). (Washington, D.C.: Government Printing Office.)

Udry, J. R., 1964. Increasing scale and spatial differentiation: new tests of two theories from Shevky and Bell. *Social Forces*, 42, 403-413.

Van Arsdol, M. D., Jr., S. F. Camilleri, and C. F. Schmid, 1957. A deviant case of Shevsky's dimensions of urban structure. Proceedings of the

Pacific Sociological Society in *Research Studies of the State College of Washington,* 25, 171-177.

————, 1958a. The generality of the Shevky social area indexes. *Amer. sociol. Rev.,* 23, 277-284.

————, 1958b. An application of the Shevky social area indexes to a model of urban society. *Social Forces,* 37, 26-32.

————, 1961. An investigation of the utility of urban typology. *Pacific sociol. Rev.,* 4, 26-32.

————, 1962. Further comments on the utility of urban typology. *Pacific sociol. Rev.,* 5, 9-13.

Wendling, A., 1954. Suicide in the San Francisco Bay Region 1938-1942 and 1948-1952. (Unpublished Ph.D. dissertation, University of Washington.)

Wendling, A., and K. Polk, 1958. Suicide and social areas. *Pacific sociol. Rev.,* 1, 50-53.

Williamson, R. C., 1953. Selected urban factors in marital adjustment. *Research Studies of the State College of Washington,* 21, 237-241.

————, 1954. Socio-economic factors and marital adjustment in an urban setting. *Amer. sociol. Rev.,* 19, 213-216.

Wilson, R. L., 1958. The association of urban social areas in four cities and the institutional characteristics of local churches in five denominations. (Unpublished Ph.D. dissertation, Northwestern University.)

Wirth, L., 1938. Urbanism as a way of life. *Amer. J. Sociol.,* 44, 1-24.

TWELVE

THE ADOLESCENT IN HIS GROUP IN ITS SETTING
I. Theoretical Approach and Methodology Required

Muzafer Sherif and Carolyn W. Sherif

This chapter and Chapter 13 report a research program on natural groups of adolescents which was initiated in 1958 and is still in progress. The research program focuses on the attitudes, goals, and behavior of individual members in the context of their group and their particular sociocultural setting. It attempts to study interpersonal relations, attitudes, behaviors and misbehaviors when these occur, in numerous interaction episodes over months. The groups under study are groups of the members' own creation or their own choosing, that is, their *reference groups*.

This chapter summarizes the theoretical guidelines and the empirical basis for a multifaceted research program requiring a combination of psychological and sociological procedures. The intimate relationship between theory and research methods will be articulated through discussion of the choice of data-gathering techniques and the timing of their introduction in the study of natural groups. We have reached the conviction painfully that free or arbitrary choice of methods is not possible in the study of actual groups which possess the essential properties defining "groupness." The nature of the groups sets definite limits on the range of methods that are appropriate.

Chapter 13 will report the methods and operational specifics used in the research program, along with representative findings to date which have general significance for youth problems. Our book, *Reference Groups: Exploration into Conformity and Deviation of Adolescents* (Sherif and Sherif, 1964) presents more details of the research program, its findings up to 1962, and the leads derived from them that are applicable to current problems of adolescent misbehaviors and the wastage of talents and energies in socially harmful channels.

This chapter is based on the senior author's invited address to Division 9, American Psychological Association, Los Angeles, September 6, 1964. Since 1961, the Research has been supported by grants from the National Science Foundation.

NECESSITY FOR MULTIFACETED RESEARCH DESIGN

The individuals studied in the research program are adolescents. As outlined in the Introduction, the dilemmas of this period, in a culture itself undergoing rapid social change, produce a broad and intense motivational base for group formations in all walks of life. The adolescent period is a paradigm for studying the individual-group-society relationship in its clearest manifestation. As such, the issues of theory and research into youthful behavior are essentially the same as those in the study of human social behavior at any period of life.

We start with a premise based on a host of empirical findings. The premise is that adequate study of the behavior of individual group members must include specification of the group properties and the part played by the individual.

Obviously, however, groups do not rise and function in a vacuum. Even though they are units with distinctive patterns of their own, groups are not closed systems defining their own universe. The claims of a group and the goals it pursues are related to the settings in which the group functions. That part of the setting which raises issues and problems about goals and collective efforts to attain them is the sociocultural setting.

Even though our interest is the individual behavior of group members, the components and events comprising the sociocultural setting cannot be reduced to psychological terms. They are *out there* relative to an individual. They are not reducible to "psychological constructs," as cogently noted by Roger Barker (1963). The sociocultural setting and its various aspects can be and are studied in their own right, by sociology, anthropology, and other social sciences, quite apart from the psychological study of particular individuals immersed in them.

Of course, there can be no denial that a person's psychological world is the world he actually experiences. But this experiential fact should not be stretched into a denial of an equally unmistakable fact: sociocultural products are *out there* as stimulus conditions for the individual, affecting his behavior and his success or failure in attaining his goals. This is the case even though he may not be aware of their impact. We cannot derive an adequate conception of the sociocultural setting merely from the psychological worlds of individuals in it without falling into a fruitless circle of reductionism.

Therefore, we must conclude that adequate study of individual behavior must include the specification of both the individual's groups and the sociocultural setting in which they form and function. The difficult research task is hitting upon concepts of analysis and procedures appropriate to each domain, namely, the individual, the group, and the sociocultural setting. Necessarily, the research task is *interdisciplinary*, to use a very fashionable term which is often misapplied. In a multifaceted research program which includes the study of individual-group-setting within the same design, the appalling gap between laboratory research and field research may narrow in a relatively short time.

If it is to achieve its purpose, such research must also interrelate its several facets without falling into a bias favoring either an individual group, or cultural approach. Proper operational procedures and the interrelationship of the various aspects will contribute to resolving a number of theoretical or doctrinal conflicts (as represented by the "institutional" vs. "behavioral" controversies in social science [cf. Sherif and Koslin, 1960], and the schisms between proponents of research on small groups and large organizations). In the present conception, individual behavior is seen in the context of groups and larger organizations. Small groups, in turn, are not viewed as units in their own right, but as parts of a larger social system. Our research program is an attempt in this direction.

THE RESEARCH DESIGN IN THREE FACETS

Mindful of the range of influences on the formation and functioning of human groups and the behavior of members, we designed our research to include operations appropriate for the behavior of individuals, for their groups, and for the sociocultural setting. In specifying the gross characteristics of the setting, as well as the prevailing patterns of values or norms within it, we relied heavily on methods, procedures, and findings of social scientists. After all, social scientists have developed tools and collected a wealth of data on the regularities of the sociocultural setting and the properties of groups. It is wasteful for social psychologists to start from scratch or to improvise tools without discovering those available in other academic disciplines.

The research program has three main facets, which may be summarized as follows:

1. Since the focus of the program is social-psychological, the concentration of procedures and data is on selected small groups of adolescents and their members. Clusters of teen-age boys (13-18 years old) are selected on the basis of their frequent and recurrent association in specified locations. Each group is studied intensively for periods from six months to a year. A combination of techniques is used in collecting data, including observation, behavior ratings by regular observers and independent raters, informal sociometric techniques, situational tests, and case history materials. The distinctive research strategy is that the boys are not aware that they are research subjects or that they are being observed for research purposes.

Behavior in the groups has included both socially acceptable activities, and deeds socially unacceptable to an extent that they would be

labeled "delinquent" if detected by adult authorities. The basis for selecting groups is their regular and recurrent association, not whether they
behave properly or misbehave, or have been labeled socially acceptable or
delinquent. For purposes of comparison, groups are selected from settings
of low, middle and high socioeconomic rank and from urban neighborhoods with different ethnic populations.

2. A second facet of the research is specification of the characteristics of the particular sociocultural settings where the small groups function. Such characteristics were conceived as stimulus conditions, relative
to the attitude and behavior of the individuals studied. Therefore, we
could not be content with a blanket, over-all characterization of the setting or with improvised descriptions of it. We relied especially on the
Shevky-Bell social area analysis (Shevky and Bell, 1955; Bell, 1958)
which yields concise indicators of what is meant by low, middle and high
social ranks, and their gradations. (These indicators are presented in
Chapter 11 of this volume.)

3. For social-psychological analysis, specification of only major characteristics of the setting is not sufficient. Certain aspects of the sociocultural setting have greater salience than others, particularly for individuals
in the adolescent period. A large research literature shows that, during
the adolescent period, individuals are particularly attuned to others in
their own age set. Accordingly, special emphasis is given in the research program to collecting data on the bounds of acceptability and
on the goals prevailing among representative samples of teen-age youth
in each sociocultural setting. These data indicate what youth in different
areas regard as "socially desirable" and undesirable, and where they set
their sights for achievement in various respects. Thus, cultural values can
be compared between areas to ascertain which are common to them all
and in what ways they differ. In turn, the concepts and goals prevailing
among youth in a given area can serve as a baseline for assessing the
relative typicality or deviance of individual members of a group being
studied within that area.

INTERDEPENDENCE OF THEORY AND RESEARCH

We sought research methods from the social sciences as well as
psychology, and we relied on the empirical findings in both as the basis
for concepts and theory. Concepts and theory enter into research from
the very beginning, when the investigator formulates the problem of
study. They influence what kind of data he gathers and what data he
disregards. They affect the selection of data-gathering techniques, the
manner in which the data are used, the analysis, and the interpretation of
findings. Consequently, it is fitting to examine the theoretical and methodological problems of interdisciplinary research, which the adequate study
of youthful behavior must be.

In social science and psychology, there are grand theories of the individual-group-society relationship. The present approach, however, did not derive from a grand theory, though that might have greater esthetic appeal. Few, if any, of the grand theories are formulated to encompass the gamut of influences shaping behavior and to guide research operations at three different levels of analysis (individual, group, cultural).

Nor does the present approach stem from theoretical models borrowed (or smuggled) from more established and prestigeful sciences. Formal models of the relationships among the multifaceted data are the *goal*, so that, ultimately, we can express events and their relationship in five pages instead of five hundred. Because of the current fad, even craze, for models in psychology and social science, we shall be explicit about the limitations placed on data gathering by premature adoption or formulation of a formal theoretical model.

The indiscriminate use of models based on analogy with other sciences has proceeded with a singular lack of concern for the crucial question of the isomorphism between the models, and the events and actualities of which they are supposed to be models. Such concern should be the basis for accepting or rejecting a model. If it is not, the model restricts the range of data collected, conveniently pruning branches of unwanted facts to the point of focusing on tiny and barren twigs of trivia.

The common pitfall in borrowed models was emphasized recently in a presidential address to the Division of Engineering Psychology of the American Psychological Association, a rather unexpected source. Chapanis (1961) observed that attempts are seldom made to validate borrowed models and that those who work with them typically end up being "intrigued with essentially trivial problems."

Model building by making analogies with a more established science is not a monopoly of our time. There was the "mental chemistry" model of Wundt and Titchener, which now lies at dead end. There was the organic analogy of Herbert Spencer, which fared no better. Some mechanical and hydraulic analogies still flourish, but a similar fate for them is inevitable. As Emile Durkheim (1915) and others put it, social life and human value systems are not on a continuum with physical and biological events. They have properties of their own, not to be found through analogy with physical sciences.

The issue at hand, however, is not model building as such, but the proper basis for building them. The first step toward adequate models of social behavior and its social setting starts with formulating the proper questions and defining problems. In order to take this first step, a period of concentration on the actualities of our topics is essential. These actualities must be explored at the level of the complexity which is characteristic of problems of individual-group and sociocultural relationships.

To gain the effective tools for the logical and mathematical formalization so essential for precise model building, we have to define our problems and their properties more clearly. Unfortunately, at this erratic stage in the study of human affairs, even the basic problems at stake have not been formulated in stable form.

This is a plea for a disciplined phenomenology as an *initial step* in formulating problems. This is only an initial step, but one which serves generously as we venture on into research and theoretical interpretation.

As an illustration, consider the study of the formation of social norms in the laboratory through utilization of the autokinetic phenomenon (Sherif, 1935, 1936). This experiment is frequently cited as an example of the precision to be gained from laboratory models (cf. Cartwright and Zander, 1960). Yet it did not originate in the techniques and procedures of the psychological laboratory—it started with a lesson learned empirically in the actualities of social life: that social norms or standards arise when conditions in the lives of men are fluid, uncertain, or in crisis. From this lesson, it was then a matter of devising an appropriate laboratory condition to represent this fluidity and uncertainty; the autokinetic setup was one of several such conditions suitable for the problem. The same concern with observed actualities was the basis for the conception of our experiments on intergroup relations, which have been presented elsewhere (Sherif and Sherif, 1953; Sherif et al., 1961). We are proceeding from such an empirical basis in studies of attitude and attitude change (Sherif, Sherif, and Nebergall, 1965).

The present undertaking on adolescents in their groups presents the investigator with much more challenging and difficult tasks than does experimentation. In the open field of actual life, event follows event, and none can be controlled and manipulated as the investigator chooses.

What guidelines do social science and psychology give us for raising crucial problems and formulating hypotheses? Necessarily, we can give only brief and essential examples of empirical findings that are established with sufficient stability to serve as a basis for research.

EMPIRICAL BASIS FROM SOCIAL SCIENCE AND PSYCHOLOGY

From the empirical findings of sociologists, especially from the Chicago school of the twenties and thirties, we learned of the universality of group formations whenever individuals interact with similar motivational promptings. These motivations may be deprivations, frustrations, or desires for earthly goods and political power. This generalization, based on empirical facts, provided the basis for hypotheses both for our experimental studies of group formation and intergroup relations, and for the present research.

As noted earlier, we also learned, primarily from findings by adolescent psychologists, of the motivational dilemmas common to this period. At the same time, we noted in anthropological reports that these dilemmas varied in their severity because of cultural arrangements (cf.

Sherif and Cantril, 1947). These reports also confirmed the generality and significance of group formation during adolescence.

From studies of both small and large organizations, we learned that human groups have properties more complex than merely an undifferentiated state of interdependence among individuals (cf. Homans, 1950; Blau and Scott, 1962). In actual groups, we learned, the interdependencies can be specified in terms of a differentiated and hierarchical pattern of positions, with decided implications as to what each individual can or cannot do in effectively initiating activities for others in the pattern without being challenged by them.

We learned from the studies of sociologists and anthropologists that every group possesses a set of regulations and standards—that is, a set of social norms—defining a latitude of acceptable behavior, including the ideal, as well as a range of unacceptable attitudes and actions which will bring forth scorn and sanction from others in the group.

Likewise, we have relied on guidelines from empirical findings in psychology. The findings from psychology have been particularly useful in developing behavioral indicators for the individual-group relationship; the hierarchical arrangements within groups, bounded by the end-positions of "leader" and "man at the bottom"; and the way members of an in-group evaluate each other and out-groups. We found invaluable leads in the accumulating empirical facts in the psychology of perception (especially on perceptual selectivity), the psychology of judgment and motivation, and child psychology. We were concerned with including the sociocultural setting explicity partly because of the unmistakably established findings on background and context effects in the psychology of perception and judgment. Because of their far-reaching implications, these findings will be summarized.

Even the simplest judgment is a comparison process, not immune to the effects of its context or background. As Helson demonstrated, the color judgment of the same patch of material "could be made anything we pleased by appropriate choice of the luminance and hue of the background color" (Helson, 1964, p. 26). Context and background effect are considerations even in a relatively simple judgment of a patch of color or a weight of so many grams. How much more crucial they should be in considering an individual's judgment, perception, and other reactions in his social relations!

Social relations constitute the context of individual attitude and behavior. Background and context intrude even into the carefully contrived confines of an experimental interview or testing situation. There is much more to a contrived laboratory or testing situation than what catches the eye or what the experimenter's instruments can record. The context is not merely the experimenter's stimulus material and special instructions. The experimenter himself, the way he is appraised by the subject, the surroundings, the presence or absence of other individuals and the subject's appraisal of them—all these intrude into the shaping of performance.

No wonder, then, that a whole movement on the "social psychology of the psychological experiment" is developing to articulate the hitherto unaccounted-for or neglected ingredients that go into the making of any situation. The trend is well represented in the experiments of Orne (1962) and Rosenthal (1961). Only a few of the recent contributions to this strengthened sensitivity to context and background can be cited here.

That the characteristics of the administrator make a difference on intelligence tests is forcefully brought to our attention once again in recent surveys by Pettigrew (1964) and Martin Deutsch (1964). Even more closely related to our own research is the report by Pearl in Chapter 5 of this book, where he compares interviews with delinquents made by graduate students with those made by other delinquents. "When graduate students conducted the tape-recorded interviews, they confirmed the usual conclusion that lower-class youth were inarticulate. But when lower-class interviewers canvassed the same persons, responses were entirely different. The subjects were animated and highly verbal."

Stevenson and Allen (1964) reported recently that the response rate in a motor task differs according to whether the experimenter is male or female; and Pishkin (1964) showed that errors in concept identification by schizophrenics were significantly affected by whether the experimenter was present or absent. Finally, we note the finding that the context of interpersonal relations in a hospital ward has produced not only behavioral variations, but also significant metabolic alterations (Schottstaedt, Pinsky, Mackler, and Wolf, 1958).

In brief, the context and background of human behavior produce significant variations, whether or not the investigator includes them in his study design. If we would understand the sources of behavioral variation, there seems to be no question about including the sociocultural and group contexts of behavior. Sober consideration of the research findings on context and background effects led to our inclusion of the sociocultural setting and group properties in the design, and to the methods chosen or developed for the study of behavior in groups.

CONCEPTS GOVERNING THE CHOICE OF RESEARCH METHODS

Since our research program focuses on the intensive study of natural groups of adolescents, the major hypotheses and data-gathering techniques for their assessment pertain to the behaviors and attitudes of individuals in such groups. The prerequisite to an adequate study of individual behavior in a group context is a definition of the properties of actual groups and their interaction processes.

Our definition of the properties of groups is based on extensive surveys of empirical findings on group formation and functioning in different social spheres, as documented in our own earlier publications (1948, 1953, 1956).

The term "natural group" is used in these chapters to designate the origins of the groups, and carries no evaluative implication. Particularly in the case of adolescent groups, it is convenient to distinguish groups formed through the informal interaction of members from those instituted by adults, a board of officers, or a council.

We are referring to groups in a technical sense, specifying the properties that distinguish a group from casual collective encounters, from temporary "discussion groups," and from experimental groups collected on an *ad hoc* basis. A formally instituted body may or may not become a "group" in the precise sense to be defined here.

In the first place, a group is a human formation formed over a given time span through interaction of individuals. It is a *social unit*. Its bounds define who is "in" and who is "not in." The criteria for membership and other properties of the group may or may not be codified explicitly as verbal rules.

The essential condition for the formation of a human group is interaction over a period of time among individuals with similar concerns, similar motives, similar frustrations, or, generally, a *common dilemma* which is not effectively dealt with through established social channels and arrangements. In other words, people in the same boat of misery or unfulfilled desires love company. They tend to interact with one another.

Repeated interaction in a variety of tasks by individuals with some common striving leads to differentiation of functions in activities, along with the coordination of effort. The differentiated functions are stabilized in time as *roles with differing status*. This differentiation of roles and statuses *over a time span* is the pattern of the human group.

Over a time span this patterned give-and-take interaction of individuals produces a *set of rules or norms* for the regulation of attitude and behavior within the bounds of the group and toward outsiders. The rules or norms that are salient in the eyes of members are those that pertain to the existence and continuation of the group and to spheres of activity related to the common motivational concerns which initially brought them together.

In summary, the minimum and essential properties of a group consist of (1) a pattern or organization of member roles, differentiated as to status or power as well as to other functions; and (2) a set of values or norms regulating behavior, at least in spheres of activity frequently engaged in by the group.

The "groupness" of a group is, therefore, a matter of degree. It is proportional to the extent that the status and role pattern is stabilized, and to the extent that member behavior is effectively regulated by a set of norms pertaining to their recurrent activities.

Now let us consider some implications that these properties of groups have in developing research procedures which will yield valid and reliable data on interpersonal relationships within the group and on the attitudes of individual members.

First, the unit character of a group implies a context for behavior which is, in some degree, "private." The "privacy" of in-group interactions develops from the motivational basis which brings the members together and the prolonged give-and-take among them.

Groups do not form and function for the benefit of an investigator. On the contrary, their very nature militates against his intrusion. The gross intrusion of an outsider into significant ongoing events will affect the usual context for behavior of members. This is particularly true if the outsider is identified as a *researcher,* an *investigator,* or anyone intent upon manipulating their behavior. We determined, then, to avoid making members aware that they were being observed and studied. This decision meant that our data had to be obtained in numerous interaction episodes at times and in places not under the observer's control. Observers were instructed to avoid, as much as possible, any interruption of the free flow of interpersonal give-and-take among members.

The definition of the group in terms of differentiation of status and role relationships and·a set of norms did not specify that the individual members could or would report on leader-follower relations or on their conformity to group norms. In fact, we have records in our research of numerous expressions of the following sort: "We have no leader." "We have no boss." "We are all equal." Despite such reports, it was possible to rank these same individuals as first, second, third, down to lowest, in terms of their *effective initiative* in activities of the group. Effective initiative is an operational index of *power* in any organization.

In brief, the properties of groups led to inferences about the procedures necessary to study them adequately—namely, that the primary source of data was to be observation of interaction episodes over a period of time, without the awareness of members, and without undue cluttering of the flow of interaction by research techniques. These decisions, in turn, required adjustments to a common problem in field observations, the problem of checking reliability of observations.

In Chapter 13 the operational procedures, including the criteria for assessing group properties, are summarized in more detail. Here it is sufficient to note that the selective bias of a *single observer* was minimized by using a *combination of methods* for data collection. The use of a combination of data-gathering techniques permits findings by one method to be checked against those yielded by another. This is the best insurance against observer bias. The methods included adaptations of techniques ordinarily considered distinctive to the controlled laboratory situation, for example, rating methods and situational tests.

HYPOTHESES BASED ON EMPIRICALLY DERIVED CONCEPTS

From the properties of groups and their formation, several hypotheses about member attitudes and behavior were deduced. The major hypotheses of our research program and a string of auxiliary predictions are spelled out in *Reference Groups* (Sherif and Sherif, 1964).

Here we have deliberately selected hypotheses of major import for youthful behavior. The research program has collected pertinent data both in the study of natural groups, as summarized in the next chapter, and in laboratory experiments based on the same conceptualization, reported in this chapter.

Here, then, are general predictions deduced from the empirically derived concept of group:

1. To the extent that a group organization (role and status relations) is stabilized, the norms or standards for behavior in activities focal in interaction become *binding* for individual participants.

("Binding" means here, psychologically binding, such that conformity to the norm occurs because the person considers the norm in question as *his personal* guideline, not as one imposed on him. One index of the extent to which a group norm is binding for the individual is his behavior in compliance to its bounds when he is out of the reach of other members, and there is no threat of sanctions for deviation.)

2. The *salience* of various groups for the individual is a function of the extent to which its activities bear on motivational concerns he shares with the membership.

("Salience" refers here to the relative importance of the group as reflected in his behavior, especially in his choices or preferential judgments.)

3. Conformity to an established norm by new participants in the interaction pattern will be a function of the extent to which the conditions giving rise to the norm continue. Conversely, deviation from an established norm is a function of its "arbitrariness" relative to current motivations and circumstances faced by members.

("Arbitrariness" may be defined operationally in terms of the difference between the established norm and a norm stabilized in the current situation by individuals who have had no contact with the established norm.)

4. The extent to which an individual's behavior in group activities is predictable is a function of his position in the status organization and the degree of the group's stability.

(The last section of this chapter will spell out the curvilinear relationship between status and predictability of behavior.)

STABILITY OF STANDARDS FORMED IN GROUP VS.
MERE TOGETHERNESS SITUATIONS

An operational distinction can be made between mere *compliance* to the demands, pressures or suggestions of other individuals in an immediate situation, and the concept of *conformity* to the group.

Conformity, properly speaking, refers to behavior within the bounds of standards (norms) stabilized in prior interaction situations. The extent to which group norms are psychologically binding for the individual member may be tested by observing his behavior when he is *not* in contact with other members. It was predicted that the extent to which standards are psychologically binding would vary with the degree of stability in the interpersonal (role) relation among the individuals who participated in their formation.

In a laboratory experiment undertaken with the support of our research program, N. P. Pollis investigated this hypothesis by comparing conformity to standards which had been formed in interpersonal relationships of varying stability. He tested the hypothesis by first establishing standards for behavior (judgment), and then putting the individual in a transitory "togetherness" situation where the others confronted him with conflicting judgments. The question, then, was to what extent would the individual comply with the immediate social influences of others, or conform to his previously established standard in a novel situation.

The experiment was preceded by sociometric study of the sophomore class of a college, conducted under different auspices than the experiment so that the subjects would establish no connection between the two. On the basis of this study, subjects were selected from the intermediate range of general social standing on the campus. Certain well-defined cliques (groups) were discovered. It was also possible to specify which individuals were not personally acquainted.

In the first session of the experiment, each of the 144 subjects participated either (a) alone, (b) together with someone he did not know personally, or (c) together with a fellow group member. These three conditions defined variations in the stability of interpersonal relationships.

The task was to judge the frequencies of auditory pulses produced by an Eico audio-generator. A series of pulses was presented, consisting of random arrangements of four different pulse rates. Each pulse rate lasted 3 seconds and was followed by a 6-second rest period.

The task was sufficiently subject to error that Pollis found it feasible to train subjects to three different ranges of judgment by identifying the slowest and fastest rates differently in his instructions. Thus, he established three different judgment ranges, each among one-third of the subjects: low, middle or high. The purpose of this variation was to provide a pool of subjects with differing established ranges for a second session.

In the second session, each subject served with two others, none of whom were fellow group members. In the first session, one had stabilized his judgment range alone, one together with another student with whom he was interacting for the first time, and one with a fellow group member. Each of these three had formed a different range for judgment in session 1 (low, middle, high). The possible effect of the source in speaking judgments within these ranges was controlled by systematically counterbalancing the range established in session 1 and the social situation in which the individual had formed it. In other words, in session 2, the group member in one triplet started giving the high range; in another, the middle range, in another, the low range.

Two measures were used to test the hypothesis. First, the percentage of each individual's judgments in session 2 that fell *within* his range for session 1 was used as the measure of his *conformity* to the standard formed in session 1. Second, the percentage of judgments by other subjects in session 2 that fell within his range of judgments was a measure of their *compliance* with him in the immediate togetherness situation.

Figure 13 presents the findings on *conformity* to initial standards formed in session 1. If the hypothesis is correct that standards are psychologically binding to the extent that interpersonal relations among those who form them are stable, conformity would be greatest for individuals who formed standards in the *group* situation. It would be next greatest for standards formed in mere togetherness situations in session 1, and least for individuals who stabilized their own standards alone. The cumulative percentages in the figure show that the hypothesis is supported. Measures computed trial by trial revealed that these significant differences were not merely a result of initial trials.

Figure 14 gives findings on the relative *influence* in session 2 of subjects who had formed their standards alone, together, or in a group. It shows the average percentage of the judgments made by the two other subjects which fell within the individual's range. In other words, these percentages indicate the relative influence exerted by the subject on others present in the session. It may be seen that those who formed their scales in a group situation both conformed to them more (Figure 13) and exerted the most influence on others, that is, complied least in session 2. Individuals who had formed standards alone were least influential and most compliant in session 2.

This experiment by Pollis verifies in more precise form a recurrent observation in our study of natural groups. Being a member of a group with shared standards for behavior renders the individual *less* compliant to outsiders in a transitory situation. To the extent that he is part of patterned interpersonal relationships, the standards formed in that pattern are psychologically binding for him. Through *conformity* to group standards, he is less easily swayed by momentary influences and pressures in a different direction.

The implication that *conformity* to group standards produces greater

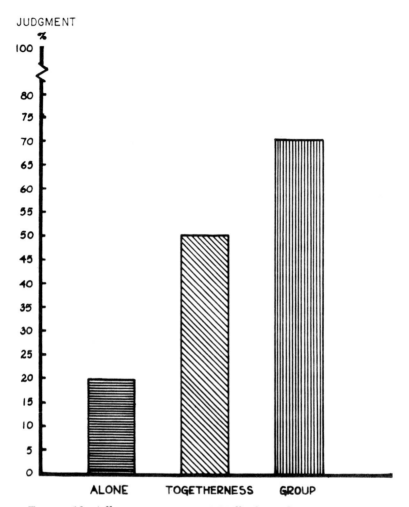

FIGURE 13. Adherence to norms initially formed in situations with varying stability of interpersonal relationships

independence by the individual in outside encounters is paradoxical only when the terms are defined without considering his social background and the context of the immediate interaction situation. The definition of the properties of a group implies definite consequences for individuals belonging over a period of time.

SALIENCE OF DIFFERENT REFERENCE GROUPS

The research program on groups of the adolescent's own choosing has yielded abundant evidence of the salience of these reference groups

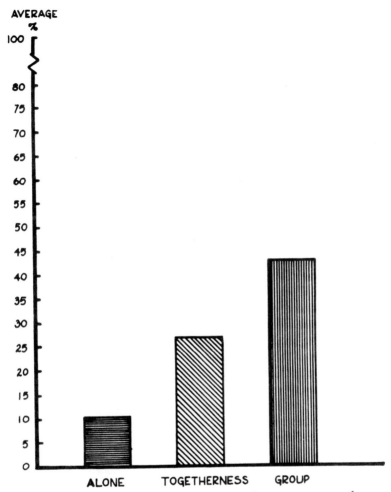

FIGURE 14. Relative influence of others' judgments in a togetherness situation by persons whose norm was formed initially in situations of varying stability

for the members. In making choices between their activities and standards and those of family, church or school, they frequently neglected the latter. As noted in the Introduction, a shift in the salience of age-mate and family reference groups is a general phenomenon of the adolescent period in this society. An experiment by Prado demonstrates behavioral consequences of this shift by a comparison of children's and adolescent's judgments on the competence of their fathers and their best friends.

Prado selected 25 boys eight to eleven years old and 25 boys fourteen to seventeen years old, who consistently selected their father as the most valued and trusted parent. This stringent criterion for selection minimized the possibility that adolescent boys were simply rebelling against unusually authoritarian fathers. Similarly, Prado obtained the boys' sociometric preferences in order to single out their best age-mate friend.

Bringing each subject to the laboratory with his father and his best friend, he had the father and the friend perform a simple eye-hand coordination task (throwing a dart at a target), so arranged that the outcome was indeterminate. Each subject judged, in turn, the performance of his father or friend with scores from 0 to 24.

If appraisal of performance indicates the salience of reference groups, it is reasonable to predict that children would estimate their fathers' performance higher than that of their friends; while adolescents would estimate their fathers' performance *lower* than they estimated that of friends.

The results showed significant differences. Of the children, 20 of the 25 did estimate their fathers' performance as superior to that of age-mate friends (mean difference $= + 3.5$ points). Conversely, 19 of the 25 adolescents appraised their fathers' performance as *lower* than that of their friends (mean difference $= - 2.6$).

Although the exact outcome was indeterminate, some real differences in the skills of the fathers and friends could have affected the boys' judgments. But actually, 17 of the 25 fathers of adolescents performed as well or better than their sons' pals, and only 13 of the 25 fathers of children equalled or outstripped their child's friend. In a reanalysis of Prado's data, we have found that, ignoring the *direction* of error, there are not significant differences in the children's and adolescents' accuracy in judging. In both age groups, average error in the fathers' performance was approximately 4.5 points, and the average error for friends somewhat less (3.5 points).

Considering the errors as overestimations and underestimations of performance, we can compare the difference between errors for fathers and errors for friends as an index of the extent to which the father is favored over the friend or vice versa, taking into account differences in performance. If the difference is *positive*, the father was favored over the friend. If the difference is negative, the friend's performance was favored over the father's, despite differences in skill.

Figure 15 presents the findings. On the average, children overestimate their father's performance, even with differences in performance controlled (Mean difference $= + 2.35$). Adolescents underestimate their fathers, with performance level again adjusted (Mean difference $= - 3.64$). (A test of the significance of these differences between errors for fathers' and friends' performances yielded $t = 3.72$, $p < .001$.)

A subsidiary finding in Prado's research supports the hypothesis

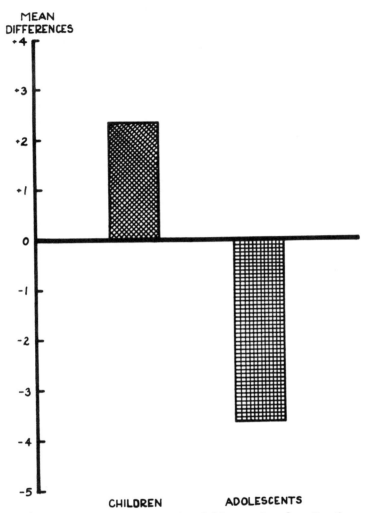

FIGURE 15. Overestimation by children and underestimation by adolescents of parent's performance as compared with best friend's

that the shifting salience of reference groups in adolescence is related to the motivational concerns the members share. He found that adolescents engaged in a significantly greater number of activities with friends than did younger boys, even though the two age groups did not differ in their consistency in choosing the friends in question. Since both children and adolescents in this study actually preferred their father as a parent, the logical inference is that the adolescent's activities and free time are focused more on common concerns with age-mates than are a younger child's.

CONFORMITY TO NORMS AS A FUNCTION OF THEIR ARBITRARINESS

If group norms become psychologically binding for individual members, without threat of disapproval, why do an individual's patterns of conformity change? Why do the values or norms of one group persist even when membership changes over successive generations, while those of another group disappear as the last member leaves?

Relative to youth problems, we suggested in the last section that adherence to group norms varies with the salience of the group. This salience shifts from childhood to adolescence, primarily because the dilemmas of adolescence in modern societies are shared with age-mates more than with one's family.

It is equally true that when adolescents gain mature roles, or are thrust into them by circumstances, the salience of age-mate reference groups diminishes. Adults say there is nothing like a job or marriage to "settle down" the wild, rebellious, or "silly" behavior of their offspring and his crowd. His motivational concerns no longer intersect so extensively with those of his age-mates.

But what of the transmission of group norms and customs over time? The transmission of a group, carrying the same identity and similar norms, to a new membership is a distinctive feature of human societies. It is observed in informal social life as well. In the next chapter, we summarize the intensive study in our research of three generations of boys living in the same neighborhood, each of whom belonged to the same group as a teenager.

When a group has established norms for behavior, and new members come as older ones depart, what conditions lead to the maintenance of the group norms in substantially similar form, and which ones are conducive to their alteration?

Our hypothesis predicts that one important variable affecting the transmission of norms and the extent of conformity to them by new members is the degree of their arbitrariness relative to current conditions facing the group. When a norm is transmitted by older members to a new generation of members, its "arbitrariness" can be defined relative to the conditions in which the new generation functions. The norm developing in those conditions *without* an enculturation process by older members can be termed *least arbitrary*.

If the arbitrariness of norms is an important variable in conformity-deviation, it will help explain the continuity of groups of boys who grow up in the same neighborhood, relative to the changes occurring in the neighborhood and the city of which it is a part.

For these reasons, a laboratory experiment was initiated (as part of our research program) to examine how differing degrees of arbitrariness affected the conformity of succeeding "generations" in the laboratory. Data were collected by Mark K. McNeil with assistance from Michael Lauderdale, both assistants in the program at the time. The autokinetic phenomenon was chosen as the situation to be appraised by the subjects.

As in the earlier studies of norm formation by Sherif (1935, 1936), a norm for behavior in this situation was defined as a common range of judgment around a modal point, stabilized over time by two or more individuals. Individual conformity is defined as a judgment falling within this norm; deviation, a judgment outside the norm.

In this situation, the degree of arbitrariness of a norm could be defined operationally as the extent to which a prescribed and transmitted norm differed from the range and mode of judgments stabilized under the same laboratory arrangements *without* the introduction of a norm transmitted by "planted" subjects.

The general sequence of procedures followed those used in a study by Jacobs and Campbell (1961), who, through instructions to "planted" subjects, introduced an arbitrary norm of 15.5 inches with a range of one inch. They followed the progress of the norm through successive generations by replacing one of three planted subjects with a naive subject after each block of judgments, and then replacing an experienced subject with a new naive subject at the start of each succeeding block.

Since degree of arbitrariness was our main interest, three degrees were standardized in our laboratory: (I) not arbitrary; (II) an arbitrary norm chosen not to overlap the range of Condition I and with a higher mode (a range of 9-15 inches around a mode of 12 inches); (III) more arbitrary norm not overlapping Condition II and a still higher mode (15-21 inch range and 18 inches mode).

In Condition I (not arbitrary), four naive subjects gave 30 judgments each of the extent of autokinetic movement; then each in turn was replaced by a new naive subject in the succeeding "generations," and so on, through eight generations of 30 judgments each. In Conditions II and III, a preliminary "enculturation" phase consisted of three generations, with the prescribed norm being given by three, then two, then a single planted subject, who in turn was replaced by a naive subject. Eight generations of naive subjects followed, the transmitted norm being traced over these.

The subjects were high school students (ages 16-19). A total of 66 naive subjects participated in two replications of each condition.

The major hypothesis was that degree of conformity over successive generations would decrease (and deviation increase) as a function of the degree of arbitrariness of the transmitted norm. In order to test this hypothesis, it was also necessary to demonstrate the following: (a) a norm formed in Condition I would be transmitted with only minor variations as personnel changed, and (b) the enculturation procedures in Conditions II and III did produce conformity to the prescribed norm by naive subjects.

The findings can be summarized briefly as follows:

1. The norm formed by subjects in the first generation in Condition I (not arbitrary) was within an interquartile range of 4-8 inches, with a median and mean of 6 inches. The means and medians of seven successive generations were around 4 inches with an interquartile range from 3 to 6 inches. In short, after the second generation, the norm in Condition I was transmitted with only minor variations.

2. The enculturation by planted subjects in the more arbitrary conditions did result in conformity by naive subjects. In Condition II, 100 per cent of their judgments fell within the prescribed range, and 90 per cent of the judgments conformed in Condition III (most arbitrary), as shown in Figure 16. Similarly, the median judgments of naive subjects in Condition II were very close to the prescribed median of 12 inches (11.7 inches); and the median for Condition III during enculturation was 16.5-17.5 inches.

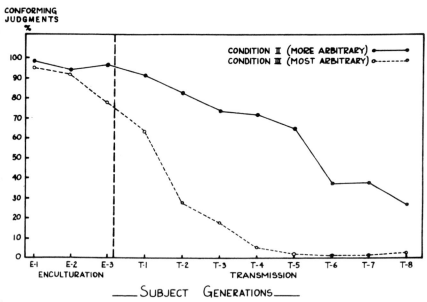

FIGURE 16. Conformity through successive generations of laboratory subjects as a function of the arbitrariness of norms

3. The prescribed norm in Condition II was transmitted to the first generation, consisting entirely of naive subjects, 100 per cent of their judgments conforming to the transmitted norm. In the most arbitrary condition (III), there was some deviation from the prescribed norm by the first generation of entirely naive subjects, but 63 per cent of their judgments conformed to the transmitted norm.

Figure 16 gives the percentages of judgments by naive subjects which fell within the prescribed norm for Conditions II and III through three enculturation and eight transmission generations. Conformity to the prescribed norm was significantly greater at every generation in the less arbitrary condition (II). The rate of increase in deviation was clearly more rapid in Condition III (most arbitrary).

Figure 17 presents the median judgments of naive subjects, generation by generation. The greatest shift away from the transmitted norm and toward the "natural" norm of Condition I was in the most arbitrary condition, with half of the downward trend occurring by the third trans-

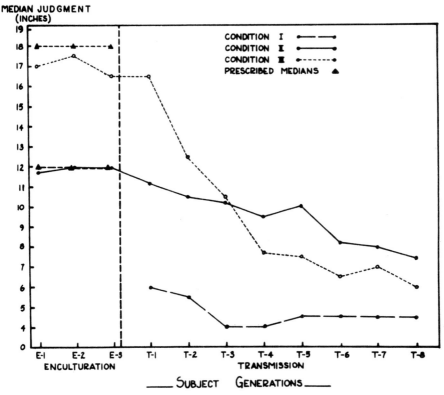

FIGURE 17. Conformity through successive generations of laboratory subjects compared to prescribed medians and "natural" norm

mission generation. The change was more gradual in Condition II (less arbitrary), with the median judgments less toward the "natural" norm even in the last generation of subjects.

The general theoretical inference from this experiment is that conforming behavior by individuals occurs in a context of social interaction which is inevitably related to the conditions, problems and tasks which confront them. The norms stabilized are products of both the interaction process and the conditions in which it occurs. With successive generations of membership, conformity to established norms for behavior is an inverse function of the arbitrariness of the norms. However, deviation by individuals results in new, less arbitrary norms which, in turn, are transmitted to new members (Chapter 13 presents an example of this process in three generations of boys belonging to a neighborhood group in a large city.)

GENERALITY OF GROUPS AND THEIR PSYCHOLOGICAL CONSEQUENCES

In the research program on adolescent reference groups, we were impressed once again with the generality of group formations in all walks of life during this age period. Whether the groups are labeled cliques, friendship circles, chums, crowds, or gangs seems to depend much more on the social rank of the neighborhood than on their essential properties.

All have differentiated patterns regulating their interpersonal relations. All have rules, customs, fads—in short, norms—regulating behavior in their activities. These are the minimum essentials of a group.

These groups of adolescents were formed, or joined, on the members' own initiative, through interactions among individuals sharing the dilemmas of status and motivation common during adolescence in this society. The status differentiation which developed was not imposed on them; the norms were not considered arbitrary impositions on the members.

The individual had a hand in creating the properties of the group, or had selected it. The group was his—a context where he could have personal ties with others, could amount to something in ways not available elsewhere, could accomplish things as a person. It contained others whose acceptance he wanted, whose yardsticks were his personal gauges for success and failure, whose approval brought inner warmth and whose disapproval left him miserable.

Psychologically, therefore, the basis of group solidarity, of conformity to group norms without threat of sanctions, of the binding nature of group rules even when they conflict with those of parents and officials, lies in the personal involvement of members. The self-image of the individual consists, in large part, of his ties with his reference group and the yardsticks it provides. The continuity of his ego identity from day to day depends to a large extent on the stability of his ties with members and on their consistency in appraising him according to the patterned relationships and norms shared in common. They are among the stable anchorages in his world. The disruption of their stability affects him as surely as the sudden lack of stable guideposts in his physical surroundings (cf. Sherif and Harvey, 1952).

Groups of the individual's own choosing are not the monopoly of adolescents. They are formed whenever people see themselves in the same boat, whether this be a neighborhood, a large organization (such as the military, industrial plant, or prison), or in a crisis situation. It is true, as Zorbaugh (1929) reported some years ago, that the slum has its gangs and the Gold Coast has its clubs. These are all human groups with consequences—good or evil—for the attitude and behavior of individuals composing them.

IMPLICATIONS FOR VALID STUDY OF BEHAVIOR IN GROUPS

Groups are not formed to be studied by outsiders. They are not formed for the benefit of a reformer. They are not formed to tolerate criticism, advice, or unfavorable evaluations by outsiders. They are formed by individuals with similar concerns. They have designs and ends of their own. They have properties of their own, which are reflected in the attitude and behavior of members toward each other and toward outsiders.

Therefore, if we would study individuals who belong to groups, the cardinal research strategy must be a design that places the behavior of members *within* their groups, and places the groups, in turn, within their sociocultural setting. The selection of methods, procedures and research models is not a matter of convenience or the arbitrary preference of the investigator. If they are to yield valid data, the methods and procedures must accommodate the properties of groups as they actually form and function.

In terms of the properties of groups, as spelled out in this chapter, certain methods are appropriate and certain are inappropriate. Furthermore, the appropriateness or inappropriateness of methods depends on the *time* at which they are used. The properties of groups require a procedural *sequence* of steps.

The issue is not merely whether or not data can be collected, for some kind of data can almost always be obtained. The issue at hand is the *validity* of the obtainable data. This issue is bound to be confronted more and more seriously as social scientists and psychologists are called upon to contribute to baffling human problems ranging all the way from delinquency and school dropouts to segregation, prejudice, and other threatening problems of intergroup relations.

The basic criterion for securing valid data on groups and their members is that procedures and techniques be *timed* so that members will not view the event as an unwarranted intrusion or imposition by an outsider. This is the reason why, from the beginning, a special effort was made in our research not to arouse the group's awareness that an observer was studying them and rating their behavior.

To the extent that a group is at odds with established routines and channels for behavior, they not only have designs of their own, but also *secrets* about these designs. Whether or not their behavior is socially acceptable to adults, most adolescent groups do have plans which they consider *private*, especially from grownups, who seldom "understand" them. (See, for example, the Introduction to this book.)

To the extent that group members consider their affairs "private," they erect walls of resistance to any outsider. The appropriate timing and sequence of research procedures are, therefore, contingent upon steps to bring down first these walls of resistance and then the walls of secrecy.

In short, the timing and sequence of research procedures must be planned in terms of the degree of *rapport* established with group members, particularly those of higher status who are most obligated to protect the group's privacy. Results from the more usual research procedures— interviews with direct questions, questionnaires, sociometric choices, laboratory procedures requiring the cooperation of subjects—are less than worthless if introduced before rapport is firmly established. They are misleading. Very early in our research, this realization was forced upon us by an incident involving the untimely use of sociometric techniques.

The observer had had considerable give-and-take with the group for several months. In securing sociometric choices, he talked individually to each boy, inquiring whom he liked to "hang around with" most. The answers seemed free and courteous, but revealed the futility of such a procedure when rapport is no deeper than surface courtesy. The boys were all telling the observer that their best pals were boys about ten or twelve years old, most of them younger brothers.

The cycle of procedures for study of groups, as developed in our research, and problems of developing and assessing rapport, are discussed in the next chapter.

PREDICTABILITY OF BEHAVIOR STUDIED IN ITS APPROPRIATE CONTEXT

A serious pitfall in research is the tendency to select a particular mode of behavior, often because it is socially unacceptable, and then to "explain" it through postmortem analysis without specifying the background and context of the events in question. In experimentation, this tendency leads to laboratory models with little bearing on the actualities of the field. In the field, it leads to failures in predicting behavior and, practically, to views impeding the development of preventive measures.

In studying youthful behavior, we have been equally interested in those attitudes and actions which are socially acceptable and those which are not. There cannot be one social psychology for acceptable behaviors and another, entirely different, social psychology for unacceptable ones. In both cases, general psychological principles must be sought which take into account the background and context of behavior.

PREDICTION AND THE SOCIAL CONTEXT OF YOUTHFUL BEHAVIOR

A research design to accommodate all the influences shaping behavior and to secure valid, reliable indicators of behavior as it actually occurs is essential in developing a base for making predictions. We have secured data on planning, decision-making, and actions that members considered secret and would not have exposed to any adult with authority. Frequently, the events had consequential outcomes for the individuals.

A case in point was our prediction of two school dropouts some weeks before they occurred. The prediction was based on extensive evidence that the two boys were highly committed members in a group in which the high status positions were held by boys who had left school. The two continued in school under pressures from parents and teachers. They were not failing. But in their group, derogation of school as a place for "sissies" was common. They had no close personal ties with schoolmates. Being in school deprived them of time when other members were doing "interesting" things. First one, then the other boy stopped attending school, a few months short of graduation.

The study of behavior in its group context has been severely hampered by a moralistic view which condemns group influence as a sign of individual weakness or even pathology. This view is blind to the fact that group influence on individual behavior may be for good as well as for evil.

In our research, we encountered numerous instances of an official tendency by community authorities (school, recreation leaders, parents) to minimize even the existence of groups within the area of their work. Apparently the tendency is nationwide in scope, as indicated in a report for the Committee on the Judiciary of the U.S. Senate in the following words:

> We further encountered difficulties when confronted in many communities with the attitude that the mere existence of any gang or gang problem constituted a failure of responsibility of the agencies, so that the type of reports made by these agencies were less than complete. In several cities we found, based on our own investigations, discussions, and contacts made with gangs, gang workers, police on the beat, teachers and citizens, a wide discrepancy between their off-the-record statements and the official reporting regarding the existence of gangs, their antisocial behavior, and the degree of problem they created. (U.S. Senate Report, 1961, p. 12)

Yet, ignoring the group context of behavior will continue to lead, as it has in the past, to failures of prediction in research and to continued "surprises" at a community level. For example, the following type of news item is not unusual:

The uncovering by police (Sunday) of a ruthless, pistol packing gang of 20 or more youthful LeDroit Park Ramblers (in Washington, D.C.), who are suspected of engineering over 80 "hustles" in 6 months has left area youth workers shocked. . . . Playground officials, the Recreation Department's roving leaders, the Junior Police and Citizens Corps, the LeDroit Park Civic Association, and the Youth Aid Division of the police department had all been unaware even that a group of youth using the name of "Ramblers" existed. (U.S. Senate Report, 1961, p. 12)

The deeds and misdeeds of youth cannot be predicted solely on the basis of class membership, nor solely on the basis of family relations, nor through any theory advocating a single sovereign cause. It should be sobering for both theorists and practitioners to read a recent report ascribed to the Pennsylvania Chiefs of Police Association (in the same Senate report) which concludes that "the broken home and unemployed and socially handicapped youth can no longer be solely blamed for juvenile crime." Several examples are cited of serious violations by youth from comfortable neighborhoods.

An equally strong case could be made that theories advocating oversimplified etiology cannot account for socially acceptable behavior. The etiology of behavior, whether acceptable or not, must include the context of membership in natural groups, in whose formation and functioning many influences participate. These influences stem from the individual and his background, from the sociocultural setting in which he develops, and from the prevailing images of success and achievement set by people who count in his eyes, whether these people are immediately present or are reflected from the mass media. All of these contribute to the natural reference groups of age-mates in which youth moves and to their directions, which may be for good or for evil.

PREDICTION AND GENERAL PRINCIPLES OF BEHAVIOR

The greatest promise for a theory to enable prediction lies in identifying general principles that are equally valid in the laboratory and in the rich context of the field. The experiments summarized earlier in this chapter are examples of research utilizing general principles of judgment with relevance for behavior in social actualities. Thus, Pollis' study showed that the tendency toward compliance with others' judgments is modified by the individual's background, specifically by whether his standards were formed in a group or in a less stable interpersonal context. Prado used the general finding of systematic variations in judgments of performance to index shifts in the salience of reference groups from childhood to adolescence. As a final example from this research program, we will mention continuity of a basic principle of judgment discovered in the interaction patterns of adolescent groups in the field.

The interpersonal relations among contemporaries are patterned affairs. To some extent, an individual regulates his behavior relative to others, and to that extent his behavior becomes predictable in a variety of situations. In comparing the ratings made by observers with the sociometric choices made by members of the relative power (effective initiative) in a group, we have found that predictability of behavior is related to the individual's position in the group structure. But the relationship is not a linear function of relative power; it is curvilinear. As Chapter 13 will show in more detail, consistency and confidence in ratings are invariably greater regarding the leader and other high status persons, followed by ratings of those with lowest status. Variability in rating is greatest in the intermediate ranks.

Thus, we see in the patterning of group interpersonal relations a phenomenon which has been extensively studied in the psychophysical laboratory—namely, *end-anchoring*. The extreme representatives of a set of stimuli are singled out most readily and used as standards for assessing the others. In natural groups, the leader position is typically the most potent anchor; the lower positions are rated with less variability than intermediate levels.

The extent to which end-anchoring of the group structure occurs, the stability of the structure, and the number of status categories (or levels) from top to bottom vary considerably in natural groups, as they do in larger organizations. The variations, in turn, are affected in a crucial way by the relation of the small group to its setting. Thus, the stability of the leader position, which is the upper anchor, as well as the extent of differentiation in the pattern, are strikingly dependent on *what* the members engage in and on what their dealings are with others in the setting— both other groups and adult authorities. The changes in the status patterns which we have observed as they happened resulted from external changes in the settings—changes in the opportunities faced by the members or exposure of their most private activities by adult authorities.

But, whatever the variations, differentiations according to the effectiveness of initiative and patterns of deference among members was the rule in these natural groups. This phenomenon is the invariant consequence of prolonged interaction among individuals facing common problems. Which individual will occupy what status position, and which individual will succeed in changing his position, rests on unique personal characteristics of individual members—their contribution relative to the demands of group activities in which certain personal characteristics matter. These are fascinating problems of individual differences to be explored in the research program as it continues.

CONCLUSIONS

The properties of natural reference groups do limit the range of procedures and the sequence of their application in collecting valid data. Much more effort and patience are required than in laboratory research. But within the approach outlined here, precise and reliable measurement is within the grasp of field research. Laboratory methods of assessment can frequently be adapted for this purpose. And with greater specification of the variables, findings in the field become the proper basis for laboratory research.

When small groups and their members are studied relative to their sociocultural settings, and the setting studied relative to the groups within it, the dichotomy between small group research and research on large organizations will disappear. The "psychological" and the "sociological" study of social behavior will supplement one another, instead of being monopolistic preferences of their respective disciplines.

The contributions of particular individuals, for good or for evil, can be studied to any desired degree of elaboration within their appropriate behavior settings. The appropriate behavior settings are patterned affairs, consisting of the individual's reference groups and the sociocultural setting of which these reference groups are parts. Personal skills and qualities are not contributed in the abstract. Unique individuality shows in the ways an individual interacts with others in activities and situations important in their concerted undertakings. These interactions provide the context for his own attitude and behavior.

On the basis of the theoretical and methodological background presented here, the research on adolescents in their groups in their settings is summarized in the next chapter. It is our conviction that the approach outlined is equally viable for the study of behavior at other age periods, taking into account the changes in the setting and their salience throughout development.

REFERENCES

Barker, Roger G., 1963. On the nature of the environment. Kurt Lewin Memorial Address, *J. soc. Issues,* October, 1963, 17-38.

Blau, P. M., and W. R. Scott, 1962. *Formal Organizations.* (San Francisco: Chandler.)

Bell, W., 1958. The utility of the Shevky typology for the design of urban sub-area field studies. *J. soc. Psychol.,* 47, 71-83.

Cartwright, D., and Zander, A., 1960. *Group Dynamics: Research and Theory.* (Evanston, Ill.: Row, Peterson.)

Chapanis, A., 1961. Men, machines, and models. *Amer. Psychologist,* 16, 113-131.

Deutsch, Martin, 1964. Guidelines for testing minority group children. *J. soc. Issues*, 20, No. 2.

Durkheim, E., 1915. *The Elementary Forms of Religious Life.* (London: G. Allen.)

Helson, H., 1964. Current trends and issues in adaptation level theory. *Amer. Psychologist*, 19, p. 26.

Homans, G. C., 1950. *The Human Group.* (New York: Harcourt, Brace and World.)

Jacobs, R. C., and D. T. Campbell, 1961. The perpetuation of an arbitrary tradition through several generations of a laboratory microculture. *J. abnorm. soc. Psychol.*, 62, 649-58.

Orne, M. T., 1962. On the social psychology of the psychological experiment: With particular reference to demand characteristics and their implications. *Amer. Psychologist*, 17, 776-783.

Pettigrew, T. F., 1964. Negro American intelligence: A new look at an old controversy. *J. Negro Educat.*, Winter, 1964, 6-25.

Pishkin, V., 1963. Experimenter variable in concept identification feedback of schizophrenics. *Percept. & Motor Skills*, 16, 921-922.

Rosenthal, R., 1961. On the social psychology of the psychological experiment: with particular reference to experimenter bias. (Paper read to Annual Convention, APA, New York City.)

Schottstaedt, W. W., Ruth H. Pinsky, D. Mackler, and S. Wolf, 1958. Sociologic, psychologic and metabolic observations on patients in the community of a metabolic ward. *Amer. J. of Medicine*, 25, 248-257.

Sherif, Carolyn, M. Sherif, and R. Nebergall, 1965. *Attitude and attitude change.* (Philadelphia: W. B. Saunders.)

Sherif, M., 1935. Study of some social factors in perception. *Archives of Psychol.*, 187.

———, 1936. *Psychology of Social Norms.* (New York: Harper and Bros.)

———, 1948. *Outline of Social Psychology.* (New York: Harper and Bros.)

Sherif, M., and H. Cantril, 1947. *Psychology of ego-involvement.* (New York: Wiley.)

Sherif, M., and O. J. Harvey, 1952. A study in ego functioning: Elimination of stable anchorages in individual and group situations. *Sociometry*, 15, 272-305.

Sherif, M., O. J. Harvey, B. J. White, W. R. Hood, and Carolyn Sherif, 1961. *Intergroup conflict and cooperation: The Robbers Cave experiment.* (Norman, Oklahoma: University Book Exchange.)

Sherif, M., and B. Koslin, 1960. The "institutional" vs. "behavioral" controversy in social science, with special reference to political science. (Norman, Oklahoma: Institute of Group Relations, University of Oklahoma, mimeographed.)

Sherif, M., and Carolyn Sherif, 1953. *Groups in Harmony and Tension.* (New York: Harper and Bros.)

———, 1956. *Outline of Social Psychology.* (New York: Harper and Row.)

———, 1964. *Reference Groups: Exploration into conformity and deviation of adolescents.* (New York, Harper and Row.)

Shevky, E., and W. Bell, 1955. *Social area analysis.* (Stanford: Stanford University Press.)

Stevenson, H. W. and Sara Allen, 1964. Adult performance as a function of sex of experimenter and sex of subject. *J. abnorm. soc. psychol.,* 68, 214-216.

U.S. Senate, 1961. Report of the Committee on the Judiciary, 87th Congress, 1st Session, Report 169, April 18.

Zorbaugh, W. W., 1929. *The Gold Coast and the Slum.* (Chicago: University of Chicago Press.)

THIRTEEN

THE ADOLESCENT IN HIS GROUP IN ITS SETTING

II. Research Procedures and Findings

Muzafer Sherif and Carolyn W. Sherif

In this chapter, we will outline the procedures and research tools developed for intensive study of natural groups on the basis of the theoretical guidelines presented in Chapter 12. Findings from our research on youth in various settings within urban areas of the southwestern United States are incorporated throughout the chapter.

The procedures and tools in this research program are not entirely distinctive—if there is innovation, it lies in procedures for studying behavior in natural groups of adolescents without arousing awareness of research intent. Nor do we propose that all the findings on adolescent youth are unique to our research. As indicated in the last chapter, we have freely utilized previous research from psychologists and social scientists as bases for hypotheses, concepts, and research procedures. We would be surprised if our findings bore no relation to those previously reported on American youth.

On the contrary, our purpose is to demonstrate the importance of incorporating the many influences on youthful behavior into single research designs. The neglect of some facets has led in the past to emphasis on one particular point to the neglect of others in theories of adolescent behaviors and misbehaviors. We have had ample opportunity to see the fruitlessness of one-facet theories, whether they focus exclusively on early childhood development, intrapsychic conflicts, sexual development, social class or local subculture.

A theory capable of accounting for the behavior of individuals interacting with others in definite habitats—that is, social-psychological theory —must be based on an integration of findings about all the significant influences affecting behavior. These include the motivational dilemma of the adolescent in his society; the person he is at the time, including his skills and his desires to be part of some scheme of human endeavor; the influences from other people who *count* in his eyes; the properties of his relationships with those people; the values and facilities of his sociocultural setting; and the setting's place in the larger social scene.

If a theory is to be adequate, its development must proceed hand in hand with the development of operational tools for research incorporating all the significant variables. Without such tools, no theory can link its concepts together and deal with empirical relationships, no matter how elegant it may sound. And without a theory to integrate the significant variables affecting adolescent behavior, practical measures for preventing the wastage of youthful potentialities can only proceed on a hit-or-miss basis.

RESEARCH PERSPECTIVE ON ADOLESCENT BEHAVIOR

Let us sum up the general features of the adolescent period, since the influences that an adequate research design must study follow from these features.

First, the adolescent is a human male or female with at least a decade of life behind him. His body and its functioning are beginning to change toward that of an adult human. As they do, he is expected to alter his behavior toward others and toward his current and future responsibilities. Although ordinarily he wants to do so, these behavioral alterations can be achieved in a consistent way only if he changes his picture of himself relative to others. Thus they demand changes in self or ego-attitudes in various respects.

Second, in modern societies, the motivational problems that come with physical changes and the necessity of changing one's self-image are further compounded by ambiguities in adult definitions of the transition period. The general characteristics of the period as defined, or left undefined, produce strong motivational problems and dilemmas which are, indeed, common to all youth in some degree.

Third, adolescent behavior under the grip of these motivational problems and dilemmas is not entirely unique to the adolescent period. Similarities may be observed among any individuals presented with a motivational problem. A frequent response, when individuals perceive that others share their problem, is to come together in regular association. Since age-mate association is both permitted and encouraged in modern societies, youth do gravitate toward one another, associating more frequently and more intensely than in earlier childhood. The domain of other adolescents becomes a reference set of greater salience than that of adults or younger children (as demonstrated experimentally in Chapter 12).

Fourth, regular associations among individuals of any age with common problems acquire distinctive properties. These include some patterning or organization of interpersonal dealings, and some agreement as to what objects and behaviors are acceptable and which are not, what is to be prized and sought, and what is "ideal." These two properties—patterned interpersonal relations and shared yardsticks for evaluation—are the minimums defining a human group. Thus, group formations proliferate during adolescence.

Fifth, what the individual adolescent desires, what he sees as the ideal, what he does in concert with age-mates, the character of their group and its products, are not *direct outcomes* of the motivational problems which bring him to his fellow group members or which he discovers he shares with them. Here, we must consider both the immediate sociocultural setting and its facilities, and the values of the larger society of which they are parts.

During adolescence, the character of the general culture and the immediate circumstances of living take on new and added significance. The radius of self-concern is expanding beyond its more limited scope of childhood and extending further into the future. Even in the immediate present, the adolescent is more tuned to sociocultural influences and his society's adult success images. He is more mobile than a child.

The point may be illustrated briefly: In our research, we found that boys and girls in the southwest come to feel, by the age of seventeen or eighteen, that it is their inalienable right to have a car. A car is seen as a *necessity*. Particular kinds, models, and colors desired are specified to the last detail. There can be no doubt of the motivational press behind these desires, nor of their relevance to other common motivational problems (including notably those related to prestige, contacts with and conquests of the opposite sex). However, it is impossible to understand this phenomenon apart from an understanding of the "car culture" in American life, with its mass salesmanship and broad impact on social life.

The general "car culture," combined with physical characteristics and facilities of southwestern cities, has made possession of a car the ideal in all kinds of neighborhoods, rich and poor. Having or not having a car, as well as the kind of car it is, affects one's status and prestige with those of both sexes. The desire for a car is certainly a "psychological need" as experienced by the individual. But this need and the resulting development of a subculture with stylized patterns of driving around, of joy rides or outright theft, would be bizarre phenomena if a researcher should attempt to study them apart from the widespread importance of a car in American life, and the differential availability of cars in different settings. The "need" for a car, as well as "needs" for thrills, or for defiance, or for "acting out," are meaningless apart from the character of the sociocultural settings in which they have been nourished and shown in action.

ESSENTIAL FACETS IN RESEARCH DESIGNS ON ADOLESCENT BEHAVIOR

If, as in our research, we wish to study adolescents as individuals, we must incorporate into the design at least the major sets of influences that affect their attitudes and behavior. This is equally true whether our problem concerns adolescent accomplishments in socially desirable directions, or their undesirable modes of activity, such as drug usage or car theft. Within the general problem of adolescence as defined in a society, we have seen that the sociocultural setting and its values are major influences, particularly those values prevailing among the reference set of teenagers. Finally, the design would be incomplete without including study of the individual's reference group of age-mates, and his relationship to them and to other groups in his ken (family, school, church groups, etc.).

As outlined early in the last chapter, the design of research included three main facets to accommodate these major influences. The next sections describe the operational steps in the three facets, with emphasis on the intensive study of behavior in natural groups of youth. Finally, findings in the three facets are summarized to indicate their interdependence.

SOCIOCULTURAL SETTINGS OF BEHAVIOR

To be sure, there must be a division of labor in the sciences of man. Study of sociocultural settings is a sociological or anthropological task. If the task has not been done as specifically as necessary for research on particular adolescents, then the investigator must "act like a sociologist" for the time. He can get help from social scientists, borrow their tools, or secure a collaborator, but he cannot ignore the task as being irrelevant to his own interests. Nor can he evade the task by assigning a blanket label to the setting, such as "lower class," "middle class," or "ethnic subculture." This evasion would be analogous, for example, to an experimenter in color vision saying: "I am studying color vision in an illuminated laboratory. But I do not know how much or what kind of illumination it is, because I am not a physicist or electrician. Information of that kind isn't my job."

Like the physical surroundings, the social habitat has regularities in structure, time sequence, and recurrence of events. For example, the range and standards of living in a neighborhood where adolescents live and meet indicate a patterned set of circumstances. These circumstances are pertinent to what youth do, how they spend their time, where they spend it, and even what they consider suitable activities during leisure hours. Boys in favored neighborhoods of high socioeconomic rank own cars, have comfortable homes, and ample spending money. They will think of leisure related to their cars, their visits and parties in each others' homes, and outlays of money for dates and professional entertainment. They are extremely mobile. In fact, the entire city is "their oyster," which makes their study unusually difficult. The contrast in mobility and attitudes is striking in an urban neighborhood where cars are not available, homes poor and crowded, and money lacking.

In our research, residential areas where the youth live are studied through first-hand exploration, mapping of facilities, available municipal statistics, and (in neighborhoods with Spanish-speaking residents) block surveys to check the extent of acculturation among residents. Looking for ways of indicating features of the setting, we found that Shevky and Bell had developed a social area analysis based on census tract statistics. A limited number of census measures, combined appropriately, serve to indicate relative ranks of areas in significant respects. These indicators seem to account for the major sources of variance in a host of discrete statistics on urban areas. Each is associated, therefore, with correlated information not included in the analysis.

Bell's chapter in this book (Chapter 11) obviates the need of presenting the three indicators in social area analysis in detail. They are, however, (1) socioeconomic rank (2) degree of urbanization and family conditions, and (3) ethnic status of the population and their concentration in an area. In addition to being reproducible and communicable, these indicators have the advantage of showing gradations in a coordinate system based on standardized scores. For example, it is possible to specify that one area of low socioeconomic rank is not as "low" as another. Or, a low rank area is not as urbanized as one of middle rank in the same city; that is, there are fewer apartments in the low rank area, more children, and fewer mothers who work. Clearly, the ecological conditions are quite different in the two neighborhoods, apart from socioeconomic level. Life in this low rank area, with its shabby two and three-room houses, is likewise different from that in a comparably poor tenement neighborhood of a large eastern city.

Specifying ethnic status of the residents is equally important, though not always sufficient for our purposes. In some areas, with a sizable proportion of Mexican-born citizens, we have conducted block surveys to assess the relative acculturation, on the basis of length of residence and style of living. Indications of relative acculturation to U.S. life were, for instance, the type of pictures on the walls and the cultivation of yards, ranging from the flower-pot culture of the Mexican to the green lawn of the "Anglo." The advantage of such specification of the setting can be illustrated, and may be similarly illuminating in other sociocultural comparisons, for example, between neighborhoods of Negroes raised in urban settings and those peopled by recent migrants from rural areas.

In this instance, we found that a group of adolescent boys in a "Latin" neighborhood had very little interest in organized sports, unlike most of their counterparts in other areas. When we found that their neighborhood was among the least acculturated to American life, they appeared as fairly representative of their immediate setting, although otherwise these boys' lack of interest in sports would have seemed extremely atypical. This information also clarified the frequent observation that whenever one of these boys spoke English to his fellows, he was chastised to remember he was "Mexican." (Their Spanish, however, would not have been altogether understandable in Mexico.)

Later in the chapter, the dangers of blanket conclusions about youth in a given socioeconomic level or subculture will be mentioned. We warn against generalizing about youth in any given stratum without sufficient evidence and against viewing any stratum as an isolated phenomenon. We stress both the importance of a comparative approach to youth from different backgrounds and the relationships among different strata in a society. After all, socioeconomic strata are characterized as "low," "middle," or "high" in rank according to social criteria as well as economic needs for physical well-being. The ill fate or good fortune of a particular stratum is, therefore, conditional in part upon the larger social system.

ADOLESCENT VALUES AND GOALS WITHIN THE INDIVIDUAL'S SETTING

For a particular adolescent, the values and goals of other youth in his ken are salient aspects of his environment. Whether his personal radius for achievement and his potentialities are in line with theirs or not, he knows full well that his actions are gauged relative to their standards, which are revealed to him time and again in episodes of action, appraisal, approval, disapproval, notice and notoriety, or, worst of all, ignominity and personal oblivion.

For such reasons, one facet of the research program assessed conceptions of propriety, of achievement, and of success in the various sociocultural settings. A paper-and-pencil form presented as an opinion survey was administered to representative samples of secondary school students in the study areas. To date, three versions of this form have been used with many identical items in each. Throughout, the aim has been to devise items on significant aspects of adolescent life in forms which will yield a *range* of conceptions, from the acceptable minimum to the personal ideal. The content areas include conceptions of leisure time and activities, work and future occupations, school and academic goals, financial and material necessities and goals, parental regulation and controls, proper modes of behavior, desirable associates, and personal success and aspiration. The data are analyzed both in terms of the bounds of acceptability and achievement prevailing in a neighborhood and of the distribution of individual responses within these bounds.

In other words, the data in this facet are sociocultural data on the adolescents themselves. In view of the school context in which the forms are administered, the data are most accurately interpreted as indicating what youth regard as "socially desirable," in Allen Edwards' use of that term (1957). However, in a school setting, young people do not always respond readily in terms of personal experiences or specific social relationships. The records contain overheard statements such as, "Boy! Did I feed them a line." In non-school situations in which the same forms have been administered, observers who have established more rapport with boys than most other adults have encountered resentment to some items, particularly those pertaining to areas where adults are usually excluded. Recent administration of the forms in detention and reformatory settings also indicates evidence of attempts at dissimulation, but the data here differ from those obtained in school settings from youth with comparable socioeconomic backgrounds.

The different pattern of responses in different sociocultural settings, and some evidence of dissimulation, support our interpretation that these data express youths' conceptions of what it is socially desirable for them to report. But even these conceptions of "lines" to give adults vary in several important ways, and are interesting data in themselves, revealing socioeconomic and cultural differences.

Since one's self-radius for achievement is, in part, a function of what one conceives as socially desirable, the differences between the bounds prevailing in different sociocultural settings have important psychological implications. Even if not followed, the prevailing bounds in a social setting are significant as stimulating (external) conditions for the individual youth. Their salience can be illustrated briefly.

In a lower middle class area suburban to a large city, one small group of boys studied in our research for nine months had all dropped out of school. Although some of them had been prevented from re-entry by school authorities, the majority had been subjected to persuasive and coercive efforts by their parents to continue in school. One parent had even given a bribe—a new car—as the reward for school attendance, to no avail. By their actions and in conversations, these boys deprecated school attendance. They were, however, fully aware that among their agemates outside their group, high school graduation was the minimum standard for achievement. Their awareness was revealed in repeated instances of withdrawal from the "school crowd" as "snobs," in their unanimous agreement about the impossibility of returning to the local high school, and by statements by all but one member that they intended to finish school in a neighboring town or "in the army" eventually, thereby reaching a par socially and occupationally with their contemporaries.

The data on prevailing self-radius and goals of youth in different urban areas are used in four ways:

First, to detect values and goals upheld by common consent of youth in different areas.

'Second, to detect differences between the areas in these respects.

Third, to assess the homogeneity or heterogeneity of standards prevaling among adolescents *within* an area.

Fourth, to form a basis of comparison for assessing the typicality or deviance of the attitudes and goals expressed by members of small groups studied in an area.

INTENSIVE STUDY OF SMALL GROUPS WITHIN EACH SETTING

Within each neighborhood of low, middle or high socioeconomic rank, the attitudes and behaviors of boys in informal groups of their own choosing are studied intensively over periods of time ranging from six months to a year. This focal facet of the research is carried out in the field —in the natural habitat of boys themselves.

In this aspect, we had to face seriously the problems of research method arising from the context effects discussed at some length in Chapter 12. The very nature of research by people into the current behavior of other persons raises issues which are by no means so obvious in the other sciences. One of these is how to establish research contact with the phenomena under study without fundamentally changing them.

Admittedly, astronomers had the problem of research contact with the heavenly bodies. The technological means for observation (telescopes, electronics, satellites) have not yet substantially affected the movements of heavenly bodies nor their nature.

In the study of human behavior, however, there is growing evidence that technological devices and instruments may be inimical to approaching the phenomena of interest. Their usefulness begins *after* the investigator has solved the problem of getting close enough to human beings to study them without letting them know they are under observation.

Therefore, the intensive study of behavior in natural groups proceeded from the premise that the timing and selection of research procedures should be such that they would have little effect on the group and its members. This is the reason for all of the efforts to keep group members from being aware that they were being observed for research purposes.

In the varied and changing field of social actualities, a single observer will inevitably choose facts selectively. It was our second premise that selectivity could best be minimized if the observer focused on one aspect of the interaction process at a time, and a variety of independent data-gathering techniques were introduced at choice points. In appropriate sequence, the observer's reports and ratings of behavior were checked against ratings from an independent observer, from sociometric interviews with group members, from interviews with adults who knew them, and from public records pertinent to their past activities. The use of a combination of techniques in a variety of situations over time is the best way to insure validity of findings, which cannot be guaranteed by sophistication in test design, or in planting recording devices, or in later analysis.

To date, the study of 24 groups of boys (ages 13-18 years) has been completed through the cycle of steps envisaged. The difficulties, and in some cases failures, in completing the study cycle would make a fascinating chapter in themselves on the rigors of social research. These difficulties range all the way from practical problems of carrying out procedures in a particular setting, to some observers' lack of persistence and interfering preconceptions on the nature of research. Many of the latter preconceptions, formed in other training, must be revised in an attempt, such as ours, to fit research procedures to the actualities of the field, rather than vice versa. The real challenge of social research is to secure precise and manageable data that faithfully reflect the actual properties of events.

THE OBSERVER BEING OBSERVED

When an observer begins to hang around in the vicinity of a group, there is always a period when the members observe and scrutinize *him*. The observer being observed by his subjects is one instance of a general phenomenon of person perception: first impressions are invariably accompanied by efforts to *place* the person and his presence in our area in some social categories.———

For this reason, the prime criterion for placing an observer is his "fit" with the predominant socioeconomic and cultural background of the residents. In appearance, speech, and manner, he must blend into the scene. Even then, the recurring presence of a strange face in familiar surroundings calls forth questions about why he is there and what he intends to do.

In our research, the observer is instructed to develop first a reasonable pretext for his presence that circumstances cannot contradict even before he makes contact with a cluster of boys. Preferably, the pretext is one which will bring the boys to the observer because of their own interest in his activities or possessions (for example, his athletic equipment, or his car).

The age difference between observer and observed is another factor to be reckoned at this stage. Our observers are ordinarily in their early twenties, slightly older than the group members they observe. This has proven necessary for two reasons: First, the observer must be trained and mature enough to follow procedures in step-by-step fashion. Second, an adolescent observing adolescents is in the constant danger of becoming *part* of their group, competing for status, and seeing the interaction process from his particular role in the structure.

Fortunately, we discovered that adolescent boys in most communities do have contacts with slightly older males and are, in fact, somewhat attracted by the possibility of contact with a person representing what they may become. The age factor, therefore, has not been insurmountable when the observer succeeded in establishing his presence as a sympathetic, possibly helpful young adult—somewhat like an older brother.

Still, for weeks or several months, the observer is observed. He is asked pointblank who he is, his connections, why he is around, and what he is doing. Over the course of time, the boys check up on his replies before they start opening up to him. The observer is still denied the luxury of direct questions to the boys. The procedures he employs are planned in step-by-step fashion to gain data while strengthening rapport.

The initial and most difficult period in the intensive field study of natural groups is making contact with the members and overcoming their wall of resistance and secrecy about their more private activities. It challenges the patience and skill of the observer. Depending on these as well as on the group, the study has sometimes not progressed beyond the period of the observer being observed. We suspect that in most such cases, the rigid walls of resistance and secrecy indicate tightly knit groups with stable organizations and binding commitments in activities of an illegal or antisocial nature.

DEVELOPING AND GAUGING RAPPORT

Once contact with group members has been made, the real cycle of procedures in the study of natural groups begins. However, the particular methods used, and their sequence and timing, are planned to coordinate with the development of rapport between observer and group members.

In the early period, no techniques are introduced that require probing questions or other assaults on the privacy of group activities. The observer simply reports on what he sees and rates member behavior after leaving the group. No other techniques are used until the observer is tolerated by members in activities and in discussion of matters considered exclusive and private.

Gauging the degree of rapport is too critical to be merely a matter of intuition. We utilize a combination of indicators in deciding on the timing of the procedures in the study cycle. Indicators of degree of rapport include these signs: the observer's success in finding the various places the group congregates when not in plain public view; the members' tolerance of his presence in these more private places; the degree of intimacy of activities the members discuss freely in his presence; the extent to which members welcome him into activities which they would hide from other adults.

Valid data on group properties and member attitudes can be obtained only if rapport is developed. For this reason, ratings by independent observers, sociometric choices, interviews and other procedures that assume cooperation with the researcher (without dissimulation or fabrication) are kept for near the end of the study cycle. Collection of case history materials is the final step in the cycle. Data obtained from all of these procedures can then be cross-checked against the mass of documentation of member attitude and action which has been collected during interaction episodes.

Developing rapport and adjusting procedures to the changing degree of rapport are continuing processes. Recently one of the observers (Mr. Lauderdale) attempted to conduct individual interviews with items from the Self-Radius and Goals schedules; this followed seven months of observation, during which he had been permitted to learn some of the more intimate secrets of the group including drinking, sexual activities, and incidents involving the police. The individuals responded freely enough about money, jobs, leisure activities, and the like. But he reported responses ranging "from apparent indifference and withdrawal to outright hostility" when he queried them about school experiences and about their special friends. "Remarks ranged from simply 'I don't know' to explanations that 'I don't like to answer questions because someone might try to get something on me,' or 'You're sure full of questions, aren't you? I don't like snoopy questions from my friends or anyone else.'"

Another observer (Eduardo Villarreal), who returned to a group he had studied about three years earlier in order to check on present membership, reported that new members were withdrawn and suspicious even though the older members introduced him as an old "camerado." The newer boys relaxed only after questioning him themselves to find out exactly what he was up to.

THE STUDY CYCLE

The complete study cycle is accomplished through ten successive sets of instructions to observers, followed as rapport warrants going on to the next step. The instructions are revised regularly on the basis of new research experiences, but they are substantially the same as those presented as the appendix of our book (Sherif and Sherif, 1964). Here, the steps will be summarized briefly along with definitions of the principal measures to be used by observers.

First, a group is singled out for observation on the basis of observed frequency of association among a specifiable cluster of boys between 13-18 years in specific locations (recreation center, pool hall, drive-in, vacant lot, etc.).

Second, after establishing rapport to the point that he is tolerated by the boys in locations and activities other than those of their initial encounter, an observer directs his attention to the status or power relations among the individuals. The prime criterion for status or power in the group is defined by the concept of effective initiative, or the extent to which suggestions made by the various individuals are actually followed at that time or later. Allied observations pertinent to ratings of status or power include concrete examples of deference, effective dominance, or submission.

Although the pattern of power relations, as defined above, is not the only dimension differentiating the attitudes and behaviors of members in a group, it is the most useful dimension for predictive purposes. If one knows which boy has most frequently suggested alternatives that the others actually translate into common decisions and actions, he has found the operational *leader* of the group. If he can rank other individuals in the same respect, he has a powerful predictive device for what may transpire among them. The observers in our research have been able to do this, and the fact that the resulting pictures of group structure are invariably hierarchical reflects something about the nature of social power. Unlike some other attributes, individual power is necessarily limited by the nature of interaction. If members adopt the suggestion of one member, those made by others are bound to be neglected for the time.

Of course, other dimensions contribute to the differentiation of individual roles in a group: popularity, special skills in activities valued by members, and special resources, such as money, a car, or a home for entertaining. However, any one of these dimensions, so frequently taken by responsible adults as *the* criterion for adolescent standing, is imperfectly correlated with status (power) in their actual interactions. (Cf. Sherif and Sherif, 1964, Chapter 7.)

Third, the observer focuses on the prevailing customs, procedures and norms of the group. He looks for collective products of their interaction—procedures typically followed in frequent activities, common jokes and sayings, signs of dress or decoration, names for "us" and "not us," and expressions or deeds denoting what is considered acceptable, unacceptable, desirable, or unsuitable enough to demand reprimand or punishment. These normative properties are assessed in three ways:

1. Observation of distinctive similarities in expressed attitude and behavior among members that differ from those in other circles or groups.

2. Members' reactions to the usually acceptable range of behavior, including rewards and approval for praiseworthy actions and various forms of punishment or disapproval, indicating deviation.

3. A new member's conformity over time with established procedures, modes of attitude and action.

Next, the observer's ratings and reports are checked through independent techniques, including ratings of a significant group activity by an independent observer, sociometric ratings obtained from the members individually in informal interviews, and situational tests devised especially to create forced choices between association with the group and other activities.

Finally, through interviews with the boys, parents, teachers and other adults, as well as any available records in school or community, a "natural history" of the group and the backgrounds of particular members are reconstructed. The observer also maps the spread of the dwellings of the members, which indicates the effort they make to associate, especially when they do not have transportation available. It is noteworthy, perhaps, that only one of the groups studied thus far has been clustered within the same block. Even "neighborhood" groups are scattered over considerable areas, which shows something about the mobility of urban life for adolescents, but also reveals a selective process in the formation and membership criteria in these groups.

MEMBER BEHAVIOR PREDICTABLE IN TERMS OF GROUP PROPERTIES

Through these procedures, we have specified the essential properties of adolescent groups and their changes over time. These group properties, and the individual's place in the group, provide a powerful basis for predicting adolescent behavior, whether desirable or not. The extent to which behavior is regulated by group membership is related to a person's standing in the group. The degree to which group norms are binding for an individual is related to the stability of his relationships with other members (as demonstrated experimentally in the last chapter).

Being part of recurrent interactions among contemporaries means, for the individual, that he will to an extent regulate his behavior relative to others. Hence, the stabilized patterns of interaction in a group and the individual's location in the pattern affect his treatment of others, their treatments of him, and how closely he adheres to group norms.

LINKING FIELD OBSERVATIONS WITH PRINCIPLES
DERIVED IN THE LABORATORY

In our earlier studies of group formation and intergroup relations in summer camps (Sherif and Sherif, 1953; Sherif *et al.*, 1961), we observed certain regularities in the formation of group structure. Invariably, the first signs of structure were the stabilization of the top and bottom levels of status or power. An observer watching the groups in a variety of activities could consistently rate the persons highest and lowest in effective initiative long before he could differentiate intermediate positions. The boys themselves also agreed more consistently in choosing who was most and least effective in initiating their activities and getting things done.

It is striking, therefore, that the end-anchoring perceived by group members (indicated by their sociometric choices) is similar to the judgments of status by an observer. On the basis of the ratings made by observers of 24 groups, we have constructed a theoretical diagram showing the end-anchoring of an observer's judgments over several blocks of observation periods. Actual data necessarily deviate in detail from the theoretical curves, depending on the number of individuals in a group, changes in membership, or shifts in activities which affect the group structure. Nevertheless, the phenomenon in question was found for each of the groups studied.

Figure 18 represents the average variations in observer's ratings of effective initiative of group members over a substantial block (10) of observation periods, each an hour or longer. Each point on the graph represents the average changes, from one observation period to the next in a given block of observations, in his ratings for members in different segments of different status (base line). In other words, the base line represents the average rating for members during a block of observations;

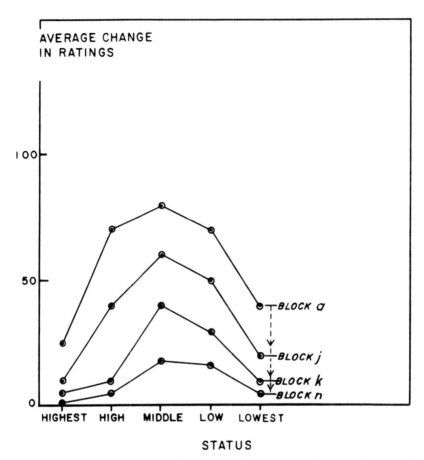

FIGURE 18. End-anchoring in observers' judgments of status in natural
groups over time

the ordinate indicates average shifts from one period to the next. For
example, if the observer changed his ratings on an average of one status
rank for each of ten periods, a point would be located on the ordinate at
.9. Or, if he changed his rating by five ranks twice throughout the block,
the average change would be 1.00. Such large shifts usually reflect a
process of change in the status structure.

Each curve in the figure represents a different block of observations,
lasting around a month, from Block a, during the early weeks of observation, to Block n, when the observer has been with a group several months.
End-anchoring is revealed in the observer's greater consistency in rating
persons in the highest (leader) and lowest (bottom) positions than in the
intermediate ranks. The slightly lower variations for high status ranks

just below the leader and for low ranks just above the bottom represent empirical findings. The intermediate ranks are typically most subject to change.

In our data, the introduction of a new member increases the variation in ratings for other persons near the status level where he first enters the group. If he is a friend of a low status member, variability increases in the low status ranks. If, on the other hand, he immediately shows some highly prized skill or possession, his presence increases variability in ratings of high status ranks. Changes in group structure for other reasons (for example, significant changes in activities, or departure of a member) are similarly reflected in sharp increases in variability of the observer's ratings.

Figure 19 represents the observers' average ratings of *confidence* in how they ranked status from time a (bottom) to time n (top), when they had become closely familiar with a group. Since the confidence ratings

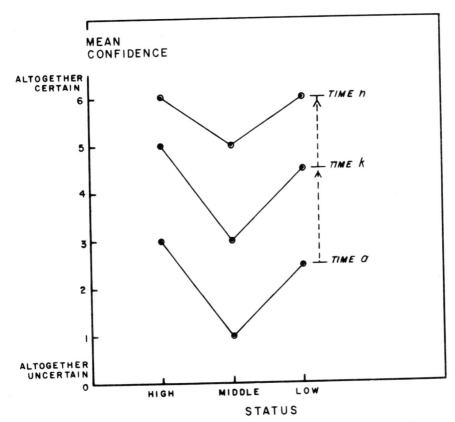

FIGURE 19. End-anchoring revealed in confidence of observers in judgments of status in natural groups

were introduced more recently, this theoretical figure is based on the ratings of fewer groups. Each time he ranks members according to effective initiative, supporting each rating with concrete observations of behavior, the observer indicates how confident he is of each rating, from "altogether uncertain" (0) through "wavering between certainty and uncertainty" (3) to "altogether certain" (6). Figure 19 shows that early in observation (time a) observers are generally uncertain of their ratings, and that their confidence increases over time (to time n). The end-anchoring effect also shows here, in the consistently higher confidence for the high and lowest positions.

Is the end-anchoring effect in group structure solely a perception of the observer, or does it reflect also a reality of group life? Independent raters have agreed closely with the observer when given sufficient opportunity to observe the group, and group members themselves agree more closely in sociometric choices at the highest and lowest levels. End-anchoring seems to be a general phenomenon in perceiving interaction patterns in a group. Furthermore, the ratings by observers can be reconstructed by a content analysis of the concrete events in which members show varying degrees of effective initiative.

We have been asked if the more dominant anchoring position of the leader indicates that groups possibly form through clustering around one individual. On the basis of our research evidence, we feel that this explanation is not sufficient. In only two or three groups have we been able to ascertain that the boys came together initially around a given individual whose initiative was accepted from the beginning. These were all fairly unstable groups. But in the majority of cases, we have found that the leader position has evolved during day-to-day interaction, rather than being the cause for interaction. Our observations include cases of leadership changes, reflected in temporarily increased variability of the observer's ratings of the high status levels, and then followed by renewed end-anchoring on the new leader.

In short, the predictability of individual behavior regarding effective initiative in interactions with others is related to status in the group, in a curvilinear fashion. The curvilinear end-anchoring effect is strikingly similar to that reported in the psychological laboratory for judgments of any series with well-defined end stimuli (for example, series of weights, lines, or sound intensities).

This finding has both practical significance for the prediction of adolescent behavior in natural groups, and theoretical significance in the study of human behavior. We see here the operation of a well-established principle of psychophysical judgment, namely that variations in judgment are smallest for well-defined extremes in a series and greatest for intermediate values. Our conceptualization underscores the operation of this general principle in field observation. The differences between judgments of series of objects and judgments of individuals interacting as members of a social unit indicate that the operation of the general principle should be analyzed discerningly.

In both the psychophysical laboratory and the field ratings of status, the extreme items (objects or persons) serve as anchors, as revealed by reduced variability in judgments. However, lower variability in judging the top position than the bottom is a peculiarity of the human organization, not found in judgments of physical series. One might conclude from this that the general principle is not, after all, general. But another conclusion is that any general principle of human behavior must take account of the context and the particular properties of the stimulus situation. This is our conclusion.

The top rank position in a human group is a more important anchor than the lowest position because of the properties of human organization. These properties are not present in a series of weights, lines, or sound intensities. So the general principle is valid in both psychophysical and psychosocial judgments if the special characteristics of the stimulus situation are taken into account: in this case, the fairly equal importance of end items for ordering a series of physical stimuli, and the inequality of the leader and lowest positions in a human group for ordering those intermediate in position. This demonstrates one way of bridging the appalling gaps still prevailing between field studies and the more precise laboratory approach to the study of human behavior.

LATITUDES OF ACCEPTANCE AND REJECTION
DEFINING INDIVIDUAL CONFORMITY

The individual's position in his group structure provides still another basis for prediction—the extent to which his behavior will fall within a range of variation defined as acceptable by other group members. This latitude of acceptance varies with the significance or importance of the activity for the group. Its limits are defined operationally by behavior indicating common disapproval, threats, or actual punishments.

In every group we have observed, the latitude for acceptable variation in individual behavior has been smallest for matters affecting the maintenance of the group and its solidarity in the face of outside threat (from other groups of age-mates, parents, school authorities, police, etc.). This narrowing of the limits on behavior in the face of outside threat has long been noted in "gangs," especially those involved in illegal activities. It is equally true for groups in activities which are not defined as socially deviant.

For example, one group observed in our research made a great point of "good sportsmanship" in encounters with other groups of age-mates. Nothing called forth disapproval, scolding, or threat of isolation so quickly as unnecessary roughness in a game with other boys or being a "poor loser," despite the fact that the same behavior was accepted when these boys played among themselves. In several groups, the common desire to do things together conflicted with parental requests to do homework. The member who dared tell his parents that they were not actually studying together, but playing records, was treated as a child at least and in some cases as a traitor. Similarly, in a high rank area, the reputation of members as "smooth" but proper young men was zealously guarded for the benefit of the attractive "nice" girls and their mothers. Members who found a younger or less cautious girl willing to engage in sexual contacts were severely chastised if they made it a public matter, outside of their private circle.

In the groups we observed who engaged in definitely illegal activities, the boy who welched out through fear or who "squealed" was treated either to a "good beating" or to ostracism. In these cases, the maintenance of the group as a unit, unsullied by adult or police surveillance, made the norm of privacy in group activities essential. "Getting caught" at an illegal act (carrying a weapon or stealing, in these cases) was a reason for group censure, since it endangered other members. Two group leaders who were caught were both chastised severely by others for being foolhardy and taking risky actions.

Figure 20 shows the relationship found between the range of individual variations permitted and the relative importance of the activity for the group. The latitude of acceptance (ordinate) is narrowest in matters of greatest importance for maintaining the group and its standing as a unit. The latitude is broadest for those matters of least importance, particularly those involving activities strictly within group confines.

The relationship depicted in Figure 20 is further complicated, however, by the relative status of members in the group. Figure 21 shows two curves of the relationship between the latitude of acceptance (ordinate) and the relative status of group members (base line). In matters of minor importance to the group (top curve), the latitude of acceptance is greater for high status members, especially the leader, and smaller for low status members. In other words, especially within the group, the leader and his high status cohorts typically have considerable leeway in regulating behavior relative to others; it is the low man on the totem pole who is continually being nagged, laughed at, or barred from play.

On the other hand, in important matters (lower curve) the leader is expected to be exemplary; even slight deviations on his part arouse questioning, criticism, or scolding from other members. For example, in several groups where money is scarce, it was observed that the leader consistently pitched in with all of his funds or with more than the others, and that this was expected of him. If he indicated that he planned to spend it in other ways, he ran the risk of being called stingy. Similarly, the high status

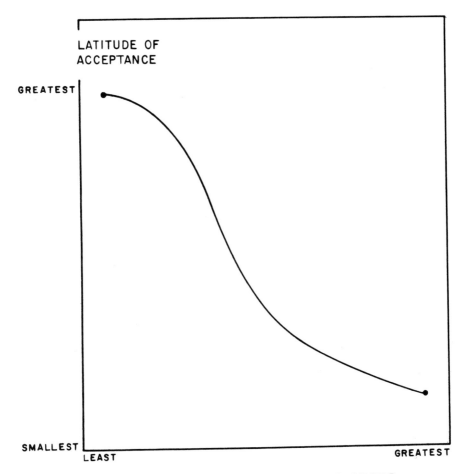

FIGURE 20. Range of individual variations acceptable in natural groups as a function of importance of activity

member with a car was expected to have it available for group activities, and conflicting plans on his part brought forth cries of "he thinks he's too good for us." In the same activities, however, a low status member could beg off without anyone expecting any more of him. He was saving money for shoes, or his sister needed the car. "What do you expect of *him*, anyway?"

To sum up: In observations of natural groups of adolescents, we have found a relationship between the person's status and the expectations others have for his behavior in various respects, as well as his expressed

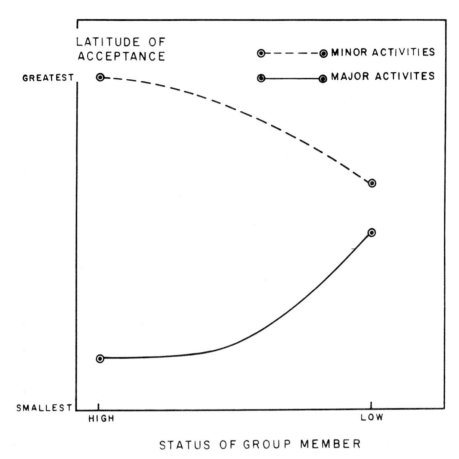

FIGURE 21. Conformity in natural groups as a function of member status and importance of activity

attitude and actions. These relationships hold promise as a base for pre-dicting adolescent behavior. Relative effectiveness of an individual in initiating activities for other members is most predictable at the top of the status structure (most effective) and at the bottom (least effective). Adherence to group norms (expressed as the range of variation in individual behavior which does not call forth sanctions from others) is most strict for all members in matters of importance to the group. However, the acceptable latitude varies with the person's status. The more significant the activity for the identity and continued maintenance of the group as a unit, the narrower the latitude of acceptance for all members, the latitude for the leader being smallest. The more incidental the activity, the broader the range of individual variations without arousal of sanctions, the latitude for the leader being greatest.

INTERDEPENDENCE OF SOCIOCULTURAL SETTING AND
GROUP PROCESS IN ADOLESCENT ATTITUDE AND BEHAVIOR

The larger social scene, the neighborhood with its prevailing values and facilities, and the informal social relationships with age-mates do not act independently in influencing adolescent attitude and behavior. The rest of the chapter summarizes generalizations from our findings, with illustrations, that show the interdependence of these influences. No one of these, considered by itself, is more important than another *in every case*. Our main generalization is that it is impossible to determine the more significant source unless all are included in the analysis.

Many of our generalizations have concerned differences between different settings. Therefore, we begin on a contrasting note: there are unmistakable similarities between youth in widely different settings in the United States.

SIMILARITIES IN ATTITUDE AND BEHAVIOR IN DIFFERENT AREAS

Contrary to some popular theories about youth of different classes, we found that certain values and ambitions unmistakably marked the adolescent in the United States. Though differing in appearance, following different fashions in dress, sometimes speaking different languages, youth in all areas cherished an image of individual success as an adult, as it is spelled out through the magic symbols purveyed by television, advertising, movies, magazines, and popular books. This was true of members of groups studied intensively. The ingredients of the image were desired by nearly a hundred per cent of every sample of high school students studied: cars, comfortable homes, attractive clothing, appliances, telephones, radios, TV sets, money for entertainment, including movies. Regardless of what they have or what is available, youth in settings of low, middle and high rank want the "good things of life," as defined in mass salesmanship so characteristic of this country today.

Another finding common to youth in all areas was their orientation toward age-mates as the reference set. This was strikingly apparent in observations in every setting. The school samples, for example, asked why "school is fun"—three-fourths of the replies pertain specifically to the opportunities that school gave to interact with age-mates.

It should also come as no surprise to find, as we have, a common and intense interest in the opposite sex at this period. Observations of the small groups of boys are peppered with references to girls. In the surveys of school students, the interest is more hidden because of the tendency to give "socially desirable" answers (a problem mentioned earlier). However, it was readily revealed in the great majority of youth by their answers to the question, "What do you and your friends talk about?" (After starting to write, then erasing, the word "sex," one boy substituted "girls."

He was overheard to say "I don't want those people to think I'm a sex fiend.")

Another similarity was the ability to distinguish what adult authorities consider "right" and "wrong." Given a list of forty-five actions, youngsters in very different settings rated their acceptability-unacceptability in much the same way. These were teen-agers attending school, not dropouts. Therefore, it was gratifying to read a recent report of similar findings by Short and his co-workers (1963), who compared nondelinquent and officially delinquent youth on a written questionnaire. Of course, some youth in both samples may have violated the precepts in question, but it seems that violation because of ignorance of what society deems acceptable, or of what deviation is considered serious, is more rare than some theories of lower class youth or of psychopathology would lead us to believe.

In the small groups studied intensively in different neighborhoods, the finding most common to all was the boys' insistent desire to do things on "our own," without adult programming or supervision. Since these expressions and this active search for "freedom" are manifested in every area, the ecology and rank of each neighborhood become very important in determining whether the "freedom" is found in a friend's house, in one's car, behind a pool room, or in the streets.

DIFFERENCES BETWEEN YOUTH IN DIFFERENT SETTINGS

Youth living in areas differentiated by socioeconomic level and cultural composition are well aware of these differences. As reported earlier (Sherif and Sherif, 1964), we have found that those living in low rank areas freely express their desire to move to a high rank area, while those in high rank areas express contentment with their present circumstances and derogate the schools and type of persons found in lower class settings.

Differences between neighborhoods are apparent to the naked eye, of course. What is not so apparent is the effect that the differences in facilities have on a youth's actual mobility, his access to adult programs designed to improve his social mobility, and his ease in entering any situation peopled by those whose appearance and manner identify them as residents of an area differing substantially in rank.

Like other investigators, we found that youth in different neighborhoods set levels for personal goals according to the socioeconomic level of the neighborhood. However, we also found that the differences in goals are accompanied by differing conceptions of achievement. Figure 22, for example, presents recent data from one city, collected in areas which are upper middle, lower middle, and low according to the Shevky-Bell index of socioeconomic rank. The low rank area is largely Spanish-speaking; the lower middle is mixed (Spanish-speaking with some Negroes); the upper middle area is mixed ("Anglos" with some Spanish-speaking persons).

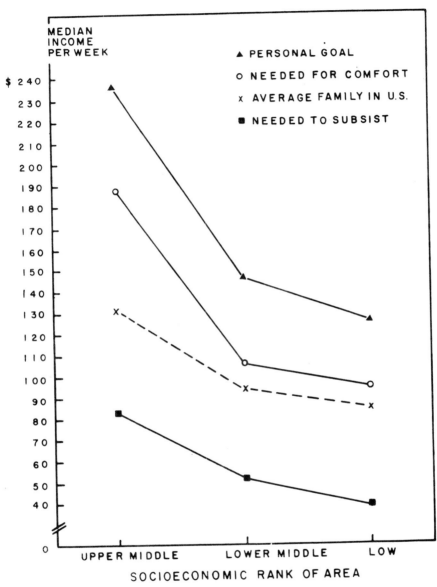

FIGURE 22. Conceptions of subsistence, "average income," comfort, and personal goals for future income as a function of socioeconomic rank of neighborhood

The triangles in the figure represent the median values of personal goals for estimated income (per week) when one is adult and married. The personal goals vary, on the average, with the socioeconomic level of the area.

The figure also shows the median estimates obtained from the youth of the amount needed per week for subsistence (bottom bars), for comfort (circles), and the estimated income of the "average American family" (X). As the figure shows, youth in all three areas are "ambitious" according to their own conceptions of achievement, that is, according to their conceptions of enough to be "really well off" (circles). However, the upper middle rank conception of comfort is higher than the goals set, on the average, in the other areas.

These, and similar data on success in school and occupation, seem to belie the notion that middle or upper class youth are necessarily more ambitious or achievement-oriented than those in lower ranks. Those from areas of lower rank are ambitious relative to their own ideas of achievement, and even more ambitious relative to their own parents' achievements (cf. Sherif and Sherif, 1964).

The data on samples of youth in school do not represent completely the values and goals of all youth in an area, because varying proportions have withdrawn or are barred from public school. A further finding on school youth in the various areas will help us in analyzing the social situation of those who withdraw from school.

HOMOGENEITY—DIVERSITY OF VALUES IN SETTINGS OF DIFFERENT SOCIOECONOMIC RANK

In analyzing data obtained from youth in schools in the areas where our small groups were found, we were not entirely prepared to find that the least diversity of individual values and goals was found consistently in schools serving areas of higher socioeconomic rank. This discovery of so many like-minded students is a comment on the residential arrangements in large cities and on the cultural situation of youth in high rank areas. In these high rank areas, students had the least individual variation in personal goals, or conception of success in education and use of leisure time.

In both middle and low rank areas, greater heterogeneity was found in the values and goals of the student body, with actual cleavages into distinct social strata being characteristic of the middle rank schools (so classified on the basis of modal parental occupation and education). Even in schools serving areas of low rank, only in matters which are strictly financial (income, spending money, and the like) did the like-mindedness equal that of students in high rank areas.

Figure 23 represents the personal goals for education in three schools, in terms of years of schooling desired. The ordinate represents

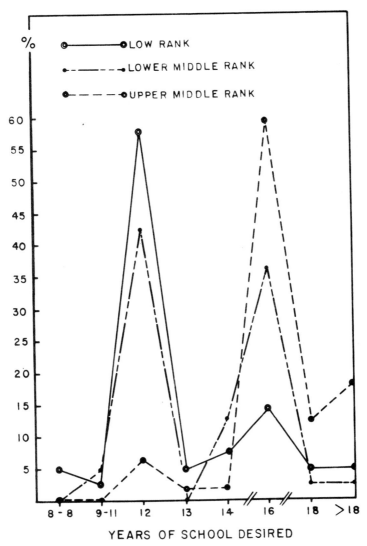

FIGURE 23. Personal goals for education in neighborhoods of different socioeconomic rank

percentage of the samples, and the curves give the distribution of goals in a school of low rank, lower middle rank, and upper middle rank in a city where free transfer is permitted. (These are the same three schools whose financial goals are represented in Figure 22.)

This figure represents one example of the greater diversity in values found in the lower rank areas. Ninety per cent of those in the high rank

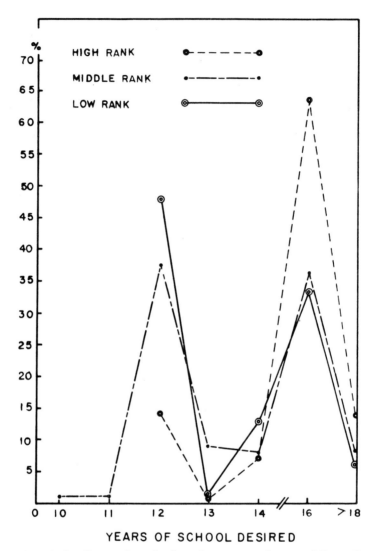

FIGURE 24. Personal goals for education in low, middle and
          high socioeconomic rank in city with higher median
          educational level

school (dash line) desire to complete college (16 years) or more advanced degrees (18 or more years). Greater diversity is evident in the
low rank area (solid line), although the mode is for high school diploma.
The distribution of responses in the lower middle rank area is strikingly
bimodal (broken line).

Figure 24 presents comparable data from a different city in which transfers are seldom granted, and the median educational level is substantially higher. The middle rank school (broken line) serves a large and diverse section of the city; but the low rank school is located in the oldest portion of the city, where most residential areas are of low socioeconomic rank, with a substantial Indian-Mexican-Negro minority. The distributions for both low and middle rank areas are clearly bimodal, while that for the upper rank area (dash line) again represents greatest homogeneity.

These findings have led us to suspect that some theorists on lower class life may have overlooked the actual diversity within lower class settings, perhaps because of their preoccupation with specific social problems. We suggest that generalizations about the characteristics and values of a class or ethnic grouping must specify carefully what values are involved, and how widely they are shared, before referring to distinct "subcultures" in different settings.

Specification of the homogeneity or diversity of the sociocultural setting proves helpful in understanding the nature of adolescent groups in that setting.

DIVERSITY OF THE SETTING AND CHARACTERISTICS OF GROUPS WITHIN IT

Let us start with a picture of what went on in the groups studied intensively in our research. What people do and talk about when they get together regularly of their own accord can tell us a great deal about them. The boys in our groups engaged in a great range and variety of activities. As noted previously, these invariably included girls, cars, and sports, in all but the least acculturated neighborhoods. During a considerable portion of the observation time, nothing seemed to happen: youth spend a lot of time hanging around, driving around if they can, while rehashing the past, planning an evening or a future scheme. The apparent aimlessness of much of the activity conceals active evaluations of things past and planning of things important to them. The discussions and plans revealed the boys' overwhelming desire to know themselves and each other as (near) adults, and to do things they wanted, on their own, without programming or intervention by adults.

Frequently, doing things on their own as adults involved activities deemed improper for the age level, even immoral or illegal. This was true in middle and high rank neighborhoods as well as low rank, even though most of the groups and their members were not labeled as "delinquent" by police.

All of the boys were concerned about their "manliness" (though this meant somewhat different things in different settings), with clothing fads, and with other cultural trends available in the larger setting. Each boy translated these trends meaningfully for himself in relation to the others in his group. For example, the discussion and consumption of alcohol were so frequent that it seemed that drinking must be considered a sign of adult-ness for a young male—at least, the ability to talk about drinking.

We have not yet found a group which specialized in one sort of forbidden activity. On the contrary, groups emphasizing drinking not only tolerated non-drinkers but had many other activities. There were groups which engaged in theft (usually in twos or threes), and others which tolerated such activities by only two or three members. Observations of drug usage were remarkably similar to those involving alcohol. Although not all members participated, it was invariably a social affair.

The observations in these respects are difficult to reconcile with the sociological classification of groups into *types* on the basis of their activities. Particularly obscure, in terms of our observational material, is the classification of drug usage or alcohol as "retreatist." If one may infer any centralized purpose, our data imply that these activities are, on the contrary, ordinarily social—a means to enhance attraction and prestige (even though they may be carried to the point where the individual becomes "withdrawn" into unconsciousness or hallucinatory behavior, as in paint solvent or glue sniffing).

Activities labeled delinquent if detected by adult authorities were not distinctive to groups in any setting, nor the exclusive specialization of any one group. Nevertheless, frequent "delinquent" activities had decided consequences for the character of the group. Roughly proportional to the frequency of forbidden activities (not necessarily illegal ones), the groups became highly *secretive*. The frequency of activities involving such violations of adult dictums was, in turn, a function of the amount of time spent together; the wall of secrecy shielding members was the most impenetrable for groups which associated most frequently.

The total amount of time spent together, the secrecy of the group, and the absorption of individuals in their group activities to the exclusion of others were related to the homogeneity or diversity of the settings. By far the most homogeneous of the settings studied in our research were the least acculturated, low rank areas populated by persons of Mexican origin, and another low rank area populated by poor whites at considerable distance from the city center and from schools.

The one group of Negro boys studied in the Southwest were in a much more diverse setting, by virtue of proximity and contact with school youth and recreational agencies, which reflected the hope from the nation-wide movement for equal opportunities. For example, Negro youth in school set their goals for education on a par with those of school students in the highest rank areas of their city, although not half of their parents had finished high school. Of course, these findings depend on circumstances in the cities in question, and cannot be generalized to other regions.

Whether labeled delinquent or not, the groups in the most homogeneous settings of low rank were also the most solid and stable. The boys' perception of great differences between themselves and anyone outside "my neighborhood," inadequate and crowded homes, difficulties in achieving in school, real deprivations of physical needs—all of these circumstances combine to make the adolescent group the central place for each boy as an individual, where he can find pleasure and entertainment and, in some cases, necessities not provided elsewhere. These boys were the least mobile. Leaving the area involved considerable planning and effort, and often subjected them to the suspicious eyes of police.

Given these circumstances, the ecology of the immediate neighborhood and its facilities become weighty matters. Interference in using the facilities is eliminated only when the group defines a territory which is its own, which it is known to claim, and, hence, which represents the group's investment in prestige. When the boys went outside the territory, or when others came in, there were occasions of gang fighting, complete with weapons. Such incidents were recalled later with excitement and pride by members. They looked for accounts of them in the papers.

To assess this love of violence and bravado, it is essential to bear in mind that it was not directed to fellow group members, even though adolescent boys are not habitually gentle with one another. Nor was violence directed to members of those other groups with whom relations were friendly. The violence occurred in conflict with individuals defined by the boys as enemies, a capsule formula used to justify the actions of one's group in conflict, whether the opponent be another informal group, a club, the police, or a nation.

We cannot share the cynical view that violence is a prime value for adolescent boys, and that their efforts to avoid it are superficial. The difficulties of avoiding violence between conflicting groups are well known in adult life today. There is little reason to expect small groups of adolescents to succeed better, even when they genuinely desire not to get into trouble.

In fact, there were repeated observations that groups involved in conflict had made efforts to avoid it. Avoiding trouble was frequently discussed; precautions against it were quite as observable as the violent actions, though less dramatic. They "cased" a place for the presence and location of antagonists before entering. They avoided going into places where trouble might start. Joel Garza, one of the observers, recorded a half-hour episode during the intermission of a drive-in-movie, to which he had driven a group by no means noted for shrinking from conflict. A rival group was spotted between their car and the rest room; with considerable self-control, the members laid a strategy to use the facilities without encountering the rivals.

Much attention has been devoted to the pleasure, or even "thrills," which adolescent youth say they derive from violent encounters with an enemy, from a forbidden joy-ride, or theft with one's fellows. We suspect from our observational data that these "thrills" have something to do with the effect of interaction among individuals who feel they "belong" together, who are open with one another, and who derive satisfaction from concerted efforts not available to them in the formal arrangements of living. Such exhilaration and "thrills" have also been reported by members of groups engaging in concerted activities toward desirable ends. In such a group situation, it is thrilling to win a ballgame, to elect a member to the student council, or to hold a party.

GREATER VARIETY OF GROUP CHARACTERISTICS IN DIVERSE SETTINGS

Most of the groups studied intensively in our research came from more diverse settings, which were characterized not only by greater variations in values but more opportunities for mobility and choice. In such settings, we find groups composed of individuals with differing backgrounds and aspirations; groups whose activities place them in opposition to the predominant values in their setting; and groups of boys directed outside of their immediate settings by the pull of opportunities seen elsewhere.

Using the prevailing values of the immediate neighborhood as a yardstick, we find that one group of boys in a lower rank neighborhood is quite atypical in several respects. Because of success in grade school athletics, these boys were imbued with the goal of "making" the high school team. Unlike the local "toughs" on their streets, they not only continued into high school, but chose a school far across the city because it had the best teams. Dubbed "Escuelantes" (school boys) by others in their neighborhood, they have not performed well academically and have not made the school team. Most of their leisure time is spent together, warming up, practicing, talking about sports and glorifying the heroes of their school teams. It would be gratifying to report that the aspirations of this group reflected their parents' efforts, but their personal histories offer no such reflection. Three of the boys are illegitimate sons of servicemen, and none of the families provides the "solid, middle class" concept of achievement.

After being with this group for several months, the observer concluded that their chances of making the school teams were slim, for they were smaller than most varsity athletes. He reported that the intensity of their concentration on the school team and their own skills was so great that, at times, it seemed (in his eyes) to be almost fantasy. But the group process has kept the boys in school, and he predicts they will complete it.

By contrast, another group, composed of lower middle class boys in a predominantly middle rank area, had all dropped out or been expelled from school. In terms of their future hopes for jobs and income, the members proved to be quite typical of school students in their community, with their goals in these respects clustering around the median.

But their own initial encounters and continuing activities have focused on the pursuit of pleasure in cars, pool halls, and with girls. This kind of group activity required considerable outlays of spending money (over ten dollars a week), more money than 99 per cent of the students in their former school feel is needed. Together, these boys have their "fun" and secure spending money to support it by sporadic odd jobs. Meanwhile, the joint pursuit of such fun has resulted in several members being sent to "training schools" by the authorities. None of these boys is "mentally handicapped" in terms of standardized tests, and the parents of some have exerted strong but unsuccessful pressures on their sons to return to school and keep away from "the boys."

Still another group, which met regularly at a public center in a low rank area, was primarily recreational. In many respects, the members were diverse in their attitudes and aspirations. For example, two boys dropped out of school in 10th and 11th grade, two intended to graduate, one planned to go to further training, and one wanted to finish college. Although this was not a very solid group, its pull on members is so strong that the parents of the boy with college ambitions moved out of the neighborhood, where they had lived many years, in an attempt to break the association.

These examples are sufficient to indicate the variety of adolescent groups to be found in areas providing some diversity and, especially, some mobility to members. The immediate neighborhood, the family, the school, the images of success in society are not clearly "to blame" for the directions taken by any of these groups, yet they are all involved. To some extent the directions taken hinge upon the selective process of interaction among adolescents who, for the time, find some significant psychological identity within the group circle. The directional power of such groups must be included in the picture in order to understand why the Escuelantes are so directed outside their neighborhood, why the dropouts have resisted persuasive and corrective efforts to bring them into line, and why a recreational group seems threatening to the parents of a boy who wants to go to college.

Ordinarily, most of these groups last only a few years, until members leave the area, get jobs, go to school or military services, or marry. Their transitory nature makes their little "organizations" and their little "cultures" no less real, nor does it lessen their impact on individual members as long as they last.

THREE GENERATIONS OF A YOUTHFUL NATURAL GROUP

The reality of the little "cultures" of adolescent groups may be seen more clearly if one could see what happened when at least some of the members "stayed put," did not leave the neighborhood, or did not enter into formal social relationships fundamentally different from those of adolescence. Such an opportunity arose in the research project in a neighborhood of low socioeconomic rank with a population of Mexican origin. The transmission of a group identity and its culture (norms) through three generations of adolescents was traced.

Early in the research project, a group of adolescent boys called "Los Apaches,"[1] was observed for several months by Eduardo Villarreal. Subsequently, he has carried through the observation cycle on an "older generation" of former members, ranging in age from 23 to 36 years, still living in the same area. Then he returned to find the current membership of Los Apaches, which had changed in the interim. Thus, it is possible to compare the norms and status relationships in three generations of members during a period when the neighborhood itself was essentially the same, but life in the city underwent considerable alteration (roughly, since the postwar period).

When first observed, Los Apaches consisted of twelve boys, with other occasional hangers-on. (See Sherif and Sherif, 1964.) Most of its members were known to police and detention home officials for stealing, carrying weapons, and engaging in fights with a rival group—the Lakesiders. Currently, nearly three years later, those who were members at that time have apparently escaped serious convictions. Some of them have jobs, are thinking of getting married, and are not active as Los Apaches members.

The observer could find very little change in the customs or norms of Los Apaches during this time. A "lieutenant" took over the leadership position when the old leader got a job and a steady girl whom he is thinking of marrying. Several new members have been added, some at high status levels. The rivalry with the Lakesiders continues, and seems to be even more important in group discussions. Occasionally, the members steal (always in twos or threes); a member of the older generation remarked, "These boys have more money than we used to get." Beer, solvent-sniffing, and marijuana are included at group get-togethers; there is always as much beer as money and ingenuity permit.

The young adults (now the older generation) meet regularly at favorite beer joints, a member's house, or night spots. They all quit school in the elementary grades, and all have unskilled jobs, with the exception of an auto mechanic and a shoe repairman. With very few exceptions, the observer reports, they seek sexual relations frequently while they are out together, even though most of them are married.

The members of the older generation belonged to Los Apaches at different times, when each was in his teens. Although the name *Los Apaches* was adopted when one of the younger adults was a member, all the men refer to the age-mate group by this name. They all still refer to to the Lakeside as the rival group, even though few of them now en-

---

[1] Like other identifications in published reports of this research, this name is fictitious.

counter adults who were Lakesiders when they were Los Apaches. Those who did belong to the group at the same time reveal closer attachments than those who did not, as revealed by patterns and frequency of visits, lending money, or borrowing a car. A former leader (El Apache) is among the highest in status in this older generation group.

By observations over a considerable period of time, and at an arranged picnic for older and younger generations, it was ascertained that the older generation of young adults has very little contact with the recent or present membership of Los Apaches, except in the parental home of one member of each of the three generations. One other possible exception is that the present generation has, on occasion, sought help or a car from the older generation during conflict with the Lakesiders, which the older generation refused. The former leader (second generation, now almost twenty) and other older adolescents make moves to be accepted by the older generation. But the present membership (13 to 18 years old) preserves a respectful distance from their elders, in line with cultural expectations.

Older generation adults say that the present generation is not as tough as they were and does not get into as much trouble, chiefly because they have more money from parents and can borrow cars. But, they say, Los Apaches and Lakeside will "always" be rivals, and the younger members agree. All ages hold an implacable dislike for "perros" (police), but the older generation says the police are also less tough now than they used to be.

These are some changes in the group as seen through the eyes of former members. The observer reports other differences traceable to the changing times: The younger generation places a much higher value on education, although none has gone further than the ninth grade. The younger generation uses slang identical to that of the older generation (Spanish), but speaks English more frequently. Unlike the adults, who strongly prefer Mexican popular music, the younger generation both prefers and sings the current popular songs in English.

In short, as a miniature culture, Los Apaches has endured with minor changes, but has reflected the impact of broader culture change. The impact of the group may still be seen on the young adults who no longer see themselves as members, but in fact continue to interact in a group with a broader age range.

IMPORTANCE OF ADOLESCENT REFERENCE GROUPS
TO INDIVIDUAL MEMBERS

The groups studied in this research, formed by individuals of their own choice, are important to their individual members. Our evidence shows many instances of individual preference for group activities and values over those of family, church, school, girl friends, and even reasonable considerations of personal safety.

It is also undeniably true that the informal groups of age-mates were of greater import for boys whose past history and present circumstances offered few other sources for a stable definition of self in relation to other human beings. These were not just boys from broken homes, for some had stable homes and were devoted to their parents. They were not only the poverty-stricken youth, for some had more than the necessities of life. They were not just school failures, for some were progressing in school. They were not all members of subordinated cultural minorities. When the entire set of such unfavorable circumstances prevailed in extreme degrees for some boys, they produced the strongest attachment to an adolescent group. However, these circumstances did not guarantee that a boy would belong or would be attached to his group.

Attachment to a group meant that the individual also had to be accepted by the others, live up to them, and prove himself a reliable and worthy member. Many boys who had unfortunate social circumstances in home, school, and community did not belong to a group because they could not achieve this necessary acceptance. Some had been expelled from groups.

The boy who was accepted, could live up, could prove himself reliable over a time, was usually among the more able, the more sociable, the more responsible to his fellows. Such personal attributes were necessary to gain status in any of the groups, regardless of other prerequisites for particular groups (for example, smoothness, or toughness, or daring). Having a secure place, especially a high place, among one's fellow-members further enhanced the importance of the association for the individual.

Thus, we have an apparent contradiction: Those to whom the group became most important as individuals, those most devoted to its tenets and outlook (whether socially desirable or undesirable) are likely to be individuals who display, *within* their groups, certain qualities usually prized by society. These qualities include loyalty, responsibility, and consistency in dealing with one's fellows. These very qualities may contribute to the individual's performance of antisocial actions directed toward outsiders or the larger community.

This generalization in no way condones those activities and norms of a group which are socially undesirable. If these are malicious, undesirable, or destructive, they should be denounced. But generalization does imply that adolescent attitudes and behaviors which are traceable to interaction in their reference groups cannot be defined within the traditional lexicon of psychopathology, or by new labels for the same pigeonholes.

CONCLUSIONS

In reporting on the research program, it has been our aim to emphasize the multifaceted nature of influences shaping social attitude and behavior of individuals, for good or for evil. We have focused on participation in reference groups of age-mates because of a conviction that many aspects of the immediate and larger sociocultural setting are filtered to the individual adolescent through this highly salient medium.

The findings have shown that adolescent reference groups are patterned affairs, with power relations and "cultures" (norms) of their own. Attitude and behavior of particular individuals vary in terms of their places in these informal social schemes. The larger social scene, the immediate setting, and the age-mate group are interdependent influences in the life of particular adolescents. Especially when the immediate setting offers diverse alternatives, the interaction patterns and goals of the groups may become decisive in choosing among these alternatives.

For the single individual, participation in a reference group of age-mates may be beneficial for his future, or it may have disastrous consequences. In either case, an adequate theory of his attitude and behavior cannot rest with assigning labels of social approval or disapproval, mental "health" or "illness," to the individual. It is necessary to develop an adequate theory of individual behavior in close alignment with empirical findings on personal background, on associations with other humans who count in his eyes, and on the sociocultural setting. The social conditions in which he acts do not merely offer opportunities or hindrances to his strivings as a human individual; they also offer success pictures which affect *what* he will strive toward.

REFERENCES

Edwards, A. L., 1957. *The Social Desirability Variable in Personality Assessment and Research.* (New York: Dryden Press.)

Sherif, M., O. J. Harvey, B. J. White, W. R. Hood, and Carolyn W. Sherif, 1961. *Intergroup conflict and cooperation. The Robbers Cave experiment.* (Norman, Oklahoma: The University Book Exchange.)

Sherif, M. and Carolyn W. Sherif, 1953. *Groups in harmony and tension.* (New York: Harper.)

——, 1964. *Reference Groups: Exploration into conformity and deviation of adolescents.* (New York: Harper, Row.)

Short, J. F., R. A. Tennyson, and K. L. Howard, 1963. Behavior dimensions of gang delinquency. *Amer. Sociol. Rev.*, 28, 411-428.

SUBJECT INDEX

AUTHOR INDEX

CPSIA information can be obtained at www.ICGtesting.com
Printed in the USA
BVOW040313040612

291614BV00001B/7/P